THE ECOLOGY AND EVOLUTION OF ANIMAL BEHAVIOR

THE ECOLOGY AND EVOLUTION OF ANIMAL BEHAVIOR

ROBERT A. WALLACE
University of California, Santa Barbara

GOODYEAR PUBLISHING COMPANY, INC., Pacific Palisades, California

Design: Bernice T. Glenn
Illustration: Jane Larson

Current printing (last digit):
10 9 8 7 6 5 4 3 2 1
ISBN: 0-87620-261X
Library of Congress Catalog
Card Number: 72-97669
Y-261X-2

Printed in the United States of America

For Bonni

ACKNOWLEDGMENTS

Here, as in any synthesis of a wide range or material, strong reliance is placed upon the efforts of others, and I am deeply indebted for information acquired as a result of their careful research. I am particularly appreciative of those times afforded me when, poring over their material, I was suddenly able to see new implications in what they had done. What began as curiosity often changed to respect and, at times, to an exhilarating admiration. I will be most pleased if I can convey only a small part of that sense of discovery to the readers of this book.

I cannot mention every author to whom credit is due in a brief paragraph, but I must, of course, acknowledge the influence of Professors Konrad Lorenz and Niko Tinbergen. Others upon whose work I strongly relied are N. E. Collias, J. H. Crook, I. Eibl-Eibesfeldt, R. A. Hinde, P. H. Klopfer, D. Lack, R. H. MacArthur, A. Manning, P. Marler, M. Moynihan, A. J. Nicholson, T. C. Schneirla and A. Watson.

I also recall appreciatively many fruitful discussions with graduate students and faculties of various institutions, including R. H. Barth, P. Chabora, R. Garrett, T. H. Hamilton, R. Huey, C. Kropach, J. Madden, R. Madden, L. Marcus, M. Menaker, R. Salsbury and, especially, R. K. Selander who advised me during the writing of my doctoral dissertation at the University of Texas. My thanks to the members of the Deaprtment of Ornithology at the American Museum of Natural History for their assistance and fellowship during most of the period of writing, especially D. Amadon, M. Gochfeld, W. Lanyon, M. LeCroy, and L. Short. Any errors in the book are, of course, mine.

For their expert aid in preparation of the manuscript I thank, most of all, A. Feldman and S. Feldman. A special appreciation is due S. Wilkins.

Lastly, I would like to acknowledge the rare blend of professionalism and camaraderie exhibited by the editor of Goodyear Publishing, C. J. Stratton, who stayed at my house one night in Atlantic Beach and gave us all a cold.

CONTENTS

Contents (continued)

PREFACE

The modern study of animal behavior is no more recent than several other scientific areas. Therefore its age does not necessarily explain the vigorous dissension which has marked its history. After a rather unanimous decision to call the nature-nurture argument finished, it seemed the ranks would be pulled together and unifying concepts could be developed to base new, more integrated and realistic programs. In a sense, this has happened. The result has been increasingly fruitful approaches to the study of animal behavior. Perhaps the radiation of the approaches to the study will prove beneficial in the long run because it has provided an opportunity for each area to develop rigorous techniques within its own philosophical framework. On the other hand, as each approach developed its own supportive evidence, a certain crystallization must have taken place which now hinders rethinking through old problems. The separate development of each field also makes it hard to find those who can absorb the great amount of information available, integrate the findings, synthesize a useful way of looking at things, and explain it to the rest of us.

Perhaps the divisions which exist in this field continue because there are too few who are able to grasp the amount and variety of material which has been presented. Or perhaps arguments continue because of a recent interest in learning about man's "true nature" by studying animal be-havior and it is hard to be rational about data with such import.

I make no attempt here to integrate the diverse areas of animal behavior. The approach to the material is based on ethology but will hopefully go past traditional ethological constructs. The search to understand the behavior of any species, I believe, should include the environmental influences on the animal, (1) as an individual, (2) as part of a population and (3) as an evolutionary product. The mechanism I will primarily stress as a way to provide such information is the *adaptiveness* of behavioral patterns.

This book, I hope, will find its greatest use among students of biology and psychology. However, I am a great admirer of that elusive "intelligent layman"—thus no prior knowledge of biology or psychology is assumed. All terms are defined and an effort has been made to make the material as readable as possible.

1

INTRODUCTION

In one way or another, man has been studying animal behavior for thousands of years. The behavior of animals was important to him in earlier ages for some of the same reasons it is important to him now. The most skillful hunters and fishermen of any age were those who were able to make certain predictions regarding the behavior of their prey. It was important to know that when salmon are spawning they will not respond to the fisherman's bait, that many rodents escape toward dark areas while most birds escape towards light, and that many kinds of animals will fight, some with awesome effect, if they are trapped.

The study of animal behavior may have occupied the fringes of man's consciousness for centuries on just such a practical basis. Later, when animals were domesticated and put to work, it was necessary to understand new things about them. Dogs could be used for the personal protection of individual humans; cats could not. Cats were found to be capable of great stealth, but dogs used their greater endurance to run down their prey. Both dogs and cats were easier to teach than fish.

Recently, as we shall see, the study of animal behavior has taken on new dimensions. The goals as well as the techniques have changed. Animals are no longer studied simply to enable us the better to exploit them (although this is certainly a major reason for our attention); now we study them, in some cases, simply because they present unsolved problems (and this is the "purest" motive) and, in others, to enable us to know more about ourselves. There are undoubtedly a host of less appealing reasons, but these shall not be acknowledged here.

The techniques of the study of animal behavior have proliferated during the last 70 years. No longer are animals simply observed and their behavior recorded anecdotally. Today, even simple observations are subject to statistical argument. The environment of the animal (or plant) is now carefully controlled as variables are introduced in an effort to discover to what component of the en-

1

vironment the animal responds—and how. In some cases, the neural apparatus of the animal is dissected and analyzed in the minutest detail. Other researchers go one step further, and attempt to describe how the animal interacts with its external and internal environment at the molecular level.

COMPARATIVE PSYCHOLOGY AND ETHOLOGY

Basically the array of investigative techniques have sprung from two major philosophical camps, and the result of their disagreement has been for each to disregard even the most valid tenets of the other group. These major branches are generally called, comparative psychology and ethology.

Comparative psychology has traditionally been an American discipline. The training of its proponents has basically been grounded in psychology and, somehow, the most widely used animal subject has come to be the Norway rat. Comparative psychologists usually carry out their work in the laboratory and the emphasis in their research is on learning and the development of theories of behavior.

Ethology was born in Europe and the training of ethologists is traditionally in zoology. Generally, the research animals of the ethologists have been insects, fish, and birds although, recently, more emphasis is being placed on mammals, especially primates. The ethologist has been concerned with the study of the evolution of behavior and, as a part of this concern, he has devoted much of his effort to the study of instinct. The ethologist usually acquires his information through field work—studying animals in their natural habitat—and through observation of the mélange of animals usually surrounding the zoologist in his own environs.

Such categorical descriptions are not quite as valid as they once were. In spite of the sporadic and often vitriolic disagreements of the recent past, each group is increasingly accepting certain tenets of the other. Hopefully the result will be the development of a more complete and unified theory of animal behavior.

ECOLOGY AND BEHAVIOR

It would be shortsighted to place all our hopes on the possible reconciliation of two fully developed disciplines, particularly since there are other important new advances occurring in the study of animal behavior. Perhaps the most important of these stems from the recent emphasis on ecology. To the biologist, the very term ecology has almost staggering connotations. Ecology is sometimes defined as the study of the interrelationships of organisms to their environment. The definition is simple, the concept is fascinating, and the practical problems of developing theory and gathering data are enormous. The key word is *interrelationship*, a term that implies reciprocal influence. The animal can influence the environment and the environment can influence the animal, which may cause the animal to change its influence on the environment, ad nauseum.

Also, what is environment? It is not simply habitat or substrate subject to definition in physical terms. It also includes other organisms. Organisms which can change in space and time and can adapt, on an individual level, to meet their own specific needs.

An animal's biotic milieu may include not only parents and siblings, but also other members of its own species, with which it must compete, its predators or its prey, as well as a variety of species of other adaptive types with which it might interact to one degree or another. Whereas for many animals the "physical" part of the environment may change slowly, or at least regularly, the biotic components may change rather quickly and unpredictably as sensitive cytoplasm responds adaptively to the changes in pressures placed upon it.

Also, it must be realized that interaction in a living system is not simply reciprocal, or between two components; nor can it be described as the sum of such reciprocal interaction. Instead, in any such system any individual may be interacting on various levels with a number of other types of organisms in an exceedingly complex feedback operation. As a hypothetical example, species A might act to increase the numbers of species B. Species B, in turn, might then reduce the numbers of species C. But the presence of species C is necessary for A to act effectively on B.

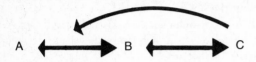

And even this scheme neglects the operation on A, B, and C of yet other species, and the effects of physical influences such as weather on the numbers of any species (Figure 1.1).

As we begin to understand more about at least the basic principles of environmental systems, we can no longer be content to restrict the study of animal behavior to learning mechanisms, the inheritance of behavior and its evolutionary descent. We must begin to try to integrate our findings so that they might reflect more closely what is happening in the real world. The interpretations of our data must be made in light of accumulating ecological information, involving finer descriptions of the habitat and the niche, population dynamics, social structure, and the overall effects of altering any one of these. The real problem is how to integrate our expanding body of knowledge in new ways to produce more accurate descriptions of nature. While increasingly detailed data is pouring in, the synthesizers among us are faced with greater problems trying to make some sense of it. At the same time, the problem is, paradoxically, compounded by critical gaps in our levels of information. So, it seems that as long as we continue to investigate our world, we have basically two (not exclusive) options: First, we might continue to concentrate on the gathering of data whose real import we may not fully

understand; or, we can give impetus to the growing trend to place our information in its ecological perspective. Admittedly, it is too early to expect much real success from such trials, but the effort at least focuses general attention on the need.

The aim of this book is to introduce the ethological concept of animal behavior with attention to certain findings of comparative psychology and, more importantly, once certain ideas are established, to attempt to place them in some sort of ecological and evolutionary context. In other words, we want to try to answer a few simple questions as to what the overall effect of certain behavioral patterns are and how they came to be.

We will begin, in this chapter, by describing certain of the techniques and the operating theory of observing the behavior of organisms as they are usually defined. We will then consider the importance of the "ethogram" as a behavioral description of an animal. In the following two chapters we will discuss the ethological concepts of instinct and learning as bases for discussions. Other chapters ("Biological Clocks," "Animal Navigation") are intended to provide some insight into the search for the mechanisms of specific patterns without delving too deeply into the complex principles of physiology. Basic principles of ecological and evolutionary theory will increasingly be introduced in later chapters. Hopefully, the result of such a format will be, first, to acquaint the reader with certain principles of behavior, and then to show how these might operate in nature. We have established the awesome nature of ecological studies, so our goals must remain modest. We cannot hope to solve great problems or even define with any confidence the important questions. We can only indicate how such a start might be made.

A note should be added here regarding my choice of certain phrases. Occasionally (although I hope it is kept to a minimum), I will refer to an animal's performance of an act *to* achieve something or other. Such a statement is not intended to imply intention, unless specifically stated; it is simply a shorthand way of saying that when a particular pattern is completed, a specific result usually follows. The account thus becomes more readable. It is a ploy often used when one biologist is addressing another or when one is certain the real meaning is understood.

THE DESCRIPTION OF BEHAVIOR

The description and classification of behavioral patterns presents several problems to the observer. First, he must be able to know when a certain type of behavior has occurred. In some cases this is relatively simple as, for example, in certain types of displays. One can easily count the display "push-ups" of a lizard or the flashes of a firefly. In other cases the classification may be more difficult. Is the heron "bowing" or simply "looking down"? At what point can a dog be said to have changed from a belligerent to a submissive posture? Is a woodpecker excavating a hole for a nest or is it simply looking for insects?

To what degree can we ignore the context of a certain pattern? A crouching dog may be crouching in fear or in preparation for a spring. We can usually ignore respiratory patterns if we are describing a tern putting together its simple nest, but we might not wish to ignore such patterns in the building of bubble nests by the air-breathing Siamese fighting fish.

Such problems can be solved to some degree by putting behavioral patterns into their proper adaptive context ("adaptive" refers to those patterns that produce a net benefit to the individual), and by carefully designing a system of description. The adaptive context can be described in terms of time. We might ask what immediately preceded a certain action in an effort to determine what might have produced the pattern ("causal analysis"). In such a case, we would be interested in the physical and biotic components of the animal's immediate environment and any change in them that might have occurred prior

to the behavioral action. A male bird in the area of its nest in spring may suddenly show aggressive behavior at the appearance of another male. It might be deduced that the intruder caused the show of aggression. (We might then experiment to see what aspect of the intruder's appearance elicited the response.)

We might also approach such problems in terms of the individual's history. To what could any animal have been exposed which could bring about the observed pattern? Are animals in parks more approachable because of some special character of parks or because they have not been chased or shot at?

Then, thirdly, we might ask what the evolutionary history of the animal has been. In other words, what has been the experience of the species? Many island species are so tame that they can be picked up by hand and show no sign of fear. Is this because they have not individually experienced harm by humans? It is more likely that they are fearless because, for generations, they have had nothing to fear. There is nothing in their genetic makeup which could inspire aversive behavior. In other words there has been no "selection" for such characteristics in these island species. On the other hand, continental species show great fear of man's approach. Their species have been exposed to man and other large predators for untold generations. Whenever certain changes appeared in the genetic makeup of offspring which might cause them to tend toward tameness, these individuals were caught by predators and, therefore, left no offspring of their own with "tame" genes. So, in continental species, there is selection *for* "wildness," and "tameness" is selected *against*. (We may also say tame individuals are selected *out*.) More will be said about all this later, but the reader should be familiar with this basic terminology before we go on.

There are, basically, two ways to describe behavior: by operation and by consequence. Description by operation simply refers to what the animal does. A quick straightening of the leg may be called a "knee jerk." There is no statement or implication regarding whether the tendon of the knee was tapped first, and no statement regarding what neural events preceded the action. The description only involves the speed and the arc of the swing of the lower leg.

In classification by operation, one simply places all behavioral patterns of a similar spatiotemporal organization into a single group. Thus, sleeping patterns in animals may be grouped together although there may be wide differences in the various animal groups. One may also utilize this kind of classification to place patterns of greater similarity into subgroups. For example, sleeping postures in arctic dogs are relatively uniform, as are such postures in many tropical birds.

In some cases, this classification is rather simple, such as in describing knee bends. In other cases, when a number of muscles are involved in a highly coordinated sequence, a range of movements within a single type becomes possible and thus classification becomes more difficult. In complex patterns at low intensity certain components may also be left out entirely and, thus, the overall appearance of a pattern may be drastically changed.

The second method Hinde (1970) calls description by consequence. Instead of describing bending down and grasping motions, "picking up nest material" is used. Such descriptions also have their limits. "Pressing down a lever" says nothing about whether the lever was pressed by a nose or a foot. "Approach behavior" does not specify whether the animal is tiptoeing or somersaulting.

Often, classifying by consequence is further clarified by modifying with operational description. "Approaching by hopping" is an example. In some cases, behavioral patterns grouped by consequence are extremely varied, such as is demonstrated in "hunting behavior." In other cases, they are exceedingly restricted, such as is demonstrated in "retrieval behavior" in geese

(Chapter 2), where a goose always attempts to return eggs to the nest by reaching out from the nest and rolling the egg with its chin. The goose's "retrieval behavior" is always performed with this peculiar chin movement in spite of the fact that this behavioral pattern is very inefficient for its purpose. It seems perhaps the wing or the foot could serve better.

Description by consequence is advantageous in that it reduces the room for error. For example, one can say with certainty that a dog did, in fact, bury a bone, or that a squirrel did open a nut. The attempt to define the motions involved might lead to argument.

Another advantage of description by consequence is in the reference to environmental variables. A lioness may pick up her kittens with the same motions she uses to crush the skulls of her prey. However, the adaptiveness (or advantage) of the two acts are quite distinct. The observer may differentiate the functions of the motion on the basis of the animal's orientation to its environment.

Description by consequence, however, is not always appropriate. Is a mouse entering the hole or escaping from the cat? Also, such descriptions lend themselves, perhaps, too easily to overinterpretation. Such possibilities usually arise when the consequence is assumed to be understood or even desired by the animal. "The rat is pushing the lever in order to obtain food" could be said of a trained rat, but not of a completely naïve one in an experimental situation. At what point could the last five words of the description be added?

THE ETHOGRAM

One of the key concepts in ethological studies is the establishment of the ethogram—the "behavioral profile" of a species. For example: How could escape behavior in rats be studied without knowing that rats show a marked tendency to run along walls and places where their bodies are in contact with a vertical substrate? The interpretation of any experimental data is open to question in the absence of information regarding the normal behavior of the subject's species, and supplying this information is the first task (if not the first love) of the ethologist. The need for this information gives him the opportunity to spend time with his animals and to record their behavior without interfering with them as they go about their daily activities. Once their normal patterns and tendencies have been established, meaningful experiments can be devised which can yield insights into the causation and results of their behavior.

As an example of the establishment of an ethogram let us consider Tinbergen's (1951, 1952) description of the behavior of the three-spined stickleback, *Gasterosteus aculeatus*.

The stickleback is a common little fish, only a few inches long, found in the ditches of Europe and when, as a young lecturer at the University of Leyden, Tinbergen was asked to organize an undergraduate course in animal behavior, he chose the stickleback as his research animal.

The choice was a fortunate one. He found that the fish were not only hardy and unafraid (for the same reason that porcupines can afford to be bold), but they proved to be excellent subjects for studying innate behavior. Their displays were dramatic, their reproductive behavior was intriguing and unvarying, and they responded strongly and predictably to certain environmental cues.

Tinbergen found that the behavior of the little fish was the same whether they were in aquariums or in their ditches. They begin to mate in early spring when the males, which have been in schools all winter (like the rest of us), leave these groups and stake out individual territories from which they drive out any intruder, male or female. Each male then builds his nest in his own territory. First he digs a shallow pit, carrying away mouthfuls of sand until the depression is about two inches square. Then he gathers up weeds, preferably thread algae, and places them

in a heap over the pit. The weeds are then coated with a sticky material from the kidneys of the fish. The stickleback then sets about shaping the weeds into a mound by repeatedly circling the heap and poking it with its snout. When the weeds have been fashioned into a mound, the male bores a tunnel by wriggling through it. The tunnel is usually only a little shorter than the fish. This, then, is the nest. After the nest is completed, the male changes color. He was grey and inconspicuous all winter long, but now his chin begins faintly to blush pink and his back and eyes take on a greenish gloss. Then the pink becomes a bright red and the back turns a bluish white. The male is now highly conspicuous and is ready to mate.

While the male has been preparing to mate, the female, too, has changed. Her body is now shiny and swollen with up to 100 eggs. Whenever one of these wandering females enters a male's territory, he swims to her in a series of zigzags, first swimming away toward the nest and then turning and darting toward her.

Finally the female seems to notice the displaying male and swims toward him in a curious head-up position. The male swims quickly toward the nest and she follows. At the nest, the male makes a series of quick thrusts with his nose into the entrance of the nest. Then, he turns on his side with his raised dorsal fins pointing toward the female. At this she quickly enters the nest and lies there, her body protruding from either end of the tunnel. The male then swims to the rear and prods her tail base with rhythmic thrusts. The female then lays her eggs. The whole affair has taken less than a minute.

Egg laying completed, the female slips out of the nest and the male rushes in quickly to fertilize the eggs. The male then chases the female out of his territory and looks around for another partner. A male may escort up to five females through his "tunnel of love" until, finally sated, his mating behavior subsides, his color darkens and he grows increasingly threatening toward females. He now spends his time hovering at the nest entrance fanning oxygen-laden water over the eggs with his pectoral fins. For a day or so after the eggs hatch, the father keeps the brood together, rounding up stragglers and retrieving wanderers in his mouth. The young grow increasingly independent and, in time, they swim off to join the young of other broods.

This, then, is the ethogram of the three-spined stickleback. The description provided the starting point for much of the experimental work which was to follow by N. Tinbergen, J. van Iersel, R. Borowsky and others. In the following chapters we will refer to certain experiments based on the ethogram, which illustrate the nature of innate-behavioral-patterns experiments and which could not have been designed without knowledge of the animal's normal behavioral patterns.

2

INSTINCT

A young long-tailed tailorbird, *Orthotomus sutorius*, has managed to acquire a mate and is in the process of building its first nest. The bird finds two large, hanging leaves and sews them together by first punching holes in the margins of the leaves with its sharp beak, and threading strands of spider webs, cocoons, or bits of string through the holes. Stop-knots are somehow tied in each piece of "thread" and it is pulled through until tight. The eggs will be laid in the nest material held between these two leaves.

The tailorbird has not witnessed nest building by older birds and it has had no previous experience in such a task. But on its first try it builds a nest which may not be perfect, or even as good as those of older birds, but it is adequate, and the tailorbird is able to raise its young (Figure 2.1).

There are many such instances of elaborate behavior in the nesting of birds which shows adherence to a behavioral "plan" that is relatively constant throughout a species and is not acquired through previous experience or learning. These types of behavioral patterns are considered to be "instinctive," a term which, through the years, has had many meanings.

It is unfortunate that even in the sciences, areas in which objectivity is of prime importance, certain ideas may come into vogue while others are unpopular and therefore excluded from serious consideration by many workers. The study of instinct has suffered from the swing of the prejudicial pendulum. A brief review of the history of the study of instinct will point this out.

HISTORY OF THE IDEA

Instinct was referred to in Greek literature over 2,500 years ago. At that time, the theory was conceived in relation to human destiny (just as today a large number of scientists study animal behavior primarily to relate their findings to man). The idea, once stated, endured in the thinking of man, with almost no empirical evidence, as very few other ideas have been able to do.

In the first century, the Stoic philosophers believed that animal behavior takes place "without reflection." This unwieldly idea was a forerunner of what much later came to be known as the reflex theory. It is interesting that this early idea, articulated by Seneca, was much closer to the true basis of some animal behavior than later anthropomorphic interpretations. The idea of primary differences in the behavioral mechanisms of man and other animals was developing.

Aristotle said, in his *Historia Animalium,* that man is at the top of the natural scale and possesses superior intellectual powers (directly above the Indian elephant). But in the thirteenth century, the natural scale was modified by Albertus Magnus. He wrote *De Animalibus,* which was based on Aristotle but was modified to suit scholastic theology. In the amended scheme man was removed from the natural scale under the assumption that man acts by reason and animals by instinct.

St. Thomas Aquinas, a student of Albertus, believed humans to be distinct from animals by virtue of a soul, divinely placed into the embryo sometime before birth. This view is, of course, not without its modern proponents. Four centuries later, Descartes supported the idea of a difference in man and animals based on religious belief.

Religion and science have often been uncomfortable bedfellows. But strangely, with regard to the development of the theory of instinct, religion was the basis of "scientific" explanation for a time. Beach (1955) reviewed the relationship of the two grand ideas. He reasoned that the theological system postulates a life after death. The continuing part of man is defined as the soul. The soul can continue under various conditions, some better than others, and the better conditions must be earned during life. In order to make the important decisions which affect the hereafter, reason is necessary. Animals do not share in the hereafter and therefore do not need reason; in its place, they are guided by blind instinct.

So, then, for many years concepts of instinct

Figure 2.1. Long-tailed tailorbird and nest. The bird sews two large leaves together and builds its nest inside. It is able to perform this complex task correctly on the first attempt. The ability is considered to be instinctive because it appears suddenly, and with adaptive results. Older birds, with more practice, however, may build better nests than those nesting for the first time. (Drawn from a photograph in Fisher and Peterson 1964.)

were not based on scientific but on philosophical groundwork. There were detractors of the instinct idea, of course. Erasmus Darwin, the grandfather of Charles, did not subscribe to the accepted idea of instinctive animal behavior and, instead, attributed all behavior to experience, or learning. Charles Darwin was to reject his grandfather's theory in favor of the idea of inborn patterns of instinct. In his book, *The Expression of the Emotions in Man and Animals,* published in 1873, he lists behavioral patterns that are not learned and are performed correctly soon after birth or hatching. One important aspect of Darwin's work was that, conceptually, he treated behavioral patterns like morphological characters. He assumed that behavior, just like morphology, is variable, and that natural selection operates on behavior just as on morphology. In *Variations of Animals and Plants Under Domestication,* published in 1868, Darwin discusses certain phylogenetic changes in behavior that are a result of selection.

Darwin thus made an important advance in bringing the consideration of instinct into the realm of scientific inquiry. Even after this step, however, little serious attention was paid to instinct. As late as the nineteenth century the instinct concept still had little empirical basis, but was generally accepted in the absence of alternate theories. During this period, there was a tendency to observe a behavioral pattern, to name it, and to consider the matter settled instead of attempting to describe carefully the adaptiveness and development of the pattern. This was one reason the instinct idea was to fall into disrepute under the critical eye of a large number of psychologists. The instinct theory was the subject of much armchair speculation but little scientific testing, and this unfortunate state of affairs did little to lend credibility to any conclusions that were drawn. Instinct was, in some circles, simply not considered valid subject material for serious investigation.

Ideas were beginning to appear, however, even

by the end of the nineteenth century, that would lend weight to the theories of innate mechanisms and make instinct respectable again. C. O. Whitman (1898:328), at the University of Chicago, wrote, "Instincts and organs are to be studied from the common viewpoint of phyletic descent," a statement very similar to Darwin's in its implication, but one which was to revitalize the instinct idea. He categorized the behavioral patterns of several species of pigeons and derived from his results the theory of an endogenous control of behavior. He further stated that instinct is based in protoplasm just as are organs. This statement strengthened the idea of the inheritability of instinct.

Other workers were adding their findings to the growing pool of information as interest in instinct began to reappear. Oskar Heinroth (1910) described homologies in behavior among various species and noted behavioral similarities of closely related species. Heinroth, Whitman, Lorenz, and others rediscovered Darwin's findings that animals, reared in isolation, often develop the behavioral patterns characteristic of the species. Various workers began to search for the behavioral patterns which appeared suddenly, without being practiced, and which were done correctly the first time. The findings pointed to an innately determined source of at least some behavioral patterns. But the nature of such a source and the mechanisms through which it worked went almost entirely unexplained during the first part of this century. Since a scientific approach to the idea of instinct was just being born, there were serious gaps in the sort of information that would be needed to construct a working theory. The important questions began to be asked, however: Is instinct inherited? Does it continue to develop after birth? Is it alterable within individuals? Does it act with, or independently of, learned patterns? Does it, in fact, exist at all and, if so, how could its study best be approached? Let us examine the findings of the ethologists as they began to construct their concept of instinct.

APPETITIVE AND CONSUMMATORY BEHAVIOR

About the middle of this century, ethologists began to see that an innate behavioral pattern cannot be ascribed to "an instinct" for that pattern. Instead of attributing continuing and complex behavior, even that which was apparently innate, to a single neurological event, a multilevel scheme was developed. Let us consider an example from nature which illustrates the multilevel or hierarchical scheme. What we will see is a series of behavioral patterns which begins as a highly variable pattern strongly subject to learning influences, and which becomes increasingly stereotyped at each level until the final pattern is performed. This pattern is entirely "fixed" and, once released, is independent of the environment.

We can begin by noting that hunting, in some birds, involves instinctive behavior. As a hunting peregrine falcon begins searching for prey, his behavior is highly variable. It is hard to predict which way he might bank or whether he will rise or drop toward the ground. The bird is hungry and might be equally "pleased" at the sight of a flying bird or a scampering mouse. Then it sees a group of teal flying below. Its behavior suddenly becomes less random as it swoops toward them in the first stage of "teal-hunting behavior." The swoop is performed in somewhat the same way throughout the species, but there is still some variability. The falcon might hit at the front or the back of the group and might strike at birds to the right or the left of the flock as it passes through them. This is likely to be a sham pass, to scatter the flock so that an individual bird may be selected for pursuit, and it is less variable in its performance than the random searching. Once an individual teal is selected, the falcon goes through a series of maneuvers to keep the hapless bird separated from the flock as the falcon closes in. The falcon's behavior becomes less variable as it goes from cutting-out behavior to a final high-speed dive. The early part of the dive is still variable to a degree and can be altered in response to changes in the teal's escape behavior. There is a point at which, however, the falcon's action is no longer variable. He is then committed to a pattern which will be performed within rather narrow limits. His actions, now, are very much the same as they have been at this stage in previous hunts. This is the brief moment at which the falcon's feet are tightly clenched into a fist as he falls at about 150 miles per hour, and performance of this strike is what caused the falcon to begin hunting in the first place. Unless the teal makes a last-second change in his pattern he will be knocked from the sky and the falcon's hunt will have been successful.

The behavior leading to the capture of the teal began as a highly variable pattern which became more stereotyped once the prey was located and the sequence leading to the kill began. It seems that the various levels of instinctive behavior, from the variable higher ones to the increasingly stereotyped lower ones, must stem from different sources in the nervous system. The entire variable part of the pattern, the performance of which is dependent, not only upon the presence of a stimulus, but its changing relationship to the environment as well, is called the *appetitive* stage. The completely stereotyped action ending a pattern is called the *consummatory* stage.

The variable appetitive behavior is considered to be a searching (the result of an "appetite") for a situation which contains a stimulus that could release the consummatory behavior or "fixed-action pattern." The end of appetitive behavior, according to this scheme, is not the attainment of an object, nor does its performance have any survival value per se. Instead, the objective is the performance of a consummatory act.

Appetitive behavior has come to be characterized as an "anxious" condition which persists and continuously increases until a specific *stimulus* can be found which releases the consummatory act. The consummatory act is followed by a state of rest. An aversive behavior has also been described by Craig (1918). It is similar to appetitive behavior but, in this case, rest comes when the stimulus has been removed.

Eckhard H. Hess (1962), at the University of Chicago, points out that appetitive behavior may be characterized in three ways: by (1) motor pattern (usually locomotion), (2) orientation (or spatial arrangement), and (3) search for stimuli to which the animal is receptive. For example, a hungry squirrel (1) climbs (2) up trees (3) looking for food. Since appetitive behavior is a search for a chance to perform consummatory behavior, it may be said that the hungry squirrel is not looking for something to fill its stomach, but something to swallow since swallowing is a consummatory act. Craig points out that many of the acts performed during the appetitive phase are not completely innate, but some acts, especially the more variable ones, may be done in association with patterns learned through experience. So a squirrel may be more inclined to forage in trees because he found an acorn there once before.

Craig stressed that in appetitive behavior the animal may be consciously striving to attain some end (*purposive* behavior). An example is a frog turning toward a fly in order to correctly release his fixed-action pattern, the darting tongue. An experienced frog, it may be said, wants to turn toward the fly and has a succulent fly "in mind" as he turns. Tinbergen (1951:106) states, "The consummatory act is relatively simple; at its most complex, it is a chain of reactions, each of which may be a simultaneous combination of a taxis and a fixed pattern. But appetitive behavior is a true purposive activity, offering all the problems of plasticity, adaptiveness, and complex integration that baffle the scientist in his study of behaviour as a whole." However, it should be pointed out that appetitive behavior may also include nonpurposive behavior as is demonstrated in seasonal migration. Even an experienced bird doesn't have in mind the lush vegetation and warm winds of Mexico when fall appears. To oversimplify, when something in his nervous system is affected by the shortening days, he just goes.

Lorenz and Tinbergen (1938) have described in detail the last level of appetitive behavior to occur before the consummatory act. The animal at this stage continually adjusts itself spatially to its environment. This adjustment is usually a locomotion or a turning of all or part of the body so that the animal is oriented correctly. The orientation is necessary for the consummatory fixed-action pattern to be effective. The change of position, which is steered by a *taxis* mechanism (Chapter 4) is, in some cases, completed before the reflexive consummatory mechanism is discharged. When the taxis is performed before the fixed-action pattern, the two types of actions may be easily distinguished. The snapping reaction of the sea horse, *Hippocampus leach*, illustrates the sequential scheme. The fish must assume a very precise posture in which the prospective prey is "exactly in the central plane of its head, in a definite direction and at a definite distince obliquely in front of and above its oral slit" (Lorenz and Tinbergen 1938:183). The sea horse may follow a small crab back and forth for several minutes. When the proper spatial relationship with the

Figure 2.2 Brooding goose retrieving an egg. The retrieval movements and the orientation of the motions with respect to the egg were separated in this experiment. (From Lorenz and Tinbergen 1939.)

crab is finally attained, the sea horse snaps the crab. The snapping action, like the tongue-darting action of a frog, is the reflexive consummatory act. Once this reaction has begun, the sea horse no longer responds to spatial changes in the environment. If the crab moves a bit to one side after the reflexive motion is begun, no adjustment is made and the sea horse misses.

If the two types of actions, the appetitive orientation and the consummatory act, are performed simultaneously, it is a difficult to determine what part of the observed behavior is due to which factor. If an egg is removed from the nest of a greylag goose, she will retrieve the egg by rolling it back under her bill (Figure 2.2). She continually makes small adjustments in direction as the eccentric egg rolls off center. If the egg is removed during this retrieving process, she will continue the egg-rolling motions until the fixed pattern is completed (or until the egg *would* have been retrieved if it hadn't been removed) but without the small correcting movements. So, here, the orientation (last level of the appetitive behavior) and the reflexive pattern (consummatory act) are performed simultaneously. Without experimenting, the two separate phases of the pattern would not have been distinguishable to an observer. Again, the fixed-action pattern (egg-rolling motions) is independent of the environment once the pattern is released. The orientation movements (corrective motions), however, are dependent upon what is going on in the environment.

Subsequent work has shown that the system operating in appetitive and consummatory behavior is actually much more complex than it has been presented thus far. For example, what seems to be appetitive in one animal may be consummatory in another. Also, complex interrelationships of environmental stimuli may exist which complicate behavioral studies. Environmental conditions which initiate an instinctive act may also serve to bring an existing pattern to an end, even when the original environmental stimuli are still present. These are, in the words of Thorpe

(1956:92), "consummatory stimuli." He adds, "The goal of an animal is not always the performance of an action; it may sometimes be the perception of the environmental situation; the achievement of such a situation may in fact be as effective in bringing a particular piece of behavior to a close as is the satisfaction of what is more crudely thought of as a philosophical need."

THE BEHAVIORAL HIERARCHY

We have seen that generalized appetitive behavior leads to increasingly specific behavioral levels until, finally, the inflexible fixed pattern of the consummatory level is released. Tinbergen (1951) proposed a hierarchical model which defines the relationship of the different behavioral levels. For example, to explain his model consider the reproductive behavior of the male stickleback (described in the ethogram in Chapter 1). In spring, the gradual increase in the length of day brings the male stickleback to an internal physiological state of readiness to perform reproductive behavior. The fish migrates into shallow water, where the temperature is warmer, and here establishes a territory. When the male settles on a territory, his erythrophores expand, turning him a bright red; he reacts to strangers in a hostile manner and begins to build a nest. It is difficult to predict which component (aggression or nest building) of the reproductive drive will be manifest at any particular time. Each is released by its own special set of stimuli. For example, fighting may be released by the sight of a red male intruding into the territory, and nest building by the presence of an adequate site.

Increasingly specific stimuli may elicit behavioral patterns lower on the hierarchical scale. In Figure 2.3 it may be seen that there is more than one type of fighting behavior and the intruding red male may provoke any of these. The type of fighting behavior is determined by what the intruding red male does. If he bites, the defending male will bite back; if he threatens, the defender will threaten back; if he flees, the defender will

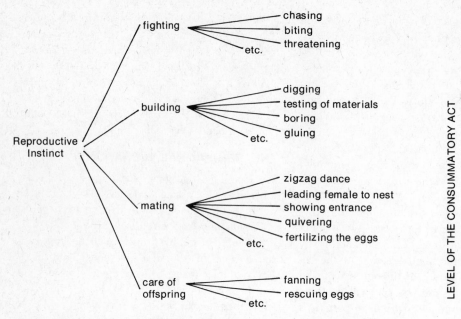

Figure 2.3 The hierarchical organization of the reproductive instinct of the male three-spined stickleback. See the text for an explanation. (From Tinbergen 1942.)

chase him, and so on. Thus, when environmental conditions cause our male to prepare physiologically for reproduction, the visual stimulus of a suitable territory elicts the propensity for either fighting or nest building. An intruder releases fighting behavior, but the type of fighting depends on even more specific stimuli involved in the activity of the intruder.

Tinbergen's hierarchical model (Figure 2.3) involves a mechanism by which each center passes the energy of the general reproductive drive to more specific centers when a neural block is removed. The center that accomplishes this is the part of the nervous system which reacts to specific environmental stimuli (the innate releasing mechanism, about which more will be said later). Tinbergen attempted to couple his model with a hierarchical theory proposed by Weiss (1941) showing the pathway of motor patterns that are activated by the consummatory act. In the integrated scheme (Figure 2.4) general behavior patterns (e.g., reproduction) are released by environ-

mental stimuli. As the "energy" flows to lower levels (its path being determined by which blocks are removed through the presence of stimuli specific for those blocks) each act is less flexible than the one before until the consummatory level is reached. The consummatory act activates motor centers of specific activities, for example, a particular nest-building motion. This center activates subordinate centers, such as the fin in fish, which in turns activates a specific set of fin rays, then individual muscles in the fin rays, and finally the motor units (motor end plates and the fibers they activate) themselves. It has been pointed out that certain imperfections exist in a too strict application of the Tinbergen-Weiss model. For example, upon close examination, it is not clear just how appetitive behavior could be fitted consistently into this scheme.

Although every facet of complex innate patterns are not accounted for in the model, the idea was theoretically important because it furnished a bridge between observed instinctive patterns

Figure 2.4 The theoretical organization of the instinctive centers and their relationship to the motor patterns. Motivational impulses (shown as straight arrows) "load" the centers (shown as circles). These impulses may begin in the external environment as well as in higher centers. The heavy lines show blocks which indicate inhibiting influences which prevent a steady discharge of motor impulses. The action of the IRM's remove the blocks. This enables the animal to show a specific appetitive behavior until more specific releasers trigger the next lowest center with its increasingly specific appetitive behavior. The curved arrows between centers of the same level show mutual inhibition and the presence of displacement activities. Below the consummatory level, several motor centers are activated at the same time. (From Tinbergen 1951.)

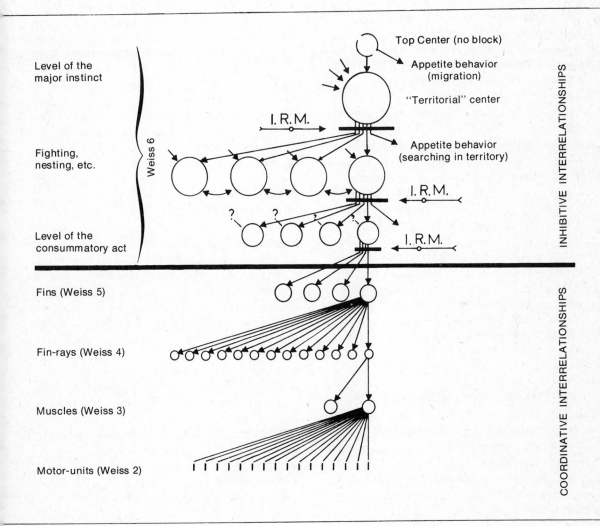

and their physiological interpretation. In 1943, W. R. Hess began a series of physiological experiments which gave credence to the basic plan of the model. He implanted tiny electrodes in the brains of cats and found that certain parts of the brain could be stimulated causing the animals to execute instinctive patterns. By administering a slight shock to a proper brain center, a cat could be made to fight, eat, or sleep. It was interesting that the normal appetitive behavior was shown in these cases; in other words, the cat would actively search for the food if the "eat" center was stimulated. The entire coordinated instinctive pattern (with its normal appetitive and consummatory parts) appeared only when parts of the hypothalamus were stimulated. If the electrodes were implanted lower, say in the medulla or spinal cord, disjointed behavior resulted—parts of instinctive patterns. These parts were, interestingly, lower on the hierarchical scale. It would be expected that the more variable higher centers would be located closer to the brain. For reviews of recent electrode implantation experiments see Marler and Hamilton (1966), Corso (1967), and Hinde (1970).

In the hierarchy model, then, the higher levels control the purposive and flexible behavior. The lower levels are involved in increasingly simpler and more stereotyped movements until, at the consummatory level, the orienting taxic component operates with the rigid fixed-action pattern. Hormones and internal stimuli are thought to operate on the higher centers as do the environmental stimuli which "motivate" behavior rather than release it. (See the discussions of drives and releasers.)

ACTION-SPECIFIC ENERGY

Lorenz, in 1937 and 1950, advanced the concept of *action-specific energy*. He found that the ease with which a stimulus released its consummatory act was dependent upon how long it had been since the act was released. ("Released" is the proper choice of words in this case.) He postulated that action-specific energy, or energy for a specific action, is constantly being produced in the animal's central nervous system. This energy is held in check by the inhibitory mechanism discussed above until the appropriate stimulus releases it. The released energy activates certain muscle systems and a particular behavior pattern results. If the proper stimulus is not found, the action-specific energy continues to build up until it can be contained no more, and then it goes off on its own, without a stimulus triggering it. This is called *vacuum activity*, and has been described in a variety of animals. Lorenz noticed it when one of his hand-reared starlings flew to a perch on a statue in his house, and began to "catch insects." The professor climbed up on the furniture several times to see what the bird was catching until he was finally satisfied that no insects were there. Lorenz's explanation is that in the absence of a stimulus the innate motor pattern was discharging due to the buildup of its own energy.

There is a progressive increase in the number of situations which will act as releasers as time goes by. Hinde (1952) found that nest-building behavior in tits is released when the bird finds an ideal site. If the bird fails to find the ideal, the threshold of acceptance becomes lower and lower, presumably due to a buildup of reproductive drive, until finally the tit will make do with a less-than-perfect site. One of the most important ecological implications of this phenomenon is its effect on animal dispersion. Animals may be forced to occupy a previously unoccupied geographical area after being displaced by storms or being driven out of a better area by territory holders. In the absence of ideal nesting sites, inferior ones are accepted and, thereby, a new area is colonized and, in time, adaptation to its particular characteristics may take place.

Progressive lowering of the threshold for a fixed reproductive motor pattern has also been described by Lorenz. A male blond ringdove was deprived of the female of its own species. After a while, it would court females of another species when they were presented. Then it showed a willingness to court a stuffed pigeon, then a rolled-up cloth, then a corner of its cage (the linear perspective of the converging lines at least presented a point at which the bird could focus its gaze). The "damming" effect is an example of one characteristic of instinctive acts which is not found in purely reflexive acts, in answer to those who wish to call instinct an elaborate reflex.

DRIVE AND MOTIVATION

The concept of drive is currently undergoing major changes based primarily on neurophysiological studies. The term has been variously interpreted and defined to the extent that it may at present mean many things. However, it will be discussed here in the sense that it has come to be defined by most ethologists.

Drive has been generally regarded as the force behind the seeking for a consummatory stimulus. It may be considered the "motivation" of appetitive behavior. Hinde (1956, 1959, 1960) reviewed the concept of drive and decided it should be considered simply a description of behavior without physiological implication. It is apparent that such a broad definition places serious limitations on the usefulness of the concept as a research tool. However, the development of the concept of drive has provided a useful way of looking at appetitive behavior. For example, conceptually, the importance an animal places on the performance of a consummatory act may be determined by measuring its drive.

One of the problems in studying drive stems from the fact that in spite of its theoretical utility, it is difficult to quantify. Nice (1937) described an attempt at such a measurement which utilized the observation that cold weather inhibits songbirds from singing. Nice correlated temperature with song frequency (Figure 2.5) in order to determine "how badly the birds wanted to sing." Hinde (1970), however, questioned the general utility of this sort of analysis by indicating some drives do not lend themselves to this experimental technique.

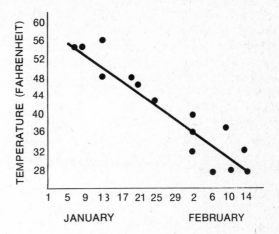

Figure 2.5 Changing threshold for temperature as a song suppressant in the song sparrow *Melospiza melodia*. (From Nice 1937.)

Some drives appear in sequence, the appearance of each dependent upon the successful performance of a specific preceding act. Tinbergen (1951) found that the male stickleback will not start to build its nest, although material is available, until he has defended his territory for a while. Nor will he court females until he has built the nest. If his pit is filled up after he has dug it, he will dig it again a few times, but then the external stimulus of a filled pit will have no further effect on him; the next drive takes over and he will build the nest without completing the pit.

An interesting characteristic of some drives is their rapid appearance and disappearance, which may result in alternately performed acts. The zig-zag dance of the male stickleback (Chapter 1) is considered to be an example of such alternation. Swimming away from the female is apparently an attempt to lead her to the nest. Swimming toward her is the aggressive behavior shown toward an intruder into the territory. The aggressive drive is replaced by the reproductive as he nears her.

Howard (1929) mentions "waxing and waning"

of drives. He is obviously referring to fluctuations of a relatively longer duration than those previously mentioned and they may be considered, therefore, to be higher on the hierarchical scale. An example is the seasonal appearance of reproductive behavior. The internal physiological changes which occur as a result of seasonal environmental phenomena is due to the influence of hormones. Their appearance is triggered by some external stimulus such as changing day-length. Their presence changes the internal milieu of the animal and affects the nervous system in a general way. These changes may make the animal responsive to different stimuli from its surroundings and thus accomplishes the seasonally correlated fluctuation.

Hormones are very important to some types of behavior such as the reproductive drive, but are less important to some other types such as foraging. In some cases, behavior which is not directly under hormonal control may be indirectly influenced by changes in hormone levels. For example, an animal in which the sex drive is strong is less disposed toward flight or eating. Witness the gaunt stallion which is penned within sight of a herd of mares. When flight is released, however, the thresholds of foraging and reproduction are raised so that they are not as likely to respond to their drives. A similar type of relationship apparently exists between drives for lower centers also. For example, nest building renders the stickleback less susceptible to stimuli which release fighting.

Drives, as we have seen, may play a great part in determining the behavior of an animal, and when a drive is strong the animal may have few behavioral alternatives. A drive may be strong enough to cause a brooding hen to fight an enemy she would normally flee. A drive may become so strong that it "breaks through," in the absence of a stimulus to produce the vacuum reactions or "explosions." All drives, however, are not as strong as those we have mentioned. There are also weaker drives which, under repeated stimuli, rapidly wane in strength. Lorenz (1937b) describes "in-

jury feigning" in a whitethroat. This response may cause a predator to forsake his search for the nest in favor of catching what is apparently a wounded bird. The response is clearly adaptive; however, Lorenz found that after the threatened bird performed the reaction three or four times, the response could no longer be elicited. Dogs or wolves, even those that are being continually fed, will gradually develop a drive to hunt. After being allowed to hunt, they show very little interest in this activity for a while. Such a condition, it sometimes seems, may exist in man. Not many wives are able to understand why a husband is willing and even eager to forsake a warm house and slippers to go hunting with "the boys," although after such an expedition he may be content to remain home for a while. Lionel Tiger (1969), the anthropologist, strongly argues that such tendencies may be innate in human males. The hunting drive, as far as the four-legged wolves are concerned, appears to be a rather weak drive which responds to a slowly accumulating internal factor and which is easily fatigued.

INTERACTIONS OF DRIVES

Lorenz (1963) points out that several types of interactions can occur between the various drives: One can accelerate the other, one can support the other, they can be superimposed on one another and give simultaneous and identical expression, and, rarely, one can negate the other. In this last case, it has been noted that the escape drive usually, but not always, subjugates the other drives. A closer examination of simultaneous drives will reveal more of the nature of the interaction. Hess (1962) described four types of simultaneous interactions. Alternation between two incompletely expressed drives, such as in the zigzag behavior of the stickleback, is called *successive ambivalent* behavior. It may also be seen in the quick attacks and retreats of territorial birds fighting at their common borders. The drives are not really simultaneous, but occur in rapid alternation to produce the typical response. *Sim-*

ultaneous ambivalent behavior is the expression of multiple drives occurring simultaneously. Leyhausen (1956) gives as a rather remarkable example of the threat posture of the cat. He allows that the back paws advance more rapidly than the more "timorous" front paws, causing the cat to "hunch" and to appear larger to enemies. *Redirected behavior* occurs when one drive is suppressed by another. An animal feeling aggressive toward its mate may attack another animal. A nesting bird may swoop at an intruding human, but, at the last minute, be overtaken by fear so that he swerves and attacks another bird instead. His aggressive act has not changed, only the object of the aggression. The last type of drive interaction is called *displacement activity.* Here, when two drives are in conflict, a third and completely unrelated pattern may appear. Tinbergen and Kortlandt reported this behavioral phenomenon independently in 1940. Hostile gulls which are disposed toward both fighting and flight may suddenly begin preening. A man who can't decide between two things he wants to do may scratch his head. The responses appear to be nonadaptive in that they are unrelated to the problem at hand.

Behavioral patterns resulting from displacement activity may not be performed as they normally are in their usual (adaptive) context. In other words, the irrelevant displacement pattern may show small differences from the normal functional pattern. In fighting sticklebacks which suddenly begin displacement digging, the digging is different from its normal model in that the spines are erected. The digging stickleback with erect spines is understood by other sticklebacks to be in a threat position. So, here the displacement activity has come to have an adaptive value in communication. Actual fighting in territorial species could be held to a minimum by developing a displacement "signal" which would indicate a readiness to fight without potentially dangerous aggressive behavior. (See the discussion on ritualization below and Chapter 6.)

In cases where the displacement activity appears to be nonadaptive, many explanations have been made for its maintenance in the behavioral repertoire. Some promising research is being done with electrophysiological studies of the central nervous system. The results of these studies indicate that displacement activities may not be due to a conflict of drives at all, but may be more properly described as the result of heterogeneous control in the central nervous system. Recent thinking has determined the overused term "drive" is not considered an appropriate term for the complex neural activity it attempts to describe. Although, we have, in this discussion, considered drive to be a measurable motivating force, it should be remembered that it is being considered as such only because it is useful in explaining behavior. For the time being, it is an operational theory only; one that works in helping us to understand *why* animals do what they do.

RELEASERS

A hen will not attempt to rescue a chick under a bell jar although the chick is visibly in distress. The same hen will very excitedly try to seek out her chick when a recording of its distress call is played. The releaser of rescue behavior in this case is auditory, not visual. The indifference of the hen to the sight of her distressed young compared to her immediate reaction to its call shows, first, that insight is not involved, and second, that only part of the situation presented reaches through to that part of the hen's nervous system that says, "rescue."

The parts of the environment that act as stimuli for instinctive actions are called *releasers.* A particular response may be elicited by more than one releaser. It has been found (Seitz, 1940) that fighting behavior in the male cichlid fish is elicited by five stimuli: (1) silvery blueness, (2) dark margin, (3) highness and broadness, (4) parallel orientation to opponent, and (5) tail beating. It was found that any one of these stimuli would elicit hostile behavior, and any two would elicit "twice" the reaction of one (although the precise

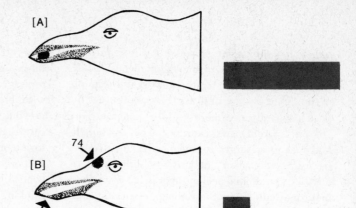

Figure 2.6 The columns show values of the two positions (A and B) in releasing begging pecks in chicks. The numbers in B show how many pecking responses were directed at the displaced red spot on the head and at the bill. Constraints on the model are described later. (From Tinbergen 1948a and 1948b.)

degree of relative strengths of reactions would be very hard to measure). Therefore, responses to releasers appear to be additive, so that the whole is equal to (not greater than, as in the case of the gestalt perception discussed in Chapter 3) the sum of its parts. The additive effect is called the *law of heterogenous summation*.

In some behavioral patterns, different stimuli are necessary to release the consummatory act and direct its orientation. Daphnia in a dish of water will swim to the top when CO_2 is high. The adaptiveness is probably related to the fact that surface water usually has a higher oxygen tension. If the dish is lighted from the bottom, and CO_2 is added to the water in which Daphnia are swimming, the little arthropods will swim to the bottom. So CO_2 increase releases swimming behavior which is then directed by light. The spatial response is more likely to be nonadaptive than is the released response, a condition which is probably due to the number of alternatives open to an animal making a spatial change. Once, when Tinbergen was spotted in his blind by a herring gull, the startled gull gave the alarm call to its young and they scrambled into what appeared to be the nearest safe place, his tent!

Some stimuli serve both as releasers and directors. Tinbergen, in one of his early experiments with releasers, found that young herring gulls, in their food-begging, peck at a red spot on the mandible of the adult. In models, if the red spot is

shifted to a place above the eye, the new model elicits only one-quarter the number of pecking responses (Figure 2.6), but of the responses elicited, about half are directed to the mandible and half to the new site. It has since been found that the responses are due partly to other factors, such as the height and the direction of movement of the model, but such experiments provide examples of the directing influence of certain releasers. The above example also illustrates the importance of configuration and spatial arrangement in visual releasers. Consider another classical experiment which illustrates this principle more clearly, the reaction of young ducks and geese to a silhouette model of a flying bird (Figure 2.7). The wings were symmetrical, at one end there was a short protuberance, at the other end a longer one. When it was pulled along a guide wire in one direction it appeared to have a long neck and a short tail like a goose. Flown the other way it resembled a short-necked bird of prey. In the first case, its appearance was noticed and ignored. In the second case it elicited escape reactions in the ducks and geese. The configuration hadn't changed, only the relationship of direction to configuration.

Tinbergen's experiments with gulls show the importance of relative sizes in releasers. Nestling herring gulls will gape at any part of a model which breaks the contour. This break is apparently considered by the chick as the head of the parent. Thus, consider the models represented in Figure 2.8. In *a*, the chick gapes at the smaller "head." In *b* it gapes at the larger. The difference is obviously a function of the relative size of the "head" to the "body." These experiments point out a difficulty in designing and in interpreting laboratory experiments with animals. The sign stimuli in the wild are complex and highly inter-related, and so valid measurements of isolated factors are extremely difficult to obtain. Experiments must, therefore, be designed very carefully with an ethologist's understanding of his subject.

The problems of studying sign stimuli are compounded by other factors also. Many reactions, even short simple ones, depend on a *set* of sign stimuli to elicit an entire adaptive response. For example, bees may initially be attracted to a colored paper flower, but they will not land unless the flower scent is there, so the visual releaser alone, in this case, will not initiate a behavioral pattern that has survival value.

The male of the grayling butterfly, *Eumenis semele*, is attracted to virgin females on the basis of their darkness (the darker the better), their nearness, and their fluttering movement. Color seems to play no part. The male would court a red as easily as a blue if both were of the same degree of darkness. It would appear then that the butterflies are color-blind. However, in tests using paper flowers of various colors, *Eumenis* reacted positively to blue and yellow and thus showed real color discrimination in feeding (Tinbergen 1951). So here is a case of sense organs being differentially employed in the search for specific releasers. (Perhaps we should avoid suggesting that love is *color*-blind?)

It is not surprising, then, that a knowledge of the sensory capacities of an animal will not tell us what part of his environment is releasing his behavior, since, as we have seen, animals may only react to a small part of their environment and these parts may be dependent upon what action in the animal's behavioral repertoire is being released. *Dysticus marginalis*, the carnivorous water

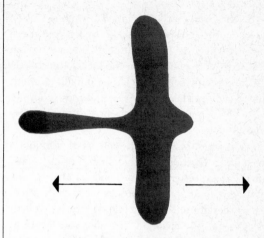

Figure 2.7 The silhouette model resembles a long-necked goose when pulled from right to left. It resembles a short-necked bird of prey when pulled left to right. Lorenz reported that when the model was pulled at the proper speed through the sky an escape reaction was elicited in young turkeys. Tinbergen later included gallinaceous birds, ducks and geese. (From Tinbergen 1948a.)

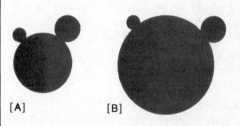

[A]   [B]

Figure 2.8 Models with two "heads." When model a is presented to a nestling, gaping responses are directed toward the small "head." When b is presented, the large "head" elicits gaping. The results indicate that the size of the head relative to the body is important in releasing the gaping response. (From Tinbergen and Kuenen 1939.)

beetle, has very well-developed compound eyes, but a tadpole suspended in a sealed test tube does not stimulate him to attack. However, when meat extract is poured into the water, the beetle will capture any solid object. The unfailing repetition of such mistakes is one of the most conspicuous characteristics of purely instinctive behavior.

Some types of patterns such as the foraging behavior in *Dysticus* can be elicited at any time, but there are other types of behavior that can be released only at special times as we have learned. Let us reexamine the principle in terms of releasers. Courting behavior in the male stickleback is released by the sight of the female's belly swollen with eggs and the peculiar posture of the "ready" female. The female, for her part, reacts sexually to certain releasers in the male's behavior such as his zigzag dance. However, none of these stimuli have any effect at all in autumn or in winter. It would be most unfortunate if a pair were to mate and waste time and energy on a brood which would surely die! The environmental control of behavior is not accomplished by flipping some physiological on-off switch. Instead, physiological changes result in increasing drive as the environmental conditions gradually approach optimum for that pattern. If the drive is only of medium intensity, only strong releasers will evoke a response. As the drive increases, the threshold for its release drops lower and lower as was demonstrated in the caged blond ringdove. So the effect of releasers is partly a function of their environmental context.

A student of Lorenz, B. Oehlert, found that male and female cichlids have the same behavioral repertoire. This discovery gave rise to certain questions. How does a male recognize a female, or how is homosexual mating prevented? It was found that three types of behavior were elicited when two cichlids met: (1) aggression, (2) escape, and (3) sexual behavior. The sexual difference was revealed by how the three are mixed. Successful pairing demanded an "awe-inspiring" male

which showed mainly 1 and 3. The submissive and "awed" female showed mainly 2 and 3. It may be assumed that there was a sexual difference in the thresholds for each act. Also, there may have been certain subtle sign stimuli characteristic of each sex that went unrecognized by the human observer.

In a sequence of reactions the animal must know when to stop each act and begin the next. In some situations this must be accomplished when the releaser of the first act is still present, as was mentioned earlier. How can the first releaser be ignored so that the animal does not continue to perform the first step over and over again? The answer may be in the relationship of the releasers to the consummatory act. Following a consummatory act there is a period of rest or of satiation. During these times of rest, the threshold for the release of that pattern may be raised above the level which was necessary to elicit the reaction the first time so that the second act may then be released. This scheme would be even more feasible if each act were to serve as the releaser for the next act. Tinbergen (1953) describes such a system in the nest building of the long-tailed tit, *Aegithalos caudatus*. Thorpe (1956) analyzes the movements in terms of sequential releasers. He describes the bird putting moss on the tree, the first act. "Moss on site" releases a search for spider silk. "Silk on moss" releases a stretching motion which is employed in binding the nest together, and so on until the nest is completed. So, in those species for which learning is not the basis for a sequential pattern, it may be that as each phase is consummated the threshold for that act is raised and, in some cases, the completion of an act may release the next phase of the pattern.

Seitz (1940, 1942) found that, in fish, the numerous sign stimuli composing a releaser could be analyzed independently (recall the law of heterogeneous summation) and that the deficiency of one part could be counterbalanced by an increase in another. Since the releasing value of each sign

Figure 2.9 An oyster catcher, *Haematopus ostralegus*, shows a preference for a giant egg rather than a normal egg (foreground) or a herring gull's egg (left). (From N. Tinbergen, *The Study of Instinct,* The Clarendon Press, Oxford 1951.)

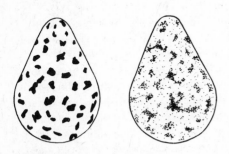

Figure 2.10 A supernormal egg which is unusual only in the size of its spots (left) is preferred by the ringed plover, *Charadrius hiaticula,* to a normal egg (right). (From N. Tinbergen, *The Study of Instinct,* The Clarendon Press, Oxford 1951.)

stimulus is modifiable then, a question arises regarding the extent to which a releaser may increase its effect. Interestingly, each part can be artificially "increased" so that it is preferred over its normal condition by the animal. Oyster catchers prefer eggs larger than normal and will try to sit on "eggs" too large to incubate (Figure 2.9). Ringed plovers, *Charadrius hiaticula,* prefer the more strongly spotted egg over their own eggs (Figure 2.10). Exaggerated stimuli which are "preferred" over normal stimuli are called *supernormal releasers.*

Magnus (1958) found supernormal releasers in the butterfly, *Argynnis paphia L.* The fluttering of females' wings showed alternately light and dark wing parts. Magnus put yellow-orange (normal wing colors) and dark strips on a rotating cylinder and found that excitement in the male increased as the frequency (rate of turning) exceeded that shown by normal females. So, in this case, the characteristic (darkness) that was important to the male grayling butterfly we discussed earlier is ignored in *Argynnis* in favor of the flashes of wing colors, and the flashes of the color increase in appeal with their frequency.

Certain parasitic birds, such as some cuckoos and cowbirds, have young that are larger and more "babyish" than the host's. This may be the reason why the host attends to the young parasite in preference to its own young in many instances. There are undoubtedly good examples of supernormal releasers among the mimicking animals also. In the cases of parasitizing and mimicking, the supernormal releasers are directed toward eliciting a response in members of other species.

Releasers have been compared to a key which unlocks a behavioral pattern in the animal's neuromotor system. The occurrence of supernormal releasers and the concept of heterogeneous summation, however, show that the lock-and-key analogy is not a good one. The analogy, however, does serve to point up the idea that an inherited mechanism (the lock) does exist within the nervous system.

INNATE RELEASING MECHANISMS

As we have seen, only a small part of the environmental situation serves as a releaser for each instinctive act. How and where are these specific incoming environmental signals decoded in the nervous system of the animal? How is a coordinated motor response achieved? The ethologists of this century have developed a concept which assumes the existence of an inborn neural mechanism that responds in a specific way to the releasers.

As has been mentioned, Darwin was one of the first to point out that instinctive behavior can be treated as a taxonomic tool, just as organs are. This concept does not seem so farfetched if behavior, particularly innate behavior, is analyzed in terms of the structure and physiology of the genetically determined nervous system. (The concept is discussed in more detail in Chapter 11.) The innate releasing mechanism (IRM) is considered to be that part of the nervous system which is the target of incoming signals set up by the animal's perceiving a releaser. The IRM responds by sending commands to the proper effectors (motor systems).

Releasers, as we know, help to control the timing of an act. It would certainly not be good if various actions were released indiscriminately under just any condition. The IRM concept helps to explain the mechanism of this regulation. Lorenz (1937) and Tinbergen (1951) postulated the inhibitory block (see Figure 2.4) to prevent unfortuitous discharge of the internally produced energy. Theoretically, the IRM is the mechanism which functions in removing the inhibitory block when it receives sensory impulses from the appropriate releaser in the environment. The IRM, then, may be the site which is influenced by the action-specific energy mentioned earlier.

How is the proper stimulus gleaned from the myriad of environmental information flooding the animal's receptors? Two obvious possibilities present themselves. First, the animal may be insensitive to those parts of the environment that are

irrelevant. The receptors may be specialized to pick up only a certain part of the total environmental picture and to ignore the rest. These specialized receptors are called *peripheral filters*. If two species of frogs are calling at different sound wave frequencies in the same bog, each individual may hear only the call of its own species, or if it hears both calls, only the call of the proper frequency may make it through the afferent (incoming) nervous system to its IRM. The "incorrect" sound is filtered out somewhere before the impulses reach the central nervous system.

The other mechanism is one employing *central filters*. In this case, a wide range of environmental signals are picked up and all are sent to the central nervous system. There, discrimination of the signals takes place and only a certain type of signal is acted upon. Tinbergen (1951) points out that the strict dependence of an instinctive reaction on a specific set of sign stimuli leads to the conclusion that a neurosensory mechanism (the IRM) does exist. This mechanism, whether peripheral or central, signals the effectors to perform and is responsible for the very precise character of sign stimuli.

From Tinbergen's principle of heterogeneous summation we learned that IRMs may be stimulated by more than one sign stimulus. Which part of a set of stimuli may be missing is not important, but *how much* may be missing is, since one part can be compensated for by other parts. Although the various sign stimuli for a certain response may be functions of entirely different aspects of the environment, they do not differ in their qualitative effects on the motor response as a whole. The important principle to be gathered from this is that somewhere in the CNS (central nervous system) they are added and, if their *total* effect is strong enough, the IRM sends an impulse to the effectors. There are indications that the summing takes place in the IRM itself.

Certain changes may occur in the IRM during the postnatal life of the animal. In some cases selectivity of the IRM for releasers may increase. In other words, it may narrow the range of stimuli which will affect it. An escape reaction may be released in a young bird by moving leaves, but later they cease to elicit any response. A young toad may snap at any insect within range, including wasps. In time, it becomes more selective. The most obvious inference to be drawn from these examples is that learning has occurred. However, there are many warnings in the ethological literature against too simple an interpretation of what, at first, appears to be modification of an instinctive act by learning. Lorenz emphasizes that since instincts are inherited, just as organs are, they must mature just as organs do. A newly fledged bird does not suddenly begin using his sex organs in mating. Instead, the organs and associated drives appear as the bird becomes sexually mature. Many ethologists very strongly stress that instinct (or the IRM) cannot be modified by learning although it can be argued that increased selectiveness in releasers is a type of learning. This is not to rule out the possibility that instinctive acts can be performed with learned patterns.

As an animal matures, the IRM may also show a strengthening in its response to a certain releaser. In animal socialization, this effect may be associated with a phenomenon known as imprinting. A gosling will follow almost any moving object until, at some point early in its life, it "selects" a certain type of object, usually an adult goose. After this, it will attempt to associate only with the selected object. Imprinting is discussed in more detail in the chapter on learning.

RITUALIZATION

Julian Huxley, Lorenz's teacher, in his pre-World War I study of the behavior of the great crested grebe, found that, in the course of evolution, certain behavioral patterns lose their original functions and become purely symbolic or useful only in communication. He called the process by which the symbolic function arises *ritualization*. In the

evolution of ritualization two coordinated series of events must occur: the first, regards the motor pattern and releasing effects of the "actor" (the ritual performer), and the second, the response patterns of the "reactor" (the ritual observer).

Daanje (1950) showed that ritual displays are not often derived from the entire original behavior sequences, but from only a small part of it such as *intention movements*. Intention movements are incomplete and useless motions which are only part of an overall adaptive pattern (such as the quick crouches made by a small bird just before flight). They may occur just before the entire pattern is carried out or, as in some cases, they appear before the complete pattern has developed ontogenetically (within the individual). Conceivably, these movements may simply be reactions to environmental stimuli which are not strong enough to instigate a complete response. If ritualization developed from the intention movements, according to Klopfer and Hailman (1967), then natural selection could develop the display gradually since the adaptive response would not be affected. The adaptive (useful) parent movement could be retained while developing the display from its nonadaptive (adaptively neutral) intention movement. Ritualized patterns could also conceivably develop from displacement activities (remember, a fanning stickleback with its spines erect is considered belligerent by other males).

Not all ritualized behavior develops from nonadaptive originals. In some cases, a pattern might first become innate while it is serving its original function. The pattern is recognized as a ritual act when it is apparent that it is no longer a flexible response composed of many separate parts and reacting to various segments of a wide spectrum of environmental stimuli. Instead, in ritualization these parts become welded into a stereotyped pattern which is responsive to fewer aspects of the environment.

The evolutionary development of a ritualized pattern is easier to imagine when it is remembered that innate patterns are evolutionarily conservative (not easily changed). Innate patterns, unless selected against, may persist in the behavioral repertoire long after they have ceased to be useful. Our dogs still turn around several times before lying down on a rug. Their ancestors probably performed the act to drive out insects or spiders from their beds; since there is no strong selection against it, the act is still performed. Therefore, once an act is innate, if it were not strongly selected against, there would be plenty of time for it to alter its adaptive value.

In behavior which has become ritualized, while all or part of the original pattern is still present, it is hard to know how much of what one sees is the original and how much is the ritual copy. The two types of patterns may overlap and, if this occurs, the movements can be identified only where the ritual differs from the original in some respect. The point in their evolution at which sticklebacks *instinctively* fan in response to other males is the point at which the act may be considered ritualized. To the observer it would appear that the fanning male is nest building (albeit at an inopportune time) were it not for the erect spines. As the act became ritualized in the actor,

corresponding changes must occur in the reactor as the intruding male begins to recognize the pattern as a threat. In some cases, conditions may so change that the original no longer is adaptive and, eventually, the pattern is performed *only* as a ritual signal. Lorenz believes many of civilized man's cultural gestures have arisen by a similar process. A man may wave as a friendly sign, but perhaps at one time it was a gesture to show that his hands were empty of weapons.

An example of the separation of the original adaptive behavior and its display derivative may be seen in the *inciting behavior* of certain species of ducks such as the European sheldrake. In the pattern's original form, if the female felt the territory was being threatened by, for example, an intruding pair of ducks, she responded by running toward her protective drake. She usually stopped in front of him and looked back over her shoulder at the intruders. Figure 2.11 depicts her effort to cause the male to attack the object of her concern. In the original pattern, the angle of the body and neck of the female was a function of the position of the two males. As the pattern became instinctive, or ritualized, the female

Figure 2.11 Inciting behavior in ducks. See the text for an explanation. (From Konrad Lorenz, *On Agression,* Harcourt Brace Jovanovich, Inc. and Methuen and Co. Ltd. 1963.)

looked over her shoulder no matter where the two males were. Adaptive orientation is still seen in the female's eye which is fixed on the strange male but she is apparently unable to resist moving her neck in what has become an innate pattern.

Some decidedly ritualized behavior patterns have retained their original function. These are best seen in symbolic fighting, which is considered later.

The development of the ritualized inciting pattern in ducks can be traced by observing differences in the pattern in closely related species. There are examples of intermediate stages, from highly flexible (nonritualized) to completely stereotyped ritual patterns. In some species of ducks, the ritualization of inciting behavior may not be identical to the original because the development of the ritual is incomplete. In other species the ritual has been lifted out of its original context and serves only as a means of communication in pairing behavior. It is interesting that in the cases where a pattern has become ritualized it may appear *in vacuo*.

There is an interesting example of ritualization among the insects. In empid flies, *Hyperborean empis*, the male brings a dead fly for the female to eat while he mates with her. Such behavior may be adaptive in keeping the female from eating the male when he approaches her. In a North American species, the courting male spins a white balloon with a few small insects trapped in it. In the southern empid, *Hilara maura*, little veils are carried between the legs which may or may not have food in them. The male Alpine tailor fly, *H. sartor*, spins a little veil but never carries food in it to the female. The veil is held between the middle and hind legs to which the female responds sexually. So, the simultaneous existence of varying degrees of original and ritual helps point out the evolutionary development of certain patterns. As Lorenz (1963) asks, who would have guessed the origin of the "lovely little viels"?

Lorenz makes an interesting proposal regarding the development of rituals. *Phenocopy* is a term used when, through environmental factors, a phenotype or physical character is produced which is identical with one that is usually produced through heredity. In ritualization, however, a new hereditary characteristic copies behavioral patterns which were formerly caused by environmental factors. He proposes the term *genecopy*.

David Blest gives an interesting account of ritualization in Thorpe and Zangwill's (1961) book.

3

LEARNING

We have all undoubtedly been confronted and even confounded by accounts of animal intelligence, insight, and understanding. While it is unlikely that Aesop's stories are universally viewed as history, there are, at the same time, great differences of opinion among scientists as to whether certain animals can learn much, what they can learn, and how important it is to them. There is also some argument as to just how one should go about testing learning in animals. Clever Hans was a horse owned by a European some years ago which amazed the scientific world with his ability to solve a number of types of problems, the answers to which he communicated by tapping the ground with his forefoot. Clever Hans withstood the most rigorous tests of the skeptics for some time until it was finally determined that he was reading extremely subtle clues given inadvertently by his owner. Today even preliminary tests would rule out such a factor, but, whereas scientific method is not usually the subject of argument, the formation of hypotheses and the methods of testing them are the subjects of some disagreement. We will not concentrate on the arguments, but we will assume the ethological approach to the concept of learning.

As we have seen, certain patterns of animal behavior may be, in the final analysis, seated in the genetic constitution of the animal. Such patterns are the product of patient and unprejudiced, yet blind and compromising, influences of natural selection. The patterns which survive this selection are the product of severe trials and are indelibly stamped into the nervous system of the species. In a sense, then, the members of any species may, to some degree, be "programmed" to behave in a certain way.

However, we also know that in a complex and ever changing world, it is not reasonable to assume that all possible problems may be anticipated genetically so that an immediate and proper response is already programmed into the animals' behavioral repertoire. Instead, some degree of individual behavioral flexibility is important. The degree of this flexibility, of course, could be expected to vary widely between and within species. Some species show very little variation in their behavioral patterns and, as might be expected, they are usually very specialized for a particular life-style. Intestinal parasites, as an example, probably are not able to profit greatly by individual experience. They live under very constant conditions as adults and, to insure new generations, rather than depend on their individual cleverness, they simply lay thousands upon thousands of eggs and leave the rest to the law of averages. Other animals may show greater flexibility of behavior. Many land vertebrates live under a variety of conditions during their lifetime and their behavioral patterns are more affected by their individual experience. The success they achieve in solving their problems is in part dependent upon how well they are able to make associations based on past experience.

In this chapter we will consider the acquisition of new information through individual experience, or *learning*. In light of the great biases and schisms in the study of behavior, it is not surprising that there are a number of approaches to the study. However, we will develop the concept within the general framework set out by Thorpe (1963) with consideration of certain modifications and expansions of the plan. The concepts we will consider are the bases for much of the current biochemical and neurophysiological studies, and the provision of such bases might well prove to be one of the most important functions of ethology.

Because the old nature-nurture controversy has provided much grist for scientific mills we might briefly review the history of the concept of learning.

HISTORY OF THE IDEA

The consideration of the central nervous system as the "instrument" of behavior was implicit in Darwin's theorizing and was carried on and strengthened in the writings of Lloyd Morgan (1894), Loeb (1901), McDougall (1905), and Sherrington (1906). Morgan was undoubtedly the most important writer of the period and has been called the first of the modern students of animal behavior. His most important contributions were his refutation of the Lamarckian concept of inheritance and the revival of Occam's rule (which, in its reappearance, came to be known as Morgan's canon: never assume an action to be due to conscious decision when an alternative hypothesis is possible which avoids that assumption).

Scientists, about the turn of the century, were greatly interested in exploring the "mind." The idea was that valuable information could be acquired by learning the subjective thoughts of animals as controllers of their behavior. Of course it was necessary to assume certain basic similarities between the minds and emotional makeup of man and the lower animals. Obviously, this sort of subjective attempt to determine "what goes on in the mind of animals" was bound to chaff many scientists who realized the futility of the approach.

Within a few years, the consideration of the relationship of the nervous system and behavior caused a shift in the approach to the study of behavior. The idea was basically simple: instead of studying the subjective "mind," it was considered more appropriate, given the limitations of experimental techniques, to study the behavior of animals and to determine, through inductive reasoning, the nature of the neural activity responsible for these actions. The German zoologists, Theodor Beer, Hans Albrecht Bethe, and Jakob Johan von Uexküll, published a manifesto in 1899 denouncing all attempts at the subjective interpretations of the animal's mind and proposing new terms which did not imply a knowledge of the animal psyche. This declaration was the beginning of the objectivist movement. Their attempt to remove overly subjective or anthropomorphic interpretations was commendable; however, their new restrictions were considered too limiting and, in fact, unrealistic. The Germans assumed the psyche of animals is not knowable and, therefore, they would have prematurely excluded a variety of evidence that was to come along and which was to prove valuable. The influence of this type of objectivism was not great, but it was an indication of the movement toward the rejection of great assumptions in the study of behavior.

A more influential movement toward objectivism was beginning in America. In 1913 John B. Watson introduced the idea of *behaviorism*. There came quickly into being a wide range of behaviorists with philosophies ranging from Watson's rather simplistic view to that of E. S. Russell who admitted the presence of feelings and strivings within the animal, but who focused his attention, not on these subjective phenomena themselves, but on their part in the animal's overall natural history. The behaviorists based their interpretations somewhere between the subjectivism which had gone before and the overly strict view imposed by the German objectivists. It was asked, why speak only of a stimulus when we know that the animal reacts to more than a stimulus, namely, a perception? Why ignore the feelings and strivings of the animal or, at the best, summarize them as "unknown internal factors"? Such appeals for flexibility in approach imply the recognition that there are certain things that are knowable regarding the animal's feelings and motivations. This middle ground was the basis for many ideas (such as "drive") which were important in the development of current theory and which assumed some knowledge of the animal's feelings.

Behaviorism continued to exert its influence long after Watson, primarily through his brilliant student, Karl Lashley. The behaviorist approach came to be based on the premise that all behavior is the result of individual learning and so, the consideration of instinct as a major determinant of behavior was neglected. This premise was to bring the behaviorists into conflict with the ethologists.

In the early clashes between the behaviorists and ethologists, Lorenz argued that behaviorism assumes the simplistic view that the central nervous system is a homogeneous and equipotential structure, ready to be molded by experience—a blank sheet, as it were—and that a variety of evidence indicates that this is not the case. Lorenz also strongly criticized the idea that all behavior is attributable to learning on the basis that it is simply not possible to learn the amount that is necessary to perform complex adaptive acts. A swift, it was pointed out, which is reared in a small dark nest, is able to fly perfectly, focus its eyes, judge distance, avoid obstacles and make pinpoint landings its first time out. It would take a *superhuman* effort to learn these things in a brief period of flight time. In clarifying his concept of a basic difference in instinct and learning, he pointed out that most ethologists do not attribute behavioral patterns to either learning or instinct exclusively, but that the two, while emanating ultimately from different neural sources, are probably intertwined in most behavioral actions.

Lorenz has postulated an interesting idea regarding the relationship of evolutionary and individual development as they are related to learning. His premise is that there are two, and only two, different mechanisms for adaptation of behavior: (1) the phylogenetic, based on evolutionary change within the nervous system of a species, and (2) the ontogenetic, based on adaptive behavioral modification within the individual. To oversimplify, it can be said that a species experiments by mutation, and an individual by trial and error. These two entirely different processes, evolution and learning, both alter the nervous apparatus with precise and different adaptive effect. We have no difficulty visualizing changes in the neuroapparatus through evolution: learning must also be considered to be related to selection in the central nervous system. It is feasible that evolutionary changes occur in the learning centers so that learning propensity is selected for. Selection might move toward both regulating the amount of learning that is possible as well as what type of learning may take place. Relative intelligence (according to some concepts, such as those held by the "connectionists") may be thought of as differences in the abilities of centers in the central nervous system to interact (or interconnect), and as differences in the types or numbers of pathways within a certain type of center. When the physical basis of learning centers are considered, it is not difficult to conceptualize the possible evolutionary modification of these centers. Thus learning (or its means, intelligence), like instinct, is considered to be a function of a special neurophysiological seat built into the organism's central nervous system during evolution.

WHAT IS LEARNING?

There have been many attempts to define learning precisely. According to Hilgard (1956), learning occurs when the probability of certain behavior patterns in specific stimulus situations has been changed as a result of previous encounters with this or other similar stimulus situations (not due to maturational or fatigue processes). Hinde (1970) focused on the exclusive part of this definition and defines learning as "changes which cannot be understood in terms of maturational growth processes in the nervous system, fatigue, or sensory adaptation." Simply "adaptive behavioral modification," an often used definition, is too broad to be useful and, perhaps, "a relatively permanent change attributable to practice" is too narrow. The increasing indications of interacting neurological centers make a definition of any of their effects very difficult. We shall incorporate aspects of the above definitions in forming one of our own. We now define learning as the adaptive changes in behavior that result from individual experience, probably physically evidenced in the central nervous system, and which may function with innate patterns but which are ultimately distinguishable from these patterns. In the following discussions it should become eminently clear that although learned and innate patterns are distinguishable, adaptive patterns are usually comprised of elements of both and, at our present level of knowledge, debate over the relative con-

tributions of each is not usually particularly fruitful.

MEMORY

The information gained from experience must be stored and then recalled at the appropriate time in order for there to be any advantage to experience. The storage and retrieval process is what is known as *memory*, and its characteristics are important in any consideration of learning.

No one yet knows just how memory works but various hypotheses have been proposed. J. C. Eccles (1953) proposed that memory consists of reverberating circuits which, when once activated through sensory experience, continue. Others have shown that morphological changes appear in nerve cells, such as changes in the number of microsomes, the size and shape of apical dendrites, and changes at the synapses themselves (Gerard 1961). Recently biochemical hypotheses have been proposed which are based on a fascinating set of experiments with planarians, *Dugesia*. When a planarian learned a task, its head was cut off. When a new head was generated, the animal still retained the task (McConnell et al. 1959). The changes that occurred, then, must have been distributed throughout the animal's body and must not have been restricted to its primitive central nervous system. If the tail sections were regrown in solutions containing an enzyme that destroys ribonucleic acids (RNA), no memory survived the regeneration (Corning and John 1961). So attention has been focused on RNA as the key "memory chemical." In other experiments, trained planarians were fed to untrained ones, and the cannibals learned the same task faster than those on a normal flatworm diet (McConnell 1962). It has been argued that the experiments are not conclusive however, since it was found that even if a planarian ate an untrained brother, it learned somewhat faster (Hartry et al. 1964).

When trained rats were killed and RNA extracted from their brains and injected into untrained rats, the latter showed the learned pattern in a significant number of instances. Other experiments indicated that not only was a specific response transferred but the tendency to react to a specific stimulus (e.g., light, sound) was also transferred. These experiments have all been severely criticized and the findings, for now, must remain tentative.

Apparently, there are two separate mechanisms by which information is stored, as evidenced in the difference in *long-term memory* and *short-term memory*. The phenomenon was first noticed in humans with brain concussions who did not remember what happened just before an accident, but could remember what happened much earlier. Two memory centers were postulated whose information could be affected independently. These two centers function in long-term memory and short-term memory. Information stored in the long-term-memory "center" system is relatively permanent (or subject to very slow decay). Once information is processed into the long-term system, it is not easily disrupted and therefore may be recalled with minimum confusion after long periods of time, even if subject to disuse. Short-term memory, on the other hand, is rather easily disrupted and is subject to rather rapid decay. (This is the reason "cramming" for exams is not a good idea. If the examination is postponed, all is lost; or if the student is suddenly disturbed or frightened on the way to class, he may forget parts of the material.) Also, there is evidence that the short-term memory can be overloaded whereas the long-term cannot.

There is interesting evidence that short-term storage may be necessary before long-term storage can occur. In a series of experiments with the octopus, Wells (1959) found that if an inedible object is presented to one arm of an octopus over and over in rapid succession the arm will come to reject it. If it is then immediately presented to other arms, they will accept it. If some time is allowed to expire before the second presentation, all the arms will reject it. This is interpreted as meaning the information gained from one arm is only locally adaptive and must filter from the

short-term center to the long-term system before a general adaptive pattern can appear.

Most studies of memory are still in the exploratory stages and, as more data appears, the picture grows increasingly complex. Hinde (1970) warns against attempting to formulate an oversimplified model at this time.

REWARD AND REINFORCEMENT

Before the various types of learning are considered, it would be well to mention a much-debated concept that enters into many types of learning. It is the concept of *reward* or *reinforcement*.

In evolution, changes are preserved through their survival value. If their net effect helps the organism to survive, they are "good" and are preserved. But how does an individual ascertain which behavioral patterns are good? Thorndike (1911) said if an act fulfills or relieves body needs it is good, and that act is thereby reinforced so that it will be likely to be repeated when that body need appears again. Others postulated that "good" should be defined as that which reduces a drive (such as the hunger drive), in other words, that which relieves physiological tension. It should be pointed out, however, that the reward need not actually be of biological advantage (as in the case with addicting drugs). It should also be pointed out that reward may be in the form of reduced psychological tensions as is exhibited in the performance of nonadaptive habits or superstitions. Although there is no real biological advantage in these acts, when performed they may relieve psychological tensions—perhaps simply because of their familiarity.

At what level does reinforcement operate? Lorenz proposes that the mechanism which directly brings about the good or adaptive effect is the fixed-action pattern, or consummatory act. The completion of the act (e.g., eating) has a reinforcing effect through *reafference* or sensory feedback. As an example of such a learning-instinct interaction, consider nest building in the crow family. A crow, standing on a suitable nest site with nest material in its beak, performs a downward and sideward sweep of the head which forces the material against the substrate, and later against the partially completed nest. When the twig meets resistance, the bird shoves harder, thrusting repeatedly, as would a man trying to push a pipe cleaner through an obstructed part of the pipestem. When the twig is wedged in, its resistance is increased and the efforts of the bird are heightened until, when it sticks fast, the bird consummates its activities in an orgiastic maximum of effort and then loses interest for a time. Some species of crows possess no innate mechanism to guide their selection of nest material and, so, young birds will attempt to build with anything they can carry. Most of the unlikely material, which may include light bulbs or pieces of ice, will not wedge firmly into the nest and so they are prevented from reaching the consummatory stimulus situation that means both relief and biological success. Such failure quickly extinguishes the bird's acceptance of inadequate material until, finally, the birds become true connoisseurs of twigs. In such situations, then, the reinforcer of a learning situation is the performance of an innate consummatory act (Lorenz 1969).

It has also been shown that learning may function in placing innate patterns into their proper adaptive sequence through reinforcement mechanisms. Eibl-Eibesfeldt (1970) found that nest building in rats is accomplished by the performance of three motor patterns. First, the rat brings nest material to a selected site. Then, it stands in the center of the material and, turning to and fro, stacks the material into a roughly circular wall. Finally, it pats the wall, tamping it down and smoothing the inside. Naïve rats, offered paper strips, will get into a frenzy of all three activities—running about with nest material, patting, and building all at once. Each act is performed perfectly—but no nest results. The naïve rat, after carrying a few paper strips, will stand above them performing heaping movements in the air and tamping down a wall which doesn't exist. The failure of the pattern to provide a rewarding reaffirmation by its resistance to the rat's paws teaches the rat not to attempt heaping before the nest material is carried in, or patting before the wall is built. Lorenz (1969) has pointed out that the structure and functional properties of the consummatory act were never fully understood until their teaching function was realized. He also notes that there does not seem to be any case in which conditioning by reinforcement could be demonstrated in a behavioral system not including appetitive behavior.

Reward, according to Thorndike (1911), is the major factor through which the stimulus-response (S-R) bond is strengthened. Of course, the reinforcing effect of some commodity, such as food or water, is not a function of properties of the commodity, but rather the properties of the animal. Water may reinforce the behavior of a laboratory rat, but not some species of desert rodents which derive water from their food and never drink.

We shall now consider some of the types of learning. Although in ethological theory the process is generally divided along the lines proposed by Thorpe (1963), it must be made clear that no such distinct divisions actually exist in nature. Individual adaptive modification of behavior may involve several of these "types" and, in fact they may all eventually be proven to be based in the same neurological mechanism, or in neurological events not yet imagined.

SOME WAYS ANIMALS LEARN

Habituation

Habituation may be defined as the relatively persistent waning of a response as a result of repeated or continuous stimulation which is not followed by any kind of reinforcement (Thorpe 1963, Hinde 1970). In its widest sense it is simply learning not to respond to specific stimuli which tend to be without significance in the life of the animal. A bird must learn not to take flight at the sight of windblown leaves. So habituation is simply dropping responses instead of adding or changing them. It appears to be a universal phenomenon among animals, and is undoubtedly of major importance for animals in the wild.

The adaptiveness of habituation may readily be seen in social or colonial animals. If colonial birds, such as seabirds, which often nest within a few feet of each other on rocky coasts, did not habituate, a great part of their time and energy would be spent quarreling with neighbors. Instead, they learn to reduce their aggressive responses to the presence of a neighbor as long as that neighbor remains outside a certain territorial limit directly surrounding the nest. In many species this limit is defined by how far a bird sitting on the nest can strike with the bill. Lorenz (1963) noticed that in "nonanonymous" communities, in which each individual animal is recognized by the rest of the community, habituation may take place only with regard to immediate neighbors which are, of course, the ones most frequently encountered. In such communities, an animal from another neighborhood will receive harsh treatment from residents into whose turf it wanders.

Lorenz (1969) theorized that in the process of habituation, an innate releasing mechanism becomes associated with an individually acquired perception so that the primary or key releasers in that situation cease to be effective. However, the altered effect of the perception (or habituation) is dependent upon a number of variables occurring simultaneously—variables which are characteristic of a certain situation. Thus, ducks will mob a well-known dog if he should appear in a stretch of shore where he is not usually seen.

Habituation in nonanonymous communities illustrates another principle, one that deals with interspecific relationships and which is extremely important to animals in the wild. There is some evidence that animals which are harmless are encountered much more often than predatory ones. Habituation, therefore, may occur to the harmless species, but not to the harmful ones such as predators. The difference in the behavior of birds in their reaction to Tinbergen's long- or short-necked model (Figure 2.7) has been explained on this basis. Geese may be seen more often than hawks and, therefore, the latter are not habituated to. The difference in the numbers of times the two types of animals are encountered does not imply that there are more geese than hawks. Selection for adaptive behavioral patterns may enable potential prey to avoid situations in which predators are likely to be found, and may cause predators to move about in a more cryptic manner than innocuous species.

Lack of habituation to short-necked or "predator-type" birds does not entirely explain the escape behavior elicited by them. On several occasions I noticed that the Jamaican woodpecker, *Centurus radiolatus*, immediately after uttering a warning cry, drops from high limbs into dense undergrowth at the approach of the large turkey vulture, *Cathartes aura*. There are no reports of the woodpeckers being attacked by the slow-flying vultures and the latter usually fly at low altitudes, just above the treetops, so there is little possibility of a high-speed dive which would be necessary to catch a wary woodpecker. Although it is not unusual for the woodpeckers to take the evasive measures several times in a single day, habituation apparently does not occur. The woodpeckers seem to be just as alarmed after the fifth encounter as they were after the first. The pattern may be a vestigial response from the period when the woodpecker's ancestors lived in a different type of biological community; or it may be a useful pattern which, although it wastes some energy, is adaptive in its net effect in that real predators with a similar image, such as hawks, are also avoided. Both interpretations of the presence of the pattern imply that the situation in which the woodpeckers now exist is a relatively new one which has not yet been well adapted to.

Klopfer and Hailman (1965) point out that habituation may play an important role in habitat selection. An animal placed in new surroundings may show a general wariness and fear response. Once habituated to an area, however, it may feel at ease only in that familiar surrounding. If the habitat is rewarding in any way, such as through supplying food or warmth, the animal's positive response to it may become firmly established.

There are some fascinating puzzles associated with the study of habituation. Habituation is, in many cases, a selection (usually a selecting out) of releasers which elicit fixed patterns. In other words, it is a mechanism which reduces the instances in which a certain IRM (such as that associated with escape behavior) is activated. In experiments, there have been found a number of innate responses which, in spite of their great survival value, wane rapidly if released a number of times in quick succession. Hinde (1960) found this to be true in the owl-mobbing reaction of the chaffinch. Not only was the mobbing reaction reduced in birds which were allowed to repeatedly mob a stuffed owl, but the response did not regain its intensity even after a rest of several months. Furthermore, no reinforcement could restore the mobbing behavior—not even being chased by a real owl. Certainly, such an effective defense mechanism is not made to function only once or twice, losing efficacy after that. Such puzzles are scattered throughout the ethological literature and await new interpretation or redesign of the experiment. Lorenz (1969) believes such anomalies indicate experimental error.

Habituation must be considered as distinct from sensory adaptation and fatigue. Sensory adaptation is due to repeated stimulation of the receptors until the receptors fail to respond. The sense of smell quickly adapts to odors so that they go unnoticed. An *effector*, such as a muscle which effects an action, may fail to respond simply because of fatigue. Both sensory adaptation and fatigue are very short-term phenomena, factors which, in part, distinguish them from habituation.

Certain changes occur in reflex responses which are associated with fatigue and/or sensory adaptation. These changes may result in a lessening of the responses and may become manifest in distinctly different ways. Knee jerks, for example, if repeatedly stimulated become slower, but change little in amplitude—the leg continues to move the same distance. Eye blinks, on the other hand, change little in timing, but decrease in extent or amplitude. It is not known whether different mechanisms also function in habituation to different environmental factors. It is believed, however, that the neural mechanism probably differs widely between different groups of animals.

Habituation is probably one of the more widely occurring types of learning responses and it has been considered to be among the simpler types of learning. However, in the final analysis, the phenomenon cannot be shown to be the result of a "simple" mechanism and, in fact, new evidence is appearing which indicates increasingly complex facets of the problem. For example, Hinde (1970) describes certain factors which can result in increases and decreases in response strength when chaffinches mob a predatory owl.

Classical Conditioning

Pavlov's widely heralded experiment involved a situation in which a bell was rung just prior to feeding a dog. The dog came to associate the sound with food so that, for a while, even when the food was not present the dog would salivate upon hearing the bell. The phenomenon is called the *conditioned reflex*. "Conditioned" is an unfortunate translation from the Russian. The term should be "conditional," implying that the behavior is conditional upon the environment.

In Pavlov's experiment the food is called the unconditioned stimulus, and the bell the conditioned stimulus. Because the unconditioned stimulus is necessary in the training process it is said to "reinforce" the conditioned response (salivation).

It is interesting that there may also be a conditioned and unconditioned response. In other words, the response to the food and to the bell are not identical in all respects. Usually such differences involve the response to the conditioned stimulus being incompletely performed. Another difference is that the conditioned response may be anticipatory; the animal may look around as if expecting the unconditioned stimulus (e.g., food) to appear. So the conditioned response is not simply a duplication of the unconditioned response.

Thorndike (1911), in testing a variety of differ-

ent animals, found that when a response was learned through conditioning, a new stimulus somewhat like the original stimulus would elicit the response to some degree. The process is called *stimulus generalization*. Usually, the more characteristics the new stimulus has in common with the original stimulus, the stronger will be the response.

Irradiation is a theoretical variable Pavlov ad-

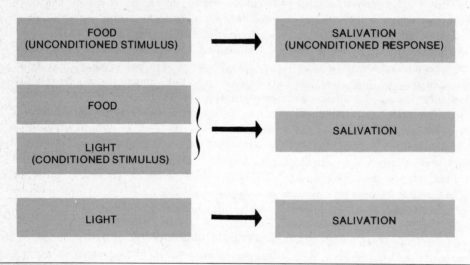

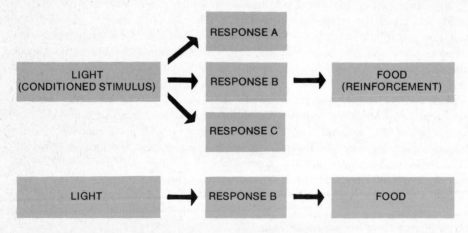

Figure 3.1 The organizational differences between classical conditioning (top) and instrumental learning (bottom). Note that in classical conditioning, an unconditioned stimulus becomes paired with a conditioned stimulus. The conditioned stimulus then becomes a substitute for the unconditioned stimulus to produce the unconditioned response. In instrumental learning, when a conditioned stimulus occurs, there is an opportunity for the animal to respond in various ways. However, only the "correct" response is reinforced. Finally the stimulus produces a specific response (After DiCara 1970.)

vanced to explain the empirical variable of stimulus generalization. Irradiation involves the acquiring of conditioning effects by receptors not involved in conditioning trials. If touching a certain area of the skin is the conditioned stimulus, touching other areas of the skin may also produce a response. It is a not unexpected rule that the farther the stimulus is from the conditioned area, the weaker the expected response.

Operant Conditioning

In 1938, B. F. Skinner published his landmark work, *The Behavior of Organisms*. The basis for his approach to the study of learning is called *operant conditioning*. Thorpe (1963) called it Type II or instrumental conditioning as opposed to Pavlov's Type I or classical conditioning. Type II differs from Type I in several important respects. In Type II the conditioned response is a *voluntary* action of an animal and is a result of appetitive behavior. Also, in establishing Type II conditioning, both the stimulus and the response must precede the reward in time (Thorpe 1963).

The basic differences in classical and operant conditioning may be seen in Figure 3.1. Skinner preferred to call the food "reinforcement," not "reward." Reward and satisfaction imply sensations which might be intuitively inferred but are not measurable. Reinforcement, on the other hand, is defined operationally; it alters the probability of a response. This delineation is an example of Skinner's "operational" viewpoint.

Skinner's approach to scientific method was an unusual one. Rather than set up and test hypotheses he suggested testing all possible stimulus-response situations, analyzing the results, and inductively arriving at scientific principles. Many psychologists do not subscribe to Skinner's approach since most types of behavior are far too complex for interrelationships of components to be tested randomly.

The mechanical test situations Skinner devised have been widely used to test operant conditioning. Typical tests of this type of learning involve running mazes or opening boxes. The important thing is that upon cue, an animal must do something to receive his reward. A typical test situation might be run as follows: the researcher wants the animal to press a bar while a buzzer is sounding. The hungry animal moves randomly, at first, until he accidentally pushes the lever while the buzzer is sounding and, lo! food is delivered. The reward thus appearing under a certain set of circumstances each time increases the probability that the proper sequence will be repeated until, finally a stimulus-response chain is established.

Actually, the effects of classical and operant conditioning are very hard to distinguish experimentally. In classical conditioning there may be skeletal responses (perhaps undetected) accompanying the conditioned response. There is also a strong likelihood that when operant conditioning is achieved a classically conditioned response may be occurring at the same time. Researchers were able to separate the two responses in an interesting set of experiments. A dog was taught to respond to one stimulus by performing an action in order to receive a second stimulus which was, in turn, rewarded by food. The first stimulus evoked an instrumental response without salivation; the second evoked salivation. Thus the two types of conditioning are distinguished.

Trial-and-Error Learning

Although probably neither classical nor instrumental conditioning alone is important in natural learning situations, the two processes occurring together may be a part of learning which occurs in the wild. Thorpe (1963) refers to this process as trial-and-error learning. Instrumental conditioning and trial-and-error learning are considered one and the same by many researchers, and Thorpe admits that the greater component of trial-and-error learning, even according to his scheme, is instrumental conditioning. He points out that no clear difference exists, but that trial and error usually contains an element of classical conditioning as well. Thorpe (1963) defines trial-and-error behavior as "the development of an association, as the result of reinforcement during appetitive behavior, between a stimulus or a situation and an independent motor action as an item in that behavior when both stimulus and motor action precede the reinforcement and the motor action is not the inevitable inherited response to the reinforcement."

Thorpe described an experiment in which Types I and II conditioning were distinguishable in a trial-and-error learning situation. A guinea pig was placed in a special harness so that when he turned his head in a certain way the movement would release food from a container. The head movement would only deliver food if the movement occurred directly after a bell was rung. At first, the movements that occurred after the bell were highly disoriented, but when the head was finally moved in the correct way food was delivered to the hungry animal. After several repetitions of the sequence, the general irrelevant motions were eliminated and, upon hearing the bell, the guinea pig immediately moved his head in such a way that would bring food. It could be shown that the guinea pig experienced anticipatory Type I conditioning (such as salivation in response to the bell). The gradual selection of the proper motor pattern demonstrated operant or Type II conditioning.

The general nonspecific "trials" which were first attempted should not be considered as random movements but rather as appetitive attempts to solve a problem of bodily need. The problem is realized by the animal in the form of a drive (here, hunger), and the trials are attempts, however simple, to cope with the problem situation. Appetitive motivation, we see, is necessary before trial-and-error learning can begin.

In the study of wild animals, such separation and delineation of the components of trial-and-error behavior are not possible. Conceptually, however, the same sort of conditioning experience in nature is not hard to imagine. A young animal could be expected to come to associate certain environmental signals with the presence of food and to react with an increasingly fruitful pattern of motor responses. Consider a young quail. In the period just after hatching, the chick pecked at anything, until it hit upon something edible. He gradually learned to associate the sight of certain objects with food until, when he located an object which had the "food image," he pecked at it and then performed the consummatory act of swallowing. The reinforcement, then, is preceded by the stimulus (hunger), the expectation (based on experience) that he will soon be satisfied, and the active response (pecking)—a necessary sequence in trial-and-error learning. The reward is retroactive and influences future pecking. This process, together with habituation to inedible objects, causes increased efficiency in foraging.

Just how important is conditioning as a learning process in nature? Most of the research on conditioning has been performed under such artificial conditions that little light has been shed on its actual level of importance. It is likely that conditioning, or the "conditioning-like processes" referred to by Thorpe, are an important part of individual accommodation to a changing environment. Thorpe theorized regarding the specific behavioral level at which conditioning could be operating: conditioning is, he said, ". . . a method by which the innate releasing mechanism is elaborated or modified to fit the environmental situation more exactly" (1956:84). He added that conditioning also apparently plays an important part in adapting the receptor to specific stimuli as a result of experience. So, here again, we see the close interrelationship of learning and instinct and how experience may modify the entire adaptive response without necessarily acting upon the neural seat of instinctive action.

In nature, conditioning may be important in escape reactions when environmental signals are associated with an attacking predator. This type of response would probably best be learned by flocking or gregarious animals which could learn the sign of impending danger and effect a proper response without being personally attacked.

In trial-and-error learning, different types of patterns may be elicited depending upon whether the reinforcement is positive (e.g., palatable prey) or negative (e.g., noxious prey). In the case of the latter, the animal not only neglects the noxious stimulus but develops an active avoiding action. A blue jay, after swallowing a noxious monarch butterfly, will vomit and thereafter carefully avoid anything that resembles the insect.

There is a variety of information that indicates that trial-and-error (or operant) learning is an extremely complicated phenomenon, if in fact it can be thought of as a single type of neurological process at all. As an example of a perplexing finding which indicates the complexity of the problem, consider the following experiment described by Pritchatt (1968) and others. A small part of a cockroach, which included only a ventral ganglion and a pair of legs with their muscles, was arranged so that when the leg was extended, an electrical circuit was completed thus shocking the animal. After this happened a few times the leg remained flexed and showed signs of "remembering" for several hours. Controls receiving random shocks showed no such flexion.

Schneirla (1959) demonstrated that trial-and-error learning may be accomplished by a different sequence of neural events in different animals. He pointed out that insects learning a maze first learn the important turns individually, and later integrate the information. Rats, on the other hand, learn and integrate the patterns at the same time. These sorts of findings should stand as a warning against any tendency to develop simplistic learning models and as encouragement to continue to conduct cross-species examinations with an eye toward finding the common, as well as the diverse, learning principles.

Latent Learning

The term latent learning is, to some extent, unsatisfactory in that it refers to only one phase of what is a broad and rather complex learning process. For reasons that are discussed below, Thorpe (1963) perfers the term "exploratory learning" and defines it as the association of indifferent stimuli, or situations, without patent reward.

First, consider the rather undefined motivation for latent learning. It has been found that rats will learn a maze even when there is no obvious reward such as food or water. A monkey will perform work such as pulling a lever simply to be able to look out of the box in which he is kept. The motivation in latent learning situations seems to be a drive simply to get to know the surroundings. It is such an unspecific sort of motivation that, at first, animal psychologists were at a loss to explain why their animals were willing to do work when the only reward seemed to be just to be able to look around. The exploratory drive should not be equated with curiosity. Curiosity is considered a characteristic of higher animals only, and latent learning, the adaptive result of the exploratory drive, has been described in some lower animals, including the insects. Also, curiosity implies a very general condition while exploratory drive may be considered the application of that condition more specifically to an adaptive pattern.

If rats are allowed to run a maze without any sort of reward at the end, they will complete the maze anyway, but the number of trials necessary each time decreases very slowly. In other words, they don't appear to be learning the maze very quickly. If food suddenly appears at the end of the maze, however, these rats will master the maze in only a very few trials. Learning was, therefore, apparently occurring all along, but it was latent—it did not appear until it was activated by a reward.

Some critics say there is no difference between latent and trial-and-error learning. The basis of their criticism is that they doubt that reinforcement is necessary in order for trial-and-error learning to occur. Hinde (1970) submits that trial and error involves learning the characteristics of a situation *and* putting this knowledge into action, thus gaining a reward; latent learning involves only the former. These reevaluations of Thorpe's (1963) divisions serve to point up the close interrelationships (and the arbitrary separations) of the learning types under consideration.

Latent learning is undoubtedly very important in wild animals. Many young mammals undoubtedly benefit greatly from exploring the area around their protected den (Figure 3.2). At the time that information is being gained regarding the general character of the area, the animals are being cared for by parents. When the animals are on their own, their first experiences at self-maintenance may then be conducted in familiar surroundings. Latent learning may also be important in adult animals. A mongoose (Figure 3.3) may range several hundred yards from its burrow, and it is important that he learns where food is likely to be found so that he may be exposed to predators for the shortest possible period of time. He must also know where the openings are into which he can dart at the approach of a predatory cat. So survival value of an exploratory drive may, at first, not be obvious, but its adaptiveness becomes apparent when the need for some commodity arises, such as food or protection, and the commodity is then seen to be acquired quickly. After establishing the location of a commodity, the animal can reasonably expect it to be there when he returns. This principle of *expectancy* is important in the next type of learning to be considered.

Insight Learning

The lines separating the various types of learning are, of necessity, arbitrarily drawn because of (1) imperfect knowledge of how learning is really accomplished (the ethologists serve importantly in furnishing clues to those who are best in a posi-

Figure 3.2 Young coyotes venturing from their den. As they explore their surroundings and gain confidence they explore farther away, always gaining information regarding their surroundings. At any sign of danger it is important that they be able to quickly find their den and scramble into its safety. They may learn the location of the den relative to other parts of their environment through latent learning. (Photo: Alfred Bailey. From National Audubon Society.)

tion ultimately to solve the problem of mechanisms, the neurophysiologists), (2) the natural intertwining and intergrading of the various types of learning, and (3) the interrelationship of learning and instinct necessary to produce an adaptive response. As an example of the latter consider that the innate appetitive behavior may be the basis of the "trial" part of trial-and-error learning. Also, the trials are nonrandom in that they are innately (instinctively) restricted so that only certain trials are attempted. However, we are more familiar with the effects of learning on trials. In an experienced animal a trial may be nonrandom, to some degree, because of the principle of expectancy. In this latter case the trial is clearly based on an "if . . . then" hypothesis.

Reinforcement in trial-and-error learning comes to be a confirmation of an expectancy. At first an animal may not know what a certain behavioral pattern will lead to, but trial-and-error learning may cause a certain result to be expected to follow a certain type of action. This is the basis of insight—a "what-leads-to-what" expectancy, to quote Tolman (1937).

In what ways might expectancy be adaptive? Berlyne (1960) refers to expectancy as a device which cuts down the "cost" of adjustment. The device works best when the events are in a regularly occurring sequence so that the element of predictability may develop. The anticipation experienced by the animal is necessary in order for a reward to be associated with an action.

Expectation is also adaptive in that it opens the way to a prior selection of responses before the situation which calls for a response arrives, so that the likelihood of choosing the proper response is increased. Expectation, too, may reduce stress by making adjustments less abrupt. If an animal has an idea of what may be about to happen, the actual occurrence may be less traumatic so that he is able to act from a more normal psychological set than if he were completely surprised.

At times, complete environmental cues may be

Figure 3.3 A hunting mongoose. The mongoose is a voracious carnivore which must range rather widely to satisfy its demands. It is also potential prey for a number of animals. Any wide-ranging terrestrial prey species could be expected to benefit from latent learning as it must be able to find hiding places quickly. (Photo: Van Rackages, New York.)

lacking or the cues may be incompletely learned. In either case, the result may be "anticipatory arousal." The cues may indicate an impending situation without telling exactly what it is. The animal may then brace for the event and react to it more successfully than if no warning had been given. Anticipatory arousal may explain the fabled sixth sense claimed by those adventurers with a flair for the dramatic.

How important is the principle of expectancy among wild animals? The problem may not yet be answered in definite terms. Expectancy may be one of the less common aspects of behavior when the entire animal kingdom is considered, but it is probably a fairly prevalent one among vertebrates and is present in at least some forms of invertebrates. Expectancy is not likely to occur in the most degenerate (a biological not a sociological term) internal parasites. But in higher animals, such as the primates, expectancy may be easily demonstrated. In an experiment, monkeys were shown various foods being placed under inverted cups. Before they were allowed access to the cups a favorite food, such as a banana, was secretly replaced by a less desirable but perfectly edible one, such as lettuce. When the monkeys were allowed access to the cups they lifted the ones under which they had seen the bananas placed. Upon finding lettuce they refused to eat it. They had obviously expected bananas and were not about to accept lettuce instead.

The principle of expectancy is the basis for *insight* learning. Insight (also discussed in Chapter 2) is that part of the mental process which relates to understanding relationships; insight learning, as Klopfer and Hailman (1967) remind us, is demonstrated in the behavioral solution of the problem.

Gestalt Perception

The concept of insight originated with the Gestalt psychologists. Kohler called it the "ah-ha erlebnis," a term that conveys the sudden perception of relationships. Simply, gestalt is the consideration of the whole rather than its parts. Perception is not considered to be simply the recognition of a stimulus, but how the stimulus is interpreted in the central nervous system. A broken circle is seen as an entire circle (Figure 3.4). The viewer supplies the missing lines in symbolic drawings (Figure 3.5). We have all as children seen examples of gestalt perception in the books in which, when the pages were flipped rapidly, figures appeared to move in a continuous motion. The motion was disjointed, not continuous, but we had learned through experience that motion is continuous and therefore we supplied the missing parts.

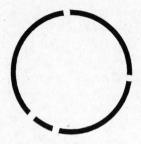

Figure 3.4 We see this incomplete circle as an entire circle because our eyes "supply" the missing parts.

Figure 3.5 We see these lines as a horse although no such configuration is actually shown. Again, our mind is willing to furnish the missing parts.

Gestalt psychology was born in Germany about the time of Pavlov, and was based on the work of Wertheimer (1912). The Gestaltists believed that insight involves the perception of relationships and is a high order of mental ability. An interesting implication of their work is that an organism acts as intelligently as it can and, therefore, the natural solution to any problem should be provided by insight in higher animals. Trial and error, according to the theory, would only be employed as a last resort in problem solving.

Gestalt psychology assumes that psychological organization moves in a given direction: toward organizing what is learned and perceived into an integrated and tightly knit scheme. In other words, animals move toward organizing their world into a good gestalt.

There are differences in the degree to which stimuli are perceived as wholes (gestalten) or parts (sign stimuli) among species, and even, at different times or in different contexts, within a single individual. Some birds, as we have seen, are known to recognize a biologically important object by the perception of a small part of its total observable characteristics. Lack (1939) showed that a territorial robin will attack a tuft of red feathers placed at a certain height as readily as a stuffed male. The sign stimulus is "red at a certain height." On the other hand, as Lorenz has pointed out, caged birds may show alarm when approached by their keeper who is wearing a hat for the first time. The "keeper" configuration has changed and he is not recognized. So perception may be based on sign stimuli for some types of environmental objects and on gestalten for others.

There may be some sort of preformed perceptual abilities and limits in certain animals, and that possibility should be mentioned. Such preformed patterns may function in mate or habitat selection or in a number of other social contexts. Perhaps such predispositions are established in a newborn animal's central nervous system and need only to be activated. Klopfer and Hailman (1965) point out that hormone treatment can

elicit behavioral patterns in young animals which would normally not appear until much later in life (in other words the neural patterns exist and need only to be activated). Perhaps, also, perceptual organization lies dormant in the nervous system although this is yet to be proven.

There is some evidence (see Hailman's discussion in Klopfer's 1962 book) that the relative importance of gestalten and sign stimuli may change as an individual matures. Young gulls may, at first, only respond to such sign stimuli as the spots on the parents' bills (see Chapter 2), but as they gain experience they begin to show greater recognition of the parent as more of the configuration of the parent appears in their field of vision. Also, it has been shown experimentally that as the young mature and gain experience they respond better to those artificial models which are more normal in their proportions.

Lack (1933) suggested that habitat selection in birds is based primarily on gestalt perception. In a complex habitat, probably no single clue or set of clues are clear indicators of habitat conditions. Pielowski (1961) supported this assessment as a result of his study of the vertical distribution of birds in pine-oak woods. He found seasonal changes in their preferred level and, as Klopfer and Hailman (1965) maintain, such responses are more immediately explicable in terms of responses to relational characters than to some absolute cue.

Any study of habitat preferences in animals must be preceded by an analysis of the animals' sensory abilities. We must keep in mind that man's perception of the world is uniquely his own. In a sense, we live side by side with animals who live in a different world. If a planarian were asked what the world is like he might describe it in terms of vague sensations of heat and cold, changing chemicals, and light and dark accented by hazy shadows. An insect, able to perceive ultraviolet rays, might describe the beautiful colors in what to us is a white flower. The perceived environment is the animal's *Umwelt* and we must have some knowledge of it before we can effectively discuss what elements in it the animal might be reacting to. (See von Uexkull 1909.)

Insight, as described by the Gestaltists, is distinguishable from trial and error in that, using insight, not all the possible simpler and inadequate solutions to a problem are attempted. For example, in a test situation in which food was placed outside the arm's reach of a chimpanzee (true insight is best demonstrated in higher primates), the animal used short sticks, which were placed within its cage, to reach longer sticks placed outside, and then used the longer sticks to reach the food. If the food were suspended well above its reach, the chimpanzee, after careful perusal of the situation, stacked boxes so that a short stick would reach. It appears that the chimpanzee in such a situation tries a number of possibilities mentally until it hits upon a likely one, and then tries it physically. Once popular was the notion that insight learning was not possible below the primate level. This is probably wrong. It is apparently a property of some birds, for example, such as the wily crow which has survived in the face of a largely unjustified effort by man to eradicate him. Insight may exist, not only at the vertebrate level, but may be found in some lower groups which have simply been neglected as research subjects.

Learning Sets

Insightful behavior has been defined as "the sudden production of a new adaptive response not arrived at by trial behavior," and "the solution of a problem by the sudden adaptive reorganization of experience" (Thorpe 1956:110). Of importance is the word *experience,* only implied in the first definition. In problem solving, any factor that reduces randomness by eliminating the possibility of unfruitful trials is adaptive, and one such factor is experience. The experience need not be directly associated with the problem at hand. Sometimes, when presented with a new problem, the animal will solve the problem without delay on the first attempt. It is making use of experience in dealing with the component parts of the problem although it has never seen them put together in just such a way before. So, unlike trial-and-error behavior, insight learning is strongly dependent upon experience.

A principle elucidated by Harlow (1949) relates trial-and-error learning to insightful learning in a rather interesting way. A monkey is shown two boxes of different shapes, one with food under it. He is able to make a choice and may or may not be rewarded according to his selection. He is then presented with several more pairs of boxes, in shape identical to the first pair, with the food always under a box of a certain shape. At the end of this set of experiments, a new set is begun in which he is shown a pair of boxes of two different shapes from those used in the first set. In several trials, the food is again always under a box of a particular shape. When the results of many such successive sets of experiments are considered, it is found there has been a steady improvement in the percent of correct choices over the successive trials until, finally, the score goes from that expected by random choices to nearly perfect discrimination after only one trial. In effect, the monkey has learned to learn. This *learning set,* as Harlow called it, is very important to any consideration of the importance of learning and experience in the wild because it describes how experience, during the lifetime of an animal, facilitates its ability to solve problems when confronted with a new situation, and, in nature, few environmental situations will be similar in all respects.

Imitation

Among some animals insight learning need not be directly related to personal experience. Thorpe (1963) refers to insight learning which occurs as a result of the influences of the behavior of other animals, and calls the process *imitation.* Thorpe warns that this is a rather nebulous classification with a variety of learning phenomena often being placed under the label. One type of this kind of learning is *social facilitation* (see Chapter 9). This is the inclusion of an established behavioral pattern into a new situation. In this case the pattern is already in the behavioral repertoire of the animal. Only the timing of its employment is altered as a result of watching another animal. A dog may learn to "speak" after watching another dog simply barking on command. The phenomenon is evidenced in human behavior in the contagion of yawns (try it).

Behavior may also be altered by *true imitation*. True imitation may be considered as the copying of an act which is unlikely to appear in the behavioral repertoire by another means. Thorpe believes this sort of behavior is limited to birdsong (see Chapter 6) and aspects of primate behavior.

Another type of imitation involves tradition. Here, there is a tendency to alter the usual response to parts of the environment after watching another individual. Milk bottles left on porches had been ignored for years by a population of tits, *Parus spp.* Hinde and Fisher (1951 described how the members of the population learned to open the bottles to get to the cream after watching other birds do so. Of course, somwhere along the line some bird must have employed a different learning process in order to remove the first lid. There are other examples of this learning phenomenon. Gregarious birds may learn to avoid predators by observing the flock's behavior toward certain potentially dangerous species. (We have mentioned how a bird may learn the clues of impending danger by watching actual attacks on other birds.) There may be strong differences between species as to the degree to which such learning may be achieved. For example, Lorenz has described how jackdaws pass down information from one generation to the next. The birds travel in flocks, and it is likely that at least one bird will be able to recognize any form of danger. When it gives the alarm and the flock takes wing, there is probably an increased likelihood that others in the flock will show an aversion to that same stimulus the next time it is encountered. On the other hand, birds which exist singly, such as thrushes, must rely to a greater degree on an inherent system of recognition and they are, therefore, probably much less adaptable than gregarious species. It should also be pointed out that there are important differences in learning abilities of these types of species. Under experimental conditions, the inquisitive and exploratory tits showed no adverse effect to being trained in pairs, but in the greenfinch, single birds learn food-discrimination tasks much more rapidly than pairs of birds. Klopfer (1961) maintains that such behavior as that demonstrated in the greenfinch can only fail to be maladaptive in species with relatively conservative food habits or those of a solitary nature.

Probably the best known instance of tradition learning involves the Japanese macaques, *Macaca fusca*, on Kôshima Island. These monkeys were fed sweet potatoes, beginning in 1952. A year later Imo, a young female, was observed washing the sand off her potatoes by holding it in one hand and rinsing it with the other. The pattern then spread throughout the community over the next few years—first through the closer families, then through playmates. By 1962, three-fourths of all monkeys who were at least two years old were potato washers. Some had even specialized to the point of salting their potatoes by dipping them in sea water before each bite.

These same monkeys were also fed wheat, which they sorted laboriously from the beach sand where it was spread. The enterprising Imo discovered that by throwing handfuls of both sand and wheat into the water, the lighter wheat could be quickly separated out. At last report, 19 of 49 monkeys had adopted the technique (Itani 1958, Kawai 1965). It might also be pointed out that, experimentally, the presence of naïve animals has been shown to reduce the effects of learning in trained animals. For example, a greenfinch, trained to avoid unpalatable food, will begin to make mistakes if it is allowed to watch an untrained companion.

Thorpe also includes imprinting (see Chapter 2 and beyond) under the insight-learning phenomenon. Hinde (1970) reminds us that imprinting, although apparently a peculiar process, is mainly unusual in its context rather than in the learning process itself.

As has been emphasized in the foregoing discussion, the various types of learning are not at all as clear-cut as is suggested by the various classifications. Thorpe (1963) himself emphasizes that complexities may arise because the categories may broadly intergrade and because each category contains examples which may differ greatly in their complexity. There are other complicating factors as well. For example, each category may involve an element of *perceptual learning*. The influence of perceptual learning is widely debated, but basically involved is information that has been inconspicuously gathered during the development of the animal. A certain experience may produce no effects at the time but may affect subsequent learning. A rat, given early non-reinforced experience with a triangle and a circle, will later be able to discriminate between geometric figures more easily than a rat with no such experience. An animal (or a baby) given an enriched environment full of playthings with various properties may learn with an increased facility later in life. If perceptual learning is involved in Thorpe's categories, the complexity and indefinite boundaries of the categories are emphasized.

Play

Play is a phenomenon observed in many species of animals and one which probably has been subjected, more than any other type of behavior, to the greatest anthropomorphic interpretations. It is a phenomenon, primarily, of higher vertebrates, those animals in which learning is an important determinant of behavior.

Part of the problem of investigating playful behavior arises in finding a good definition of the term "play." We all believe we can recognize play

in the animals around us. Mason (1965:530), in describing play in primates, states, "In spite of the difficulties in arriving at an acceptable and comprehensive definition of play, the fact remains that observers show considerable agreement in judging 'playful behavior.' " However, in the lowest animals in which playfulness exists, it may very well exist in forms which are not recognizable to the human observer. As always, it is not advisable to attempt to rigidly interpret behavior patterns in lower animals because of the error that may be involved in relating the patterns to human subjective feeling which may have no parallel in the minds of the animals. For the present, we can only discuss some of the results of the study of play in a few groups of animals, and in the light of subjective interpretations with human behavior as the basis.

Playlike behavior has been described in fish. Van Iersel (1953) reports such behavior as expressed in low intensity nest building actions. Thorpe (1956) mentions reports of "shooters," *Jaculator*, squirting water at their aquarium keeper. Other accounts of playful behavior in fish are given in Beach (1945). The argument for fish play is not completely convincing, but enough evidence has been presented to warrant further investigation.

It was believed for a time that birds do not play, but, in recent years, play, or something like play, has been reported in birds. Roberts (1934) describes eider ducks "shooting the rapids" in Iceland. They walked up the bank, jumped in, careened through the rapids, got out, walked back up, and jumped in again. Stoner (1947) observed an Anna hummingbird repeatedly floating down a small stream of water which was flowing from a hose. Also, it is said that some passerines (perching birds) may sing out of sheer exuberance. Such an argument would indeed be difficult to prove, but it is offered in the absence of a better explanation of behavior in some cases. If birds do sometimes sing for some reason not related to mating, territoriality, threat, etc., then it might be considered a form of play.

Lorenz has mentioned playful behavior in his birds, but probably play is not an important learning technique in most birds. It would be extremely difficult to imagine anything as starkly humorless and unplayful as a chicken! There may be an explanation for the unplayfulness of precocial birds such as chickens. These species must run about and forage successfully for themselves a few hours after hatching and have no time or energy for behavior which is not immediately productive. On the other hand, playful behavior might be expected in altricial species, such as crows, which are cared for by parents as they face their first weeks of life. Also, crows are omnivorous, eating a wide variety of food including animal and vegetable substances, and relatively wide-ranging and, therefore, behavioral flexibility may be selected for. To animals that are adaptable and labile in their behavior, play might give the opportunity to become familiar with the surroundings and to develop facility in dealing with a variety of conditions.

There is good reason to believe play does not exist in animals below the vertebrates. Play can only be expected to be found, to any great degree, in those species for which learning or practice is important and those which show relatively great flexibility in behavior. Also, play should only be expected in those species in which appetitive behavior is not strongly bound to a consummatory act. In lower animals, and for some behavioral patterns in vertebrates, appetitive behavior must lead to a consummatory act. In higher animals appetitive behavior is flexible enough to be broken off without leading to the consummatory act. One of the characteristics of play is that it is not necessarily relevant to any environmental situation existing at the time it is performed. It appears without environmental cues and without the normal appetitive occurrences which precede the type of behavior shown in the play. A young kitten may suddenly arch its back, spit and appear terrified of something that is familiar and

presents no threat. Then, just as suddenly the defensive attitude may be dropped with no attempt to follow through with the normal avoidance or escape behavior.

Since the goal of play is not an adaptive consummatory act, play would be expected to appear in domestic animals whose needs are provided by man. Adult dogs have been labeled "neotenous" (at a permanently immature stage of development) by some researchers because of their propensity for play. It is believed that closely related animals in the wild do not play frequently. It would be interesting to compare time spent playing in equally well fed dogs and "tame" wolves.

In ordinary appetitive behavior, as obstacles are overcome, learning takes place so that the consummatory act becomes more easily reached as time goes by. If the consummatory goal (such as food) is provided for an animal, the obstacles may become ends in themselves and, when this happens, the learning which takes place may not be directed toward reaching the consummatory situation but, instead, may become strictly exploratory. Here we have the beginnings of latent learning and the adaptiveness may not be in helping the animal to learn to reach a goal, but instead the advantage may lie in expanding his horizons, in giving him a better overall understanding of his world. This understanding, of course, is important to another behavioral process, namely, insight.

One of the most persistent and apparent interpretations of play behavior is that it provides practice. Puppies play-fighting and kittens stalking a ball of yarn, give credence to the practice theory. They are obviously learning motor patterns which will be important later. However, there are examples of play behavior which cannot be explained as practice since they appear *only* in play. Why would a bird practice shooting the rapids? There are many accounts of otters racing uphill just to be able to slide down again. To include such behavior, the practice theory would have to be modified to include patterns which are not practiced to improve a specific pattern but rather to improve coordination or some other general faculty. Puppies and kittens in play-fighting often grab each other by the throat in just the manner they will later use in making quick-kills of their prey (Figure 3.6). Eibl-Eibesfeldt (1970) found that meerkats, *Suricata*, employ the same sort of bite when playing, copulating, or killing prey.

In the light of what is known regarding the development of appetitive behavior, there are other interpretations of the appearance of disjointed behavior which seems to be play. As examples of patterns which appear to be play, but which are not, consider the following: In the ontogenetic (individual) development of instinctive sequences, the more stereotyped of the appetitive patterns, or even the consummatory act, usually appear in

the behavioral repertoire of young animals before the more general ones, so the irrelevant pattern may actually be so only temporarily. Also, remember that "damming" may cause unadaptive in vacuo patterns (see Chapter 2) which would be difficult to distinguish from real play. And, when a series of patterns is the result of a rising hormone level (for example, increasing levels of sex hormones as spring approaches) appetitive behavior may be incomplete during the rising phase, or, if complete, it may be out of phase with the optimum period for its occurrence and, therefore, would not be adaptive. Even in the face of the various explanations it may still be argued that all out-of-context or incomplete patterns of behavior afford practice so that motor patterns are strengthened and randomness is reduced when the pattern is called for in a "real" situation.

Figure 3.6 The cheetah has a tight hold on the throat of a male reedbuck. The success of the neckbite in a number of predators has been shown to be partly a function of practice through play. (Photo: Mark Boulton from National Audubon Society.)

Play behavior can change to serious behavior in some cases. A cat may, as a normal sequence, play with its prey, then kill and eat it. When two mismatched puppies (or dogs) are rough-housing, the "underdog" may change to serious defense if he is buffeted too hard. It is interesting, though, that play-fighting almost never leads to real fighting.

Imprinting

In 1910 Heinroth described a surprising behavioral pattern in goslings. He found that they tend to follow the first large moving object they see after hatching and to relate in specific ways to that object later in life. In the wild, of course, the first moving object they would see would probably be a parent, so the adaptiveness of the pattern is obvious. Lorenz later called the process *imprinting*. It has been described in a variety of types of animals including some mammals.

Imprinting has been described as a rapid learning of certain general characteristics of a stimulus object. The learning appears to be limited to a relatively fixed developmental stage. Also, it is relatively independent of the reinforcement which is required for most other types of learning. This trait, and the fact that the adaptive responses to the stimulus may not appear until long after the original exposure, show marked similarities to latent learning.

The phenomenon has been characterized by three attributes, each of which has received some criticism:

1. The individual must be exposed to the model at a certain "critical period" in its development. However, it has been pointed out that this period varies from one individual to another, even within a single species.
2. Once a preference is established through imprinting its effects are irreversible. There is some evidence, however, that reversal may occur and that one model may be substituted for another. So the imprinting may not be as fixed as some have suggested.

3. The attraction to a model is proportional to the effort expended in the original exposure. Thus, a duckling which was forced to crawl over hurdles while following the model would later have a stronger attraction for it than one which followed unhindered. However, this principle has been demonstrated for few species so no generalizations can yet be made.

Imprinting, then, shares certain characters in common with both innate and acquired behavioral phenomena. For a discussion and criticism of the phenomenon see Klopfer 1962 and Klopfer and Hailman 1967.

Autonomic Learning

There is one last type of learning which should be mentioned—one that is just beginning to be explored but that may have enormous implications. This learning process is called *autonomic learning*. The sympathetic and parasympathetic centers comprise the autonomic nervous system and are located in the brain and spinal cord. They control many of the involuntary motor patterns of the body. The nature of their control can possibly best be illustrated by an example. If an enraged bear suddenly rushes into the room in which you are quietly reading, certain changes will take place throughout your body. Impulses will pass over the sympathetic neurons causing (1) the iris of the eye to dilate, with the result that the bear is more easily seen; (2) the blood vessels of the stomach and intestines to contract, so that the running muscles receive a greater supply of blood; and (3) the heart rate to accelerate, allowing more oxygen-laden blood to reach the muscles which are about to propel you out the window. If the bear just as suddenly rushes out, the parasympathetic nerves passing to the same structures cause the reverse effect and the system returns to normal. All these changes have taken place involuntarily and it was assumed for years that, in fact, there could be no voluntary control over these types of responses.

It was agreed that visceral responses (those

under the control of the autonomic nervous system) could be classically conditioned, an example being Pavlov's conditioning his dogs to salivate. But it was not suspected that the dog could be instrumentally conditioned to salivate in order to receive food. The theory was that classical and instrumental conditioning operate by different neurophysiological mechanisms, and that visceral responses could only be learned through classical conditioning. There were those learning theorists, all along, who argued that the mechanism for learning is the same for both types and that if an arm could consciously be trained to bend, an iris could consciously be trained to contract.

L. V. DiCara (1970) described a set of experiments performed by him and N. E. Miller of Rockefeller University. He reports that they were able to produce, through instrumental training, increases and decreases in heart rate, blood pressure, intestinal contractions, control of blood-vessel diameter, and even rate of urine formation.

Basically, their experiments involved using rats which were paralyzed with a curare derivative (the arrow poison of South American Indians). The effect was that movement of voluntary skeletal muscles was impossible although the animals remained fully conscious. Reinforcement was accomplished positively by an electrode implanted in the "pleasure center" of the brain, and negatively by a mildly unpleasant electric shock. The minor physiological variations that occur naturally throughout the body were the starting points for the experiments. For example, if they wished to train the animal to slow his heart rate, as the heart temporarily slowed naturally, a reward would would be given; when it speeded up the animal received a shock. Soon the heart rate remained slow. The reverse effect could be achieved also. When a rapid heart rate was rewarded, the animal learned to maintain the increased rate.

Some recent experiments have shown that brain-wave patterns can be altered by training. Miller and Carmona trained rats to raise or lower the voltage of their brain waves. A. H. Black of McMasters University in Canada trained dogs to alter the activity of one kind of brain wave, the theta wave. (Yogis, in practicing certain types of meditation, usually increase the number of certain brain waves, particularly alpha waves. In this country, novices are sometimes tested with simple electroencephalographs to determine whether they are properly controlling their thought patterns).

To rule out the possibility that such changes were due to some general phenomenon produced by changes in the autonomic nervous system, other tests were performed. For example, when heart rate and intestinal contraction were tested separately it was found that changes could be brought about in one without altering the other. Also, it was found that visceral changes can be made in very specific areas without affecting other parts of the body. The blood vessels of one ear can even be trained to dilate more than those of the other ear.

The question arises, is this sort of learning ability useful, or does it simply exist as a by-product of voluntary skeletal muscle learning? DiCara offers a possible explanation of the adaptiveness of autonomic learning: skeletal responses operate according to what happens in the external world, so, possibly, the autonomic system functions in responding to the internal environment.

Another possible adaptiveness of visceral conditioning is in maintaining homeostasis (the steady state or constant internal condition which is so necessary to higher animals). In the event of injury or disease to normal homeostatic mechanisms, the body could "learn" to take over these functions. Such redundancies are not at all uncommon in the vertebrate body.

In the wild, the implications of autonomic learning are enormous. Perhaps such learning plays a far more important role in animal physiology than has yet been imagined. For example, suppose gulls swimming in frigid North Atlantic waters learn to respond to unusually cold temperatures by constricting the vessels in their feet, which then reduces the amount of fluid in that area and renders the foot less susceptible to the dangers of freezing. Suppose an arctic fox learns to withdraw blood from his ears for the same reason. Such learning, of course, would function only as part of an overall adaptive pattern which involves morphological specialization as well. For example, the gull has circulatory "shunts" which permit blood to bypass extremities under certain conditions, and the ear of the arctic fox is small and a minimal surface area is exposed to the elements. We need only point out here the implications of autonomic learning in habitat selection. This ability would permit any animal to exist in highly variable or changing habitats by adding flexibility through expanding the physiological tolerance of the animal.

What are the implications of such learning for humans? Aside from the benefits extolled by the practitioners of Yoga and the bizarre feats accomplished by certain cultists (certain of these phenomena may, it is believed, be based on autonomic conditioning) there are certain very practical therapeutic benefits of the process. Already, teams of doctors have shown some promising results in helping heart patients to control their rate of heart beat and in training epileptic patients to control a type of abnormal brain wave, to suppress paroxysmal spikes.

On the other hand, visceral learning may be at the root of certain psychosomatic illness. If prolonged tension, for example, brings about headaches, the appearance of the discomfort may be "rewarded" by rest, a round of ale, or even (for some) a gratifying feeling of martyrdom. The appearance of the headache is therefore reinforced until finally certain internal changes may be brought about (such as the constriction of certain blood vessels) in order to cause a headache which will be rewarded.

For further information on autonomic learning the reader is referred to Miller (1961), Miller and Carmona (1967), Trowill (1967), Miller and DiCara (1967), and Miller (1969).

RESTRICTIONS ON LEARNING

We have become aware, by this time, that what is learned and how much is learned are, to a large degree, a matter of innately determined qualities of the animals. Lorenz implied such influences in his discussion of the evolution of learning centers (see above).

The often-asked questions regarding relative animal intelligence are, for the most part, nonsensical; and the concept of an "animal I.Q." is unrealistic. Probably no test will ever be devised that would test intelligence without being biased somehow by variations in innate tendencies or physical abilities. A cat is no less smart than a bird because it can't learn to chirp. Nor is a cat smarter than a dog because he uses stealth in approaching his prey, since hunting by stealth is an innate pattern in cats, while dogs run down their quarry.

At the same time, it cannot be denied that there are marked species difference in the learning ability of animals. Some, as we know, are genetically programmed to respond to releasing situations with certain relatively stereotyped patterns and there is little room for individual adjustment in their nervous systems. Certain spiders "know," through their genetic constitution, that certain prey types are to be bitten first and then wrapped while other prey types must be handled in the reverse sequence. Such specialization, of course, is possible only when conditions are stable and the characters of the prey types do not change.

It is interesting that the same degree of stereotypy does not prevail for all behavioral patterns even in species of rather fixed actions. For example, Eibl-Eibesfeldt (1970) has found that squirrels learn very little when hiding food, but that they show great improvement, through learning, in opening nuts. The former pattern is relatively fixed, the latter is not. Another example of action-dependent stereotypy was provided by Baerends (1941). He found that when the digger wasp carries caterpillars to its burrow for its larvae to feed on, it first drops the caterpillar near the opening, goes inside, inspects, then reaches out and drags the caterpillar in. If the caterpillar is moved away some distance from the burrow while she is going in, she will come back out, locate the caterpillar and repeat the sequence. She will not vary her pattern for thirty or forty trials, but then she will finally enter the nest *with* her prey. Here is a highly stereotyped behavior. In other situations however, this same wasp shows remarkable learning abilities. She can care for as many as fifteen nests at a time, each with larvae at a different stage of development with specific needs related to that stage. Before she begins hunting for the day she checks all her nests on a morning inspection tour. If caterpillars have been removed before she inspects the nest, she will bring more that day than she normally would. If caterpillars have been added she will bring fewer. She remembers the condition of each nest after her morning tour and changes made after she has begun her work do not affect her behavior further. She is only influenced by the conditions of the nests on her first visits of the day.

Other types of animals rely strongly on learning. These species are usually characterized by having extended parental care so that there is time to learn specific behavioral patterns and proper responses before having to meet critical situations alone. In some cases, the parents perform behavior the sole result of which is to teach their offspring. Female meerkats, *Suricata*, present food to their young and the young thereby develop food preferences. Schaller (1963) observed a mother gorilla removing an inedible hagenia leaf from the mouth of her offspring. "Learning animals" are also usually characterized by the heterogeneity of their habitat or their "niche." A variable or changing habitat requires flexible behavior, and it is more likely that flexibility would be maintained through heightened learning rather than through alternate stereotyped patterns. It is sometimes theorized that chimpanzees are more intelligent than gorillas because of the greater precariousness of life in their particular habitat.

Species differences in learning abilities can sometimes be revealed only by careful experimentation. For example, Braemer and Schwassmann (1960) report that the sunfish, *Centrarchidae*, which live only in the northern hemisphere, can orient by the sun upon their first exposure to it provided the sun moves from left to right (through the southern sky), but they are unable to orient to a sun moving as it would in a southern hemisphere. On the other hand, the cichlid, *Aequidens portalegrensis*, whose range includes both hemispheres, can orient by either a northern or a southern sun depending on the direction the sun was moving when it was first seen (Lorenz 1966).

Bitterman (1965) described the results of experiments which showed inherent learning differences in various species of animals (monkeys, rats, pigeons, turtles, and fish) and which differed sharply from earlier assumptions. It had often been assumed that as we go up the phylogenetic tree there is a continuous increase in learning ability. For example, Thorndike, writing at Harvard in the early 1900s, assumed no intellectual uniqueness anywhere in the evolutionary hierarchy and said species differences were only a matter of degree. The theory of intellectual continuity has been based largely on the results of curves called learning functions. Experimental psychologists give an animal a choice between two alternative courses of action. One consistently rewarded, the other never. After a number of trials the animal will choose the rewarded alternative and the trials are plotted against the errors. The results for monkeys and fish, for example, have similar shapes, a relatively steady increase in the number of correct responses in every set of trials, with monkeys showing simply a more rapid improvement than fish.

The theory of intellectual continuity, stated simply, says that an animal is born with certain tendencies to react in certain ways to certain stimuli. These tendencies are functions of inherited neural connections between sensory and motor systems. Learning ability, then, is simply the ability to make or break these connections as environmental circumstances dictate. The assumption in the first half of this century has been that higher, more intelligent animals can simply form more of these connections because of a more complicated central nervous system. This idea means, of course, the evolution of intelligence simply involves refining the old learning equipment. The result of such a theory, as Bitterman points out, was to discourage tests on a wide variety of animals and to concentrate on an interesting representative of animals, such as the rat.

Bitterman was able to illustrate important qualitative differences in learning ability in several instances. In "habit reversal" experiments, once an animal learns to discriminate between two alternatives for a reward, the reward is transferred to the opposite choice, and learning function is determined by the decrease in time it takes to make the switch. Monkeys and rats show a steady improvement in performance; fish do not. In fish, later reversals are accomplished no more easily than earlier ones. Turtles show an intermediate ability by showing progressive improvement in spatial (e.g., high versus low choices) but not in visual (e.g., red versus green, circle versus square) problems. Therefore, habit reversal requires an intellectual ability present in higher animals, not in fish, and manifested in the turtle in only a restricted class of problems.

It was also found that different species showed differences in probability-learning experiments. In the experiments, the rewarded alternative is changed within a given trial session (not from session to session). For example, a given alternative would be rewarded randomly 70 percent of the time, the alternate choice 30 percent of the time. In these experiments both spatial and visual clues were used. Rats and monkeys tended to "maximize" by choosing the most frequently rewarded alternative every time and, therefore, collecting 70 percent of the time. Fish, on the other

hand, "match." This means that if an alternative is rewarded 70 percent of the time, they will choose it 70 percent of the time. In some cases the rats and monkeys did not maximize but matched, although in a different pattern from fish. Fish matched randomly, but rats and monkeys, when they matched, tended to choose the alternative which produced the reward in the preceding trial or to choose, rather consistently, the opposite ones. Both mammals and fish solved both spatial and visual probability-learning tests in their particular manner. The turtle, on the other hand, matched in visual problems and maximized in spatial problems. Therefore in both habit reversal and probability-learning it is rat-like in solving spatial problems but fishlike in solving visual problems. Bitterman concludes that the modes of adjustment evolved by the higher animals appear earlier in spatial than in visual contexts.

The ability to maximize, it should be mentioned, produces a higher percentage of correct choices than does matching. For example, in an experiment where the reward ratio is 70 to 30 the probability of success is 70 percent if the subject is maximizing, but only 58 percent $(.70 \times .70) + (.30 \times .30)$ if the animal is matching. It is concluded that the rat and monkey show learning ability of greater adaptive significance (assuming the problems presented by the environment of the fish and mammals are similar in certain critical respects).

There may also be sexual differences in what constitutes learning situations. An estrous female is reinforcing to male rats. The males will learn a maze to be able to copulate. However, the female responds equally to sexually active and passive males. It has, therefore, been concluded that mating does not reinforce operant conditioning in the female rat. Sexual differences in behavior may also be a function of anatomy and unrelated to reproduction. The female Hispaniolan woodpecker, *Centurus striatus*, has a shorter, thinner bill than the male and she gleans food primarily from the surface of trees, whereas the male more often uses his strong bill to excavate burrowed larvae. Whether behavioral differences arise as a result of learning to employ different anatomical specializations or whether there are innate behavioral differences pertaining to foraging in the sexes is not known.

Other learning constraints may be a function of maturation. Young chaffinches will hop over the ground when they are about two weeks old, occasionally pecking at it. But in the midst of food they will starve to death unless fed by an adult bird. It is not possible to train them since if food is gradually lowered to the ground they will stop looking at it. If it is held in front of them they do not take it, but only gape, waiting to be fed (Sevenster, reported by Hinde 1970).

Since there are limits to what can be learned, especially in some types of animals, it may be assumed that there are also differences in what is taught them by their parents. There is some evidence, for example, that fish hawks (ospreys) are taught fishing behavior by their parents. Among woodpeckers, the young learn to forage on their own, but the parents continue to feed them while they are learning the technique. In some pelicans, on the other hand, the parents abandon the nest before the young leave, yet the young forage normally.

For summaries of the theoretical implications of various learning experiments and extensive bibliography it would be useful to consult Estes et al. (1954), Hilgard (1956), Koch (1959), Hilgard and Marquis (1961), Klopfer and Hailman (1967), Prilbram (1969), and Hinde (1970).

THE NATURE-NURTURE ARGUMENT

The operational model of instinct as described here was laid out, in its basic structure, by Lorenz and his co-workers in 1937 and 1950, and amended by Tinbergen (1942, 1951) and others. What they proposed was an explanation of the operation of inborn behavioral patterns which result in adaptive behavior. The model, in spite of its imperfections, demanded serious consideration, and the arguments began immediately. The result was a strong polarization of views in the scientific community partly based on misunderstandings of position and subscription to dogma, but partly on honest differences in interpretation of the same material.

The argument centered over not only whether certain behavioral patterns are inborn or develop as a result of learning, but particularly whether there is any value in attempting to segregate and identify the contributions of these two phenomena. The strong dichotomy of views resulted in what has been termed the nature-nurture controversy.

As is often the case, the principal proponents of each side probably disagreed less than the vigor of their supporters' arguments would have indicated. Neither side had any information that the other lacked and, probably, in those early days (the 1950s) the beginnings of a realistic model for the basis of adaptive behavior could have been designed which incorporated the best information from each camp. However, shortly after Lorenz's (1950) paper, which did not differ substantially from Tinbergen's (1951) views, criticisms were raised and answered which began an unfortunate crystallization of positions.

The first volleys were intended to be warnings against attempting arbitrarily to place behavioral actions into one category or the other (Hebb 1953, Lehrman 1953, Schneirla 1956). These were rather vehement attacks upon Lorenz's assumption that if behavior could ever be broken up into its individual elements it would then be possible to name each as either "innate" or "learned." Lorenz's critics argued that the dichotomizing was artificial and that the more important question involved the overall ontogeny of behavior.

Lorenz seemed to dismiss his critics as "American psychologists"—rat-runners—who were not prepared to ask the important questions. The charge might have been directed with more justification against some others of that (and this) period who subscribed to the positions of the Americans, but the gauntlet had been thrown down and the response was in kind.

There has been much discussion of the argument in the ensuing period (Lorenz 1961, 1965; Eibl-Eibesfeldt 1961; Thorpe 1963; Tinbergen 1963; Schneirla 1966; Lehrman 1970). The very persistence of the argument for twenty years seems to indicate that (1) it is a problem outside the scope of science, (2) our investigative technique is inadequate, or (3) we are treating the available data in a biased or irrational manner. It is far too early to assume the first. Our problem is probably the second (which might be more nearly resolved by closer cooperation between ethologists and physiologists) with the added influence of the third, more or less.

It is currently popular to decry the existence of the hoary argument and to maintain that there is really no argument at all. However, the positions of the major proponents have changed little. Lorenz, as late as 1965, stated, "it would be hard to exaggerate the importance attributed by ethologists to the distinction between the innate and the learned." Lehrman (1970) proved no less apologetic when he said of his 1953 criticism, "I do not now disagree with any of the basic ideas expressed in my critique."

Lehrman (1970) attempted to discuss rationally the problems of semantics which have too often led to artifactual disagreement, and it is all too clear that such clarification is eminently necessary. There is one case of a confusion of terms, however, which is actually more conceptual than semantic and the difference should be made clear. Throughout the book I will refer to "experience" when I mean learning situations and in the contexts of the usage there will hopefully be no problem regarding meaning. However, Schneirla (1966) considered experience to include a wide range of stimulative effects from biochemical influences on the developing nervous system to learning. If this meaning is accepted then one must certainly admit the influences of experience on instinct. Considering the developmental interaction of cells, not even one neuron could develop normally without the experience of its proper milieu. Such an interpretation of the term is supported by certain experiments. For example, flight in insects is considered to be an innate pattern and fruit flies, *Drosophila melanogaster,* can fly normally, erratically, or not at all, depending on the temperature of their environment during incubation.

In spite of the hardened attitudes on the part of many workers, there have been several studies which attempt to analyze the innate and learned components of adaptive patterns. One such study by J. P. Hailman (1969) is boldly entitled "How an Instinct is Learned." In this report, Hailman describes his work with the feeding behavior in gull chicks wherein he extends, and in some cases repeats, certain of Tinbergen and Perdeck's (1950) earlier experiments. He argues that in gull chicks the feeding instinct is not completely developed at birth, but that its normal development is strongly affected by the chick's experience. As evidence he cites his findings which show that experience is necessary in order for the gull chick to properly peck the bill of the parent to induce regurgitation. He also finds that the chicks quickly learn the visual characters of the parent so that increasingly "natural" models must be used in order to release the pecking responses. Let us examine the results of another experiment which points out the problems involved in designing and interpreting such experiments. At least part of the improvement demonstrated in Hailman's chicks is attributable to increased coordination of the muscles, which results in more accurate pecks. Such coordination might be a result of learning to hit their target through practice—and this is the most obvious explanation. However, the improvement, in other cases, might also be due to the "maturation of an instinct" described by Lorenz. An interesting experiment conducted by E. H. Hess (1956) demonstrated the maturation of the aiming mechanism in domestic chicks.

Figure 3.7 Chick wearing prism goggles as part of a test to demonstrate the maturation of an instinct. A nail was embedded in soft clay to serve as a pecking target. The scattered impressions around nail A were made by a one-day-old chick without goggles. A four-day-old chick without goggles had tightened the pattern around nail B. Prism goggles shifted the appearance to the left, and a one-day chick showed a scattered pattern to the left of the target (nail C). A four-day-old chick with goggles (nail D) tightened the pattern, but did not learn to compensate for the diffraction. See text for an interpretation. (From Hess 1956.)

Newly hatched chicks tend to peck at objects around them, but their aim is not very good. The head of a nail pushed into soft clay provided a target in the experiments and imprints around the nailhead showed how well the chicks were doing. At first the imprints were scattered around the nailhead (Figure 3.7a), but by the fourth day they were clustered closely around the target (Figure 3.7b). Hess was able to show learning was not involved. He fitted his chicks with prismatic goggles (Figure 3.7c) so that the objects they viewed were displaced to the right. Figure 3.7d shows that their aim had improved by the fourth day, but it had little relationship to the position of the nail since the cluster was still displaced from the target. The birds were never able to learn to hit the nail.

In view of these findings showing the intercalation of innate and learned patterns to produce an adaptive response, it has been suggested that Lorenz's scheme be applied with any rigidity only to invertebrates and lower vertebrates (Crook 1970). Such suggestions should not necessarily be taken to assume instinct operates on a different principle in higher vertebrates. Instead, we should be reminded that in such animals the strong influences of learning on any "innate" pattern would be likely to obstruct objective analysis of the separate components.

It is not probable that evidence of any sort will suddenly end the enduring argument. Rather, what will probably escort it to its long-awaited rest is the slow accumulation of experimental data, carefully analyzed, gradually yielding bases for generalities. Even these generalities will need to be carefully qualified, however, since we already know that certain types of animals are more likely to rely on innate patterns than others and that in various types of animals the normal interaction between innate and learned patterns may be quantitatively and qualitatively quite distinct.

NAVIGATION AND ORIENTATION

Many of us have been strangely moved while standing on a crisp autumn day shrouded in the reds, yellows, and browns of the season, watching formations of ducks or geese flying strongly against a steely sky. An observer might have noticed that if it is early in the day the flocks may be heading almost due south. If it is nearing dusk or fields of grain are nearby they may be temporarily diverted to resting or feeding areas. But when they resume their flight they will head southward again.

The following spring we may stand beside a swift-moving river in the Pacific Northwest and watch salmon below a dam or fish ladder. As they lie in deeper pools resting before the next powerful surge which will carry them one step nearer the spawning ground, they all face one way—upstream.

Both the birds and the fish are responding to a complex and changing environment by positioning themselves correctly with respect to it and by moving from one particular part of it to another. The questions which concern us here involve the ways animals meet their very specific spatial problems. Although we will discuss space here and time in the next chapter, in terms of the adaptive responses of animals, the treatment is admittedly artifactual and is done only for the sake of simplicity. It should be pointed out that the study of animal navigation is one of the most dynamic areas in modern biology, and the body of evidence is growing at a prodigious rate. We can only hope to review some of the most general tenets.

KINESIS

Animals may adjust themselves spatially in a number of ways and with a variety of adaptive effects. Perhaps the simplest type of movement is kinetic. *Kinesis* may be defined as a type of movement that is related to the intensity of the stimulus but is independent of its spatial properties. To illustrate, consider the humidity kinesis of the wood louse. If these arthropods are distributed over the floor of a chamber which has both humid and dry areas, they will soon be found congregated in the humid part of the floor. The explanation is rather simple: they are more active in the drier areas and they scramble about until they reach the more humid part where activity slows down until some individuals may stop altogether (Edney 1954). The receptors need only be able to register variations in humidity. So the response, in spite of its appearance, is nondirectional.

Kinesis may also be shown in vertebrates. The ammocoetes larvae of the brook lamprey, *Lampetra planeri*, spend much of their time burrowed head downward in muddy streams or on lake bottoms so that light receptors, located near the tip of the tail, are completely covered. Tests were performed in which the larvae were placed in an aquarium which was lighted on one end and which graded into a darkened portion. The lamprey became very active at the lighted end. The activity increased with the amount of light to which the animals were exposed, but the activity was independent of the direction of the light. Since the larvae were not able to burrow as they randomly moved about, they sooner or later ended up in the darkened end where activity was reduced causing the darkened area to act as a trap.

TAXIS

Of much more interest biologically are directed movements, movements which occur with reference to the direction of the stimulus. The simplest of these types of movement is the *taxis*. Tactic responses are becoming increasingly important in behavioral studies, especially those undertaken by the behavioral ecologists. Very little is known about the degree to which taxes function in the behavior of animals, especially the higher animals, the bases of most of whose movements we are disposed to describe in terms of "preferences."

There are almost as many lists of specific taxes as there are authors and there is little need to confuse the issue further here. Suffice it to say that taxes are described in terms of whether an animal moves toward or away from certain environmental characters. Thus, an animal that moves toward light, away from gravity, and toward water is positively phototactic, negatively geotactic, and positively hydrotactic.

The directed movements of animals and plants have interested biologists since the beginning of the nineteenth century. At the end of that century, Loeb proposed that all animal movements could be understood in terms of tropisms (a term which has come to refer to plant movement and which, in animals, has been replaced by the term taxis). He argued that, in bisymmetrical animals, a stimulus that registered unequally on the sides would cause the animal to turn until the stimulus was equalized. Loeb's mechanistic theory was discarded as new information began to indicate the varieties and complexities of animal movement. Fraenkel and Gunn (1940) have summarized the early work on taxes begun by Loeb.

A few examples will illustrate the complexity of tactic responses. First, consider the behavior of the grayling butterfly, *Eumenis semele*. To escape from pursuing predators it flies upwards toward the sun. If blinded in one eye, it will "escape" in circles as it attempts to equalize the stimulus, just as Loeb would have predicted, but the same half-blinded butterfly will follow a female in a straight line. So not all taxes, even within the same individual, are dependent on the same type of mechanism (Dethier and Stellar 1961).

Taxes are not always simple responses to all levels of a single stimulus. The peculiar little unicellular flagellate, *Euglena*, which requires light to carry on its photosynthesis, moves toward a dim light but away from a very bright one (strong sunlight is known to destroy chlorophyll in plants). So the type of response, in this case, is dependent on the intensity as well as the direction of light.

An animal may also change its tactic response with time. Newly hatched blowfly larvae are positively phototactic — a response which facilitates dispersal from the dark hatching area. As the larvae mature they become negatively phototactic and begin to hide in darkened areas. Of course, along with changes in behavior, changes in habitat and morphology may also be expected. Hawkmoth caterpillars keep their lighter colored dorsal surface toward the sunlight when they are young, but, as they grow older, they show a ventral light reaction and their habitat changes to the underside of leaves. The coloration of these older larvae changes accordingly, so that they are harder to see in their new habitat.

The tactic response of any organism is not necessarily reflexive and unvarying. The response or the degree of the response may be dependent upon the motivational state of the animal. For example, water beetle larvae, *Dytiscidae,* swim toward the illuminated surface of their water. Normally this takes them toward air. After they have replenished their oxygen supply, however, they are no longer positively phototactic. In other words they actively change their reference to the stimulus.

Most tactic responses are considered to be innate, so one of the obvious questions to ask is: To what degree can the response be altered by learning? It has been found that tactic responses can even be reversed by conditioning. A cockroach which is fed under light and given a mild electric shock when it approaches darkened areas will begin to avoid its usual habitat. There are reports of a similar type of conditioning being accomplished in the lowly planarian.

Investigations of taxes must be controlled very carefully because tactic responses are often not as simple as they may appear. Poorly designed experiments may, at best, be inconclusive. For example, an experimenter should be aware that tactic interactions may occur and these must be separated by experimental design in order for a single component to be analyzed. The upright position of a fish may depend upon dorsal light *and* the effects of gravity. When these two are altered

in relation to each other the results may indicate their individual effects (Figure 4.1). For an example of how two tactic responses with identical behavior may come to have a special adaptive significance see the discussion of the honeybee in this chapter.

The last point regarding taxes is that orientation is not always simply toward or away from a stimulus. Ants and bees may move on a course at a certain angle from a light source, usually the sun. An innate timing mechanism enables homing ants to change the angle of movement with respect to the sun as the sun moves across the sky. There is some basis for arguing that this sort of movement should not be considered a taxis but rather a compass orientation of the type discussed below.

Animals show much more complex orientation than simple kineses and taxes. We will primarily consider orientation ability of three types in the following discussion. *Piloting* is the ability to find a goal by referring to familiar landmarks. The animal may either search randomly or systematically for the relevant landmarks. *Directional compass orientation* is seen in those animals which are able to head in a geographical direction without the use of landmarks. And, lastly, some animals show true *navigation,* which is the ability to maintain or establish reference to a goal without the use of landmarks. Navigation may be accomplished by reversing the path of the displacement process of animals from their homes or by comparing bicoordinate readings. In the case of the latter, two or more coordinates (such as latitude and longitude) of the displaced position are compared with the known coordinates of the goal and the animal moves so that the conditions of the goal-situation will appear.

Investigations of animal orientation have been made on a wide variety of animal species and it would be impossible to attempt to summarize all the work here. Instead we will consider a few species which show a variety of sensory capacities and which utilize various environmental proper-

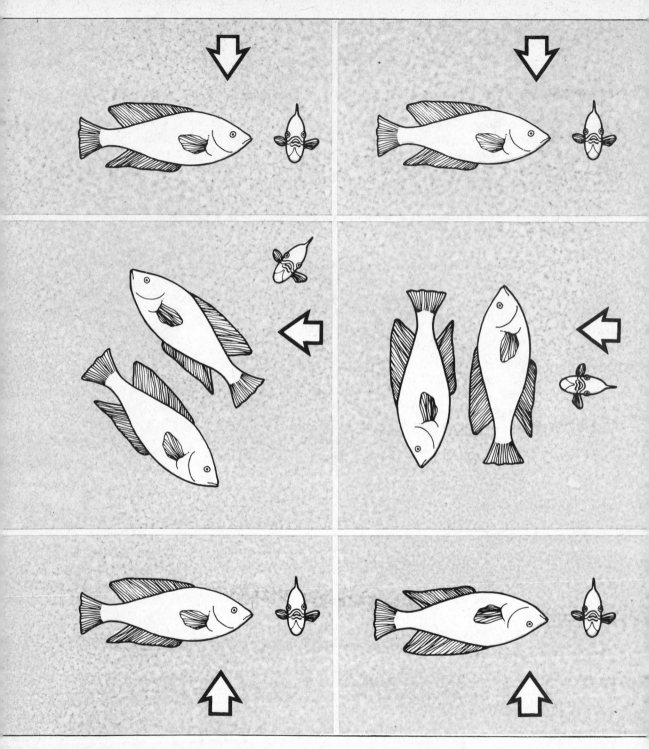

Figure 4.1 The orientation of *Crenilabrus restratus* to light coming from different directions with respect to gravity. Gravitational pull is downward. The direction of the light is shown by the arrows. The fish on the left is normal and orients correctly with regard to both light and gravity. The fish on the right has had the ear labyrinth removed and is unable to sense the direction of gravity. It responds only to light. (From von Host 1935.)

ties as their directional clues. We will direct the greater part of our attention to orientation in birds, first, because of the wealth of information available in the literature, and also because the experimental techniques themselves have often been fascinating examples of scientific imagination.

NAVIGATION

Birds

It has been known for centuries that birds disappear from certain areas annually only to reappear the following year. Over the years, many theories have been developed to account for this phenomenon. Included among them were ideas which claimed the birds had been to nether areas or the moon or had temporarily changed into another kind of animal. These suggestions have been largely discredited.

Migration

The best answers as to where birds go when they migrate has come from banding experiments. The birds are caught, a metal band with the address of an agency is fastened to the leg, and the bird is released. When the bird is found, caught, or shot, the finder is requested to send the band to the proper address. Information begins to build up, indicating the bird's range, its seasonal habitat, and something of the rate at which it can travel. Some of the results have been startling. For example, a lesser yellowlegs was banded one August day in Massachusetts and was shot in Martinique six days later. Since the distance was 1,930 miles, the speed the bird reached was *at least* 322 miles per day. Many members of the world's enormous army of birdwatchers have become involved in bird-banding and so a very large body of evidence has accumulated regarding the movements of certain species.

Other methods of detecting migratory movement in birds are also employed. Daytime (diurnal) migrants may be seen with the naked eye or with the use of telescopic aids. Nighttime (nocturnal) migrators have been counted by focusing a telescope on the moon and recording the birds that crossed the field of vision. Also, it was found that during peak migratory periods, a patient observer could count the numbers of bodies of birds (often many thousands) which crashed into radio towers or other tall structures on nights of low visibility. One of the most valuable sources of information, however, is radar. The "angels" that plague military men or flight controllers are often groups of migrating birds, and while no species identification can be made, migratory routes can be described as well as the heading, speed, altitude, and number of the migrators.

The incoming data have furnished many surprises and some of the feats performed by migratory birds seem incredible. If there were not indisputable evidence in many of these cases they would be denied on the basis of common sense. As an example consider the Arctic terns which nest within 10 degrees of the North Pole in the barren Canadian Arctic. Where do they go to spend their winter? Some tropical retreat? Actually some fly via the west coast of Africa to winter on the Antarctic ice pack. In the spring they return to the same nest sites in the Arctic. The distance, of course, is equal to circumnavigating the globe and it's done by the fragile birds once each year.

Another example of migratory prowess is shown by the greater shearwater which ranges over the vast expanses of the entire Atlantic Ocean and returns to the isles of Tristan de Cunha, tiny islands only thirty square miles in area and 1500 miles from the nearest land. Also consider the bristle-thighed curlew which nests in coastal Alaska and winters on Pacific islands 6000 miles away. Each leg of the journey necessitates sea crossings of 2000 miles. The sheer physical power involved in these feats seems astounding and has been the subject of much research of a histochemical nature in order to determine where the cellular energy reserves are and how these are utilized so efficiently. We are concerned, however, not with the physical but with the mental. What system of navigation have birds developed in the course of their evolution?

First, it might be well to ask how the pattern started to begin with. A common, but almost totally unsubstantiated, answer is that migration was initiated by birds fleeing southward before advancing ice-age glaciers. The genes of those individuals not having inherent tendencies to retreat southward were eliminated from the population. Other theories include the effects of continental drift and adaptations which permit the exploitation of temporary or moving food supplies. Welty (1968:449) writes, "Without question, ecological stresses have been the most frequent cause of the migratory habit. Birds are driven out of their breeding areas by periodic climatic cycles, which bring on food shortages that are aggravated by the annual increase in bird population. Although the original impetus to migrate may be entirely external, the ceaseless repetition of seasons of famine, brought on by arctic frost or tropic drought, may eventually, through natural selection, winnow the sensitive protoplasm of a species until the urge to migrate at a particular time of year becomes innate, and comes into play at the appropriate season even in the absence of the original impelling threat of starvation." For a review of the theories of how migration may have developed see Dorst (1962).

What are the ecological implications of migration? Certainly there must be significant advantages involved in order for such a system to have evolved in so many animal groups. The energy expenditure is great; large areas of inhospitable terrain must be passed; the weather is unstable in the migratory periods; and, for some, dangerous man-made obstacles appear attractive at this time. In addition to such dangers, a migratory bird must relinquish the rights to a hard-won territory each year and compete vigorously to become reestablished the following year. So what

rewards could possibly override such disadvantages?

We can intuitively understand the advantages of animals moving from approaching arctic winters to the sunny tropics. We can even see why birds might move shorter distances, for example from Nebraska to Oklahoma, for the winter. Only a cursory familiarity with the elements of nature could also convince us of the advantages of simply moving from a mountain top to a valley every winter. In each case the birds are trading a less hospitable habitat for a more hospitable one.

There are factors other than weather involved in the development of migration. For example, during the northern winters the food supply drops low and forces any resident species into increasingly severe competition for such commodities. Some species have very narrow food preferences and their food may even disappear from parts of their range each year. The pennant-winged nightjar, *Semeiophorus vexillarius*, breeds during the rainy season each fall in southern Africa. Then, in February, it follows the rains across the equator to winter in the area from Nigeria westward. This movement places the birds in the proper habitat at the time of the appearance of their preferred food, flying termites (Stresemann 1927-1934).

If there is so much food in the warmer winter habitats, why do not migratory species stay there? Why do they return to their summer homes at all? First, there are certain important advantages to rearing broods in these habitats. For example, days in the far north are long, and so the birds' working day can be extended, they can bring more food to their offspring in a given period of time, and thus perhaps rear the brood faster. Another result of long days is that, in essence, more food is available for offspring and so more young can be raised. It is known that, generally, the farther north from the tropics a species breeds, the larger is its brood (Welty 1968).

Another advantage in returning to the temperate zone is to escape the high level of competition which exists in the warm species-packed area (see Chapter 8). The annual flush of life in the temperate zones provides a predictable supply of food which can be exploited readily by mobile species such as birds.

In the far north, breeding periods are very short because of the weather cycles and this "inconvenience" works to the advantage of nesting birds which are in danger of falling prey to predators. The short season results in a great number of birds nesting simultaneously. Thus, the likelihood of any single individual being taken by a predator is reduced. Also, since there is not an extended period of food availability for predators their numbers are kept low. By leaving certain geographical areas each year, migratory species deprive many parasites and microorganisms of permanent hosts to which they can closely adapt. Long harsh winters in the frozen north act further to reduce the numbers of these threats in that area. By the same token, predators which are unable to escape such rigorous conditions might also be expected to be fewer in number the following spring.

Migratory movement may also bestow certain advantages to the populations of the migrators. The "scrambling" of the population each year might result in parts of the population ending up in new habitats where they might be able to establish themselves and thus extend the species' range. Because of the strong differences in summer and winter habitats, migrators might be expected to have high behavioral flexibility—an important quality for colonizers as we shall see.

Dispersal may result in the isolation of a small population of birds, and such pockets may then rapidly increase their evolutionary rate. Mutations have greater effect on smaller populations than on larger ones since they are not so overwhelmingly outnumbered and thus subject to being swamped by other genes (Chapter 8). Not only are such small-population effects important in quickly adapting an isolated group to its new surroundings, but new genes thus established in

a population may furnish important new material for other populations should cross-breeding occur.

The English mallards apparently followed their foster-parent group, but in some species the young are left to make the trip alone. In Europe, as in other places, the parasitic cuckoo, *Cuculus*, lays its eggs in the nests of other birds which then care for the young birds. The cuckoo thus grows up without ever seeing its own species. When the season approaches, the adult cuckoos migrate even before the young leave their foster-parents' nests. As soon as the young birds can fly, however, they migrate 2,000 miles to the cuckoo wintering ground, and they do it alone. The young Atlantic puffin, *Fratercula arctica*, is deserted by its parents in the last days of its nestling period. Before it has even learned to fly well it tumbles from its nest, flutters to the sea and begins to swim toward the adult birds already at the wintering area a thousand miles across the sea. So young birds are able to navigate.

It was found that when first-year birds of some migratory species were displaced experimentally they flew in the same direction of the parent group and, importantly, they flew for the same distance. In some cases this meant that they ended up in an ecologically unsatisfactory place. Schüz (1949) took storks from nests in the Baltic region, reared them in West Germany and released them after the local storks had left. He found that they had a strong tendency to head south-southeast, the direction of their parent population, while the West German storks headed southwest. It seems, therefore, that the tendency to move in a certain direction is innate and continues for a set length of time. When the drive is fatigued, the animal stops. Apparently the continuance of the drive is a function of time and not of distance. It has been found that the restless activity in caged migrators diminishes at about the time they would have reached their goal.

There are several puzzling facets of the general problems of migration in birds. Some individuals within a population may be sedentary, some migratory, and some may change their migratory status. Also, in some cases, stock which does not ordinarily migrate at all can be induced to migrate. Hatchlings from nonmigratory English mallards were allowed to mix with Baltic and Finnish migratory mallards and, of 116 young, nineteen were recovered up to 1500 miles away in the wintering grounds of the migrators (Matthews 1968). Other tests were made to find whether migratory direction in young migrators can be influenced by experienced birds of another population. It was found that, in some species, displaced first-year birds abandoned their normal migratory direction and flew with their foster-parent population in a different direction.

It should not be assumed, however, that the migratory route is learned from older birds. The urge to stay with others of the same species is a strong one and may overcome normal directional tendencies in the young; however, the migratory route has been demonstrated to be instinctive in several species.

The direction and distance ability which have been demonstrated should be enough to permit birds to migrate successfully between wintering and breeding grounds provided no mishaps occur. In the wild, though, mishaps do occur. Violent storms may take birds far off their migratory course. If they were only able to continue on a set compass direction for a certain distance, they might never be able to return to the parent population. However, some birds have appeared back in the home area after being experimentally displaced. There are indications that navigational ability improves with age in a way that permits correction for such disasters. Birds which had successfully completed a round-trip migration were experimentally displaced and it was found that they would ignore the movement of local migrants and their own normal direction as well and would fly in the direction of their proper home at that time of year. Apparently, learning has occurred and has resulted in increased navigational ability.

How do they navigate? What directional clues do they use? A great amount of time and energy has been spent in trying to unravel the secrets of the avian navigators, but the problem is far from solved. Some of the evidence is contradictory and for some questions of navigational behavior no answers, other than conjecture, are forthcoming at all. However, some of the most promising evidence has come from the analysis of navigation in homing species.

Homing

The ability of some species of birds to return to their nests when displaced has been known for centuries. The ancient Greeks and Romans were aware of this ability in their pigeons, *Columba livia*, and they used the birds to carry messages home as they journeyed across the land. It was not until about 1825, however, that homing ability began to be selected for by Belgian breeders. Since that time, the breed has changed a great deal from the Rock Dove stock from which it sprang. Pigeons are rarely used as messengers today (although they saw some service in World War I). Today, they are bred primarily for racing, as pets, and as subjects for navigation experiments.

There is much folklore and anecdotal material regarding the abilities of homing pigeons. However, the truth is that homing pigeons do not home very well naturally and must be trained. Training is accomplished by taking them longer and longer distances from their nests (usually nests in which they have reared young) and releasing them. The birds are always taken in the same direction. A pigeon taken in a new direction and released may be lost. It should not be assumed that lengthening the training distance in the same direction simply permits the birds to accumulate knowledge of landmarks. Trained homing pigeons released well out of sight of any known landmarks are also able to navigate homeward.

Strangely enough, individual homing pigeons differ greatly in their ability to home. Some birds show no ability to navigate at all, while others (a very small percent) are able to home long distances at high speeds on the very first attempt. Only 5 to 10 percent of pigeons are *ever* able to achieve long-distance high-speed homing.

Inconsistencies have been shown in the homing ability of individual birds in different trials. Of 122 pigeons tested by Matthews on 549 sorties (a sortie is a single flight by a single bird), 57 percent vanished into the horizon in the correct direction within 2½ minutes of release at least once, but *not one* had a consistent record of such swift starts.

Matthews (1968) points out that true homing in pigeons is best demonstrated in older birds which, when displaced laterally from the training direction, show a greater rate of returns than younger birds. Whether the older birds have learned to navigate better or whether their homing instinct has simply matured (see Chapter 2) is not known. Young trained birds are able to get their initial heading just as well as older birds, but older birds reach the nest faster. One partial

explanation is that they are more familiar with the landmarks once they have reached the general area of home. The importance of recognizing landmarks is indicated in experiments in which birds are reared in a cage so that they are unable to see the horizon or surrounding landmarks; when these birds are displaced and released they are unable to home.

It was thought for a time that perhaps pigeons do not possess navigational ability at all, but simply fly in random patterns until a familiar landmark is sighted. The unpredictable results of homing experiments seemed to lend credence to this idea. Wilkinson (1952) published a mathematical analysis of the percentage expected to home if random flight were the mechanism. His results were very close to those shown in Figure 4.2. It was also thought that perhaps birds had a directional tendency, although very weak, and this, coupled with random flight, would bring them home. G.V.T. Matthews, beginning in 1953, described over 500 bearings from various release points of over 50 miles in one of the most statistically significant series of homing experiments. He found that 56 percent were within 45

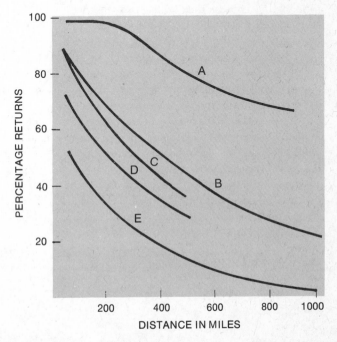

Figure 4.2 The effect of distance on homing returns in several species of birds. As distance increases there is a decline in the percentage of returns. The birds involved are the herring gull (A), the swallow (B), the common tern (C), Leach's petrel(D), and the starling (E). (From Matthews 1955. Reprinted by permission.)

degrees of the homing direction compared to the 25 percent which would be expected in a random scatter. The entire argument for random flight has been weakened by data showing homing ability over extremely long distances and it is now thought that random flight is not even a significant factor in homing.

Matthews (1955b, 1963b) has shown an interesting phenomenon regarding homing: highly experienced pigeons can home from 50 to 100 miles away and they can home from short distances 2½ to eighteen miles away, but they are unable to home from intermediate distances of 25–35 miles. This information indicates that the navigational mechanism is only functional when the animal is displaced over great distances, and is not sensitive enough to detect minor (25–35 miles) displacement. One explanation is that very different coordinates would be easier to compare than more similar ones. Short-distance homing probably is due to landmark recognition.

The view is, then, that in homing pigeons navigational abilities are not of phenomenal accuracy, but that under proper internal and external conditions, the bird is able to fly in the correct general direction and so make use of landmarks.

Homing experiments are often done with domestic pigeons because they are easy to work with; the best homers, though, are wild seabirds. Homing in the latter species has probably been the subject of strong natural selection since these birds are often blown far from their homes when ocean storms arise. There have not been as many experiments with seabirds as with homing pigeons, but the data that have been collected show a remarkable homing ability in some species. For example, a Manx shearwater, *Puffinus puffinus*, was taken from its burrow nest and sent by air to Boston, over 3,000 miles away, in a "black-box" (a carrying case that does not permit the animal to see and thereby gain visual clues regarding the direction it is being taken). It was back on its nest 12½ days later. There are other remarkable records of shearwaters' homing (Figure 4.3).

The longest homing flights were made by two Laysan albatrosses, *Diomedea immutabilis*, which were taken from Midway Island in the central Pacific, released in Washington state, and were home in 10 and 12 days. A third returned 4,000 miles from the Philippines, but that trip took 32 days.

Since, regrettably, it is not possible to follow birds on these homing flights, little is known about what they do en route. Regarding the third Laysan albatross, why did his flight take so much longer? Most birds home at rather slow speeds. Each day they fly distances that can be covered in only a few hours of flying time. The delay is not necessarily related to navigational problems since they may be spending time in feeding or resting or even soaring.

The route taken would, of course, be a factor in the time involved in homing. Perhaps some species are inclined to fly over certain types of familiar surfaces such as land or sea, or even along coastlines. In experiments with the strictly marine Leach's petrel, *Oceanodroma leucorhoa*, however, it was found that the birds would take the shortest route homeward even if it meant flying overland, but they still homed at the widely different speeds of 40 to 217 miles per day (Billings 1968).

There is an interesting phenomenon characteristic of some populations of birds which may affect studies of navigational ability. Certain populations show a directional tendency which is called *nonsense* or *fixed* orientation. This tendency is expressed by the birds of a given population all traveling in the same direction no matter where they are released in reference to their home. The direction is consistently the same under various experimental conditions. However, after an initial nonsense heading, the bird may appear back on the nest. This means the wrong heading is eventually checked and the animal begins to correctly navigate homeward. If the bird disappears in a nonsense direction it may mistakenly be recorded as a loss.

Nonsense orientation is a population, or "sub-

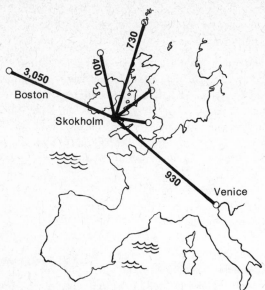

Figure 4.3 Results of homing experiments with Manx shearwaters, *Puffinus puffinus*. The map shows the distance over which individual birds successfully returned to their Skokholm breeding ground. The numbers indicate the distance (land miles) and the lines show direction that the birds traveled. (From *Animal Navigation* by R. M. Lockley. 1967.)

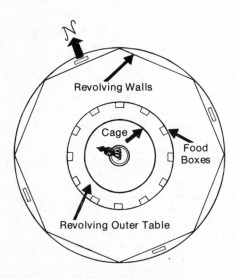

Figure 4.4 Kramer's orientation cage. The bird can see only the sky through the glass roof. The bird is trained to expect food in the box which lies at a particular compass point (such as due east). Kramer found that birds rely on the sun for directional clues. (From Kramer 1957.)

group," tendency rather than a species characteristic. Populations within a given species may or may not show nonsense orientation and different populations may show different directional tendencies.

Nonsense orientation is found in a wide range of animal species; Emlen and Penney (1964) and Penney and Emlen (1967) found the characteristics in Adélie penguins and it has been described in some arthropods. Some species, such as bank swallows and Manx shearwaters, which are excellent navigators, show no such orientation at all. The adaptiveness of this sort of behavior is not known. Although there seems to be no reason for nonsense headings, the tendency is so regular and predictable that, once determined, it is a useful tool in orientation experimentation.

Thus, although it is not known what transpires en route in migrating and homing flight, the navigational abilities of some species of birds is firmly established. It would now be in order for us to examine some of the evidence regarding the mechanisms of navigation and orientation. For recent discussions of navigational mechanisms the reader is referred to Kramer (1957, 1961), Adler (1963), Lindauer (1964), and Schmidt-Koenig (1965), Lockley (1967) and Matthews (1968).

Diurnal Navigation Clues

Gustav Kramer (1949) found that caged birds show directional tendencies in the restless activity which occurs at migration time. In other words, they huddle in that part of the cage which lies in the direction they would normally take. Also, in their fluttering about they launch themselves most often in the proper migratory direction. In noting these tendencies Kramer set the stage for a series of experiments which would yield valuable evidence in the quest for the navigational mechanisms of birds.

Kramer set up experiments with caged starlings, *Sturnus vulgaris*, (daytime migrators) and found that they oriented in the normal migratory direction unless the sky was overcast, in which case

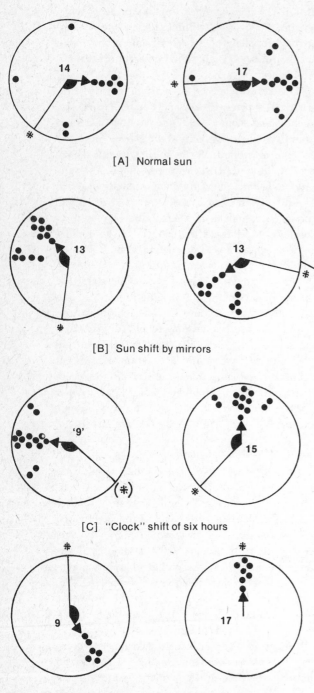

[A] Normal sun

[B] Sun shift by mirrors

[C] "Clock" shift of six hours

[D] Stationary artificial "sun"

they lost their directional ability and moved about randomly. When the sun reappeared they oriented correctly again. Apparently they were using the sun as a compass. Kramer tested his "sun-compass hypothesis" by blocking the sun from the birds' view and using mirrors to make the sun appear to be in different directions. In each case the birds oriented according to the direction of the new sun.

In another set of experiments, Kramer trained his birds to expect food in a box which was no different in appearance from other feeding boxes that encircled the enclosure (Figure 4.4), but which lay in a certain compass direction. As long as the birds could see the sun they would approach the proper food box. Even when objects in the enclosure were moved about the birds were not confused. When the feeding boxes were rotated and the wire cage enclosing the birds was lifted, the birds walked over to the box which lay in the proper compass direction. However, Kramer reported that on overcast days the birds were often disoriented, further evidence of a sun-compass. When he placed an empty box in the direction in which the birds had been trained to expect food according to the position of the artificial sun, the birds would try the box several times

Figure 4.5 The analysis of sun-compass orientation in starlings tested in Kramer-cages. (A) The birds take the same direction at different times of the day. (B) The orientation may be changed by changing the sun's apparent position by use of mirrors. (C) The orientation is also changed by shifting the birds' internal clocks. (D) The direction taken up with reference to a stationary artificial sun changes throughout the day. Time is indicated by the numbers. Dots represent periods of activity in (A) and (B) and food-box choices in (C) and (D). The asterisk indicates the perceived direction of the sun whether real or artificial. (From Kramer 1957.)

before they gave up. Kramer said it was amusing to see their puzzlement at the empty box, but they were not easily persuaded that they had made an orientation error.

The ability to measure time is characteristic of a great many species of plants and animals, but the physiological basis of the ability is not entirely known. Clocks are discussed in the next chapter; however, a brief reference to how clocks are important in navigation should be made here. Kramer noticed an interesting pattern emerging in his artificial-sun experiments. If the sun remained stationary, the birds would continually adjust their angle with reference to it as though *it* were moving. This reaction became much more pronounced when the sun was raised and lowered at the same rate of the apparent rise and fall of the real sun. He had noticed earlier that when the real sun was used, the birds were always able to orient in the proper direction even as the sun moved across the sky. The birds were able to compensate for the sun's apparent movement, and the compensation meant they possessed some sort of independent timing mechanism.

Clocks can be reset by artificially altering the light regime. This is done by beginning with an artificial light-dark period which corresponds to the natural diurnal period outside. The light period is gradually shifted, over a number of days, until it occurs earlier or later than the natural light period. In one set of experiments, the internal clock of pigeons was shifted six hours (¼ day), and when the birds were taken from home and released under the sun they departed 90 degrees (¼ circle) from the home direction (see Figure 4.5). Hoffman (1954) reared starlings with

time retarded by six hours under artificial light. He placed them outside when the sun was at the same altitude (3 P.M.) as the artificial sun inside (set at 9 A.M.). He found that their orientation changed 90 degrees clockwise. The rate of change was 15 degrees per hour, or the sun's rate of apparent movement. A converse test was performed by Emlen and Penney (1964) who moved Adélie penguins which showed a northward nonsense orientation to a different longitude (at the poles small lateral shifts result in large time changes). The nonsense orientation changed, as expected, by deviating counterclockwise when transported eastward and clockwise when transported westward. Nonsense orientation may be changed also, by resetting the biological clocks of birds.

Just how do birds utilize the sun in navigation? There are several ways directional information may be gained from the sun's position, but it isn't clear which clues are used. The sun may be used as a simple compass; but knowing "which way is north" is not the solution to navigational problems. Imagine being suddenly blindfolded, taken to some remote place and left with a compass. You would want to know in which compass direction home lay.

The compass direction of any celestial body is described in human navigation by taking the number of degrees measured clockwise from a known compass direction—usually north. This reading is called the *azimuth*. A second reading may be taken of *altitude*, or the vertical distance from the horizon to the celestial object (see Figure 4.6). Simply observing the altitude of the sun places the observer only on a *circle of Sumner*. This circle includes all those points on the

Figure 4.6 The position of a celestial object as determined by azimuth and altitude readings.

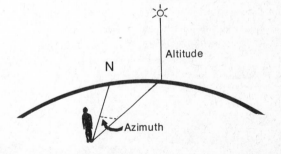

earth where at a given time the sun is at a given altitude (See Figure 4.7). The circle may extend for thousands of miles and so is of little use by itself. The bird could restrict its location to a part of the circle if it knew which way the sun was moving; but can a bird detect the movement of the sun along its arc? The sun's rate of movement is such that it might be easier to see movement in the minute hand of a watch. In fact, Meyer (1964) found that the pigeon's eye is able to detect the sun's movement. His birds could distinguish a stationary artificial sun from one moving at 15 degrees per hour, the sun's normal rate. (Humans are unable to distinguish movement slower than 60 degrees per hour.) The necessity for determining the direction of the sun's movement may account for the delay shown by some birds before orientation (50 minutes or more for some species according to Walcott and Michener's 1967 observations). It may also explain why even the best homers often start on courses 60 degrees to 90 degrees from the correct course.

Theories of sun navigation assume the bird knows where the sun should be at a certain time of day according to what it remembers about conditions at home. Homing is, then, an effort to move in such a direction as to restore the sun to its proper position for that time of day. If a bird were able to extrapolate, from a brief glimpse of the sun's movement, just where the sun will be at its peak (or when the sun will arrive at due south in its arc), as Matthews (1968) suggests, it would be possible for the bird to determine its latitude. If the sun were going to be lower at noon than it would be at home, then the bird is too far north (see Figure 4.8). Lockley (1967) reports that there are indications that birds, as well as bees and lizards, have this ability to project the sun to its highest point.

The bird could also detect longitudinal displacement by use of the sun's arc (Matthews 1968). For example, if the sun were on a course such that at noon (home time) it would be lower than if observed from home, the bird could cor-

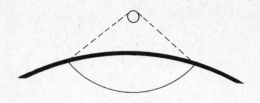

Figure 4.7 Circle of Sumner. The sun appears at the same angle with reference to the earth's surface from any point on the circle.

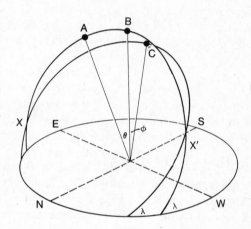

Figure 4.8 Perceived changes in the sun arc due to a move in a southwest direction at noon (home time). The altitude of the highest point of the arc B is greater (by 0) than at home, C. The inclination of the arc is also greater. The observer could be aware of the shift since the sun A would not have moved as far along its arc as it would have at home. In order to avail itself of such information, a bird would have to be able to extrapolate a new arc from observing movement of the sun after the bird had changed geographic positions. The bird would also have to memorize the home arc and be able to use it as a reference. (From Matthews 1955.)

rect for this by flying eastward. There are those who argue that extrapolation to the sun's highest point in its arc is beyond the ability of birds. Some of these critics argue that correct bearing can be taken from azimuthal position alone. Even this simpler idea, however, is complicated by the fact that the rate of change in azimuth varies with the time of day. The sun changes its compass direction more slowly when it is rising or falling than at about midday.

Are there possibly other diurnal celestial clues that could be used in navigation? In experiments with pigeons described by Keeton (1969), resetting the biological clocks caused the birds to orient incorrectly in homing tests when the sun was visible. Yet when he tested these birds under overcast skies they homed correctly. Keeton interprets this as evidence of a redundant mechanism built into the navigational system which is not time dependent, and which is not employed when the sun is visible.

Implicit in Keeton's interpretation is the possibility of diurnal celestial clues other than the sun. The evidence for such clues is inconclusive, but at least two other possibilities exist: the planets and the daytime moon. It is true that either Mercury, Venus, or Jupiter is above the horizon most of the time and, although the positions of the planets are not nearly as stable as those of the stars, the planets do not change position much at a given hour over a period of a few days. Brids' eyes do show adaptations for reading celestial clues (see Matthews 1968), but there is no good evidence that they are able to see the planets in a daytime sky. Although the daytime moon has been suggested as a possible celestial clue there has been no direct evidence to substantiate this suggestion. Also, many problems arise in attempting to explain how the daytime moon might be useful. The stars, moon, and planets would be expected to best be utilized in nighttime navigation and certain evidence has been presented to show that the night sky does in fact hold navigational clues.

Nocturnal Navigation Clues

It has been known for many years that birds migrate both by day and night. Some species are more inclined to fly at one time than the other, but many species fly around the clock. After the evidence for daytime celestial navigation began to appear it was assumed for a while that nocturnal migrants took their bearings at sunset and made it as best they could through the night. Then Sauer and Sauer (1955) reported results of experiments that changed this notion. They exposed two sylviid warblers, blackcaps and garden warblers, in Kramer-cages to the autumn night sky of Germany. The cages were variously modified with devices to record the direction of the birds' activities without the necessity of continuous observation. The Sauers' birds had been handreared indoors and had never seen the sky, but after one glimpse of the stars they oriented southward. When the test was repeated in the spring they oriented northward. So here was evidence that the night sky could provide navigational clues.

Franz Sauer then began a series of experiments aimed at discovering just which objects in the nighttime sky the birds use as clues. He moved his Kramer-cage inside the Bremer planetarium so that the nighttime sky could be controlled. He first lined up his planetarium sky with the sky outside and found that the birds oriented themselves in the proper migratory direction for that time of year. The lights were turned out and the "sky" was rotated various degrees from normal. The birds oriented according to the new direction of the "sky." When the dome was diffusely lit the birds became disoriented and moved about randomly. In some of these experiments the moon and planets were not projected and the birds oriented correctly so, apparently, they were taking their bearings from the stars (Figure 4.9). Sauer concluded that the birds were not relying on the stars themselves, but on the altitude and azimuth of the starry sky. They were able to derive a "fix" by determining longitude from the azimuth and latitude from the altitude, a rather complex set of calculations as skeptics have consistently pointed out. (Some evidence of lunar orientation is indicated below.)

Of course human navigators have long been aware of the usefulness of stars in direction finding; constellations may provide rough information even to the amateur navigator. For example, when Orion's belt is perpendicular to the horizon it is in the eastern sky. The angle is 45 degrees when it is in the southern sky, and it is parallel to the horizon when it is in the western sky.

The apparent motion of stars presents serious problems to our understanding of nocturnal navigation. It is not known whether birds use constellations or individual stars by which to navigate, but simplicity would dictate that they use those stars which show the least apparent movement. Stars do not show the seasonal rise and fall of their arcs as the sun does, but they rise four minutes earlier each night (two hours earlier each month). So the stellar day is 23 hours 56 minutes long. The star sphere continuously slips westward until a given star returns to the position where it was a year ago. This means a bird would have to fly at a different angle relative to a certain star, depending on which night he flew. This also means

that new stars appear and others disappear below the horizon through the course of a year. The only group of stars that are always above the horizon are those within 35 degrees of Polaris, the relatively stationary North Star. Emlen (1967) has provided preliminary evidence that this star group is the most important to navigation.

Many birds cross the equator in their annual migrations and in so doing they see an entirely new sky come into view with its myriad celestial patterns. Out of this sky the bird must pick its navigational clues and it must do this accurately the first time. Polaris is lost from view as the Southern Cross (Crux Australis) comes into view. The Southern Cross, however, is not as stationary as the Polaris group and is therefore not as good a navigational clue. So the theory of star navigation becomes increasingly complex.

If birds are able to compensate for the apparent motion of the stars, a biological clock must of course be assumed. As is the case with diurnal navigation, a clock would permit the bird to alter its direction relative to its changing celestial clue. A night clock, as Emlen (1967) points out, is much more demanding than a diurnal one which uses a single celestial clue. If individual stars are used in navigation, the rate of compen-

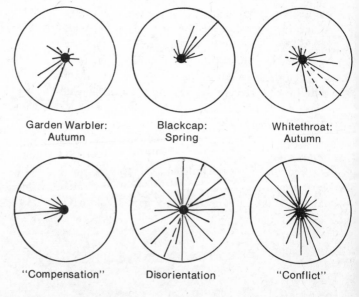

Figure 4.9 The migratory orientation of warblers in cages under the dome of a planetarium. The top row shows what happens when the dome is aligned with the outside sky. The bottom row shows the directional activity of the warblers when the dome has been rotated. Compensation occurs when the birds orient correctly to the new pattern. Disorientation occurs when the birds show no directional activity. Conflict is the result of a multidirectional phenomenon. Note that the longest ray stands for the direction most often taken. The remaining rays are proportionate. (From Sauer 1957.)

Garden Warbler: Autumn

Blackcap: Spring

Whitethroat: Autumn

"Compensation"

Disorientation

"Conflict"

sation for apparent movement must differ depending on which star is used. A star appearing near Polaris moves through a smaller arc than one farther away and therefore it seems to move more slowly. So if a bird uses stars of different declinations, the compensation rates must vary accordingly. The same sort of difficulty arises if star groups are used. In the latter case, however, the issue is further confused by changes in relative positions of stars in a group due to differences in their distance from earth. The same type of phenomenon is seen when trees nearest the highway on which you are riding zip past faster than those farther away.

There is some evidence that nocturnal migrants show a constant azimuth compensation of approximately 15 degrees per hour. This is the apparent rate of motion of some stars across the sky relative to a celestial axis through the North Star. If only those stars which show an azimuth motion of 15 degrees per hour were accepted by birds as cues, the necessity of compensation for the various rates of apparent motion of different stars would be relieved. Of course such a system would necessitate some ability to recognize specific stars unless, as Emlen (1967) has suggested, the birds are reacting to gestalt stimuli provided by the star patterns. A complicating factor in such a system is that the direction of compensation must vary, being clockwise for the northern sky and counterclockwise for the southern.

It must be pointed out that the evidence that biological clocks function in nocturnal navigation is far from conclusive. Some experiments seem to show that timing is irrelevant to nighttime orientation. Matthews (1968) reset the clocks of mallards, *Anas platyrhynchos,* a species known to migrate both by day and night. Three groups of birds were tested by setting group I six hours ahead, group II six hours behind, and group III twelve hours out of phase. When released in daylight the controls flew northwest as expected, group I flew southwest, group II northeast, and group III flew southeast. When re-

leased at night, however, the same three groups went northwest with the control group. Griffin (1964) interprets this as evidence that birds can get more reliable information from stars than from the sun and therefore cannot be thrown off course by clock resetting. Matthews observed on some occasions that his mallards flew northwest when thin clouds obscured the stars but not the moon. So, possibly, mallards as well as other birds show "moon-compass orientation."

On the basis of experiments with nocturnal migrating indigo buntings, *Passerina cyanea,* Emlen (1967) suggests that time compensation for stellar motion is not an essential component in the nighttime orientation mechanism. He arrived at this conclusion by shifting planetarium skies 3, 6, and 12 hours advanced and retarded from local time and finding that 25 of 28 buntings tested maintained their original heading. Subsequent experiments showed that the birds were orienting by clues from the planetarium itself, but the results still indicated that the birds were not relying on a time clock. These results conflict with the results of some of the experiments performed by Sauer which seemed to indicate that clocks are important to nighttime navigation. If clocks are not employed in nighttime navigation, then just how birds utilize the stars is certainly not clear.

For further discussion and criticisms of the planetarium experiments see Adler (1963), Schmidt-Koenig (1965), and Matthews (1968). Unfortunately, much of the experimental evidence is contradictory but these discrepancies will doubtless be cleared up as experimental techniques are perfected and more sensitive statistical procedures are developed.

Other Types of Navigational Clues

It is possible that birds can orient by clues other than visual ones. Gordes (1962) and Fromme (1961) have reported orientation in birds in the absence of any celestial clues. In their experiments dissociation occurred only when the steel door to the birds' chamber was closed, an effect that would be expected if the birds were orienting magnetically. Wiltschko (1968) reports experiments with captive robins, *Turdus migratorius*, which chose a normal migratory direction when in a room subjected magnetically only to the earth's normal field (0.41 Gauss). In an artificial magnetic field of about the same intensity, a change of direction of magnetic north produced a corresponding change in the direction of orientation. Fields weaker or stronger than normal were not responded to and this may be one explanation of why other, more crude, magnetic experiments have failed. It is too early to report conclusively that the phenomenon is important in the navigation of birds, but the early indications are that the idea deserves more serious attention. Magnetic orientation in planarians is discussed in the next chapter.

Once a bird has begun a migratory flight, it might conceivably use a number of types of clues to maintain the proper course when the sky is overcast. There are theories involving the Coriolis force, or the sensing of latitudinal changes in subtle forces due to the earth's rotation. Inertial receptors of the inner-ear labyrinth have also been hypothesized but, as yet, not discovered, which might allow the bird to feel subtle changes in speed or direction. It has been suggested, also, that birds which call to each other in flight might detect wind movement by differences in the sound produced by members of different parts of the flock. These theories are almost entirely unsubstantiated by experimental evidence.

One of the interesting problems of migratory flight centers on how the birds maintain the proper altitude even in completely overcast skies and when the ground is not visible. Radar observations show that they continue to move inside and between cloud layers, and that they vary only about 40 vertical years for distances of 2 miles at altitudes of 700 meters to 1100 meters (Griffin 1955). It has been suggested that perhaps they listen for sounds or echoes from the ground

such as those reported by balloonists. Some cave-dwelling birds are able to use echolocation to fly in the dark in much the same way a bat does (see below) so the idea of such a system being developed by migrating birds is not unreasonable. Another theory states that the birds may be sensitive to small changes in atmospheric pressure. We have all felt these changes in our ears when driving over mountains. Griffin (1955) suggests that they may be the function of the Vitali's organ, sometimes called the paratympanic organ.

The strong bias at present in favor of visual navigational clues is expressed by G. V. T. Matthews (1968:26): "We may conclude that birds do not orientate with reference to any unknown, magnetic, rotational or pressure stimuli, and suggest that visual stimuli of paramount importance."

Since the ability to orient in space is probably found to some degree throughout the animal kingdom, it would be impossible to attempt to discuss the phenomenon in all groups here. Consideration of orientation in a few other groups of animals is in order, however, to show something of the range of animal life in which directional ability has been demonstrated and to indicate some of the ways animals gain directional information. These animals are not discussed in the usual phyletic sequence to dispel any notion of progressive development from one species to the next. There is almost no information, as yet, regarding how many times orienting and navigating ability has arisen anew in the animal kingdom.

Fish

It has been established that some fish can navigate long distances, but our knowledge is extremely limited regarding which species possess this ability and what types of mechanisms are involved. Fishermen are aware that certain species of fish appear in certain areas at a given time of year and, in many cases, this is the extent of our knowledge. Where do the fish go at other times? And how do they find their way? Fishermen find the first question of great interest but we are more concerned with the second.

Migration of fishes is somewhat different from that of birds. Fish migration may be defined as a behavioral pattern in which the animal spends the early part of its life in one locality, journeys to another locality where it reaches breeding condition, and then returns to the home locality where it breeds. The time spent away from its home locality may involve years. As an example of migration in fish let us consider the fascinating case of the salmon.

Salmon hatch from eggs in the redds, or spawning areas, of North America and Europe. The redds are usually in the cold, clear headwaters of gravel-bottomed rivers. The young slamon may spend two years in these home waters where they grow large and mature. Then they swim to sea. They fan out in all directions once they reach the ocean, but many of them eventually show up in certain feeding grounds far out at sea. They spend two to seven years in the ocean (depending on the species) where they reach their breeding condition. Salmon in breeding condition are large, glistening, beautifully colored creatures and, in this state, they head from their feeding grounds back through the trackless sea to the river from which they came. When they reach their river, they swim upstream, always turning up the correct tributary until they reach the very riverlet where they spent their youth. It is a remarkable journey from the depths of the open ocean back to the home redds and it is performed flawlessly. They return to their own grounds with such consistency that streams which are near each other may hold strains of fish that are following separate evolutionary lines.

Once home, the females shed their eggs which are fertilized by the males. The journey is over and the fish are no longer the beautiful specimens they were. Their fat stores are gone and their color has faded. Fish of the Pacific species, *Oncorhynchus spp.*, completely spent, die. The European Atlantic species, *Salmo salar*, may feed for a while and return to sea to make the breeding journey again as even larger specimens.

One very interesting set of experiments was conducted in British Columbia. Two branch rivers, the Upper Columbia and the Willamette, converge into the Columbia River which flows into the Pacific Ocean. The king salmon of the Upper Columbia are autumn-run fish while those of the Willamette swim upstream to spawn in the spring. Eggs were collected from the Willamette fish and hatched in the Upper Columbia. The fish grew well in their new home and eventually made the journey to the sea. They returned from the sea and swam up the Columbia with the Willamette fish in spring; but when they reached the fork in the river, they left the Willamette fish and turned up the Upper Columbia, although this tributary was not suitable for breeding at this time of year. Their behavior was interpreted to mean that the time of movement is instinctive, but the characteristics of the home waters are learned.

One of the pioneer workers in fish navigation, Arthur Hasler (1960), pointed out that the fish learn, or are imprinted to, the odor of their home waters in the first few months of their lives. The evidence he and others give which shows the importance of olfaction is convincing. First, it has been shown that many fish have phenomenal abilities to distinguish certain types of molecules in water. Salmon can be halted in their spawning by certain organic smells, such as the scents of predatory seals and otters. A fisherman dipping his hand into the river upstream may cause migrating salmon below to reverse their direction. In tests, salmon and other fishes have shown the ability to be conditioned to respond to very small amounts of various soluble chemicals. Other tests have shown that when the salmons' sense of smell is destroyed, they are unable to home. So salmon are able to use their sense of smell to swim upriver to the waters where they spent their youth.

Hasler believes the fish do not follow a gradient because constant exposure to the odor would result in its being adapted to. Instead, he believes, they crisscross the scent, much as a trailing dog might, and constantly move upstream in tactic response to the direction of the current.

Do streams have their own odors? In some places strong differences in stream solutes are known to exist because of geological differences in the stream-bed material. Other scent differences could arise through the type of plant material which decomposes in the water, or by various effects of its physical characteristics such as the depth of the water, its speed, and its degree of oxygenation (which might vary according to whether large rocks break the water surface and cause rills or bubbles).

Olfaction cannot be the answer, however, to the question of how salmon navigate from far at sea to the mouth of the river. Marked Pacific salmon have been caught at sea as far as 2,375 miles from their home river. European salmon are known to travel hundreds of miles out to sea after leaving their rivers. The river effluent would simply be too diluted by the salt water to be used in navigation. So how do they manage to navigate so unerringly back to their river mouth? As Hasler (1960) points out, there are strong indications that they may use celestial clues. In tests with a device similar to a Kramer-cage, white bass, *Roccus chrysops*, were conditioned to swim into an enclosure which lay in a certain compass direction. Under a clear daytime sky they were able to perform correctly, but under overcast skies they were unable to orient. In conclusive tests with mirrors it was shown that the white bass is able to orient by the sun's position in association with a biological clock. Although the ability to orient under test conditions should not be equated with the ability to navigate in the wild, the possibility of sun navigation is very real.

There is one other possibility that should be mentioned in regard to possible navigational mechanisms in fish: magnetism. Salmon have a high sensitivity to electric currents. They can detect (and presumably avoid) sea lampreys which use electric currents to locate their prey. Given their acute electric sense, it is possible that salmon can get directional information from the earth's magnetic fields. No such ability has yet been demonstrated, however.

Bees

One of the most amazing stories of how animals find their way about has been described by Karl von Frisch (1953 et seq.) in his exquisite studies of the honeybee, *Apis mellifera*.

Honeybees are, of course, highly social animals and, as such, they exhibit a high degree of coordination and cooperation in their behavioral patterns. They work together to build a hive, care for the young, keep the hive at the proper temperature, defend the hive, and gather food. In regard to the last, they work together in a very direct way. They "tell" each other where food may be found.

According to von Frisch, scout bees, upon finding a good food source, bring back a full load of pollen and nectar to the hive. They may have found the food by a very roundabout course though, so they fly out again to the food and thereby establish the most direct route. When they return to the hive they communicate their find to the other bees by "dancing" on the vertical combs inside the dark hives. The dance describes the direction and distance of the food source. Distance may be communicated by several methods. The round dance (Figure 4.10) is performed when the food is less than 100 meters from the hive. The waggle-tail dance (Figure 4.10) is done when the food is farther away. In the latter case, the distance is communicated by the time spent in "waggling," by the tempo of the dance, and possibly, by sounds produced by the bee, either by pulse rate or period of sound production. The pulse rate is about 2.5 times faster than the waggling rate. Substrate vibrations set up by the dancing bee may also function in relaying information.

Distance is described by bees in terms of the energy expended in covering it. This means if a bee must fly into a headwind, or uphill, or if she

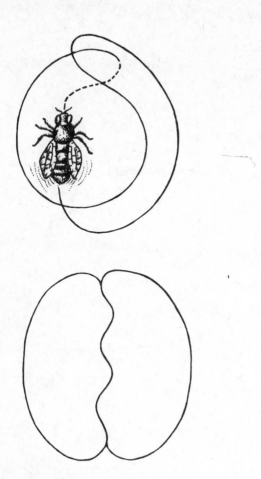

Figure 4.10 The dances of the bees. Successful foragers show the position of food by these dances. If food is less than 100 meters from the hive, the round dance shown on the top is performed. If the food is farther than that, the waggle-tail figure eight dance shown on the bottom is performed. (From *Biology* by Karl von Frisch, translated by Jane M. Oppenheimer. Copyright © 1964 by Bayerischer Schulbuch-Verlag. By permission of Harper and Row, Publishers, Inc.)

is forced to walk, she will report a farther distance than the actual distance.

The direction of the find is described by the angle made by the "waggle" part of the dance and a vertical line. This angle indicates the position of the sun relative to the food. Of course this angle changes as the sun moves across the sky.

The bee's system of communication appears even more complicated when it is realized that the dance is performed in the darkness of the hive and that the other bees apparently pick up the information by touching the dancer. The information gained tactilely is employed visually when the sun's position is determined and the bee sets out at a certain angle to it.

Even more complex, theoretically, is the communication of the angle of the food relative to the sun since the dance is performed inside the dark hive, out of sight of the sky. What happens is this: the waggling part of the dance is not performed with direct reference to the sun since the sky is not visible. Instead, the dance is performed with reference to gravity (Figure 4.11) on the vertical face of the comb. An angle of 40 degrees from vertical means the bees should fly at a horizontal angle 40 degrees from a line running from the hive to the sun's position.

The evolutionary basis for the transposition was explored by Vowles (1954) working with ants. The sensory transfer was concluded to be probably based in the positive phototaxis (normally upward toward the sun) of disturbed arthropods, and the negative geotaxis which normally has the same adaptiveness. An alarmed bee, then, may fly toward the sky and away from gravity in what might be considered a redundant system of escape orientation. The association of the two taxes may have served as the evolutionary basis for one coming to be described in terms of the other.

It might be asked if, in such a complex system in arthropods, learning can be involved or if the entire scheme is under the control of instinct. In fact, learning is important to the system. Marler and Hamilton (1966) describe experiments which

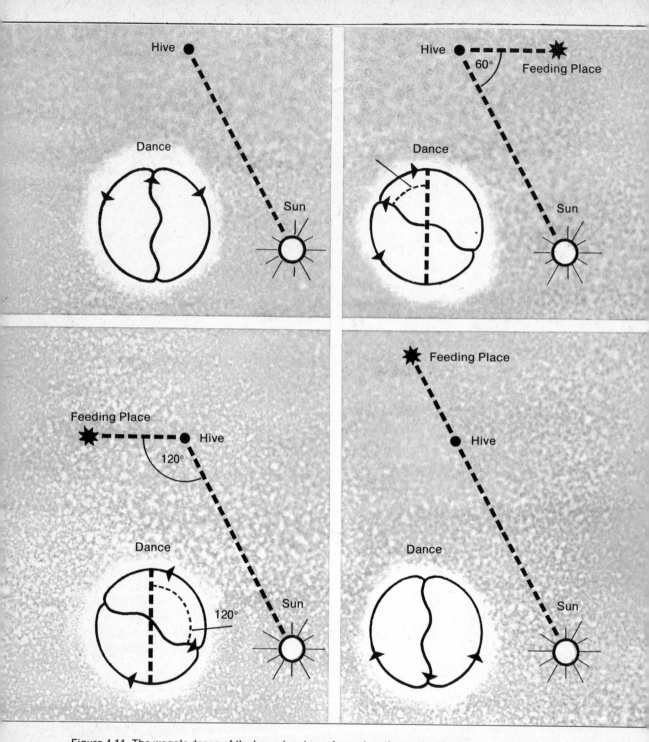

Figure 4.11 The waggle dance of the honeybee is performed on the vertical face of combs inside the dark hive. The direction of the waggle run across the diameter of the circle shows the direction of the food discovery. In the hive the direction is relative to the vertical, in flight it is relative to the sun. Therefore the other bees in the hive must transpose the angle of the dance and the vertical to an angle relative to the sun before they set out to locate the food that the scout has announced. (From *Biology* by Karl von Frisch, translated by Jane M. Oppenheimer. Copyright © 1964 by Bayerischer Schulbuch-Verlag. By permission of Harper and Row Publishers, Inc.)

show that bees must learn the sun's track as demonstrated by the fact that only experienced individuals compensate correctly for the sun's course. It is noteworthy that in order to learn the sun's course bees need only be exposed to less than one complete journey of the sun across the sky. Also, if insects can learn, they can also forget. In the ant, *Formica rufa*, ability to compensate for the sun's apparent motion is greatly reduced in spring after hibernation. It seems the ants lose some of their navigational ability during their long winter's "sleep."

It should be pointed out that von Frisch's description of communication in bees has fallen under serious criticism by Adrian Wenner (1971). In an outstanding example of the scientific method in action, Wenner has accumulated impressive evidence indicating that among bees communication may take place through odor; he recommended the rejection of the bee-language hypothesis. The issue has not been resolved among bee men as yet, and much vigorous debate appears to be in the offing.

Frogs and Salamanders

It has been found that some species of frogs and salamanders can orient by the use of celestial clues in conjunction with biological clocks. In any search for an orientation mechanism, the first factor to be considered is visual. However, displacement experiments with newts, *Taricha rivularis*, showed that they were able to home over relatively long distances even after they had been blinded. So it was then thought they homed by olfaction, but in experiments designed to preclude olfaction they were still able to home. Then a remarkable set of experiments revealed some rather startling information.

Taylor and Ferguson (1970) reported that a group of blinded southern cricket frogs, *Acris gryllus*, were able to orient with respect to their learned shoreline at home. Also, in other experiments, their biological clocks were altered by a changed light-dark regime so that when the cycle

was advanced six hours the animals shifted their direction 90 degrees. They were obviously reacting to light so a system of extraoptic photoreceptors (EOP's) was hypothesized, but such a system would need to be sensitive not only to light, but to the direction of the light source. Then it was found that when an area of the skull between the eyes was covered with opaque teflon, the sightless frogs lost all directional ability.

The part of the skull that was shielded lay over a peculiar little structure that has been the subject of much debate by comparative anatomists and physiologists. This structure is the pineal complex. The pineal is generally thought to be the vestige of a third eye which was functional in the distant ancestors of many extant vertebrates, including man. In some lizards a small lens and retina are still present at the tip of the structure (Weichert 1965). The complex develops embryonically as an outpocketing of the forebrain, just as do the eyes. Both photoreceptive and secretory cells have been found in the pineal, but very little is known about the function of the structure. Many vertebrate evolutionists dismiss it as just an interesting, but no longer useful body, but Taylor and Ferguson's experiments indicate that its present adaptiveness in some species should be reconsidered.

EMITTED-ENERGY ORIENTATION

Most orientation and navigation is accomplished by organisms perceiving environmental features which exist independent of the organism, such as sunlight. Another type of orienting mechanism, however, is the clue that is derived from the action of the orienting individual. Remember the theory that night-flying birds which continually call in flight may be listening for the deflection of the sound wave to determine their altitude or their relationship to the rest of the flock. Marler and Hamilton (1966) call the general mechanism of "reading" self-produced energy patterns *emitted energy orientation* and it has been found to be a feature of widely diverse species of animals.

At present there is no evidence that emitted-energy orientation functions in any other way than (1) simply giving an animal information about the topography of his immediate environment and (2) making known the presence of other objects in the air or water through which the animal is moving. There is no indication that this type of orientation functions in navigation other than in merely permitting the organism to move through his immediate environment successfully.

As would be expected, the species which have evolved such systems are generally those which cannot utilize light in orientation or those which live in places where light energy is not present in sufficient amounts to be utilized. As examples we will briefly consider bats, water beetles, electric fishes, and porpoises.

Bats

In 1793 and 1794, Spallanzani performed a set of experiments which showed that blinded bats could find their way about a room. It was then demonstrated by Juvine that if the ears of blinded bats were plugged, that ability was lost. The subject was essentially one of conjecture until, in this century, the mechanism was confirmed to be echolocation (see Griffin 1958). In studies of several species of bats it was found that the animal simply bounces sound waves off any object in its immediate environment and, by noting the time taken for the echo to reach it, it calculates the distance to the object. The size of an object may be determined by the distortion of the sound wave when it is deflected. The bats are thereby able successfully to move through elaborate darkened mazes of their home caves without flying headlong into the walls as would a visually orienting creature.

The frequency of the echolocating call was found to be far beyond the range of hearing for man. The sounds, however, are of high intensity, so for animals that hear in that range the sounds are very loud indeed. They are composed of very short pulses lasting only a few thousandths of a second. When the bat is hunting, the pulses are longer and relatively slow until the animal senses the presence of prey (such as a flying moth). Then the pulse rate immediately increases and the duration is sharply reduced. This change, of course, produces more accurate readings of the prey's position and increases the efficiency of the hunter.

Some species of nocturnal moths have evolved a very interesting mechanism to escape hunting bats. They have developed a sensitivity to the sounds of the bat and, depending on how close the bat is, they take appropriate evasive action in response to the sounds.

Not all bats forage on airborne creatures. In addition to the fruit-eating flying foxes, *Megachiroptera,* and the fabled vampire, *Desmodus,* there are the fishing bats. The best known of these is *Noctilio leporinus,* the bulldog bat. These bats take small fish near the surface of the water. The toenails are elongated and sharply curved to act as gaffs and the bats often trawl by flying along dragging their hind claws in the water. The search is not always random, however. It seems they locate fish by echolocation. Surface-feeding fishes often break the surface of the water causing ripples. The small deviations in the pattern of the echo caused by the ripples aid the fish-eating bats in locating their prey.

Water Beetles

Some insects, such as the whirligig beetles, *Gyrinus,* also utilize surface ripples. We have all seen groups of these small beetles whirling crazily over the surface of fresh-water ponds and may have wondered how they keep from crashing into each other. It has been demonstrated that as long as the beetles keep moving they are able to avoid contact with each other, but if one stops he may be bumped by another beetle. It seems each beetle is aware of the location and direction of the others by the vibrating waves they set up. The impulses are registered by a modified second antennal segment.

Electric Fish

The dark, turbid waters of the rivers of South America and Africa are the homes of two unusual species of fish which have evolved separately, but which are remarkably similar in some ways. The mormyrid and gymnotid fishes swim with equal ease either frontward or backward by simply reversing the direction of their undulating fins. They avoid obstacles when swimming either way and when they enter a crack or crevice they enter it backwards. Backward movement should not be surprising in animals which do not primarily utilize sight in orientation and these fishes do not.

It was found by Lissmann (1951) and others that orientation, obstacle avoidance, and recognition of the presence of other animals are a result of sensitivity to changes in electrical fields which these fish produce in a tail organ. Conducting objects, such as other animals, distort the electrical field differently than do inanimate objects such as jutting rocks. Other electric fishes distort the field in a characteristic manner also and so the animal is able to recognize the presence of members of its own species.

Porpoises

The development of antisubmarine devices during World War II permitted scientists to begin studies of underwater sounds. The early workers in sonar were surprised to the find the ocean a rather noisy place with much of the sound produced by animals. This finding should not have been so surprising, however, since the physical properties of water cause sound to attenuate less and to travel more rapidly than in air.

Porpoises, *Phocaena*, are among the marine species which are believed to use echolocation. Captive porpises are able to move about and locate food in very turbid water which renders vision almost useless. It is now known that porpoises continually emit high-frequency pulses at intervals of 15 to 20 seconds and that these pulses function in orientation and in location of other bodies in the water. Interestingly, porpoises have no vocal chords and apparently produce sound by transferring air from one nasal sac to another.

5

BIOLOGICAL CLOCKS

Perhaps you have noticed that the small carnivore sharing your home becomes restless each evening. The eyes of the cat are dark-adapted and the claws are sheathed in silent pads. If you were not feeding it, this animal would find its greatest foraging success at night when its stealth and quickness would enable it to catch smaller animals. For ages, the ancestors of your cat hunted at night and now the pattern is firmly fixed in the entire group. The question arises, How does an apartment-dwelling cat know when it is night? A more unanticipated question would be, How does a *potato* "know" when it is night? In this chapter we will follow the search for the mechanisms of timing in living things. The reason for this emphasis lies in the fact that this has largely been the bent of scientific research thus far, and because the process has been a fascinating example of the scientific search.

Just as living things must arrange themselves spatially, they must also arrange themselves in time. Since time itself is apparently not segmented so that we can measure the rate at which the units pass, we measure time in terms of regularly occurring events instead. (Notice that in our attempts to conceptualize time, we think in terms of space, thus accenting the arbitrariness of the division.) Because the earth revolves around the sun with regularity, rotates at a constant rate on its tilted axis, and has a predictable and recurring position relationship with the moon, life on earth is subjected to cyclic fluctuations in its environment. Of course, the life that exists in the changing environment must change also, so as to behave in the most adaptive manner according to the conditions.

The rhythmical nature of life comes as something of a surprise—even to many biologists—but such should not be the case in the light of the evolutionary principle. Life developed under cyclical conditions, and the differences in phases of the cycles are often so pronounced as to place a high adaptive value on life being able to accommodate itself as specifically as possible to each phase.

Even very subtle environmental rhythmicity may be responded to if life is exposed to it over long periods of time. We are all somewhat taken aback, from time to time however, as new data appear indicating the organizational levels at which cyclicity appears and the myriad ways the rhythmic nature of life expresses itself. Such revelations only serve to point up our level of ignorance on the subject. Admittedly, this level is somewhat higher than might be expected since observations on the cyclicity of life began to appear over 2,000 years ago.

About 300 years before Aristotle, men first wrote about plants which raise their leaves to the sky during the day and fold them at night (we will depart, somewhat, in this chapter from exclusive consideration of animals). It wasn't noticed for another 2,400 years that the leaves would rise and fall even when the plants were inside and therefore deprived of environmental information regarding the time of day. Then it was found that even in plants which were kept in total darkness and at a constant temperature, the leaves would continue to rise and fall with a startling regularity (Figure 5.1). This meant, of course, that the organisms possessed some means of keeping time, and so the search for the "biological clock" was on.

The first reports of biological clocks in this country came from John Welsh at Harvard (working with crustaceans) and Orlando Park at Northwestern (with insects) in 1934. The response to their work was unfortunate. The scientific community greeted their reports with distinct coolness, and their evidence was almost ignored. For the most part, biologists simply found it very difficult to accept either of the two proposed hypotheses: independent internal timers or the ability to read exceedingly subtle environmental clues. It was generally thought that the fault lay with experimental technique. Then, in 1948, Dr. Frank A. Brown, feeling his status secure enough in the scientific world to approach an unpopular problem, took up the sword. Based on his own work, he announced his opinion: organisms time themselves by environmental clues. These clues, he theorized, are not the obvious ones such as light and temperature, but environmental variables which are able to pervade man's best attempts to provide constant conditions. His statements generated discussion and the opposite interpretation was, of course, upheld by other workers who said that timing is by internal mechanisms and independent of the environment. The issue is unresolved to this day. We shall consider evidence for the two arguments, but before doing so it would be useful to discuss a few general aspects of what is now known regarding the phenomenon.

As would be expected, considering the various known types of environmental cycles (e.g., stellar, lunar, and solar), there is wide variation in organismic rhythms. Such rhythms may vary in time from the rapid beatlike staccato of firing neurons (nerve cells) to yearly seasonal changes as demonstrated in some animals building up fat or storing food before winter. There are even rhythmic aspects of events which occur only occasionally or just once in populations. For example, human births are more likely to occur in the very early

Figure 5.1 The normal "sleep movements" of plants. The leaves rise at the beginning of daylight (left) and fall when dark approaches (right). These movements persist even when the plant is placed under constant light and temperature.

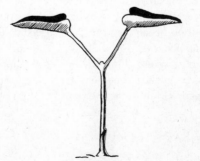

morning than in the early evening. Probably the most obvious and best-known cyclical changes, however, occur on about a 24-hour basis and these will furnish most of the material for our discussion. Of the various cycles, the biological rhythms that correspond to geophysical periods are distinct from the others in several important characteristics, such as temperature independence and propensity for "entrainment," as we shall see.

It should be pointed out that rhythms may not be directly related to abiotic influences such as temperature and light. They may, instead, be coordinated with the activities of other organisms, which may be, in turn, regulated directly by the environment. Bees time their visits to flowers so that they arrive at the time when the flower is beginning its daily period of nectar secretion. This means the bee can gather the maximum amount of food with a minimum effort and it means the flower need not waste energy by continuously secreting. There are other examples of rhythms of one species being coordinated with other members of an ecological community.

Some animals show age-dependent rhythmicity. They may operate on one time schedule early in their lives and another one later. For example, young badgers play in the sun in front of their den when they are young. As they grow older they gradually shift their period of greatest activity toward evening and night. Such shifts are accompanied by changes in behavior. The younger badgers are quite calm during the day, but as they change to nighttime activity they become more nervous or fearful during the day as they gain confidence at night (Eibl-Eibesfeldt 1950). Differences in the rhythms of two species occupying the same range may function importantly in reducing competition. Flycatching birds and bats are not in direct competition because of the time differences in their feeding behavior.

It is not entirely correct to speak of *the* rhythm of an organism since several cyclic events may be taking place simultaneously within a single organism. Such rhythms may be entirely out of phase with each other. In mice, for example, body temperature, glycogen, and DNA content of regenerating liver may each reach their maximum values at different times of the day, according to Michael Menaker of the University of Texas.

Proper coordination in timing (called *phase relationships*) among the various internal physiological processes are very important (Menaker 1969). Substrates, enzymes, energy sources, and information-carrying molecules must appear in a properly spaced sequence if the body is to function as a coordinated whole. The importance of the phase relationship of cellular constituents is indicated by the sudden appearance, over about a day, of a great many enzymes in developing chick embryos. After their appearance they begin functioning in proper phase relationship to each other.

As an indication of the complex nature of the biological clock (or clocks) it has been found that multiple cycles occurring within a single individual may not be in phase with the same aspects of the environment. An example of this aspect of the phenomenon is demonstrated in intertidal crabs. These animals exhibit a light-dark coloration of their "shell" which corresponds to the day-night local cycle. They also exhibit cyclic variation in their running periods, the time of greatest activity. Interestingly, the light-dark period is about 24 hours and corresponds with the appearance of the sun, but there are two running periods, one usually at night, the other during the day. These arrive 50 minutes later each day and correspond with the rise and fall of the tide. (The crabs come out to scurry around on the beach and forage at ebb tide.) So the crabs are able to time both solar day and lunar day.

Biological rhythms are not always coordinated to appear in conjunction with the onset of some ecological event. In some cases the advantage or adaptiveness of a particular rhythmic pattern is not apparent at the onset of the pattern. There are instances when the the period of activity must begin at such a time that it will *end* at a critical period. Here, the environmental event is "predicted." For example, a wide-ranging nocturnal animal must stop hunting and begin its trek home so that it will reach the protection of its burrow before daybreak. Such changes in pattern may well be a function of time rather than distance. Remember the bee which describes the distance of food in terms of the time taken to reach it.

Another example of predicting ecological changes is seen in the time of onset of breeding. Breeding usually occurs so that the young will be born at the time of maximum food abundance. The timing in this case has come to be through *photoperiod* effect. Photoperiod is a description of seasonally changing day-length. In order to utilize such environmental changes animals must often differentiate between ten-hour days (winter) and thirteen-hour days (spring). It has recently been found that photoperiod effect is possible because of differences in susceptibility to light of different *parts* of a daily rhythm. An animal may be insensitive to light, in terms of a breeding cue, for ten hours a day, but sensitive for the next few hours. When light continues to fall on the animal during his sensitive period in the spring months certain hormonal changes are instigated and the onset of breeding occurs (Pittendrigh and Minis 1964).

One of the fascinating facts revealed in the clock studies is that rhythms are even found in isolated parts of organisms. For example, cell-division rhythms and contraction rhythms are found in tissue cultures (cells growing on an artificial medium). Also, mammalian hearts and adrenal glands maintain a daily rhythm for several days after removal from an organism. Even a single neuron in a ganglion, or group of nerve cells, continues to exhibit a daily rhythm. So far no circadian rhythms have been shown at any level below the intact cell.

As further evidence of the complexity of rhythmicity in animals, some organisms are more sensitive to biological agents at certain times of the day than at other times (Halberg 1960). A given amount of the toxin produced by the intestinal bacteria, *Escherichia coli,* will kill about 80 percent of a group of mice when given in the early evening, but will have little effect when administered only eight hours later. Interestingly, there are sensitivity rhythms for some common pharmaceutical agents in humans also.

It is obvious that rhythmicity exists in a wide range of animals, is expressed in many different ways, and may be coordinated with a number of different cyclical environmental events. It should be stressed at this point that the rhythmic behavior of all but a few species is unknown, as is the degree to which individuals may vary. However, Menaker (1969:683) states, "For nearly all organisms at any level of organization, most behavioral, physiological, or biochemical variables which one might choose to measure can be expected to exhibit a daily rhythm."

THE PHASE, PHASE SHIFTING, AND, ENTRAINMENT

Many of the natural biological rhythms are about 24 hours in length corresponding to a solar day, as mentioned. When rhythmic organisms are placed under constant conditions where, theoretically, no aspect of the environment is allowed to vary, their rhythms may drift slightly to 23- or 25-hour periods. These periods of about a day are called circadian rhythms (*circa*, about; *diem*, day).

It is interesting that the alteration in the rhythm of organisms under constant conditions may depend upon the type of conditions under which they are placed. For example, constant light of increased intensity may cause the rhythm to become longer or shorter, depending on the species (Figure 5.2). "Aschoff's rule" states that an increase in the light intensity lengthens the high-activity phase (free running period or FRP) for nocturnal organisms and shortens it for diurnal organisms. Thus, with an increase in light intensity the FRP of a mouse increased while that of a sparrow decreased.

Altering the environment can bring about other

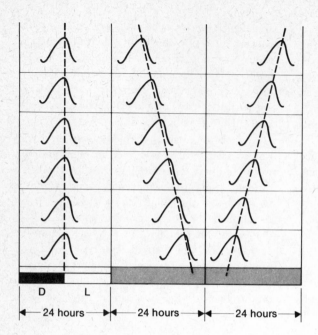

Figure 5.2 Diagram showing the circadian variation in a biological rhythm. The column on the left shows a hypothetical rhythm which appears in response to a normal light-dark cycle. The period cycle of such a rhythm repeats itself every 24 hours. If the light and temperature are maintained at a constant level in the laboratory, the rhythm will shift becoming longer or shorter. The cycles may lengthen to 25 hours as in the middle column or shorten to 23 hours as in the column on the right (From Palmer 1970.)

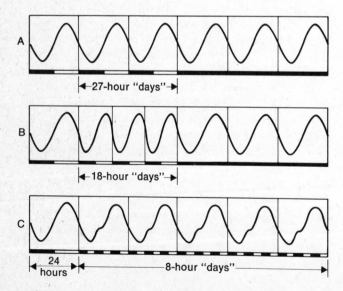

Figure 5.3 Diagrammatic representation of some effects of light-dark cycles on the period of a typical biological rhythm. In A, after many days on a regular 24 hour day regime (the last of this regime is shown at the left of each row), the day is lengthened to 27 hours for several days and the organism adjusts accordingly. However, the effect is superficial. When the treatment is followed by constant darkness (darkness is indicated by the dark areas along the base lines), the organism reverts to its 24 hour rhythm. In B, the organism adjusts superficially to an 18 hour day. In C, however, when the organism is subjected to an 8 hour day, the extreme change is registered only in a distortion of the 24 hour rhythm. (From Palmer 1970.)

changes in biological rhythms also. If a plant exhibiting normal "sleep movements" (daily rising and falling of leaves) is placed into a situation where the nights are light and the days dark, the plant quickly changes its pattern to fall into line with the new schedule. It comes to raise its leaves when it is actually dark outside. If the plant is then placed into a constant environment, the new rhythm will persist for a few days and it will then gradually return to its normal schedule. It is apparent that the clock was temporarily reset. Such *phase lability* is characteristic of biological rhythms. An important effect of resetting clocks can be a change in the migratory direction, as we learned in Chapter 4.

The time involved in the completion of an entire cycle may also be altered by changing the environment. By lengthening the period of a cycle (see below) in controlled environment chambers, the leaves of plants can be made to rise and fall every 27 hours. Their "day" may also be shortened to 18 hours (Figure 5.3). There is a limit, however, to how far the cycle may be altered. For example, if very short "days" of about eight hours are offered, the organisms will ignore them and continue in their 24-hour cycles.

The effects of altering biological clocks can best be conceptualized by considering a mechanical model, devised by Menaker (1969), on the basis that daily rhythms behave in much the same way as do some physical oscillators (Figure 5.4). In this model we are considering the behavior of a coiled spring with a weight attached to one end and the other end attached to a rigid surface. For purposes of discussion we will assume there is no friction so that once the oscillating (up and down) motion of the spring has started it will continue without change unless disturbed by some external force. Various positions of the weight are shown as they would occur at different times. Time is shown along the horizontal axis. We have already employed certain terms such as "rhythm" and "cycle" according to their common usage, but perhaps we should now tighten our definitions to comply with the restricted senses of clock models. The recurring oscillations comprise a *rhythm*. The repeating unit of the rhythm is referred to as a *cycle* and the length of time necessary to complete one cycle is the *period*. In the diagram the period of the rhythm is five seconds. *Phase* refers to a specific part of the cycle (or the position of the weight at a given point in the cycle). *Amplitude* describes the displacement of the mass or the distance of the weight from the resting (coiled) position to the farthest point below the resting line.

We may now describe clock alterations in terms of the model. Figure 5.4B shows what happens if external force is applied at some point in the cycle. The result is a *phase shift*. Phase shifts can occur in either direction or to any degree. If the external force increases the velocity of the oscillator, the phase is advanced by causing the "weight" to reach a point earlier than it would have normally. Conversely, retarding the oscillation, as is shown in the model, leads to a phase delay.

If one applies sufficient continuous external force with a different period the oscillator will take up the period of the applied force. This phenomenon is called entrainment. Notice that the entrainment does not occur immediately; instead, the new period is taken up gradually. Also, there is a fixed relationship between the phases of the oscillator and the external force. When the external force is no longer applied (consider the plant placed under constant conditions), the oscillator returns to its normal period.

Experiments may be done which demonstrate control of both the phase and period of cycles. A sparrow was kept under constant conditions of darkness and showed a natural circadian rhythm of 26 hours. A cycle was imposed upon this bird with 3 hours of light and 21 hours of darkness. The onset of activity (FRP) then began 35 minutes before the light went on each day (so the period changed to a 24-hour basis entrainment). When the light period was extended to 11 hours, with

13 hours of darkness, the onset of activity began directly with the light. Here we have an example of phase-shifting.

In plants, phase-shifting can be demonstrated by reversing the light-dark cycle of a bean plant. The result is a reversal of the phase in the sleep-movement rhythm. So both the phase and the period of the rhythm are controllable. The limits within which entraining cycles can vary and still alter the normal period are different among species and even among individuals. As Menaker (1969:682) says, "Oscillators are controllable, but only within certain limits determined by their physical characteristics and the characterisitcs of the signal."

So a basic pattern in the timing of living things is emerging. Plants and animals show rhythmic behavior even when deprived of the more obvious environmental cues. These cycles are modifiable, within limits, by known environmental factors. The modifiability of the cycles is ecologically imperative. As mentioned, the natural cycles are rarely of a 24-hour period and so are somewhat out of phase with environmental events. The sensitivity to daily cycles keeps the organisms' clocks continually "set" so that behavioral phases occur at the adaptively appropriate time of day. We shall now consider some of the arguments regarding the nature of the ultimate control mechanism.

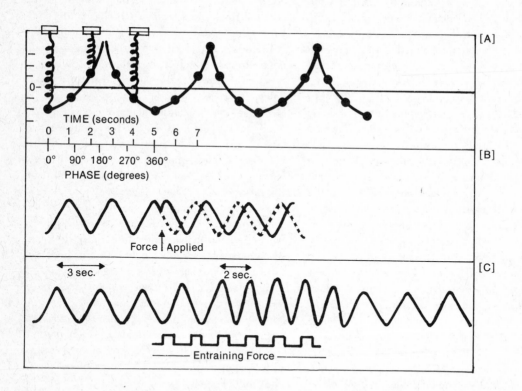

Figure 5.4 An oscillating model showing, in physical terms, the general characteristics of biological clocks. See the text for an explanation. (From Menaker, M., *Bio Science* 19(8):682 (Fig. 1), 1969.)

ENDOGENOUS CONTROL THEORIES

Crickets chirp at dusk. The most obvious explanation is one involving cause and effect: the crickets chirp in response to the sun's going down. However, there is some good evidence that any causation involved operates primarily on an evolutionary level and not within the individual. In other words, a cyclic nature within the cricket has appeared in response to a regular photoperiod over the eons and the nature of these cycles cannot be altered basically by individual experience. Such a system of recurring behavior cannot be considered simply as "instinct" according to the ethological concept since there is no evidence of releasers, IRM's, or other aspects of instinctive patterns involved. Learning or imprinting are also probably not involved, since, even when several generations are reared under constant conditions, rhythms persist. The more prominent theories involve a rhythmic system within the cell based on a cyclic nature of the chemical constituents of cells.

Aschoff (1963) has said that for the organisms which had been investigated thus far rhythms are innate and inherited characteristics. Such a statement regarding the heritability of clocks is supported by such evidence as successful artificial selection in the laboratory for stocks of insects with certain rhythms. In other experiments, it was found that plants and animals which had been reared entirely under controlled static conditions became rhythmic *de novo* or turned out to be arhythmic (showing irregular fluctuations). In some of the latter cases they could be induced to become rhythmic in response to a single stimulus. As an interesting example consider the fruit fly, *Drosophila*. In nature, fruit flies emerge from their pupal cases only at dawn and from thenceforth show the usual 24-hour rhythm. If eggs are kept under constant laboratory conditions they will hatch at any hour of the day. It was found that even when a strain was kept continuously under constant conditions for 25 generations, with each generation hatching randomly through-out the day, when the developing pupae of any generation were subjected to a single flash of light, that generation all hatched 24 hours later (or multiples of 24 hours). Only the single stimulus was necessary to synchronize the clocks of all the insects for the rest of their lives.

Circadian rhythms which persist under constant conditions are considered as evidence for an endogenous (or internal) control mechanism. A flying squirrel may show a period of 23 hours 36 minutes and, since there is no known natural cycle of 23 hours 36 minutes, the control is presumed to be internal. Also, other flying squirrels may show longer or shorter periods, further evidence that the rhythms are not originating in the environment. The evidence of individual differences is incorporated into the argument of the endogenous-control theorists. The lack of precision or synchrony, they feel, upsets their theory not at all since evolutionary pressure could be expected to develop a clock which only approximates the 24-hour day. Normal day-night cycles could then operate to make the small corrections necessary to adapt the system to local conditions. Flexibility, according to this interpretation, is essential.

The endogenous rhythm theory, then, does not rule out the possibility that organisms are sensitive to geophysical factors or that timing is influenced by such factors. It only states that the basic timing mechanism is not dependent upon any periodic change in such factors. Menaker (1969) points out that the earth's environment cannot be expected to furnish adequate timing clues because of the variable nature of the environment. As examples of variable geophysical factors he cites variations in light intensity, temperature, barometric pressure, magnetic field, and ionization of the air.

As was mentioned, any innate internal biological clock must be conceived in biochemical terms. The concept is basically simple. Biochemical reactions proceed at a given and predictable rate. There are cyclic systems known in which the end-product of a reaction is just the material needed to initiate the reaction again. By-products, of course, could be expected to appear in the course of a reaction, and these could affect specific "targets" in a target-system and account for the phases of a cycle.

There have been objections raised to a strictly biochemical interpretation of the mechanism. For example, it is known that temperature greatly affects the rate of chemical reaction. An increase in temperature of only 10° C doubles the rate of many reactions. If a clock could be made to run twice as fast by a 10° C increase in temperature, then it could be assumed that clocks could be used as peculiar thermometers, as Palmer (1970) points out. Temperature, however, seems to exert very little effect on most biological rhythms. A change in temperature of 10° C seldom even causes a change of 20 percent in the period. Even these small effects might be the result of a change in the ease with which the rhythm is expressed in its milieu rather than a change in the basic mechanism. As Hastings (1970) states, however, a feedback mechanism could account for the temperature independence of biochemical clocks (Figure 5.5). It is adaptively very important, of course, that clocks not be affected by temperature. If they were, cold-blooded animals, whose body temperature fluctuates with that of the environment, would be unable to develop reliable clocks.

It is not correct to assume, however, that clocks are entirely independent of temperature. Whereas clocks are not easily advanced or retarded by temperature changes (phase shifting) alternating temperature changes may influence the period (entrainment). Twelve-hour periods of 28° C alternating with 20° C can entrain a rhythm which will persist for a time when the organism is shifted to constant environmental conditions (see Palmer 1970).

Figure 5.6 shows the relationship of the basic *mechanism* to the appearance of its observed *effects*. An analogy may be drawn to a clock and its hands. So far, the problem is not unlike trying

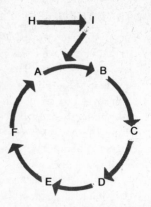

Figure 5.5 Diagrammatic representation of hypothetical mechanism. A chemical cycle is show in which the product F is starting material for the first step of the reaction. Temperature independence is achieved through a feedback mechanism (H→I and A→B). The mechanism can work if A→B and H→I are temperature dependent as are most chemical reactions. This means that B and I would increase as the temperature is raised. However, if I is a specific inhibitor of the A→B reaction, the heat-induced production of I would slow down the production of B, thereby stabilizing the rate of the entire reaction. (From Hastings 1970.)

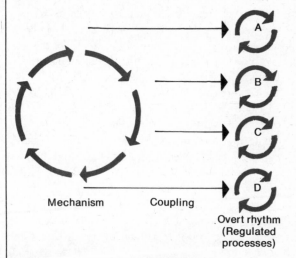

Mechanism   Coupling

Overt rhythm
(Regulated
processes)

Figure 5.6 Diagram of a model for the hypothetical mechanism of a circadian rhythm. The model shows a self-regulated mechanism which could be sensitive to environmental variables such as light and temperature. Such a mechanism would serve as the drive behind a number of observable cellular phenomena such as A, B, C, and D. (From Hastings 1970.)

to determine how the mechanism of a clock works by manipulating the hands. The target system (the hands) can be altered without affecting the basic mechanism. Considering the analogy, it may be said that there is an accumulating body of evidence regarding the nature of the hands, but a dearth of information regarding the mechanism.

Gonyaulax, a dinoflagellate, provides an example of how the hands may be altered without affecting the mechanism. The organism has a glow-rhythm of bioluminescence, and a rhythm of photosynthesis (timed to correspond to the presence of sunlight). Chemical inhibitors can block the rhythm of photosynthesis while not affecting the bioluminescence. When the inhibitors are removed, the photosynthesis picks up right in phase (as shown by its relationship to the glow rhythm) showing that the basic mechanism was not affected.

The clock-and-hands analogy also shows how multiple rhythms with different periods could operate by the same mechanism. Recall the crab whose color period was in phase with the sun and whose running period was in phase with the tide. The two hands of a clock have different periods also but are driven by the same mechanism. The existence of a clock-and-hands scheme would mean that different mechanisms need not have evolved for every rhythmic system and thus would make the endogenous theory more plausible. This is not to rule out the existence of multiple systems, however, since it is possible that more than one mechanism may be involved in producing the many known rhythms (Figure 5.7).

Manipulation of the hands of a clock does furnish some information about the nature of the mechanism, but such indirect information is, of course, of limited value. For this reason there has been a great effort to "get behind" the observable patterns to the source of the rhythm. The problems involved in such efforts are enormous. For example, biochemical inhibitors have been used to try to alter the mechanism and thus to provide insight into its nature. However, if an inhibitor is

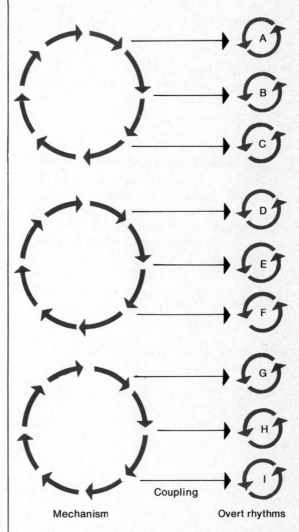

Mechanism   Overt rhythms

Figure 5.7 A multiple-mechanism model for circadian rhythm which has been offered as an alternative to Figure 5.6. (From Hastings 1970.)

to be successful its effects must be reversible and it must throw the clock out of phase by as many hours as it is allowed to remain in the system. (If the rhythm picks up again in phase after the inhibitor has been removed, then only the hands have been altered.) A true mechanism inhibitor should be able to suspend the activities of a mechanism for extended periods of time (limited only by the effect of the suspension on the viability of the organism).

Inhibitory agents have, in spite of such demands, provided some clues regarding the biochemical nature of clock mechanisms. It has been found that clocks are generally insensitive to a great variety of chemical inhibitors, such as narcotizing agents and sublethal amounts of metabolic poisons. Some of the results have been startling and very difficult to interpret. For example, poisons such as sodium cyanide may alter the *amplitude* or a rhythm while the *period* remains essentially unchanged (Figure 5.8), thus the clock itself has not been altered.

It is clear that simple inhibition experiments are not likely to produce definitive answers to the question of biochemical mechanisms. Even simple metabolic pathways are often replete with complex systems of shunts and feedbacks so that blocking a specific pathway may have very little effect on the general cellular oscillation. The administration of general or multiple inhibitory agents is likely to produce unanticipated, unseen, or severe effects which would render the agents less than useful as a research tool.

Some promising information is based on the effects of agents whose influence on the system is not entirely known. Deuterium (D_2O) has an unusually interesting but unexplained effect on clocks. It was found that the phototactic rhythm of the flagellate *Euglena* was changed from 23 to 27 hours when water in the medium was largely replaced by D_2O. An effect has also been noticed in mammals. Deuterium in the drinking water of a deer mouse increased the period of activity rhythm as a direct function of the D_2O concentration. It is believed the deuterium is affecting the mechanism since it has caused phase shifts (see Hastings 1970).

The biochemical mechanisms of clocks remain clouded in mystery with only occasional tantalizing glimpses of what is really there. Educated guesses by careful and highly trained researchers have often proven valuable in providing working hypotheses until more data are forthcoming. The guess of those who work with clocks is that a mechanism involving protein synthesis is operating. Such a system would involve the very regular building and tearing down of extremely complex molecular proteins, or enzymes. Such a scheme,

Figure 5.8 Diagram of the effect of a sublethal dose of sodium cyanide, a metabolic inhibitor, on both the period and amplitude of a biological rhythm. It was expected that the period would be lengthened. However, the period remained the same but the amplitude was decreased. (From Palmer 1970.)

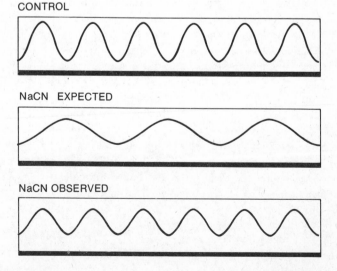

CONTROL

NaCN EXPECTED

NaCN OBSERVED

unfortunately, is ridden with unknowns. How can protein-based rhythmic systems be turned on and off? What is it that actually oscillates, enzyme quantity, enzyme localization, or enzyme activity? Or are enzymes directly involved at all? Perhaps substrates, the substances which enzymes act upon, are the rhythmic component. Enzymes are known to appear in response to the presence of their substrates.

Perhaps the system does not involve an enzyme-substrate system at all. It is thought that bioluminescent rhythms in *Gonyaulax* are not derived from such a system. Hastings (1970) believes that the control is from a complex cellular particle, or organelle. He has isolated such a particle and has derived and purified its working substance. This particle is called the *scintillon*. But even if this sort of model proves valid, the difficulties of the problem are not much reduced. The "simple" enzyme-substrate model might have to be abandoned in favor of a complex physiological control mechanism. The multiple target hypothesis would be strengthened by such a concept, but the basic problem would remain: how does it work?

The exogenous (environmental) control proponents accept the idea of a cellular clock mechanism, so the biochemical approach is of interest to both groups. We shall now consider some of the arguments for exogenous control. The proponents of this theory are fewer in number than the endogenous control people, but provoking arguments for the case are concisely and well presented by Frank A. Brown (1970).

EXOGENOUS CONTROL THEORIES

Some of the support for exogenous control stems from different interpretations of the same data cited by cellular control theorists. For example, two flying squirrels, *Glaucomys volans*, were kept in total darkness. One showed a 23-hour 58-minute period and the other a 24-hour 21-minute period. This was presumed by some workers to show that each had its own endogenous clock which was independent of the environment. However, Brown (1970) interprets the data another way. He argues that it may be demonstrated that animals may generate periods other than 24 hours while using a 24-hour clock based on environmental cycles. (A man may get up later on weekends, but he is still using a standard 12-hour clock.) The timing of a rhythm having a period different from 24 hours with the use of a 24-hour clock, is called *autophasing*.

The environmental control theorists do not deemphasize the importance of biochemical endogenous clocks. The argument surrounds the ultimate source of the timer. Those who support the exogenous theory maintain that the intracellular rhythm occurs in response to cyclic geophysical changes, although there is no general agreement as to just what part of the environment is furnishing the clues.

Brown (1970) conceptualizes the system as a two-layered ring (Figure 5.9). There is a "core" of unchanging geophysical timers which exists under a changeable rhythm affected by as examples, light, temperature, and food. The geophysical forces, he believes, penetrate all experimental conditions so that what were thought to be constant conditions are not at all. According to the scheme, only the outer conditions can be experimentally controlled.

It is known that several diverse geophysical phenomena are cyclic in nature and therefore could be furnishing information. The most important, for purposes of this study, are those which fluctuate on a daily basis. The more obvious daily changes, of course, include temperature (discussed in the previous section), and light-dark cycles. There are more subtle geophysical cycles. For example, the atmosphere is subjected to tides just as are the oceans. (Atmospheric tides can be measured as barometric highs and lows.) Atmospheric tides might have secondary effects on such geophysical entities as gravity, geomagnetism, electrostatic field, and background radiation. These tidal pressure changes are cyclic due to the regularity of celestial events and therefore they can be predicted on a daily, or even an annual, basis. There is some interesting evidence of the correlation of atmospheric tides and biological rhythms. One such report stems from Brown and his group regarding work which was done about ten years ago on what some might regard as a peculiar area of interest: potato behavior. It was found that the metabolism of the potatoes (which were kept under "constant" conditions and shielded from the direct effects of barometric change and temperature) showed changes which could be correlated with the weather. The relationship was so dependable that one could tell by looking at the respiratory charts of the potato whether the outside temperature was 50° above or 5° below for any day, and whether the barometric pressure was high or low. The potato could not have been getting the information directly but, it was reasoned, somehow environmental information was filtering through. The evidence supported the premise that organisms in standard constant conditions can still receive and read exceedingly subtle environmental clues.

Another example serves as a fascinating illustration of the receptive abilities of some organisms. Fifteen oysters were sent from New Haven, Connecticut to F. A. Brown's laboratory in Evanston, Illinois. Brown and his co-workers were studying the shell-opening activities of the oysters under constant light conditions. The oysters were expected to open (as if feeding) during what would

have been high tide in Connecticut, and to close at the time of low tide. The oysters opened and closed in the expected way for two weeks, but then there was a surprising change. Their phases suddenly began to alter until they were opening and closing in keeping with what would have been high and low tide if Evanston were a coastal city! Somehow they were gaining information regarding their new location in spite of their controlled environment.

There are good indications, also, of clues being provided by other phenomena associated with the rhythmic pulling of the sun and moon. Fiddler crabs, according to long-term records, show a diurnal change in metabolism which fluctuates in a semi-monthly pattern. Careful monitering for several years showed that their metabolic rates rose and fell with a regular two-month period year after year. Then, in July 1954, a strange thing happened. The graphs of the rhythms showed that their metabolic rates were mirror images of what they should have been. Although there was a wide search for possible causative factors, there was no explanation for the change. A year later, it was found that at the time of the shift there was a mysterious inversion of the daily rhythm of primary cosmic radiation, the particles from space which strike atmospheric molecules. This variation couldn't be the answer to the metabolic change, however, because the secondary cosmic

Figure 5.9 Schematic representation of the twofold nature of biological rhythms. The outer ring is the source of patterns which more precisely fit the organism to its environment. The outer ring controls circadian, tidal and annual rhythms. The inner ring however, is the source of other more underlying patterns. These respond to the subtle rhythms of the geophysical environment. (From Brown, "American Astronautical Society," 17:29-39. 1964.)

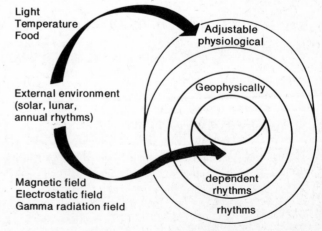

Light
Temperature
Food

Adjustable
physiological

External environment
(solar, lunar,
annual rhythms)

Geophysically

Magnetic field
Electrostatic field
Gamma radiation field

dependent
rhythms

rhythms

THE RHYTHMIC ORGANISM

rays which actually strike the surface of the earth at such phenomenal speeds are not related, in time, to the primary particles in any predictable way. However, the primary radiation *is* directly related to fluctuations in the earth's geomagnetic field. The stronger the field at any time, the fewer the secondary cosmic rays that strike the earth's atmosphere. The idea is exciting. Could organisms be reacting to daily fluctuations in the earth's geomagnetic fields? In order for such an explanation to be considered seriously it would have to be shown that organisms are sensitive to exceedingly small changes in environmental magnetism.

Brown (1970) discovered that, in fact, some organisms are very sensitive to magnetic fields of the amplitude found in nature. He found that the pathway of the lowly and negatively phototactic planarian would vary according to the compass direction in which the apparatus (Figure 5.10) was pointed. Then he found the path could be altered by placing a bar magnet across the top. This evidence indicated that the worms could read compass direction by magnetism.

A second directional phenomenon which was discovered was that the worms show a recurring monthly variation in the angle of their turns and that the direction of the turn can be altered by changing the direction of the light source or the magnetic fields (Figure 5.11). Here, an apparent turn of 180° causes a phase shift of half a cycle. So, Brown believes, the monthly rhythms are apparently timed by subtle geophysical forces.

Brown's third finding in this set of experiments was that the degree of turning could be affected by previous trials. In other words, the worm is able to "remember" the directions of light stimuli in relation to geophysical clues (Figure 5.12). After establishing that the planarians possess these three abilities, Brown stresses that they are just the characteristics that are essential for an organism to be able to set timed events by recurring directional events. The problem becomes not one of time, but of space, and the data are given as support for the idea that, ultimately, timing is

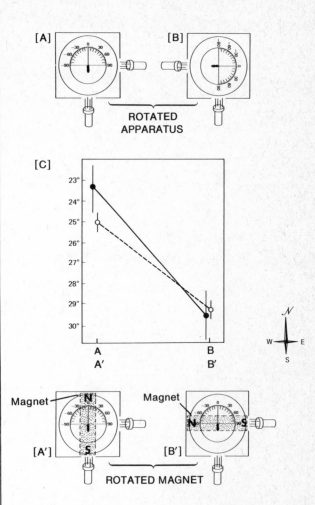

Figure 5.10 Results of experiments demonstrating that flatworms can use magnetic fields to orient themselves geographically. In A and B the apparatus is oriented north and east respectively. The worms moved in a 25° direction in A and in about a 28° direction in B, as is shown by the open circles connected by the broken line in C. In A′ and B′ a bar magnet augments the earth's natural field and the worms move in a direction of about 23°. In B′ however, the apparatus is not shifted but the magnet is moved 90° counterclockwise to simulate a rotation of the apparatus with respect to the earth's magnetic field. The worms move as if the apparatus had been shifted as shown by the circles joined by an unbroken line in C. Notice the close correlation of the two pairs of points in C. Standard errors are shown by the vertical lines intersecting the circles. The worms respond to magnetic changes irrespective of the direction of light as shown by the flashlights. (From Brown 1970.)

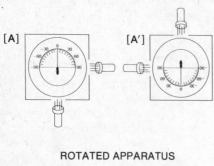

ROTATED APPARATUS

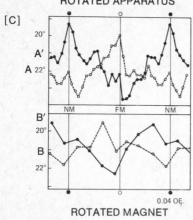

ROTATED MAGNET

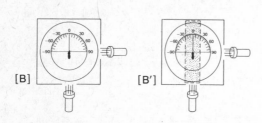

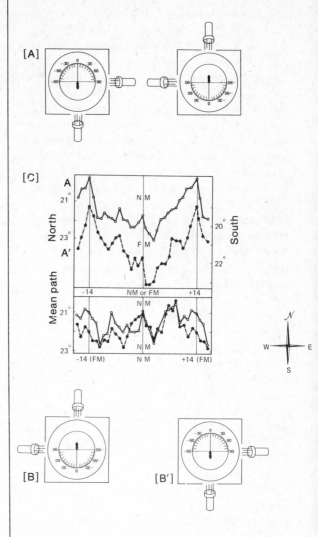

Figure 5.11 Diagrammatic summary of experiments in which the phase of the monthly variation in turning of the flatworm can be altered by changes in magnetic fields. In A and A' the changes in direction are reversed according to the compass-card in the apparatus. The results are shown in the top portion of C where the curves are 180° out of phase. In B and B' the apparatus is not rotated but the poles of the magnet are reversed. The worms behave in B' as if the entire apparatus was directed southward. The results of a comparison of B and B' are shown in the lower graph of C. The turnings are 180° out of phase. In C, the circles indicate the average turning direction each day. NM designates the new moon and FM the full moon. (From Brown 1970.)

Figure 5.12 Diagrammatic evidence of a form of learning and memory in flatworms. A and A' are experimentally identical to A and A' in Figure 5.11 as is the upper pair of graphs in C except that one has been shifted by half a month. The result of the shift is that the curves may be superimposed showing that the shape of the two curves is similar. In B and B' the worms were first directed southward with respect to the lights. After they had established a pattern relative to this direction they were quickly rotated so that they were oriented northward. The lower graph in C shows that the curves are different from A and A' but they are similar to each other. The worms continue to orient themselves as if the apparatus had not been rotated. (From Brown 1970.)

by the perception of subtle rhythmic geophysical changes.

Part of the problem in arriving at an agreement regarding the basic source of timing is that much of the data can be interpreted as supporting either premise. The data collected by one group may usually be used by the other simply by inserting it at the variable control stage, the outside of the two-layered ring of Brown.

The evidence that has been forthcoming, we can see, indicates a very complex system is operating—one which may employ multiple interacting mechanisms. The widespread occurrence of the phenomenon among living things indicates the high adaptiveness of the clocks, and also suggests that several types of mechanisms could have developed through parallel evolution. This latter possibility serves as warning that the search for the mechanism may prove to be incredibly complex and that when promising evidence does appear, extrapolation to other species may not be warranted. For further information regarding the nature of biological clocks the reader is referred to Aschoff (1965 a and b), the Cold Spring Harbor Symposium (1960), Brown 1962, Bunning (1967), Goodwin (1963), Harker (1958), Mayersbach (1967) and Sweeney (1969).

6

COMMUNICATION

A little screech owl moves on its branch and, suddenly, splits the deep quiet of the woodland night with a piercing shriek. In the cool African highlands a big male gorilla sits quietly and stares directly at a smaller male. A colorful sage grouse assumes a bizarre posture and steps and whirls crazily on the American plain. Farther north, a spotted skunk walks on his front paws, tail high, toward a retreating lynx. In each case the animal is communicating with other animals although in different ways and for various purposes. The owl's screech and the grouse's strutting have the same function, to gain a mate. The gorilla's stare may be a threat to another male, who quickly retreats. The skunk is also threatening, but here the communication is between animals of different species. Thus, communication is a diverse and widespread phenomenon.

In its broadest form, communication may be defined as any activity which alters the behavior of other organisms. Since it may be assumed that such a widely existing phenomenon is highly adaptive, we may search for the "reasons" animals have developed ways to alter the behavior of other organisms. In the foregoing examples we can see advantages accrued to both the signaler and the recipient. The owl shrieks and gains a mate. The gorilla does not even need to rouse himself, much less fight, in order to cause another male to retreat. The skunk is not attacked. On the other hand, the recipients may also fare better. A female owl who hears the male gains a mate; the smaller gorilla retreats, and is not attacked; and the cat is saved from despair. In each case the recipient adjusted itself to its environment in the sense that other animals comprise an important part of any environment. The behavior of the recipient could thus become more adaptive based on an increased level of prediction. The perceptive cat could "predict" what would happen if he continued to approach the skunk.

In addition to signals that communicate intentions to act, there are those that permit a negative prediction. An animal, in other words, may signal that a certain pattern is *not* likely to occur in the near future. Darwin referred to this sort of behavior as the *principle of antithesis*. As an example, a cringing dog with tail tucked, ears back, and head down has assumed the characteristics opposite to a stiff-legged, bristling, belligerent dog with his head held high and his ears forward. We know the cringing dog is not likely to attack.

The methods by which communication occurs, the environmental determinants of each method, the informational content of various signal types, and the adaptiveness of each make up an incredibly complex picture and one which is only beginning to be unraveled. As in any science, the technique of investigation must yield as precise quantitative values as possible. In the area of communication, however, we are in many cases only at the stage of discovering the advantages of certain types of signals and making certain generalizations regarding their nature. For example, trained men can make few statements beyond those of a dog owner regarding the nature of the pet's facial expression. In certain areas, however, the communication of animals is being measured with a high degree of precision. In chemical communication, some signal molecules have been identified and even synthesized and, furthermore, molecular size and configuration have been related to specific functions. Animal sounds are also being recorded and converted to visual images which reveal specific characteristics and which yield themselves to more precise description.

Before investigating the various ways in which living things communicate, we should first be aware of some general aspects of the phenomenon.

LEVELS OF COMMUNICATION

If we see a man slip on an icy sidewalk, we gain information regarding our environment. Also, the man, in the absence of a misdirected sense of humor, may choose to tell the next person about the ice. In the first instance, communication is unspecific, inadvertent; in the second, specific. In this example it is clear that specific communi-

cation potentially carries much more information than inadvertent communication. The principle will become more apparent in the following discussion.

Inadvertent, unspecific signaling comprises the lowest level of communication. As an example from lower animals, consider certain protozoa which produce chemical by-products of metabolism which then cause rather general reactions in other protozoa in the medium.

A higher level of communication is seen in cases where the neuro-apparatus of an animal is programmed to respond to inadvertent signals of others, such as is seen in the schooling behavior of fish where swimming movements of a single fish are influenced by its being tuned in through highly specialized receptors to vibrations set up by the movements of other fish.

Much more complex communication is achieved in those groups where specific signaling devices and corresponding receptors have developed. The potential variety in such systems is enormous. The variation in communication is limited by environmental and anatomical influences, but a number of types of devices may develop (visual, acoustical, etc.). The possible complexity of such systems is increased further by the development of discrimination within each signal type. In other words, a fish may not only react to the visual stimulus of a red belly in another fish, but his reaction may vary according to how red the belly is; in other cases the levels of discrimination may be more discrete. For example, in ants, chemicals are important signaling devices and a number of distinct chemicals may be produced, each with its own meaning. In ants, fish, and other animals below the mammals, any signaling may be reflexive or, at least, not performed with any real intent, although the communication may be quite specific and may employ highly specialized mechanisms.

The highest forms of communication are reached in mammals and culminate in the primates. It should be pointed out that even animals capable

Figure 6.1 A goose at the Bronx Zoo "begging" to be fed. It is showing directed and purposeful communication behavior based on "information" acquired through operant conditioning. (Photo: R. A. Wallace.)

of the highest forms may also employ the lower types. As an example, Jane Van Lawick-Goodall was for a long time unable to approach chimpanzees in the wild because they showed avoidance responses to her inadvertent signals of her presence. In such animals, though, a wide range of intensities of a single signal may be possible as well as subtle and complex signaling interaction which might act to modify general statements. Also, at this level, true purposiveness in communication is most clearly demonstrated. Purposiveness, for example, may be involved in the barking of a small dog who hears a noise at the door. He may have no intention of attacking an intruder, but he may wish to make the situation known to his master.

Purposiveness in communication, it should be stressed, is by no means restricted to mammals (Figure 6.1) although probably, in general, it is a characteristic of vertebrates.

As would be expected in a biological world whose diverse members have developed a variety of sensory mechanisms, there is a wide variety of means of communication. Each has its special advantages, but these often exist at the price of the merits of other means. The ideal communication system should be specific in the nature and emphasis of messages, it should be able to reach the receiver rapidly, to travel long distances, and to show a wide range of information content. It should also be able either to start and stop quickly or to persist in the environment for long periods. Obviously no system fulfills all these requirements, so the function of the signal, the anatomy and physiology of the animal, and the nature of the immediate environment must determine which qualities are emphasized.

Signaling devices are varied and may include electrical (see Chapter 4), tactile (important in arthropods and some amphibians), visual, chemical, and acoustical signals. Probably because of the nature of our own communication systems, we know more about acoustical and visual signals. Much of the information in this chapter is derived from studies of birds since their receptive abilities are roughly similar to man's. Surprisingly, nonhuman mammals may differ strikingly from man in these abilities. Most other mammals, for example, are color-blind and rely heavily on olfaction as a signaling mechanism. In the following discussions we will concentrate primarily on communication by sight, sound, and smell because these areas have been the subjects of the most intensive investigations. We will begin by describing the physical properties and relative merits of each type of communication since such information is critical to our understanding of the environmental implications discussed later in this chapter.

METHODS OF COMMUNICATION

Visual Communication

Visual signals are an especially important part of communication in fishes, lizards, and birds and function in diurnal, and a few nocturnal, insects, some poisonous amphibians, and many primates as well. Lorenz (1935) and Tinbergen (1948) laid the ethological groundwork for the investigations of visual signaling and have since made important contributions to the study as the various facets of the phenomenon came into focus. The bulk of the data has come from work on a few species. For information and bibliography the reader is especially referred to Tinbergen's continuing work on fish and birds (1951, 1953, 1959, 1967) and Marler and Hamilton (1966), and, for a recently developing study of mammals, De Vore (1965) and Ewer (1968). A wide range of animals is included in Lanyon and Tavolga's (1960) book.

To the ethologist, visual signals are especially interesting because of the tremendous amount of information they may carry. This "information load" is possible because visual clues may be expressed in four basic ways: through color, posture or form, movement, and timing. We have seen that color is important in releasing fighting behavior in fish and birds and that it functions in mating and foraging patterns in some species of insects. As other examples, Magnus (1958) found that size, motion, and color are involved in the male-female interaction of the fritillary butterfly, *Argynnis paphia L.* Crane (1955) and Stride (1958) showed that in other butterflies males first react to females because of their color or flight movements. A good example of the importance of timing is seen in fireflies in which the sexes are attracted to each other on the basis of their flash intervals (Barber 1951).

One of the important advantages to such a potentially diverse system is the wide range of variation possible. Some signals may convey only the presence or absence of a particular condition or motivation (Figure 6.2). In other cases, such

Figure 6.2 An example of an all-or-nothing display in the male cutthroat finch *Amadina fasciata*. At left is a low intensity courtship display. At right is a high intensity display of the same type. While the differences in the displays are slight, there are no intermediate states. (After photographs in Morris, *Behavior*, 11:1-2, 1957. By permission of N.V. Boekhandel and Drukkerij.)

as in aggressive behavior, it may be useful to convey degrees of motivation (Figure 6.3). So the various elements of visual signals may significantly increase the potential information content through slight but precise changes in intensity and through mixing the visual clue sources. Of course, graded and mixed signals are only important to those animals which have developed receptors sensitive to subtle differences and which have attained such a level of nervous complexity and integration that graded cues may be differentially responded to. Signal complexity may also reduce the opportunity for error in instances where the same message is conveyed by multiple means. Such redundancy may serve to emphasize and reiterate signals and thus insure accuracy in the signal recognition.

There are other advantages to visual signals as well. For example, they can be started or stopped immediately. If a displaying bird suddenly spots a hawk and freezes, its position will not be revealed by any lingering images of its earlier movement. Also, there is never any doubt as to the exact position of the sender. The receiver can therefore respond to him in terms of his precise location as well as his general presence.

A visual signal may be a permanent feature of the animal, such as the elaborate coloration of the male pheasant and the facial markings of a male baboon. It may also be a temporary or recurring signal, such as the reddening tail area of the female baboon in estrus and the annual growth of antlers in deer. The signal may also be present or not according to the "wishes" of the animal. An angry male baboon will expose his long canine teeth as a warning, but the weapons are covered at most other times. An alarmed bird may show striking feathers when attacked or threatened which are kept discretely covered at other times such as when feeding or resting.

The dynamic properties of visual signals are often critical. Temporal patterning of the signal, for example, is important to a wide variety of species. The Caribbean fireworm, *Odontosyllis,* is about an inch long and spends its time burrowed in the bottoms of bays throughout the West Indies. However, on the fifth night after an August full moon, the worms crawl out of their burrows and swim to the surface of the warm tropical sea. Their timing is such that there is about an hour between sunset and the time the moon rises, so there is nothing to interfere with what they are about to do. When they reach the surface, for the only time in their lives, they become phosphorescent. The water sparkles and shimmers with living greenish blinking lights. This is their

Figure 6.3 An example of a graded display. At upper left the bird, *Fringilla coelebs,* is threatening at low intensity. At right it is threatening at medium intensity and intermediate to these. (From *Darwin's Biological Work,* eidted by P. R. Bell, pp. 150-206, "Developments in the Study of Animal Communication" by P. Marler. ©1959, Cambridge University Press.)

time of reproduction. Females maintain a steady light for about ten seconds while males, blinking once or twice a second swim toward them. Suddenly in a tiny phosphorescent explosion, clouds of eggs and sperm fill the water. The lights then quietly fade and the worms sink slowly to the bottom, probably to die.

Visual signals have certain disadvantages. The most obvious of which is, simply, if the sender can't be seen, his signals are useless; and vision is easily blocked by all sorts of environmental entities from mountains to fog. Also, visual signals are useless at night or in dark places (including the depths of the sea) except for light-producing species. Furthermore, visual powers weaken with distance, so visual clues are not employed for long distance communication. As the distance increases, the signals must become simpler and bolder and, of course, they therefore can carry less information.

Visual signals can only be maximized by nearness and contrast. It is not possible to increase such a signal by pumping more energy into it (except for light producers), as is possible with, for example, sound. So visual communication is strongly controlled by the dictates of the immediate environment in that its properties do not usually permit it to circumvent or overcome environmental obstacles.

As might be expected in a diverse and widely occurring system, visual signals have developed by several routes. For example, certain signals have apparently developed from intention movements. A dog with teeth bared, we know, is likely to bite. Other dogs and postmen now interpret the sight as a hostile warning, but originally the biting dog was likely only moving his lips out of the way. Some signals may have developed from involuntary events. In man, a reddening face may, depending on circumstances, mean that he is embarrassed or angry. The reddening of the wattles in courting or fighting birds may also have occurred involuntarily and only later have come to be used as a signal.

"Irrelevant" movements may also have contributed greatly to the development of visual signals. Preening in courting pigeons is now a part of the courtship behavior, but, at one time, it may have simply been the displacement activity of an excited and conflicted bird.

The nature of the habitat is an important determinant of what sort of signals the animals there will use. Because of a tendency for animals in a certain habitat type to solve problems of communication in similar ways, certain generalizations can be made regarding habitat-communication relationships. Let us consider a few general environmental influences on communication.

In woodlands birds which occupy the lower levels of the forest, canopy can be expected to be dull in coloration in comparison to the birds which occupy the upper levels or live at the forest's edge. The lower canopy is often dark and visual signaling would, therefore, not be efficient. Animals which occupy dark areas (or those which are in danger of attracting predators) might be expected to rely more on sound or chemical signaling. By the same principle, long-distance visual signaling could only be effective in unobstructed environments.

The living component of an ecosystem is an important determinant of the behavior of its members. Predators, of course, are an important factor in the development of any communication pattern of a prey species (and vice versa). Spatial distribution of nests or broods, for example, may be influenced by predation (Chapter 8), and spacing is an important determinant of communication type. Predation may also figure in signaling in another way. If the risk of predation is great, the prey species may be cryptically marked so as to reduce the use of visual signals except in displays by movement or posturing.

Predators may be cryptic as well as prey and, therefore, subject to the same limitations in visual signaling. The conspicuous hood of the brown-headed gull may be important as an intraspecific signaling device, but it may be disadvantageous at times when the bird is searching for surface fish. Here again we see a character preserved because of a *net* adaptive value. Its disadvantages are more than outweighed by its advantages.

One of the most critical environmental variables is distance between signaler and recipient, a factor largely determined by habitat, population density, and ethological influences. Long-range communication presents problems other than simply increasing the likelihood of the presence of physical barriers and these problems must be met in specific ways. In long-distance communication, the emphasis is on simple, conspicuous, stereotyped patterns. For greatest effectiveness, however, these must contrast sharply with the background in any system of communication.

There is, at present, almost no information on the ecological or reproductive ramifications of relative conspicuousness of various markings on different backgrounds with changing distances. In other words, a pattern may be conspicuous on a certain background at short range, but as distance increases the pattern may become cryptic against the same background. As an example, from close up a zebra is much more conspicuous than a horse and his markings may figure in intraspecific communication. As distance increases, however, the horse becomes more conspicuous as the zebra fades into the background.

Acoustical Communication

Studies of sound communication are an unusually fruitful source of information on animal interaction. The value of such studies stems primarily from the development and utilization of the sound spectrograph, a device that changes sound to markings which can be measured and analyzed visually (see Borror 1960).

Sound plays such an important part in man's communication that it is surprising to discover that it is limited, for the most part, in the animal world to arthropods (joint-legged creatures such as insects) and vertebrates.

Arthropods communicate acoustically in a var-

iety of ways. In some cases, for example, insects react to the inadvertent flight sounds of others, but in other cases a specific sound is produced which functions solely in communication. Arthropods utilize friction devices involving almost every movable part of the body including wings, legs (and their evolutionary derivatives), and special devices such as membranes which are vibrated. Sound communication has apparently evolved independently hundreds of times in insects and now occurs in tens of thousands of species (Alexander 1960). In spite of such strong reliance on sound by arthropods, the dimensions of the signals are severely limited. In fact the most complex arthropod sounds have fewer dimensions than most vertebrate sounds. For example, insects lack rhythmic fluctuations in frequency—or melody—in their signals. Sounds by insects are characterized by differences in time distribution of the pulses rather than by pitch or tone which is so important in sound signals of birds and mammals (see Alexander 1960).

Vertebrates, as would be expected in such an ecologically and morphologically diverse group of animals, vary widely in their application of sound to communication. In fishes (see Tavolga 1960, 1964) sounds are produced in a variety of ways, but usually by frictional devices or by manipulation of the air bladder. Since sound travels quickly in water it might be expected that underwater sound signals would be widely employed. However, such is not the case and, although the relative rarity of the phenomenon is not entirely explained, it may be due to the fact that sound sources are difficult to locate underwater.

Terrestrial vertebrates usually produce sound signals by moving air through the respiratory system to vibrate membranes. However, some nonvocal sounds are also produced. Rabbits thump the ground; grouse drum their wings; gorillas beat their chests; woodpeckers hammer hollow limbs (or drainpipes, to the distress of households).

Vocal communication is rather limited in lower

vertebrates. The limbless caecilians apparently receive sound through substrate vibration and are thought to be incapable of producing sound. However, a few salamanders emit squeaks and two genera apparently can whistle; one large California ambystomid can even bark (Bogert 1960)!

In frogs and toads sound is important in mating and territoriality. (It is interesting that these anurans have "vocabularies" which are about the same size of those of the orthoptera insects—grasshoppers and crickets.) For a discussion of the acoustical behavior of amphibia the reader is referred to Blair (1963).

Reptiles, although more advanced, have less well developed sound systems than do the amphibians. Snakes, like the caecilians, apparently rely on substrate vibration to detect sound. Snakes,

crocodilians, larger lizards such as the Gila monster and some turtles may hiss as a warning to other species (since their own species could not hear such a sound). A few snakes, such as the coral snake, *Micruroides spp.*, draw air into the cloaca (the common genital and excretory opening) and loudly expel it when irritated. And, of course, some snakes in the genera *Sistrurus* and *Crotalus* have rattles and these may be effective in repelling attacks. Certain geckos, *Gekkonidae*, however, are usually considered the only truly vocal reptiles.

Reptiles may also communicate through startlingly loud sounds. Roaring and bellowing tortoises were described by Darwin who visited the Galápagos in 1839 when the reptiles were breeding. Loud bellowing of territorial alligators could

Figure 6.4 Male and female redwing blackbirds, *Agelaius phoeniceus,* mobbing a stuffed crow. Their distinctive calls will attract other redwings from the area which will join in the attack. (Photo: S. A. Grimes from National Audubon Society.)

often be heard in the deeper recesses of our great southern swamps (see Beach 1944) until fashion decreed the depletion of their numbers.

Sound communication becomes much more complex and takes on new meanings and increasingly subtler nuances in birds and mammals. Such a striking phylogenetic shift in emphasis is accompanied, as would be expected, by distinct changes in the morphologies of the acoustical receptors. The middle and inner ears of birds and mammals are exceedingly complex and sensitive structures. The outer ears of many mammals are movable and can be shifted or focused on a sound source. This ability undoubtedly aids in locating the sound sources for these animals, but the slight difference in the time taken for sound vibrations to reach each ear is more important, generally, in locating the source.

Sound may vary in frequency (the number of waves per unit time—usually expressed as high or low pitch), in volume, and in "quality." The latter character may be demonstrated by the example of two men who are humming the same note at the same volume, but whose voices are still distinguishable. The possible variation permitted by such subtleties makes sound suitable for those higher vertebrates which have mental abilities that permit the efficient utilization of such a potentially complex system. The ability of the higher vertebrates to recognize subtle distinctions and gradations in sounds has posed special problems for the investigator who would like to be able to label each sound he has recorded as carrying a certain meaning.

Collias (1960) discusses the similarity of types of sounds in birds and mammals. An example is the use of similar low soft sounds by which both birds and mammals "speak" to their young. The significance of these resemblances is underscored by the fact that the sounds of birds are produced by a syrinx and those of mammals by vocal cords. Such convergent evolution (arriving at a common

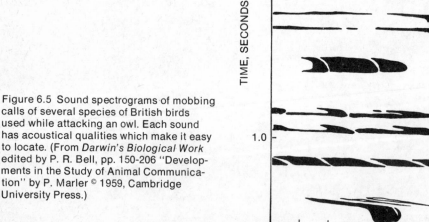

Figure 6.5 Sound spectrograms of mobbing calls of several species of British birds used while attacking an owl. Each sound has acoustical qualities which make it easy to locate. (From *Darwin's Biological Work* edited by P. R. Bell, pp. 150-206 "Developments in the Study of Animal Communication" by P. Marler © 1959, Cambridge University Press.)

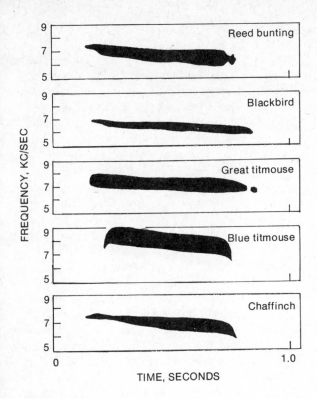

Figure 6.6 Sound spectrograms of calls of five species of British birds that occur when a hawk flies over. These calls are usually high-pitched and extended. These qualities make them hard to locate. (From *Darwin's Biological Work* edited by P. R. Bell, pp. 150-206, "Developments in the Study of Animal Communication" by P. Marler © 1959, Cambridge University Press.)

characteristic by different evolutionary routes) indicates a high adaptive value of the common characteristic.

The relationship of signal characteristics and functions is demonstrated in studies of sound communication. Perhaps the best example of this relationship is seen in the difference in two types of responses of passerine (perching) birds to predatory birds. Passerines will usually mob a stationary owl or crow by swooping down on it, displaying, and calling loudly to attract other birds (Figure 6.4). Such sounds are easy to locate and a typical sound spectrogram is shown in Figure 6.5. When a hawk is spotted overhead, the response differs. Here the call is a high-pitched *twee*. A bird in the open heads for cover, crouches quietly, and sometimes continues to call in its plaintive, hard-to-locate manner (Figure 6.6). The high-pitched warning call does not differ much between species (Marler 1961) and probably several species are able to take advantage of the

warning of a single bird.

Sounds which are easy to locate, such as the mobbing call, breeding calls, and signals between parent and young are usually repetitive, of brief duration and of low frequency with much emphasis on the first part of the song (Klopfer 1962). They may, then, be highly variable while maintaining critical adaptive qualities. The adaptiveness of such variability is discussed below.

Sound signals have, then, certain characteristics which render them suitable for specific types of communication. First, sound may vary in several dimensions (frequency, volume, timing) and it may be distinguishable at very low levels. Also, it may be raised above environmental noise by pumping energy into the system. The transient nature of sound makes possible rapid exchange and immediate modification, but it does not permit the signal to linger without the expenditure of more energy. Also, it may not be necessary for an animal to suspend other activities to transmit or receive sound signals.

Seabirds and a few other animals which live in noisy environments have a particular problem in communication. It's simply hard for an animal to be heard over the pounding of the sea or the roar of a falls. One example of the effects of noise is noted in Brandt's cormorant, a fishing bird which nests in rough coastal areas and which does not utilize vocal signals. Presumably the noise of the pounding waves renders sound communication inefficient. Instead, the Brandt's cormorant relies strongly on visual signaling. The southern cormorant, which nests in quieter areas, uses vocal displays as well as visual signaling and its visual signals are much less pronounced. A number of naturalists have maintained that the St. Kilda wren is much louder than the mainland species which lives in a quieter habitat. If this is so, it may be an example of increasing the energy of a signal to overcome background noise.

For burrowing and tunneling animals the texture of the soil may determine whether sound is used in signaling. Burrowing animals are not likely to rely on sound production for intraspecific signaling, but sound carried through the earth may signal the approach of terrestrial predators. In such cases it seems that finer, more densely packed soil particles would transmit sound better.

The type of vegetation of a habitat may figure importantly in the attenuation of sound above ground. Longer distance sound communication by animals living on a forest floor is best achieved if the wave lengths of the sound are greater than the average diameter of the trees (Konishi 1970). If an animal living on the forest floor were to make sounds of a shorter wave length, the energy of the sound would quickly be dissipated by reflection, diffraction, and absorption. Since higher frequency sounds have shorter wave lengths, denizens of the forest floor tend to produce lower sounds for longer distance communication. An example of such a sound is the cough of a leopard.

In the interest of not attracting predators, solitary or cryptic bird nests are seldom advertised by song. The nest owners sing more softly around their nests or they sing someplace away from the nest area. Colonies on the other hand are usually in protected sites, and the likelihood of predation is reduced in gregarious species in any case, so colonial nesters often blatantly advertise the presence of their nests (see Crook 1969). The likelihood of visual communication also increases with gregariousness. In ground-dwelling primates which live in cohesive groups, many visual signals are associated with the face (Hall and De Vore 1965); thus it may be assumed that gregariousness may increase the likelihood of having the ability to distinguish subtle gradations in the messages.

We learned in Chapter 5 that many of the activities of animals are dependent upon diurnal biological clocks. It is interesting that such is apparently not the case in birdsong. Birds appear to sing in response to light and not the time of day. So communication by birdsong appears in response to relatively rapid fluctuations of light in the habitat in the immediate sense, while ultimately being a result of changing day-length. Singing is inhibited by overcast skies in the morning and evening and even by solar eclipses. Singing is also inhibited by high wind, extreme heat or cold, and heavy rains. Birdsong is most likely to occur in quiet humid days when the sound carries well.

For some species the time element is even more specific. When at dusk the light intensity drops to about five footcandles, cicadas begin to sing so suddenly that the effect is startling; they fly in every direction for a short time and then, just as suddenly, they stop. The effect is especially noticeable in tropical jungles when the quiet calm of early evening is suddenly shattered as if a great wind were sweeping through the trees. The following calm, if the chorus of another species doesn't swell, gives one an eerie feeling that something terrible has just passed. Such synchronization of intraspecific communication, of course, is highly adaptive to prey species which are thus exposed to predators for the briefest period of time. It may be that signaling at dusk or dawn is adaptive in that it is a period for which neither nocturnal nor diurnal predators are well suited.

Many songbirds overcome the likelihood that their high-frequency, short-wavelength sounds might become attenuated by environmental obstacles by singing in treetops. Singing from such a perch also makes the bird visually conspicuous. Some species even launch themselves into peculiar, erratic flight patterns which can be identified from afar. In such a way, birds may increase the information content of their signaling by the simultaneous use of two media.

Humidity may affect the propagation of sound. Sound attenuates quickly in dry desert air while humid arctic air is "acoustically transparent" (Hunter 1965). The phenomenon has been witnessed by anyone who has stood on a lakeshore and clearly overheard conversations by people out in a boat. Konishi points out that this is perhaps one of the reasons desert animals have such large ears—the better to hear in an acoustically poor environment. (Heat dissipation through exaggerated appendages may be another reason.)

Long distance presents special problems in sound communication. Complexity of signals increases potential information content, and one way complexity in sound can be achieved is through the use of different frequencies. However, since high-frequency sounds attenuate faster than lower ones, frequency modulation, or changing pitch, cannot be used well in long-distance communication. Variable frequencies, however, may be expected in many of those animals which gather to breed or which live in colonies where both high- and low-frequency sounds are assured of reaching the recipient.

Harmonics (production of high and low frequencies simultaneously) are used in the signaling of colonial or semicolonial birds (Collias 1963, Hall 1962). Monkeys and apes which form social groups and do not mingle with other species show many harmonics and lack "purity of tone"; on the other hand, those species which live in forests, move in loose groups and mix with other species produce purer, even "birdlike" tones (Marler and Hamilton 1966).

Chemical Communication

We have all seen ants running single file to a distant food source. We have also taken perturbingly slow walks with dogs which stop to urinate on every bush and fence. Both activities may involve communication by use of chemicals. In fact, a wide variety of animal species, primarily insects, fish, amphibians, reptiles, and mammals employ chemical communication, usually by smell (olfaction) but occasionally by taste (gustation)—although a clear distinction between the two types of reception cannot always be made.

In insects, very specific behavioral patterns are released in response to certain chemicals produced by other members of the population. In the absence of insight or "reason," such stereotypy would be expected. The immediate and rigid responses elicited in these cases were thought to be similar to that of hormones (chemicals produced in one part of the body which cause changes in another part) so the chemicals were called *pheromones* (from the Greek *pherein*, to carry; *horman*, to excite). Pheromones are, then, "substances that are secreted by an animal to the outside and cause a specific reaction in a receiving individual of the same species in which they release a specific reaction, for example, a definite behavior or a developmental process" (Marler and Hamilton 1966:293). Interestingly, pheromones are not restricted to insects. Frank Bronson of the University of Texas and others have demonstrated pheromonal interactions in mammals (discussed below).

In order to understand more fully the nature of chemical signals, let us briefly consider the insect pheromones. The sexually receptive female silkworm moth, *Bombyx mori*, releases a sexual lure into the air. The substance is a complex alcohol called bombykol and it is so potent that it arouses males which are presented with a glass rod which has been dipped in incredibly dilute solutions of the substance (10^{-12}mg/ml or one part in a trillion). In nature such weak signals could not present a gradient for the male to follow, but once aroused he simply tactically responds by flying upwind and so approaches the female (Case 1966).

Honeybees provide an interesting example of the effects of one organism upon another's behavior. The queen produces a "queen substance" which, when fed to developing females, causes them to become workers replete with the complex array of innate patterns of the worker bee. When she dies the substance is no longer produced and new queens can develop. The undeveloped ovaries of some workers also mature and these eggs produce drones or royal consorts, one of which will mate with the new queen in her nuptial flight. The behavior of each caste is very specific and caste is directed chemically by other members of the group.

Wilson and Bossert (1963) analyzed the properties of various chemicals employed in signaling and described the characters of the types according to their function. They found that the range of carbon atoms (the "backbone" of chemical chains) should lie between 5 and 20 and that the molecular weight of the chain should be between 80 and 300. They reasoned that at least five carbons are needed for diversity. Otherwise the number of possible configurations will be too small. The maximum number however, is determined by other factors. Since the molecules must usually be airborne in order to function they must be small or light enough for this purpose. Also, large molecules require more energy for their synthesis and a larger space for their storage. As Wilson and Bossert predicted, the size of sexual attractants is larger than those used in other chemical signals since complex signals must be used to insure that only members of the same species are attracted. (For further informa-tion on insect pheromones see Collins and Pott 1932, Dufay 1957, Schwink 1958, and Barth 1961, 1962 et seq.).

Animals could, and possibly do, increase the information content of chemical signals by mixing chemicals. However, if one molecule is lighter than another it may diffuse farther and confuse distant receivers. Different chemicals could also be released sequentially but the long life of lingering chemicals generally rules out such a system.

It has been found that in spite of complex long-chained chemicals, males of some species are stimulated by pheromones from females of other species (Schneider 1962). So, apparently, chemical distinctiveness does not completely ensure private lines of communication. Instead species-specificity may be maintained in these cases by chronological factors such as differences in the time of day or the season that the signals are sent. In fact, a circadian rhythm has been found in the *responsiveness* of some male moths.

Some insects are capable of chemical discrimination within a much wider range of stimuli than is indicated in simple pheromone studies. Bees are dependent upon antennal receptors (just as are silkworm moths), but are sensitive to up to 43 odors (von Frisch 1950).

Apparently taste perception is much more limited than olfaction. Water beetles and honeybees may discriminate only four tastes, comparable to sweet, salty, sour, and bitter, but are unable to discriminate between compounds in these various classes.

So, then, of the major types of communication, only chemical signals linger in the environment. Even the shortest-lived chemical persists longer than a visual, auditory, or even electrical signal. Unlike any of the others, its effectiveness is strongly dependent upon movement in the surrounding medium, so time and space take on special meanings, making it unnecessary for the sender and the receiver to be simultaneously coordinated in time and space, as demanded in the two former types of communication.

We need only be reminded that chemicals share characteristics with sound in being able to go around environmental barriers, but, unlike sound, chemical signals are difficult to modify on short notice.

RECOGNITION

Signaling in animals may roughly be categorized according to whether the message is between members of the same species or those of different species. The methods of communication may not vary between the two cases, but there may be distinct differences in the adaptive result. For example, intraspecific (within a species) communication usually functions in species and sex recognition, in identification of populations or individuals, in alarm, and in social coordination. Interspecific (between species) signals, on the other hand, may function in alarm, in threat, in intimidation, and in crypticity (the message, "I am not here"). In some cases we see the same message conveyed between and within species, such as in the warning systems which alert members of the signaler's own species and other species as well.

Communication in the animal world has, of course, many roles, or functions. We shall explore only a few broad categories of these adaptations and, as we progress, it will become increasingly apparent that there are few, if any, instances when a pattern or character will be useful in a single narrow sense. Here, as in all biology, it must be stressed, dogmatic categorizing is presumptuous.

Species Recognition

It is, first of all, important for communicating animals to know with whom they are communicating. In many species there is relatively little need for communication to occur with animals of another species (although certain such instances are discussed below), so it is of utmost importance that an animal be able to establish its credentials within its own species. Just as impor-

tant, an animal must be able to read the credentials of other animals: "Is this individual one of us?" Certainly, a fox is not going to confuse a horse with one of its own. However, in Chapter 3 we learned that birds may be imprinted to consider even a horse or a man as a conspecific (of the same species). Confusion may occur in other cases also. We just learned that some male moths can be fooled into approaching a female of another species if only she emits chemicals similar, but not identical, to those of his own species. Some species of birds are strikingly identical and, when they occur together, they may mate or attempt to mate.

Such mating is largely prevented by each species being born with certain characteristics of morphology and behavior which are distinctive. It is interesting that some species are also born with certain sound repertoires. Nearly all insects which communicate largely by sound overwinter in the egg stage, so no individual has contact with any member of another generation. Each year the new generation produces the sounds of the species without ever having heard the songs. In insect species with simpler songs, a deafened individual can produce the proper songs without even having heard himself. In other cases it has been demonstrated that, for some types of songs, a little practice is needed before the sound organs operate properly (Alexander 1960). So we again see the close coordination necessary between inherent and acquired characteristics in order to produce an adaptive response.

In some birds such as the roller canaries, *Serinus canarius*, and the European whitethroat, *Sylvia communis*, the normal song is produced even when the birds are reared in auditory isolation. The European blackbird, *Turdus merula*, will produce the proper song even when deafened while young. On the other hand, the chaffinch, *Fringilla coelebs*, learns its song, but only in its first spring. Thorpe (1961) suggests that certain critical parts of the chaffinches' song are learned through a rapid learning process similar to imprinting. For a review of the importance of learning in song development see Lanyon and Tavolga (1960), Thorpe (1961), and Marler and Hamilton (1966).

Why is it so important that species-identification mistakes not be made? The answer is, in most cases, to ensure proper reproductive and aggressive behavior. These patterns are discussed later, but, put simply, an animal must not waste time attempting to mate with another animal when the result of such a union, should it occur, is likely to be a reproductive failure (see Mayr 1942, Huxley 1942, and Sibley 1957, 1961). Also the strongest competitor for available resources for any animal is most likely to be a member of the same species. So these competitors must be recognized and either avoided or driven away.

But how is such recognition accomplished? One method is by the mutual attraction to each other of animals of a given species. Chemical stimuli are involved in some insect aggregations. Males of one species of beetle collect around other males at places where other aggregations have recently occurred (Eisner and Kafatos 1962) and some species of butterflies aggregate in response to pheromones (Crane 1955). Schooling in fish is accomplished by sensing vibrations of other fish of the species and by vision (Keenleyside 1955). Vision is also probably important in the aggregation of birds and mammals. Certain birds also use specific calls to bring members of a group together (see Stoddard 1931, Odum 1942, Hinde 1952). We have already mentioned sounds made by groups of migrating birds which may function in keeping the flock together. "Grouping signals" are in most cases species specific, but there are notable exceptions such as occur in mixed foraging flocks of tropical birds (discussed in Chapter 10).

The likelihood of proper species identification can greatly be increased by the development of a system of filters, whether peripheral (at the level of the receptor) or central (at the level of the IRM). In such cases signals lacking certain critical characteristics of the species are simply not perceived.

Species recognition in some cases may be on the basis of any of several types of cues which may interact in rather interesting ways. For example, Lanyon (1963) set up dummy flycatchers with loudspeakers within sight of live members of the species and played two songs simultaneously. Only one of the songs was characteristic of the species, and the dummy singing the "appropriate" song was attacked. So the visual clues needed to be reinforced by acoustic ones. In another experiment Dilger (1956) presented thrushes with models of their own and four similar species and found they were attacked indiscriminately. However, when the song of the attacking species was played at the same time that the models were presented, the attacks were restricted to the model of that species. Here, sound seemed to have a directing or restricting effect, in that with sound, attacks on "incorrect" species were eliminated.

In some cases the environment or "context" of a signal may function directly as a modifier of the message. The setting may cause the parent of a young bird to know whether the offspring is crying in response to being lost, disturbed, or hungry. The honking of Canada geese may be related to defense of territory, defense of mate, competition for food, greeting of mate, a contact call, or an alarm call (Collias and Jahn 1959). Head-tossing in gulls may be elicited in soliciting food, precopulatory display, or hostile encounters (Tinbergen 1952, Moynihan 1962). So the recipient must read both the signal and the context to know whether to feed, avoid or copulate with the communicator.

When communication depends upon sign stimuli, the individuals may be strongly influenced by environmental dictates. As an example of such contextual influences recall the male robin which will not react to the red of another robin's breast outside of his own territory (cf. Lorenz 1957). It must be pointed out that the phenomenon of the same signal having many functions may not be a reversion to the simple; it might rather be a step toward the complex in that the meaning is dependent upon simultaneous recognition of the signal and the conditions under which it is uttered.

We need only be reminded that environmental effects may be expressed in another way. Some signals are only made at a certain time of the year, such as during the breeding season (Marler 1956). The clucking of hens is known to be an indicator of parental behavior which appears in response to a rising level of prolactin (a female hormone) which, in turn, is dependent upon daylength (Collias 1960).

Population Recognition

Once the species has been recognized, subtler distinctions may be made. Among the animals of many species, there is a distinct predisposition to associate not only with other animals of his own species, but also with members of his own population (or subgroup) within that species. We have seen one instance of such a tendency in salmon returning to their own redds to spawn each year. The primary adaptiveness of such behavior apparently lies in ecological advantage and may be a critical factor in wide-ranging species and in species which occupy eurytopic (diverse) habitats. An experienced ornithologist, traveling through mountain regions, can notice slight changes in the songs sung by birds of the same species. The development of such a phenomonon apparently is related to the sharply changing habitat types seen as one travels first at high altitude and then in valleys, passing from timbered areas to grassland into the rugged timberline area. Each habitat-type dictates the characters of its denizens and places different requirements upon each group, even if the animals are of the same species. Therefore, it would be advantageous for birds of a certain habitat-type, for which they are to some degree specialized, to mate with birds having the same characteristics. For example, if the birds of the wetter lowlands are darker in color, to match their background, it is to their reproductive advantage to mate with another bird which is also dark. Otherwise, the young may be conspicuous and fall easy prey to predators. Such birds may, of course, be perfectly compatible genetically with members of lighter colored populations from drier areas and some level of interpopulation breeding can be expected.

If the level of interpopulation breeding becomes sufficiently low, it is possible that the populations may diverge, each along its own line, until such a time that successful interbreeding between populations is no longer possible. When this happens the populations may (and will, by some) be considered as distinct species. At some point before this happens, however, the adaptiveness of population recognition shifts from an ecological basis increasingly toward a reproductive one. In our example, the advantage in choosing a mate from within the group was first ecological (to blend with the background); later, the advantage was reproductive (to insure the production of viable offspring). So there are species for which population recognition is important, the adaptive basis being ecological, reproductive or both.

Let us consider some specific examples of population recognition. The phenomenon has been noted in a wide variety of animals. Ants and honeybees are probably able to recognize the smell of members of their own colonies because of small differences in diet. Konishi (1970) reports that cricket frogs may employ filters not only to select the sounds of their own species, but also their own population.

The greatest amount of experimental evidence, not surprisingly, derives from studies of populations of birds (cf. Sauer 1955, Gompertz 1961, Thielcke 1961, and Marler and Tamura 1962). Song "dialects" have been demonstrated by sound spectrograph analysis (Figure 6.7). Studies of such dialects indicate that the patterns appear as a geographical mosaic. Also, certain patterns characteristic of one population may appear to lesser degrees in other populations as well.

There is another, more general, aspect of dialect formation. In birds there are dominant song patterns which affect all populations over a large area. The phenomenon has been described by Benson (1948), Thielcke (1961), Thorpe (1961) and others. As an example, the song of the chipping sparrows, *Spizella passerina,* in the United States have shorter syllables, more syllables per song, and are uttered at a more rapid rate than those of the Mexican sparrows (Borror 1959). Such differences may be due to such nonselective evolutionary processes as genetic drift or they may be due to differences in the "sound environment."

Interestingly, in some cases there are apparently no song differences between separated populations. Songs of the flycatcher, *Myiarchus tyrannulus,* vary little over extensive ranges in South America (Lanyon 1960). There was also no difference shown in widely separated populations of the house wren, *Troglodytes aedon.* As Marler and Hamilton (1966) point out, it seems unlikely that the song requirements for species are identical throughout their entire ranges, so it must be assumed either that there is little selective pressure on the songs or that song patterns for some reason resist change.

Sometimes there are even subgroups within the population. Andrewartha (1961) described "tribes" of birds which behave as an integral unit. There are instances when individual birds may be evicted from a tribe, but still remain within the population.

The caste systems of social insects (ants, bees, some wasps, termites) present interesting social schemes. Here, the individual is not recognized as such (except the queen), nor is he recognized as just a member of the population; instead, recognition is according to caste. The workers clearly demonstrate caste recognition when they methodically kill bachelor drones.

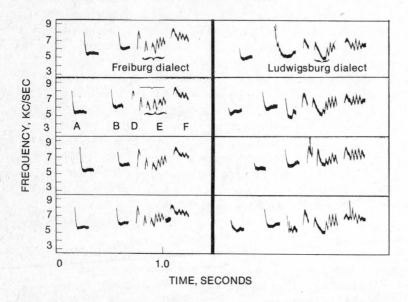

Figure 6.7 Sound spectrograms showing song dialects in the tree creeper, *Certhia brachydactyla.* The sounds differ in birds from different geographical areas. (From Thielcke 1961.)

There may be differences in the degree to which populations of a single species are able to utilize interpopulation signals. The recorded distress calls of French crows provoked no response in Maine crows. However, when the French calls were played to Pennsylvania crows, a response was elicited. Frings and his co-workers (1958) proposed an explanation for the difference. The crows in Maine migrate southward to Pennsylvania in winter. The Pennsylvania crows migrate farther south to areas where other species of crows are found. The Pennsylvania crows, then, may have learned to react to the calls of other populations. In a sense, and to no New Englander's surprise, the Maine crows are more provincial.

Individual Recognition

A man standing on the beach watching circling seabirds may, at times, easily recognize several species. However, if he looks closely at, for example, the strongly marked Caspian terns, *Sterna caspia*, he might remark at the fact that they all appear completely identical in size, markings, and even vocalizations. The observer may be a highly experienced ornithologist, but he will have little or no success telling the birds apart. In fact, however, they are not identical. Each has its own characteristics which are immediately evident to other birds of the species.

The question arises, what is the advantage in the members of a population being distinguishable from each other? The answer is apparent when we consider the problems which might arise if we could not recognize our own neighbors, spouses, or children. It is just as important in other species for an individual to react to other members of the population in specific manners according to "who" they are.

So members of a species or population must be similar enough, at least in some respects, to be recognized as belonging to the group; on the other hand, in many species members must be different enough to permit individual identification. So the problem becomes one of variation.

How much can an individual vary from the rest of the population before he is no longer recognized as a conspecific? Is natural selection pushing toward difference and uniformity at the same time? On the basis of what we have learned about instinct and learning we can formulate at least a partial answer. Those behavioral or morphological characters which act as releasers of, for example, reproductive behavior can be expected to vary only within very specific limits. On the other hand, some social interaction is based on individual recognition, such as mate identification. In such cases, the observed characters probably do not function as releasers of innate patterns but as learned characters instead. It is possible, and even likely, that the ability to learn certain characters of others has been selected for, according to the Lorenzian scheme described in Chapter 2. So, in essence, some characters are relatively free to vary, others are not and, of course, the characters which fall into each category may differ even between closely related species.

Good examples of how much individual and species characters are free to vary are seen in birdsong. The *song* (a specific type of vocalization) of birds is usually, but not always, restricted to males and is associated with territorial defense, establishment and maintenance of the pair, and control of the reproductive cycle. Some repertoires are extremely small and, in fact, chipping sparrows have only one type of song (Borror 1959). Some finches have well-defined song vocabularies comprised of several patterns. Other birds, such as the brown towhee, *Pipilio fascus*, may show so many individual differences that it is hard to find any basic similarities at all (Marler and Hamilton 1966). In these cases it is hard to know what the function of such "extemporaneous" vocalizing might be. Dr. Charles Hartshorne, ornithologist and philosopher, maintains that birds may sing for the joy of it, out of sheer exuberance (1958), and so the individual songs could be expected to vary. Such an interpretation is easy to accept for those who have listened to the chortling of small birds on early mornings in spring.

The problem is not as simple as determining the numbers of vocalization types within species, however, because individual variation is as common in birds of small repertoires as in those with large ones. On the basis of studies on a number of species, Borror (1961) concluded that two individuals rarely sing identical songs. Individual variation may thus express itself in subtle ways, even within restricted song types. It must be remembered that such variation is not simply a difference in the expression of personality or an evolutionary side effect, but it may be an important factor in the social organization of the species.

Individual recognition, interestingly enough, is often based on facial features. One is not often taken aback by the variation in the faces of chickens. However, if a hen is removed from the flock and her comb affixed to the opposite of her head, she will be treated as a stranger upon her return (Guhl and Ortman 1953). Schaller (1963) was able to recognize individual mountain gorillas by their noses.

Chemicals can also convey individual identity. Dogs can distinguish the trail of a particular dog or man, for example, although they have difficulties with identical twins (Kalmus 1955).

We shall discover in the following discussions how individual differences function in identifying mates and young, but there are, first, two other important ways individual recognition functions in social systems. As mentioned (Chapter 3), habituation may occur between animals sharing common territorial boundaries. Songs of the ovenbird, *Seiurus aurocapillus*, were played to territorial males in the field. It was found that the songs of neighboring males elicited far fewer responses than those of strangers (Weeden and Falls 1959).

Secondly, individual recognition is the basis of *linear dominance* or the "peck order." In these systems a single individual dominates all the others. His immediate subordinate dominates all the others except him, and so on. The last animal in the order is subordinate to all the other animals and may lead a frenetic life, indeed. The peck order may exist within either sex. Rarely are both sexes included in a single linear order although there may be some linear arrangement involving both sexes in the leadership cliques of certain primate species. Clear examples of such arrangements, however, have not been demonstrated. In some species, the female assumes the rank of her mate. Lorenz reports that, among some birds, if a female's mate dies and she mates with a higher ranking male she assumes new status in the population. It is interesting that the highest ranking male of polygamous species does not necessarily fertilize more females than other males. In fact, he may be less successful in romance since he spends so much time defending his position. Such a disadvantage, however, would necessarily be restricted to the highest ranking individuals. For most of the group, it could be assumed that status would influence reproductive success or the system would probably not be maintained.

One's position in the peck order usually depends upon fighting ability, but factors other than pugilistic skill may be a determinant. For example, as we all know, intimidation (or "bluff") is an important weapon. If the comb and wattle, structures used in aggressive signals, are removed from a hen, she will begin to lose more fights and may end up at the end of the pecking order (Marler and Hamilton 1966).

Linear dominance is ecologically and reproductively important. It functions in permitting each animal to know its rank so that once the system is established the number of fights and the vigor of such encounters may be greatly reduced. Animals which spend less time fighting may then spend more of their time and energy in maintenance pursuits, such as grooming and foraging, and in mating and rearing young. The ecological benefits of linear hierarchies are discussed in more detail in Chapter 7.

We shall now consider certain social interactions for which individual recognition may be important at least at some point in time. These interactions are involved in various ways with reproductive behavior.

COMMUNICATION AND REPRODUCTION

Communication between Members of the Same Sex

We have already noted several instances of fighting and threatening between males of a species. Such behavior occurs, less commonly, between females of some species as well. Usually, in fact, in the animal world hostilities are reserved for members of the same sex. Such a pattern can be seen, for example, in territorial birds. Males exclude other males of the species from the territory and females usually only attack intruding females. Such intrasexual belligerence has its own adaptiveness which may, in some respects, be quite different from that of other types of hostile interactions. Intuitively, it would seem that intrasexual belligerence primarily must be related in some way to reproductive pursuits and, perhaps, secondarily to ecological competition. This idea is more fully developed in the following discussions.

Since intrasexual interactions are often of a hostile nature, it is important that effective communication systems exist so that actual fighting need not occur, and, if it does, it need not end in death for one of the combatants. In fact, in aggressive contests a winner is often decided on the basis of his signals. Birds disputing a territorial border may never touch each other, but may stand apart, threatening and displaying, until a victor is decided whereupon the loser flies away.

Even when real fighting occurs, the winner is almost always decided before serious injuries are inflicted. Males of the Ensifera insects often spar with the forelegs, antennae, and hindlegs. The sounds produced during such encounters reflect the dominance of a male and the less noisy individual retreats (Alexander 1960).

When an animal does not wish to fight, or finds he has confronted a superior animal, it is often to his interest to turn off the aggressive behavior of the prospective opponent. The European jackdaw, *Corvus monedula,* averts attacks by turning its head and raising its silver tipped neck feathers (Lorenz 1952). This *appeasement gesture* induces the attacker to begin preening the intended victim instead. As Marler (1961:112) says, "fights may end in an orgy of mutual preening." Here we have demonstrated the *antithesis principle.* The animal which wishes to stop the attack does just the opposite of the things he would do if he were belligerent. He exposes the vulnerable back of the head which, if hit, could result in his death, and at the same time he hides his weapon, the bill. The same sort of phenomenon is noted in wolves which expose their neck to a superior animal. Lorenz (1966) stresses that the attacker is *unable* to harm the suddenly vulnerable animal. Such patterns, of course, must function innately and so the appeasement gesture acts as a releaser of nonagressive behavior. In connection with such behavior, Lorenz stresses the dangers inherent in the long-distance killing practiced in modern human warfare. Such slaughter might be averted if a gunner could see the appeasement gestures of the victims. As has been demonstrated in warfare, however, man's "intelligence" may have overcome his ability to respond properly to such gestures.

Intrasexual hostilities may also be averted if members avoid each other entirely. A singing bird may cause other male birds to avoid the area and a fight. In the field two male crickets singing the same song will move away from each other (Burkhardt et al. 1967). Recordings of the male southern toad, *Bufo terrestris,* attract females, but repel males (Collias 1960). It must be pointed out, however, that an avoidance response does not occur in every case. In fact, in some cases a male's advertisement may actually attract other males. Such attraction would probably have a different selective basis than the aforementioned aggregation and mutual calling of some species. In the satinfin shiner, *Notropis analoctanus*, territorial males produce knocking sounds during courtship display and chasing. Recorded playbacks of the knocks elicit aggressive behavior from other males (Stout 1963). The factors which determine whether an advertising male elicits approach or withdrawal in other males are not entirely understood.

There is no intent here to imply that all communication between members of the same sex is hostile in nature. Other types of interactions also occur such as grouping signals and parent-offspring communication, but these are discussed separately. Here we are primarily concerned with signaling which is specifically elicited by the recipient's sex, and it seems that the more ecologically and reproductively important of these are aggressive in nature.

Communication between Sexes

Darwin set forth the principle of intersexual communication when he stated that winning a mate is a highly competitive process and one in which displays are important. The relationship between communication and competition is an important one. Each individual must be able to persuade a member of the opposite sex to enter into reproductive activities with him or her—and *not* to take another mate instead. To this end, the highly stereotyped patterns leading toward mating have become intense demonstrations of salesmanship.

Let us examine a few specific effects of individuals' calling to themselves the attention of the opposite sex. A male chaffinch singing loudly to nearby females is letting them know several pieces of information: he is an unmated male, in reproductive condition, in possession of a territory, and near the female at that time (Marler 1961). As conditions change, the song may also change and take on new meaning. For example the calling songs of crickets attract females in reproductive condition. If a calling male runs into another

male the sound will change to the shorter rival's song. In grasshoppers, the males do not fight at this time. The rival's song serves another purpose instead. The males are so promiscuous that they will mount anything even remotely resembling a grasshopper, so the shorter call serves to keep males from ravaging each other in vain attempts to copulate. If the singing male runs into a female, however, his song changes to the courting song. He will sing this song for long periods with occasional attempted mountings as long as the female remains. The time she is willing to remain depends upon her own reproductive state (Burkhardt et al. 1967).

The advertisement by males can take on unusual forms. Several species of birds advertise themselves by "decorating" a particular area. The decorating may be done by clearing the area of leaves and grass, building a bower, putting shiny leaves or other objects in the cleared area, and, in other ways, making the area conspicuous (see Figure 11.1). Here the bird attracts attention not to himself but to an area, his territory, instead. Armstrong (1965) gives several examples of such behavior, and Gilliard (1969) discusses its evolutionary implications.

In other cases the female may not be entirely passive in communication. In insects, just as in birds, the songs of males serve to attract, advertise, and identify, but in insects the songs constitute the entire mating display. A grasshopper walking around in tall grass is not likely to be able to utilize visual clues to any great extent, as do birds. In these insects, however, identification and attraction is enhanced by the calling of the female in response to the male's sounds. The song is sexually stimulating to both sexes so that if the approaching female encounters a silent male of another species she may mate with him. These accidents are probably rare, however, since similar species are likely to be separated for ecological reasons and since alien males are not likely to succumb to the seductive advances of the ready females (Bastock 1967).

There are other examples of females signaling in reproductive behavior. Some female fish secrete chemicals which stimulate males (Tavolga 1956) just as the odor of females in heat stimulates males of some mammals. In some female primates the "sexual skin" of the perineal region swells and turns red when they are in estrus. Estrus females also may behave differently than they would otherwise, for example, by standing still for the male's approach or assuming the "ready" position for copulation.

Another way interspecific matings are avoided is by use of a complex sequence of the stereotyped sexual signals. As an example, consider the mating behavior of the cockroach *Nauphoeta cinerea* as described by Roth and Willis (1952). These individuals respond to the scent of members of their own species so they are likely to congregate in the same places. Sexually mature males scurry about touching antennae of other members until they receive a specific chemical stimulus from a virgin female. When this happens the male and female stand there stroking each other's antennae. Then the male turns his back, raises his wings, touches his abdomen to the ground and maintains the pose for up to a minute. Secretory glands on his back are thus exposed and the female comes forward and nibbles at the secreted substance. She then climbs onto his back. The male grasps her genitalia with his claspers and twists his body from under hers so that their bodies are in line but facing opposite directions, the normal copulatory position of cockroaches. It is apparent that in such an elaborate mating procedure, mating mistakes will be rare.

The phenomenon of elaborate behavioral patterns in reproduction is widespread among animals. The adaptiveness of such procedures may be in their leading directly to copulation, as was the case in the above example, or in leading to *pairing*. In the latter case both individuals usually assume some sort of responsibility in the rearing of young. In the cockroaches the remorseless male leaves the female directly after copulation.

The female develops the eggs and, once they are laid, she too is relieved of responsibility toward them.

In other animals, however, the reproductive process may not be quite so carefree. For example, in birds at least one parent must remain with the young to feed and protect them after they hatch. In some species, both parents remain with the offspring and share in the labor involved in rearing them. Differences in reproductive contributions of the sexes in bird species provide an unusually clear and fascinating insight into how natural selection may operate.

The *biological fitness* of an animal is determined by the proportion of genes it is able to contribute to the overall "gene pool" of the population. So, in one sense, fitness is measured by the number of offspring the animal leaves. The term "fitness" is somewhat misleading since no evaluation of the animal's individual well-being is implied. The meaning becomes apparent, however, when the species is considered in relation to its ecological and reproductive requirements. Those animals which maximize their reproductive success will contribute most to the gene pool, and therefore to the species, in the next generation. Those which emphasize any other aspect of their lives instead may benefit themselves more individually, but they will have less effect on the species, so natural selection is continuously favoring high reproductive success. The population at any given time is composed primarily of highly reproductive stock. Fitness, however, is not simply a game of numbers. An intestinal parasite is not necessarily more fit than a hen because it lays thousands of eggs to the hen's one. Nor is a hen which lays many eggs necessarily more fit than another hen which lays fewer. If the hen which lays many eggs has specialized physiologically for rapid production at the expense of slower normal development of the egg, none of her eggs may hatch or the offspring may be sickly and die before reproducing. In such a case the hen would have contributed nothing to the gene pool.

If only a limited niche (see Chapter 8) with its various commodities such as food and nest-sites is available to a species, then a population must sooner or later come up against certain barriers to its continued increase. Then, if the population size is limited, specialization for leaving large numbers of offspring cannot define fitness. In view of a limited niche, fitness can only be increased by contributing one's genes to the gene pool at the *expense* of others, especially unrelated individuals, in the population. Therefore fitness must be defined in terms of success in maximizing the percentage or ratio of one's genes in the overall gene pool. The principle of competition as discussed in Chapter 8 must, then, necessarily enter into any definition of biological fitness.

For now we are concerned with how fitness may be affected by communication. We have seen the importance of signaling in mate selection. So one means of increasing fitness would be to maximize the impact of one's signals and therefore one's attractiveness to the opposite sex and, in fact, such an evolutionary route has been taken by many species of animals. The peacock with his elaborate coloration, bold markings, and glaring presence must present a veritable barrage to the IRM's of the drab peahens (Figure 6.8). Since the female does react to the sight of these releasers, it may well be that the bolder the markings, the longer the tail, and the more garish the demeanor, the more likely is the female to react to them. Such a probability becomes even more likely in the light of what we know about the possibility of heightening releasing effect as demonstrated by supernormal releasers. It should be pointed out, however, that at present there is little data to verify that fitness can thus be maximized in nature; the scheme, as presented here, is based primarily on circumstantial evidence. The result of such a system, of course, would be to force males increasingly toward the rococo in order that they, rather than a competing male, might be chosen as a mate. However, conspicuousness is fraught with danger in the wild. If the splendid male peacock attracts females, he also attracts tigers. It is apparent that such a male cannot be expected to live a long time, but for a while he may lead an active sex life indeed.

Since selection of these bold sorts of males stresses the attraction of as many females as possible in a brief span of time, the males cannot be expected to assist in the rearing of the young. After copulation they move on to the next conquest, leaving the female to raise the brood alone. Some examples from birds are the ruff, prairie chicken, argus pheasant, and cock-of-the-rock in which the sexes meet only for copulation and no pair bond exists at all. The males are promiscuous and mate with as many females as possible whereas the females, once mated, no longer respond to the overtures of any male.

The female, as is well known, is usually the drabber, duller member of these sexually dimorphic species. She is therefore much less likely to be subject to predation and may live through several more seasons than the male. She has taken a different evolutionary route, one which favors crypticity so that she may make her contribution through taking care of her young. Her role is to tend to several broods over the years and to maximize the chances of each chick carrying her genes reaching maturity.

The conspicuousness of males may be not only through color or markings, but through sheer size. Male Alaska fur seals, *Callorhinus alascanus*, may weigh six times the weight of females (Amadon 1959). Male grackles may weigh twice the weight of females. Selander (1965) interprets the larger size of these males as being adaptive in aggressive interactions as a result of competition with other males. It is important to realize that any showiness in males, whether in size or markings, may be functional both in attracting females and in intimidating other males, and that the relative importance of each effect may vary from one situation or species to the next. It may even be that, in some cases, sexual dimorphism in size is unrelated to reproductive success.

Figure 6.8 The display of the peacock. Its garishness makes it highly conspicuous and increases its reproductive success. The male peafowl must maximize its reproductive effort in a short span of time because its appearance and continual displays render it especially vulnerable to predators. (Photo: The American Museum of Natural History.)

In a few bird species, such as the button quail, the Hudsonian godwit, and certain phalaropes, the sexual roles are reversed. The females are larger and more striking than the males and in these species the females compete with each other for the attention of the males. In these cases it is likely that the males take over a large part of the rearing of the young. The females, on the other hand, can be expected to be promiscuous. This condition is referred to as *polygyny*. Unfortunately, specific data on the roles of the sexes in cases of reversed sexual dimorphism in vertebrates is meager.

The relative numbers of one sex to the other may be related to the mating system of some species. In birds, the females of Wagler's oropendola, *Zarhynchus wagleri*, outnumber the males six to one and, in such a case, promiscuity on the part of the males can be expected. The female oropendola quarrels for a nest site and builds the nest alone while the male ogles down at her with his blue eyes, raising his feathers, twitching his tail and spluttering, cackling, wheezing, and gurgling. When the nest is finished she seems to notice him for the first time and accepts his amorous advances. After breeding he leaves her to her nesting duties and flies off.

In other nonmonogamous bird species of more nearly equal sex ratios, reproductive behavior in the female may not be released by the presence of a garish male or even by a gaily decorated bower, but (in a more practical vein) by a male with a nest already built. The male crimson-crowned bishop bird courts one female at a time, builds a nest for her, mates and then goes off to build another nest.

Some species show sexual dimorphism of the sound-producing apparatus. For example, in males of some ducks the syrinx (sound producer) has a long bulla, lacking in females, which gives males a distinctive sound (Johnsgard 1967). Such dimorphism would seem to be highly advantageous in that sex identification can result without the birds' being visually conspicuous.

In most bird species, sexes are almost indistinguishable in the field. Even an expert is unable to distinguish the sexes of the flycatcher *Myiarchus* by its appearance, general behavior, or vocalizations. In other species, slight differences in morphology between sexes may be apparent. The sexes of the golden fronted woodpecker, *Centurus aurifrons*, are almost identical except for subtle differences in coloration of the head and some tail feathers. In such species mate selection is probably not due, in any important sense, to differences in appearance. Instead, sex-dependent behavior may be increasingly important.

In relatively monomorphic species, the role of the female remains basically unchanged from that of the dimorphic species discussed earlier. She is cryptically marked and colored so that she may escape detection and be able to care for her broods without attracting attention to them. The male, being of the same appearance, does not attract females to him by garish visual signals but by the development of pair bonds through behavioral signals. When behavioral patterns are used in sex identification rather than instantly recognizable color and markings the development of pair bonds can be expected to be slower. One reason is that females are likely to be treated by males as other males—in a hostile manner—until their sex becomes apparent, and such encounters certainly cannot expedite pairing. Also, in those species in which there is no premium on a male's making successive conquests in a single season, the males as well as the females must move carefully in mate selection or the whole breeding season might be lost in terms of reproductive success. If promiscuous males make a poor choice of a mate, nothing is really lost since they may be more successful on their next attempt. A monogamous male must live with any mistake, however, and is not likely to be able to make up for it. (Again, we are dealing with theory—there are few data available for support.)

So, in cases where the sexes are identical in

appearance, or nearly so, the male is likely to increase his fitness, not by attracting as many females to him as possible each breeding season,
but, after slowly pairing with a single female, by
then assisting in nest building, incubation, and
rearing of young. The males of such pairs are
likely to live a relatively long time and thereby
see several breeding seasons and rear several
broods. These pairs may endure for a single season, part of a season, or a lifetime, depending on
the species. (Lifetime pairing is reported in some
mammals, for example, wolves, and in some birds,
as geese, cranes, penguins, and hawks.)

In species in which the sexes are similar, the
displays of both sexes may be identical, as seen
in the elaborate mutual ceremonies of the great
crested grebe (Figure 6.9). In such cases the
sexes may be indistinguishable to a human observer. (To further confuse field observers, in
some monomorphic species either sex may mount
the other!) Mutual signaling may reinforce pair
bonding after mating has occurred. Foraging *Centurus* woodpeckers call softly as they move through
trees out of sight of each other. Presumably, such
keeping in touch reinforces the pair bond.

These examples of communication between
sexes are by no means the only routes open to
natural selection. There are probably almost as
many variations as there are species and there
are probably exceptions to any unitary rule. As
one example, consider the whooping crane, *Grus
americana*. Both sexes are white with red and
black head markings, and so are conspicuous and
identical. Such a scheme doesn't fit anything we
have described. Probably selection for visibility
which facilitates social interaction is greater in
this case than selection for crypticity. Such bal-
ancing can only be assumed to be due to low
likelihood of predation. Again, there are no hard
data to substantiate the hypothesis. (See Chapter 7.)

As another example which does not easily fit
any simple model, consider the sexually monomorphic species of frigid habitats. Time is a very

Figure 6.9 Elaborate mutual ceremonies
in the courtship of the great crested grebe.
In the head-shaking ceremony (A) the birds
face each other, raise their crest feathers
and shake their heads from side to side.
In B, the male approaches the female with
his head submerged. Just as he reaches her,
the male suddenly lunges out of the water.
In C the birds present weeds to each other
in a mutual ceremony. (After Etkin 1964
from J.S. Huxley, Proc. Zool. Soc. 1914.)

critical factor in the breeding cycles of polar and alpine species since the season is short. As Johnsgard (1967) points out, the behavior and physiology of such species move toward a rapid completion of the breeding cycle. For birds, nesting, fledging, and molting periods under such conditions are generally shorter than in temperate regions of the world. In such cases, communication involved in mate selection and other reproductive acts must be accomplished quickly in the absence of any marked sexual dimorphism.

It is possible that identically marked sexes can use their markings in mating behavior. Such signals are called *epigamic*. When epigamic displays operate in pairing, strong sexual differences in behavior can be expected at some stage in the process. Otherwise unadaptive homosexual matings might occur.

Garden snails, *Helix pomatia,* are hermaphroditic (having both male and female reproductive organs) and so present an interesting problem in mating. In such a case the problem of sex recognition becomes one of species recognition. The mating procedure of these animals is rather unusual. The courtship begins with a series of postures and movements. The snails slowly entwine as they continue to signal by gentle touch. The pairing culminates as each snail suddenly thrusts a calcareous arrow—a love dart—into the body of the other (Figure 6.10). This action is followed by coition, or exchange of sperm.

Let us consider another unusual type of mating behavior which illustrates the complexities involved in sexual communication. In some instances a mistake in the mating procedure does not mean mere reproductive failure—it might mean instant death. The zebra-striped salticid (jumping) spiders hunt by running and jumping upon their prey. They have good eyes and can usually see visual clues. The problem lies in the spiders' habit of attacking arthropods roughly their own size. The male is smaller than the female and is in great danger of being taken for prey. So the male approaches the female with extreme caution and much signaling by leg waving and dancing back and forth until she gives signs of receptivity (Bastock 1967). In some species the antics of the male seem to put the female into a trancelike state, after which the male approaches to mate with her.

It is interesting that in spite of the strong stereotypy of intersexual signals, *compensation* between the various signal types is possible in some species. For example, captive bullfinches which have had part of the inner ear removed are still able to form pairs, go through normal breeding patterns and even to transmit alarm calls (Hüchter and Schwartzkopff 1958). Apparently vision is compensating for hearing loss.

We have learned that environmental cues, such as daylength, may be responsible for hormonal changes which then influence behavior. The re-

Figure 6.10 Garden snails in the act of mating. On the left a "love dart" is shown. (After Meisenheimer, 1921.)

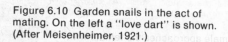

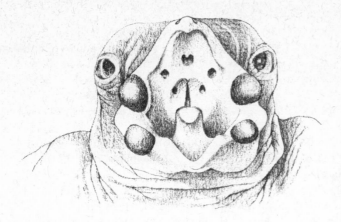

Figure 6.11 When the young parrot opens his beak wide to ask for food, four large irridescent blue spots appear along the mandibles. The appearance of these spots brings about the feeding behavior in the parents. (After Tinbergen 1965.)

verse relationship may also exist between physiology and behavior. Display may actually be a necessary step in the development of breeding behavior in that it initiates a sequence of physiological as well as psychological events culminating in copulation (Lanyon 1963). The complexity of such interactions is further indicated by Nice's (1943) findings that after a song sparrow had acquired a mate, his song frequency may be reduced by 90 percent.

There are certain pheromonal signals between sexes of some mammals which are of interest to physiologists. Female mice kept in a group free of males, will come into estrus (heat) infrequently and asynchronously. If a male is introduced, the females will immediately become receptive. They will also respond to male urine or the scent of an upwind male. If the olfactory bulbs of their brains are destroyed the female will not respond (Bronson 1968). An interesting relationship between signals and physiology is shown in such studies. Pregnant female mice, when exposed to a strange male, will abort their fetuses and become estrus again. The mechanism has been shown to be hormonal (cf. Clulow and Clarke 1968).

Communication between Parents and Offspring

In many species there is no need for the parents to be able to communicate with the young because there is virtually no interaction between the generations after birth or hatching. Insects usually leave their eggs and, when they hatch, the parents react to their offspring no differently than to any other young members of the species. Generally such species have simpler nervous systems which are able to function in an adaptive manner after a short period of development. Parental care is believed to have developed in species which are more complex and for which more time is required for the young to develop advanced types of nervous systems. Such parental behavior is demonstrated in such activities as feeding, cleaning, leading, and alarm behavior. Here we will consider only a few such patterns; other aspects of such behavior are considered in Chapters 2, 3, and 7.

In those species in which one or both parents care for the young, one of the most pressing needs for communication lies in feeding behavior. We have discussed one form of such communication (Chapter 2): the pecks of the young gulls, directed toward the spot on the parent's beak, which elicits food regurgitation. Similar signals operate in other species. For example, in the young of some bird species, such as the parrot shown in Figure 6.11, there are four large spots visible when the young gapes to be fed. These spots act as releasers of feeding behavior for the parent. In some species, the foraging of the parent is influenced by the cries of the young. The more they cry, the more time and energy the parent puts into searching for food for them.

In most species it is not likely that a parent with multiple young can recognize any of them individually as long as they are related to as off-spring and without rank or sex. Such parents are, however, able to recognize their own young from among other young animals. The signals emanating from, or associated with, offspring often act as releasers of parental behavior, whereas the same signals from other young animals do not (Rheingold 1963). There are undoubtedly several basic ways a parent may come to recognize its own young. For example, ground-nesting gulls seem to recognize their young by their cries. Other animals may use other sensory clues. Nanny goats come to know the smell of their offspring by licking the newborn animal. If a newborn goat is removed from its mother before she has had a chance to lick it and is then returned to her a few hours later, she will reject it. The ability of the mother to become associated with her young seems to be limited to the period directly after birth. A young goat apparently learns to recognize its mother by the process of elimination after being continually rejected by all the other mothers (Etkin 1967).

Specific signals may exist which function in the recognition of the parent by the young. Lorenz found that the night heron, *Nycticorax nycticorax*, bows to its nestlings when it approaches, thus displaying its bluish cap and white plumes. It thereby suppresses any escape or defense behavior in the young which they normally show toward any large figure approaching them. Of course there is no individual recognition demonstrated here—only the acceptance of a "friendly" large form.

In some cases, only restricted types of signals (sign stimuli) are used in the identification of young. Herring gulls, *Larus argentatus*, nest only a few feet from the nest of other members of the colony and the parents vigorously defend their young. However, if a young bird wanders into the nesting area of another gull and is killed, its parents may eat it. When they no longer hear its call and they see no movement, it loses all significance as offspring and becomes food (Tinbergen 1964).

Although individuals in a group of offspring may not be distinguishable to a parent, differences in the state of the individuals may be. In birds, unfed chicks call more than fed ones (Muir 1954) and this probably has an effect on food apportionment by the parents. Such a system would tend to ensure an equal amount of food for the offspring. Since the last of the young to hatch would be smaller than its siblings, in time of food scarcity the lack of vigor of its pleadings might cause it to receive less food and so it would quickly die. The parent, then, would have a brood of a size compatible with the carrying capacity of the immediate environment and could, therefore, be expected to rear more young than if it had tried to feed them all (see Chapter 7).

The question of imprinting takes on new facets when it is considered in reference to parent-young communication. A baby chick, after hatching and drying, is up and running about looking for food within an hour. Birds which hatch at a late stage of development are called *precocial*. They still require some parental care but they are independent in many respects. A blue jay, *Cyanocitta cristala*, on the other hand, is an example of an *altricial* species. These birds are born naked and helpless, they spend their early life sprawled or doddering about in their nest until a parent appears with food, when they feebly gape to be fed. The complete dependency of the young and the prolonged close relationship of parent and offspring in altricial species, could be expected to provide more time for the young to *learn* the characteristics of the species. The importance of imprinting in altricial species might therefore be reduced since time is not a critical factor.

Sexually dimorphic species do not depend as

much upon imprinting as monomorphic ones. The young are exposed to the female of such species more often than the male, as we have seen. Therefore both male and female offspring would tend to imprint on the mother and, of course, this would be disadvantageous in later interactions such as mate selection. So, as Klopfer (1962) points out, whereas precocial ducks might be expected to rely more importantly on imprinting than would altricial thrushes, among ducks selection for imprinting in sexually dimorphic species might be less than in monomorphic ones.

ALARM SIGNALS WITHIN SPECIES

Alarm signals comprise parts of communication systems at several levels, for example within populations, between parents and young, and even between species. On an intraspecific plane the consideration of alarms must involve at least two elements: how they are adaptive and how they may have developed. Its adaptiveness, it seems, would be in preserving one's offspring or relatives (see Chapter 10) with the expression of the alarm involving various levels of risk. The acceptable level of the risk is largely determined by how strongly the average recipient of the alarm is related to the warning animal as is discussed in the section on kinship selection. Any warning signal, of course, becomes part of the environment of any organism able to perceive it; so completely unrelated animals, even those of other species, may come to react appropriately to any such signals as is discussed below.

Alarm signals may vary widely in their specificity. They may be very general warnings of an unspecified threat, as is demonstrated in barking dogs. They may also be of a more specific nature, as was discussed in regard to the high pitched *twee* warnings of birds which means "hawks overhead." Alarm signals may be even more specific than this. The California ground squirrel, *Citellus beecheyi*, has three different warning chirps; each type of chirp announces the presence of either hawks, snakes, or mammals (Fitch 1948). The in-

formation content of a warning may be further increased by differences in the vigor with which it is issued. The warning chirps of a merely anxious bird may suddenly rise in intensity with the sudden, near appearance of a human observer (Nice 1943).

INTERSPECIFIC COMMUNICATION

Since the biotic milieu of any animal includes members of other species, adaptations to their presence and activities may be expected. In some cases such adaptations are critical and, so, complex systems of communication between species have resulted. It is not surprising that interspecific communication is most likely to appear in birds and mammals in light of their complex milieu and relatively increased mental capacities. Brand and Kellogg (1939) showed that they learn certain signals quickly, such as those signifying danger. Interspecific signals, just as intraspecific ones, by no means function only through learning, however. There are even examples (discussed below) of communication of a sort between plants and animals and these could certainly only function through natural selection operating independently of any learning mechanism.

Defense Signals

Let us consider one of the most common and widespread types of communication between species—one whose operating mechanism we might "intuitively" understand—the maximizing of threat. We have all seen two strange dogs approach each other stiff-legged, heads held high and hair bristling. Such behavior makes each animal appear larger and perhaps more dangerous. The advantage of such behavior can be seen in our own society in which large powerful men, somehow, initially gain our respect. Animals may employ the same principle when dealing with members of other species. A cat hunches its back in the presence of an aggressive dog. The dog's hackles are raised. In both cases the animal appears more formidable. Several displays of intimi-

Figure 6.12 Warning and intimidation displays in several species of animals.
The displays serve to make the animal look larger and more formidable to his
enemies. The animals shown here are A. frilled lizard, B. zorille, C. spotted skunk,
D. short-eared owl. (From Johnsgard, *Animal Behavior*. Wm. C. Brown Company
Publishers, 1967.)

dation through an apparent increase in size are shown in Figure 6.12, but such communication is not always visual. The adult howler monkey, *Alouatta palliata,* roars his displeasure at human intruders in a resounding and awe-inspiring manner (Carpenter 1934).

Alarm calls have been mentioned in reference to intraspecific communication and it is interesting to note that such signals may function between species as well. If two species sharing the same range are hunted by the same predator, there is an advantage in using the same alarm calls to warn of its presence. We have noted the similar characteristics of the cryptic high-pitched alarm calls of birds. Such convergent development of signaling characters may be separately initiated by environmental expediency and, later, become more similar and mutually recognizable for ethological reasons. In experiments with recorded distress calls of birds it was found that escape reactions may be triggered in a number of species which are not necessarily closely related. It should be pointed out that interspecific signals may also occur which are not based on convergence of signals. A well-known example is the relationship of the wary little tickbird and the rhinoceros. The tiny bird warns the nearsighted rhinoceros of intruders and thus protects his food supply—ectoparasites of the mammal.

Prey animals may act to confuse a predator and thus reduce his efficiency. For example a blue jay will attack an owl which ventures near the jay's nest. Under other circumstances, the owl might have attacked the jay. Although the jay can do no serious harm, its attacks are usually effective in driving the owl away. The owl, having no natural enemies, is not equipped to handle attacks. Apparently, the jay has short-circuited the owl's normal hunting pattern by attacking instead of fleeing (Tinbergen 1965).

A hunted animal may also confuse a predator by giving false clues. "Flash-colors" may appear while a moth is in flight, but these disappear as soon as it alights. A pursuing hunter continues to look for the colors and the moth goes unnoticed. A lizard may twitch its tail and thus divert a predator's attention away from the lizard's intended direction. Some species of fish have concealing stripes running through the eyes and a false eyespot on the tail so that a predator is unsuccessful when it attempts to "head off" its prey.

The well-known white rump flashes (Figure 6.13) of several species of mammals (primarily ungulates) have for years been considered as alarm signals to other members of the population. It was assumed that the disadvantages of an individual attracting the attention of a predator to himself were more than balanced by warning others among which would be the signaler's offspring or kin. A new theory of the advantages of such signals has recently been advanced, however. Smythe (1970) believes the signal is basically intended for the predator, although it may serve as an intraspecific warning as well. The system, he theorizes, would work like this: there is a critical distance from a "running prey" that a "chasing predator" must be within when he

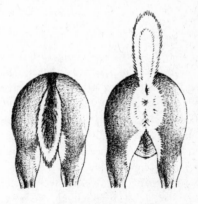

Figure 6.13 The white-tailed deer, *Odocoileus virginianus,* has a conspicuous "flag." When alarmed, the tail is raised and the hairs of the underside become erect. This very visible pattern may be an alarm system to let other members of the population know they are in danger or it may act to entice enemies to attack prematurely.

Figure 6.14 These drawings illustrate the principle of disruptive margins. Place the drawing in an upright position by standing the book up. Then move toward the back of the room until the zebra or the pseudozebra disappears. Note that the figures in the bottom square that have disruptive edges also disappear first, thus illustrating the principle of the zebra pattern. (From Cott, *Adaptive Colouration in Animals,* Associated Book Publishers, Ltd. 1957.)

begins his chase, if he is going to be successful. When a prey animal notices that he has been detected by a hunting predator he moves away in such a manner that his rump patch is most conspicuous. By so maximizing the effects of his presence upon the predator's sensory apparatus, he would induce the predator to charge prematurely, or while outside the critical distance. When the escape abilities of the prey had been demonstrated, the discouraged predator would go elsewhere to search for food.

I Am Not Here

"I am not here" is the message of cryptic species. Crypticity may range from simple markings which break the contour (Figure 6.14) to devices which render the animal almost invisible. There are many well-known examples of crypticity including reed-nesting marsh birds which sit immobile with bills pointed upward, moths which seem to disappear on the bark of a tree, and strange frogs which are almost invisible against the forest fern (Figure 6.15). Movement is also an important part of crypticity. Most cryptic animals in their hiding habitat are slow moving so that they attract little attention as they go about. The selective mechanism for cryptic species is similar to that for certain mimics discussed below. However the message of the latter is, "I am not of interest," and they are therefore considered separately.

There are also species which do not spend their lives concealed or inconspicuous in their environ-

Figure 6.15 A toad, *Megophyrus nasuta,* of Malaysia, among dead leaves. (Photo:
M. W. F. Tweedie from National Audubon Society.)

ment, but which, at certain times, must conceal themselves. As an example consider predatory cats. These animals are in some cases so formidable that they can spend much of their time lounging in full view of other animals. It is only when they begin a hunt that they seek to "disappear" (Figure 6.16).

NO!

Certain animals, notably insects, also communicate with their predators, in a sense, by saying, "No!" A wide variety of insect species manufacture noxious chemicals which are released when they are captured. Some of these chemicals are powerful toxins or irritants and, in some species, they can be shot with some accuracy in any of

several directions. Some of these chemicals are mixed just before release, the result being that their action and reactivity are heightened by very high temperatures which are produced in the mixing. Thomas Eisner (1962, 1970) at Cornell has elegantly described in some detail the remarkable defense glands of insects. (Such signal meaning is by no means limited to arthropods since the message of the skunk must be much the same.)

It is rather interesting that most of the insect poisons are not fatal to the predator. If their predators were, in the main, vertebrates with high learning capacities, nonlethal dosages would be expected. However, in many cases, other arthropods, such as ants or spiders, comprise the large part of the predatory species. It would appear that it would be more adaptive to kill these predators outright unless their foraging habits could be altered by bitter experience through a type of learning. It is conceivable, however, that it might be advantageous for a noxious prey species to allow vertebrate predator species to live, since the diets of these predators may be influenced by tradition learning or by other modifiers of behavior; also, it is likely that such predators might then switch their diet to edible competitors of the noxious species.

Mimicry

One of the most interesting types of communication based on predator-prey interaction is mimicry. Mimicry may be defined in narrow terms, but we will consider the concept broadly as referring to any organisms taking on characteristics of other species in order to alter the reaction of yet other species, usually predators.

Müllerian mimicry is named after Fritz Müller, a nineteenth-century German zoologist. The phenomenon referred to is the convergent selection for *common warning coloration* in poisonous or noxious species so that predators have fewer signals to learn. Recall the visibility of poisonous coral snakes and the similar type of color and markings in the wasp. Animals which advertise their presence so that they will not be mistaken for palatable prey have certain basic characteristics in common which include (1) bold, simple arrangements of black, white, yellow, orange, and

Figure 6.16 A hunting leopard. Its markings and coloration and behavior render the animal almost invisible in its natural hunting area. (Photo: Leonard Lee Rue III from National Audubon Society.)

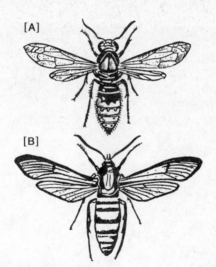

[A]

[B]

Figure 6.17 A., a hornet, and B., a hornet clearwing, a moth in wasp's clothing. (From *Biology* by Karl von Frisch, translated by Jane M. Oppenheimer. Copyright © 1964 by Bayerischer Schulbuch-Verlag. By permission of Harper and Row, Publishers, Inc.)

red combinations; (2) obvious movements in open view; (3) alarm postures which maximize the effect of the color and markings; and (4) gregarious social patterns which reduce the likelihood of capture by naive predators.

Batesian mimicry is named after the nineteenth-century English naturalist, Henry Walter Bates and refers to the type of mimicry adopted by an innocuous or palatable species of the warning characteristics of a noxious or harmful species (Figure 6.17): the harmless species is called the mimic and the noxious one, the model. Although mimicry is rare among mammals, one example from this group will illustrate its use. The tree shrews, *Tupaia*, of Borneo, taste repulsive to many predatory animals and they are therefore avoided. In the same area, the palatable squirrels, *Sciurus*, resemble the tree shrews to such a degree that they cannot be distinguished from one another by the skins alone. The squirrels are undoubtedly protected from predators by their similarity to the shrews (Wickler 1968).

In some cases, selection in signaling devices must reach a balance between the need for crypticity to reduce predation and the need for species recognition. As an example, consider the *sex-limited mimicry* among certain butterflies. In

those species in which the male attracts the female by his visual characters only, the females mimic noxious forms. In species which use olfactory clues in mate recognition, mimicry can occur in both sexes. In all cases it is probably important that the mimic maintain numbers low enough that it be exposed to predators less frequently than the model; otherwise attacks by predators would probably be reinforced often enough to cause the system to break down.

In Costa Rica, the milkweed, *Asclepias curassivica*, is avoided by cattle for good reason; if it is eaten the animals will become very sick and may die. The plant contains glycosidic chemicals similar to the drug digitalis, and one side effect of ingesting the plant is vomiting. Since vomiting will be induced before enough of the plant is eaten to cause death, the usual result is severe temporary illness. The Danainae, the family of the monarch butterfly, may spend its larval stage on the milkweed and incorporate its poisonous glycosides into their own bodies (Figure 6.18). Predatory birds made ill by catching one of these insects learn to avoid all monarchs, although other members of a population may have developed on other plants and are perfectly edible. Protection afforded an entire population by the noxious

Figure 6.18 Larvae of the monarch butterfly feeding on the leaves of the milkweed. The body of the butterfly thus becomes impregnated with powerful poisons which causes even edible members of the population to be avoided by predators. (Photo: American Museum of Natural History.)

qualities of a few operates through what Lincoln Brower (1959) calls *automimicry*. In such a case, the model and mimic are of the same species with identical appearances and, therefore, the system could be expected to be more efficient than Batesian mimicry.

The possibility exists that certain poisons (such as the alkaloids or glycosides of some insects) are tasteless to predators. These chemicals may occur with harmless but flavored chemicals and it may be that the predator uses the harmless chemicals as a clue to the presence of the poison. If this happens then certain edible forms might develop the harmless clue substance in a form of chemical mimicry as Brower (1969) has suggested.

While in Batesian mimicry the mimic may take on the general appearance of the model, in other cases only certain parts of models are copied. For example, many predatory animals such as hawks, owls, cats, and wolves have eyes that focus directly ahead rather than being situated on either side of the head as is the case in the rabbit and songbirds. (Such a predator is usually at the top of the food chain and, therefore, is less concerned about what may be creeping up on it than what type of prey is before it.) Animals which have frontal eyes utilize their effect as a defense mechanism or a threat (Figure 6.19). Gaze directly at a strange dog (a small one) and notice his uneasy behavior. Several species of harmless animals have utilized the relationship between eyes and threat and have developed eyespots as a means of repelling predators (Figures 6.20 and 6.22).

In some species, weapon automimicry has developed (Figure 6.21). In such cases hair, ears, and facial markings have developed in such a way to accent the weapons of the animals, particularly in artiodactyls (Guthrie and Petocz 1970).

Sounds may also serve as models in mimicry. Hissing and growling are sounds which accompany many truly dangerous reptiles, mammals, and even birds. Sound mimicry would probably be most successful in hole-nesting species which

[A]

[B]

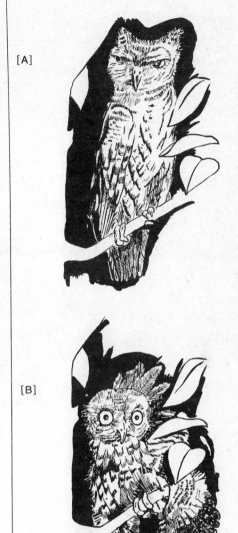

Figure 6.19 The owl in A is trying to be inconspicuous by hiding his eyes, sleeking his feathers and standing erect. After having been discovered, the owl in B is using the startling effect of staring while raising his feathers to make himself look bigger and more imposing.

Figure 6.20 An edible hawkmoth caterpillar with eyespots on its back (the real head is visible at the extreme anterior) and a stinger at the posterior end. (Photo: Robert Hermes from National Audubon Society.)

Figure 6.21 Patterns of ears and facial markings which emphasize the visual effects of the horns in *Hippotragus equinus* (top) and *Oryx beisa* (bottom). (From Guthrie and Petocz, "American Naturalist" Vol. 104, University of Chicago, 1970.)

could be heard, but not seen. It is known that hole-nesting titmice and screech owls and some nocturnal cockroaches hiss; and the coot, *Fulica americana*, growls when defending its nest against predators.

There is an interesting time element that may function in some types of mimicry. Young harmless animals may threaten in the manner of older more dangerous ones. Young lions growl, cough, and spit in a most threatening way. Burrell (1927) reported the growling of young platypuses when they are disturbed. Such threats in young animals may be more than incipient behavior as shown by the adoption of models unrelated to the mimic. Baby snowshoe hares, *Lepus americanus*, and baby European hares, *Lepus europaeus*, when threatened in their nest growl and lunge at a predator (Severaid 1942, Hediger 1948) in the manner of a dangerous species. The prospect of being attacked by an enraged baby hare might give a predator pause just long enough for the hare to escape.

In another type of mimicry, perfectly palatable individuals may not hide themselves, but may appear inedible. The twig caterpillar takes on the appearance of a broken twig on a limb. It doesn't hide its presence; it appears to be something of little interest to a predator. Certain tropical katydids have leaflike wings which are true to their model even to showing "veins" and the results of insect attacks. One species of frog approaches the upper limits of an unpalatable appearance by

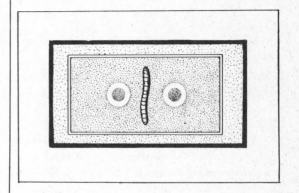

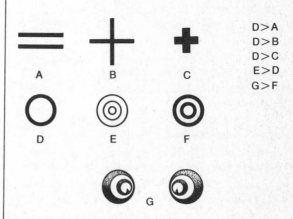

Figure 6.22 Results of tests to determine the effects of eyespot patterns on birds. These patterns appear in several species of insects such as the butterfly, *Precis almana,* at top. In the experiment, the birds were trained to take food from a slide at a certain site. When a mealworm was placed on the slide, the birds normally took it. However, when various eyespot models were projected onto the slide, the birds would not approach it. The relative effectiveness of the various models is shown at the bottom. (From Blest 1957a. With permission of N. V. Boekhandel and Drukkerij.)

crouching on a leaf in its imitation of a bird dropping. In some cases, such as the latter, the animal may not move at all; in other cases, movement may enhance crypticity—for example, in some leaf-hoppers which mimic leaves and which sway gently to and fro as a leaf might be moved by a breeze.

Mimicry is primarily a characteristic of prey animals, but in some cases it is also used by predatory animals to draw prey near. The angler fish lies on the bottom and draws small fish to their fate by wriggling a worm-like appendage just above its mouth. By human standards of conduct, one of the most ignoble of the deceivers is the blenny, *Aspidontus,* a small fish which has evolved the coloration of the helpful cleaner wrasse (Chapter 9). When a fish approaches for cleaning the blenny rushes to tear a piece of flesh from his' unwary host (Figure 6.23).

Among the more fascinating examples of mimicry are those involving plants and animals. Such interactions should not be unexpected since both great kingdoms are interdependent and subject to the laws of natural selection. Most of the signaling between plants and animals apparently occurs as a result of insect pollination of plants. Insects are usually attracted to certain flowers for physiological reasons (see Marler and Hamilton 1966) but, in some cases, certain insects approach flowers for other reasons. In one group of orchids each species mimics the odor and appearance of a particular species of insect (Figure 6.24). The insect pollinates the flower while attempting to copulate with it (also see Baerends 1950). As an other example of plant-animal mimicry there are the fly-pollinated flowers which emit odors reminiscent of rotting meat (Johnsgard 1967).

Gairdner Moment (1962) has described an interesting phenomenon in the animal world which operates on a principle opposite to that of automimicry. He cites instances where members of a population look as little like each other as possible. In such cases, the likelihood of an individual

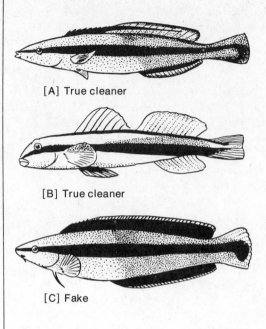

[A] True cleaner

[B] True cleaner

[C] Fake

Figure 6.23 The two fish at the top, A, *Labroides dimidiatus,* and B, *Elancantinus oceanops* are true cleaner fish. They are small and clean ectoparasites from the bodies of larger fish. Many of the larger fish even allow them to enter and clean the parasites from inside their mouths. Note the color patterns on the two cleaner fish and then notice the pattern on the bottom fish, *Aspidontes taeniatus,* which is a mimic. That is, it mimics the appearance of the cleaner fish. However, when it is allowed to approach the larger fish, it bites chunks of flesh from the would-be host.

We know that human communication systems can be "tapped" and so can communication systems between animals. Mimicry is only one example. A predator may find its prey by intercepting smells or sounds that in their adaptive context actually make up elements of a communication system. (From Wickler 1968.)

having a certain appearance is inversely related to the number of other individuals in the population having that appearance. Selection thus works on a feedback system which Moment calls *reflexive selection*. The adaptive principle was specifically described by L. Tinbergen (1960) in his discussion of *search images*. (The idea of the search image was suggested by von Uexküll after he missed seeing a *flask* of water on the table because he was looking for a clay *pitcher*.) Tinbergen argued that a foraging bird will continue to look for food which has the appearance of the type he has recently found or "has in mind." The system seems to work through principles of stimulus generalization and reward expectancy (see Chapter 3). After a predator has taken a member of a prey population, he would be likely to continue searching for others of that appearance. Those individuals of a different appearance might then escape notice. If variation is selected for in prey types such as the brittle stars (Figure 6.25), predatory shorebirds may be unable to form a search image of the starfish and so their foraging efficiency would be reduced. Obviously reflexive selection could not work for animals which signal intraspecifically by visual methods. The ecological implications of such selections are important and should be studied in more detail in highly variable species.

The principle of the search-image may have great ecological importance. It seems that search-image formation would be dependent upon the relative density of food types so that as a prey species became scarcer through being hunted, the predator would lose that particular search image and drop that species from its menu until it had recouped enough that it was in no danger of being decimated and could again be hunted.

Finally, let us briefly consider the fascinating idea behind *Mertensian mimicry*, a concept developed, of course, by Professor Mertens. The coral snakes, *Micrurus*, are highly poisonous and most species bear a characteristic red, black, and yellow banding which makes the snakes highly conspicuous. These species occur with similarly colored non-poisonous snakes (e.g. *Simophis*). It has often been assumed that the harmless species was the mimic, and the deadly one the model. It might be asked though, that if the model usually killed its attacker, how would the predators ever learn to avoid them? (There is no evidence that their major predators have any innate recognition system which would induce them to avoid coral snakes.) Mertens then suggested that neither of these species is the model, but that both are mimicking a similarly marked moderately poisonous species, *Pseudoboa*, that inhabits the same areas. Survivors of attacks by these species, could, indeed, learn to avoid snakes with the characteristic banding and, thus, the deadly and the harmless species could also profit by the lesson taught their common predators.

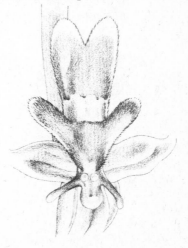

Figure 6.24 Mimicry of female wasps by *Ophrys orchids* (bee, spider and fly orchids). The result is that sexually oriented males pollinate the flowers by moving over them. (From Kullenberg 1961.)

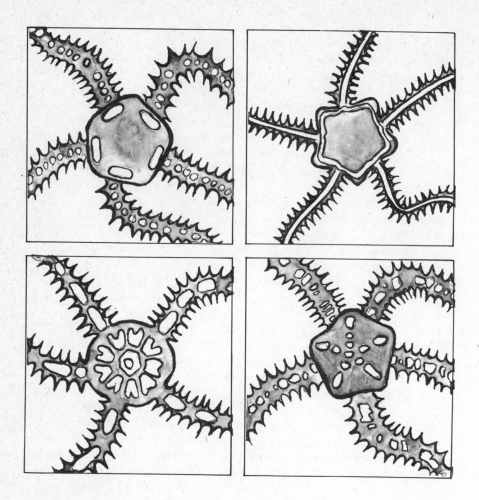

Figure 6.25 These four brittle stars, *Ophiopholis aculeata,* are all of the same species but show a variation in pattern. (From Moment 1962.)

POPULATIONS

Any careful observer who has spent time in the field knows that the number of wild animals in any area seems to fluctuate. In some cases the changes are not surprising. For example, many insect populations fall off each winter but rise anew in the flush of spring. The numbers of birds in the American forests also drop sharply each fall as certain species migrate southward. However, there are other less predictable changes. In some years, scarcely an individual of a certain species can be found which was abundant the year before. Occasionally, some species become so abundant they they rise out of control and we hear of invasions or plagues.

Although the numbers of the animal world may rise and fall, one of the most impressive phenomena is the *stability* of populations. One gets the impression that the rising and falling of numbers, whether regular or irregular, usually occurs within rather definite limits, and, if they are observed over long periods of time, well-established populations will be found neither rising out of control nor dwindling into oblivion. If, somehow, populations are maintained at certain levels through some regulatory mechanism—and some say they are not (see Ehrlich and Birch 1967)—the question arises, how does the mechanism work?

There come to mind immediately two periods in animal life histories which could serve as the points of focus for this kind of regulation; animal numbers could be limited by (1) restricting the number of young produced, or (2) by affecting the mortality or longevity of individuals in a population. Such considerations are important to the student of animal behavior for a number of reasons. A short life span or an inability to compensate for eggs somehow lost could have important influences on how an animal is likely to behave. An animal of a long-lived species which is likely to see several breeding seasons is less likely to emphasize immediate reproductive success in its life strategy than an animal which has only one chance to reproduce. The life strategies of animals determined through natural selection are a

balanced and highly integrated melange of interacting forces. In order to account for one, we
must carefully consider the others.

HOW MANY OFFSPRING
ARE PRODUCED?

It might seem that in a competitive situation an
animal could exclude his competitors by simply
overwhelming them with the sheer numbers of
his progeny. The principle has been cited by those
people who do not wish to limit their families
because of the fear that their children might be
overrun by the offspring of some other ethnic
groups. Let's examine the principle in the animal
world.

The first question is obvious. Do animals produce as many offspring as they are biologically
able? A quick examination will show that the *biotic potential* (the physiological ability to produce
offspring) is phenomenal in most animals. For
example, Table 7.1 shows the biotic potential of
the housefly, *Musca domestica*. Even large mammals show a startling capacity for increasing their
number. According to Charles Darwin, a pair of
elephants could leave over 19,000,000 descendants in only 750 years. When placed in new situations, some animals have demonstrated their
reproductive potential most graphically. For example, when the pheasant, *Phasianus colchicus*,
was introduced to an island its numbers increased
from 8 to 1,898 in five years (Einarsen 1958).

And then we are all aware of what happened when
the rabbit was introduced to Australia. These animals were taken from their normal habitat, however, and thereby released from any environmental regulation which might have been operating
there.

Some of the most interesting and best documented work on influences on reproduction which
could limit populations comes from studies on
clutch size (the number of eggs in a nest) in birds.
According to Lack (1954, 1966, 1968), most birds
rear as many young as possible. This is not to say,
however, that they lay as many eggs as possible.
Rather, the number of eggs per clutch has evolved
as the maximum number the parent can successfully feed (in altricial species in which the young
are fed by the parents). That larger clutch sizes
do not necessarily result in more young was shown
by Lack (1966). He found that in the European
swift, *Apus apus*, the clutch-size number has not
become fixed by evolution and the clutch size
varied from one to three eggs. It was found that
the average number of young that survived to
the fledgling state for 2-egg clutches was 1.9,
for 3-egg clutches 2.3, and for artificially increased 4-egg clutches 1.4. So those females
producing two eggs were better off than those
with four. Lack found that the number of young
the parents were able to rear varies with the
weather. A great proportion of the larger broods
(of three) survived in good summers when there

Table 7.1. Total Population

Generation	If All Survive But 1 Generation	If All Survive 1 Year But Produce Only Once	If All Survive 1 Year and All Females Produce Each Generation
1	120	120	120
2	7,200	7,320	7,320
3	432,000	439,320	446,520
4	25,920,000	26,359,320	27,237,720
5	1,555,200,000	1,581,559,320	1,661,500,920
6	93,312,000,000	94,893,559,320	101,351,520,120
7	5,598,720,000,000	5,693,613,559,320	6,182,442,727,320

Table 7.1 Projected populations of the housefly, *Musca domestica,* for one year
which is made up of seven generations. The numbers are based on the female
laying 120 eggs per generation and half of these developing into females. (from
Edward J. Kormondy, *Concepts of Ecology,* © 1969, Prentice-Hall, Inc., Englewood
Cliffs, N.J., p. 63.)

was an abundance of insects. In poorer years, clutch sizes of two proved more successful.

Cullen (1957) reasons that selection has allowed for mortality of young in some species. Gulls, which suffer high predation, may normally only be able to feed two young successfully, but they often lay three eggs since at least one of the young is likely to fall prey. In the kittiwake, a gull which nests on cliffs and does not suffer from predation, the usual clutch size is two. Other clutch-size adaptations to predation may also be operating. For some prey species of gulls, smaller clutch sizes may make the brood less conspicuous to hunting predators. The preyed-upon gull, *Furcatus*, lays but one egg and compensates behaviorally by nesting in cycles of less than twelve months (Hailman 1965).

It is obviously more advantageous in terms of biological fitness to rear large broods, so why do small broods appear in so many bird species? The answer may lie in the time that is needed to raise broods of various sizes. The same quantity of food can raise a small brood quickly or a large brood slowly. Rapid development of young is imperative in areas where the nesting season (or period of food abundance) is short—such as in polar regions. Also, where risk of predation is high the young are more vulnerable while in the nest. High predation, of course, reduces the number of those utilizing the food supply; so, with the resulting increase in available food, it might be expected that larger broods would appear where clutch size is dictated by predation rather than by a short season. There are no data to support such a hypothesis at this time however.

In species which have relatively precocial offspring (advanced, able to run about and feed independently soon after hatching, so that parental feeding is not necessary), clutch size probably is a function of the food available to the laying female. More food means more nutrient material which can go into egg production while still maintaining the female. However, it should be noted that moulting (feather replacement) begins and

egg laying stops while food is still abundant, so egg laying is not entirely dependent upon food. This is not to say, of course, that egg laying could not be *initiated* by high food levels and that the bird might fail to respond to the same stimulus later in the season.

The size of the egg is probably of great importance to precocial species since a large egg means more food for the embryo and therefore hatching can occur at a relatively advanced stage of development. This advantage must be weighed against the increased strain on the female in developing large eggs. A very large egg, with a very exhausted mother, is at no advantage; so where eggs are larger, fewer may be laid, all other things being equal.

Since the number of offspring attempted is so strongly affected by food abundance, there must be different strategies for species which have an abundant and relatively constant supply, those which are subject to regularly fluctuating (seasonal) supply, and those with an irregular food supply. As an example of an adaptation to the last consider the frigate bird, *Fergata minor*, which breeds in the Galápagos Islands. It is believed that its food supplies are erratic and nonseasonal and that a peculiar breeding pattern has resulted. The frigate birds have long incubation periods; the young develop slowly and have the ability to fast if necessary; they leave the nest at a relatively advanced stage and they are fed by the parents for extended periods even after they can fly. The latter trait may be an adaptation to give the young a chance to learn the fine art of piracy (robbing other birds of their catches). Finally, the birds breed only every other year and so the drain on the parents and on the food supply is reduced (Nelson 1967).

In a competitive system, the number of young appearing on the scene each year can be expected to have an effect on the mortality rate of the population and the arguments of the precise relationship can become rather esoteric. Lack, for example, believes that the evolutionary process has resulted in attempts to produce as many young as possible each season, and that the mortality rate is adjusted to the reproductive rate. On the other hand, Alexander Skutch, a noted field ornithologist, suggests that in the tropics more young are not attempted because of low adult mortality in these areas of the world. It has been suggested that the two concepts are not entirely incompatible (Fretwell 1969).

The occurrence of multiple broods in times of high food abundance provides important evidence of the strong relationship between available food and the number of offspring attempted. Lack (1954, 1966) provides references to such correlations. (Lisa Salmon, the "Bird Lady" of Jamaica, told me how she provided food for a pair of Jamaican woodpeckers while they raised three successive broods.)

Another consideration is raised by Professor Wynne-Edwards (1962) who believes birds may not lay as many eggs as possible, but that, instead, they practice a form of "birth control" at high density. The concept entails a form of "group selection" where selective mechanisms move to enhance the welfare of the group rather than the individual. The implications are contrary to our idea of fitness where each individual contributes as many genes as possible to the population at the expense of others. Wynne-Edwards has been roundly criticized (cf. Lack 1966), but so far the question, by its very nature and the current limitations of our research techniques, has firmly resisted final resolution. This is not to say there are not those willing to take up a position and argue vehemently enough to convince some that the data *are* in.

There is another interesting way the reproductive rate can be depressed—one which has interesting implications for man. High population density may depress reproductive success. At high densities, mammals may show depressed reproductive success (Christian 1963). The effect is rare in birds, but Lack (1958, 1966) found reduced clutch sizes at higher breeding densities

in great, blue, and coal tits (*Parus major, P. caeruleus, P. ater*), and others have reported similar findings for other species. Kluyver (1963) also found fewer females attempting second broods in high-density years. The mechanism by which such a control could operate is not clear, but some have attempted physiological explanations. For example, the effect of social stimuli upon gonad development has been shown for several species of birds (cf. Phillips 1964).

There are those species, also, whose life histories are such that selection has left them with one directive, "Lay as many eggs as possible." An example is the tapeworm, which lives attached to its host's intestines. It is capable of self-fertilization and, as new segments are developing behind the head region, the mature ones at the tail section are virtually bulging sacks of eggs which drop off and pass out with the host's feces. The risks are so high for these eggs however, that few will find their definitive hosts. Probably intestinal parasites come closer than any other animal (besides perhaps queen termites) to realizing their full biotic potential.

Geography may also affect how many offspring may be attempted by any species. Tropical and temperate zone influences on reproductive strategies are discussed in the following chapter.

POPULATION CONTROL THROUGH MORTALITY

Another way populations can be regulated is through the deaths of members of the group (although there is no intention to imply that regulation occurs through any single factor or that an either-or effect is operating). In living systems complexity is the rule, and it is probable that any regulation of numbers occurs through a variety of mechanisms. Regulation through mortality operates, primarily, in five possible ways: abiotic (such as through severe weather); ecological (such as in competition for food); behavioral (such as in competition for territories or nest sites); and through disease, parasitism, and predation. The first, abiotic control, is primarily of interest to students of behavior in that changes in numbers, by whatever means, affect competition. The rest may be considered together as biotic influences on populations.

Abiotic Control

It is well known that certain species fall off drastically in numbers at predictable times each year. Annual plants, for example, usually die each fall and only the seeds are carried into the next season. Some animal species suffer the same fate (Kormondy 1969). You may have noticed sluggish and dying grasshoppers on your lawn as the nights grow colder and winter draws on. In winter, their numbers are reduced to virtually zero as their hope lies in overwintering eggs. The following spring will initiate a period of rapid population growth until a peak is reached; after that the first animals begin to die in response to the coming of the next winter. The result is a population-growth curve of rather regular peaks and depressions.

Just as seasonal weather change can alter population numbers, so also can irregular or unusual weather patterns. Extreme drought may kill large parts of populations of plants and animals. Many birds have perished because they started their northward migration in spring only to be caught by a late cold snap.

It is important to realize that population change brought about by such factors is not affected to any great extent by population numbers or density. The parching sun can destroy a whole field as easily as a single plant. Such influence on populations is called *density-independent control.*

Probably the best known study indicating the operation of density-independent control is a 14-year program involving a tiny insect, *Thrips imaginis,* which lives on roses (Davidson and Andrewartha 1948 a,b). The study reveals that the population size of *Thrips* was related to the weather and was independent of the population density. The conclusions have, however, been criticized by other ecologists (Solomon 1957; Nicholson 1958; Smith 1961).

Dobzhansky (1950) proposed an interesting hypothesis regarding geographic influences on population control. He wrote that in temperate zones (see Chapter 8), mortality is relatively independent of the genetic makeup, the behavior, or the morphology of the animals and, furthermore, that mortality is not greatly affected by population density. He reasoned that temperate conditions are so severe that deaths are more often caused by weather than by competition. The adaptive response, then, should be to increase the reproductive rate of individuals at the possible expense of rearing "quality" young; leave as many offspring as possible since density independent factors are operating (this is called "*r*-selection"). In the more hospitable tropics, he believes, a greater percentage of the young could be expected to survive so most mortality would be due to other factors, such as the results of competition. Therefore, natural selection should constantly be moving toward making the individual better adapted for competitive interaction (this is called "*k*-selection"). The evolutionary accent, then, under more constant conditions, is on the quality of the individual, not on mass reproduction. Pianka (1970) notes that in the tropics birds lay fewer eggs and development is slower; therefore, through natural selection apparently, parents increase their fitness by prolonged care of the young which should then be better able to compete.

Density-independent or abiotic population control is not as distinct from what we will term biotic control as might be indicated here. Andrewartha (1961) is quite correct in pointing out that population density has no meaning unless it is considered in perspective to other characteristics, including the abiotic ones, of the habitat. For example, normally a population declines in density near the boundary of its habitat. The reason may be because the peripheral areas are not entirely satisfactory, due, for example, to some character of the habitat such as an increasingly rocky terrain. Usually, the decline of one population in any direction is accompanied by an increase in numbers of another species better adapted to that type of habitat; and so competition may increase in such areas and reduce numbers. The abiotic environmental influence may be more obvious in another example. The red-bellied woodpecker ranges from the East Coast to central Texas. Its western boundary is partly determined by a change in vegetation-type and partly by the appearance of the golden-fronted woodpecker in Texas; but competition, of course, does not satisfactorily explain its absence off the Carolina coast. Density, then, is only meaningful in the context of environmental variables.

Living organisms can, by their presence, alter the environment so that abiotic control increases its influence. The concept will not be discussed here, but the interested reader is referred to a paper by A. J. Nicholson (1957).

In discussing abiotic-control mechanisms, we cannot neglect the influences of man's ability to alter his environment far beyond his natural biological impact. It has already been demonstrated that so many dangerous chemicals have been added to the air, especially over large cities, that increased mortality rates in these areas have resulted—affecting primarily the very young, the very old, and the ill (Ehrlich and Ehrlich 1968). The Ehrlichs also describe a 1968 report by UNESCO, which states that within about twenty years this planet may be uninhabitable for man because of the quality of the air. We have *already* deposited so much mercury into our waters that by the time it has all been altered biologically, its effect may render most of the earth's water dangerous to human consumers. There is evidence that we have drastically altered weather patterns over large metropolitan areas. But for the most part, the warnings by our scientists about what we are doing have resulted in little more than some families changing to white toilet tissue. Man's phenomenal powers to alter the environment may soon bring the real meaning of density-independent mortality into sharp focus.

Biotic Control

In the discussion of the control of animal numbers one must keep clearly in mind the type of animal being considered and the various possible interactions of control mechanisms. Lack (1954) stated that numbers of birds, carnivorous mammals, certain rodents, large fish (where not fished), and a few insects are limited by food, and numbers of gallinaceous birds (which "scratch" for food), deer, and plant-eating insects (which comprise most of the world's species) are limited by predators or parasites. Lack probably should have given more weight, in his early book, to the population-limiting effects of territoriality and dominance hierarchies for reasons discussed below. It has also been pointed out (Hairston et al. 1960) that there can be no single model to describe population control because the control may be different depending on what trophic level is being considered (whether decomposer, plant, predator, etc.). This last paper has generated strong criticism from Murdoch (1966).

Lack (1970) presents four main points in his argument for food as the limiting factor in populations of birds: (1) Apparently few adults die of predation or disease. (2) Birds are usually more numerous where food is more abundant (Figure 7.1). Seabirds are scarce in the tropics, for example, except in the plankton-rich Humboldt Current. If warmer waters shift into the region the plankton die and so do the fish and the birds. (3) Birds living in the same habitat depend on different food sources (discussed in Chapter 8). When a food is superabundant, different species may forage in more similar ways and (4) fighting for food occurs more often in winter, a time of low food supply. He states that although food limits population density in most birds and a few other types of animals, there are species which are held in check by other mechanisms, such as predation, and which therefore rarely reach the food barrier.

Lack is undoubtedly correct in stressing the importance of food as a population regulator. Birds are so sensitive to food level that it may be possible to assess the abundance of food by observing the birds' behavior (Stenger 1958; Kear 1961; Kress 1967; Kilham 1958b; Wallace 1969; Ward 1965). There are those who argue that the available food is probably never depleted, or is sufficient throughout most of the year, and food, therefore, cannot be a significant factor in population control. But others (cf. Willis 1966) point out that bird populations are undoubtedly regulated by the *lowest* amount of food present during the course of the year. Lack agrees that food probably does not exert its population-limiting effect on many species throughout the year as it does in winter. Interestingly enough, if there is a lag between food increase and its utilization, there probably is a food surplus through most of the year. The role of food competition as a population-limiting factor is discussed by Hutchinson (1957) and

Watson (1970), evidence being presented for and against.

Too often, discussions center on whether one type of factor or another is operating in population regulation. Arguments, again sometimes seem to imply an unrealistic either/or situation. As an example of the complexities of the question, Crook (1970) stresses that in one period the key factor could be extrinsic, such as food; in another, the critical factor could be an intrinsic social one such as territorial behavior. There is some evidence, also, that significant population regulation may occur through a number of factors at the same time, although one may be more important than another (Watson and Moss 1970).

Where populations are regulated through mortality rates, the determinants can interact in a compensatory manner so that if the effects of one increase, another may decrease. When guppies, *Lebistes reticulatus*, were artificially culled from a population, cannibalism—the guppy answer to

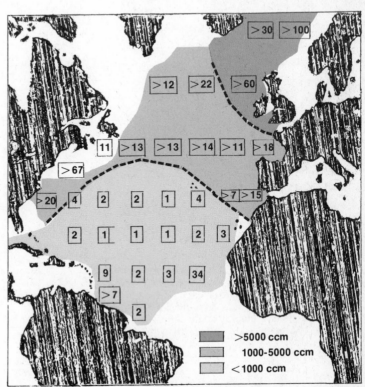

Figure 7.1 Seabird numbers as related to macroplankton density in the Atlantic Ocean. The shading of particular areas indicates the density of macroplankton. The numbers in the boxes indicate the number of seabirds observed in that area each day. By comparing the two, we can see the relationship of seabirds to the density of the macroplankton. (After Jesperson 1929.)

overpopulation—decreased, and vice versa (Watson and Moss 1970).

Nicholson (1933, 1954) suggested that the stability of natural populations could only be accounted for through a system involving the effects of living things upon each other. He explained how such a system might work in terms of *density-dependent* control. The theory is that an increasing population will increase indefinitely unless it is controlled by some factor which increases its depressing effect as the population increases. Conversely, a decreasing population will become extinct unless its controlling influence reduces its pressure as the population gets lower. Obviously, the most likely type of entity which could show such sensitivity to population numbers is a living one—such as a predator. Abiotic control could not be expected to operate in such a fashion. In times of drought, as a population decreased, the sun could not be expected to respond by reducing its effect.

What has come to be the conventional view of density-dependent mortality involving food supply, territories, hierarchies, disease, and predation is

reviewed by Lack (1954, 1966, 1970). The basic concept is not a difficult one. Let us examine how a prey species in times of high population numbers could be controlled through density-dependent mechanisms. First, as the prey species increased, so would its predators in response to an increased food supply. The predators could be expected to increase their success in the presence of abundant food through learning mechanisms (such as in the formation of search images and by spending more time searching the areas which had recently been productive). The prey species might put increased pressure on its own food supply and thus tend to reduce its own numbers. Its high-population density would increase the probability of parasites or disease spreading from one individual to another. The net effect of such pressures would be to lower the numbers of that prey. As their numbers lowered, their predators might starve or switch to different food sources thus relaxing pressure on the prey. The level of the prey's food would increase in response to reduced demand. Parasites and disease could not

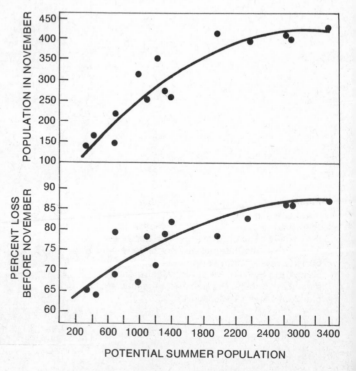

Figure 7.2 The population of the bobwhite quail, *Colinus virginianus,* and its losses by autumn. (From a census each April and November 1930-1943, from Errington 1945. *Ecological Monographs.* By permission of publishers.)

be transferred so easily as density decreased and so, at some point, the prey animal's numbers would begin to rise again.

The stability of animal numbers could most easily be accounted for by a system involving density dependence, but because of complexities such as the interaction of abiotic and biotic influences, such a system of control has been difficult to demonstrate. The difficulty in demonstrating density-dependent effect is compounded by the fact that such influences are not always reflected in the population immediately, thus impeding correlations.

Some data on density-dependent regulation of populations are available however. One type of evidence comes from field studies such as Errington's (1945) data involving a 15-year study of bobwhite quail in Wisconsin. He assumed the summer population to be ten times that of April, based on the number of first-year young that he found. These results (Figure 7.2) show that the higher the summer population, the higher the loss before November, i.e., the loss was density dependent (in this case due to changes in death-rate, not birth-rate). Lack (1968:117) demonstrated a different sort of density-dependent effect which is not apparent until considered on a long-term basis.

In a study of the feeding ecology of tits (Gibb 1954), it was found that food was especially short in midwinter and that possibly, then, mortality was more strongly related to density dependence at one season than another. High mortality could be expected in winter due to the density-independent effect of weather. But if the severe weather reduced the food supply so that a portion of the population starved, then the weather could heighten the effects of a density-dependent regulation. Here, we have not only an interaction of regulating factors, but the possibility of a shift in dominance of one to the other according to the season.

On the basis of a study of two species of barnacles occupying adjacent intertidal strata along a rocky shore, it was determined that the lower lim-its of the species occupying the higher zone, *Chthamalus stellatus*, was largely set by the action of biotic factors including competition for space with the species, *Balanus balanoides,* which occupied the adjacent lower zone. *Balanus* was able to crowd out *Chthamalus* by virtue of its higher population density and faster growth. In some cases *Balanus* more directly influenced *Chthamalus* by covering, smothering, or undercutting the latter. Whereas *Chthamalus* was limited in the lower part of its range by biotic factors, in the upper reaches it was limited by abiotic factors such as heat and desiccation at low tide (Connell 1961). So here is a clear example of a species being limited in different parts of its range by entirely different factors.

Density-dependent regulation can fail under certain conditions. Our own species has provided us with one of the clearest examples of such failure. The great whales have been so sharply reduced in number over the past few decades that, at present, their numbers are dangerously small and a few species have been placed on the endangered list. The demand for whale products has not diminished however, especially in Japan, and the whaling fleets continue to exert their depressing effect on the whale populations. A clearer example is provided by the fishing industry. In spite of increasing worldwide efforts to catch fish, the catches have begun diminishing. No relaxation of pressure is likely to take place however because of the needs of the world's burgeoning population, and fishing efforts are actually being increased. Perhaps man provides poor examples of animal behavior because of his unique position, but he sometimes beautifully illustrates certain points by behaving in ways no other animal will.

Predation

Alas, in the often paradoxical world of nature the expected does not always occur. In what is seemingly contrary to what we have learned we find, for example, that predation can actually increase prey numbers. Lack (1968) reports that when fishermen (acting biologically as predators) take larger fish, the result is an increase in the number of young fish which are able to mature. Then breeding begins earlier and more eggs are laid. The result is an increase in numbers of fish (when *overfishing* occurs, of course, numbers are reduced). This example merely serves to point out the complexity of predator-prey interaction. Such results would only occur in those species which are limited by food and which are so abundant that moderate predation does not bring the population below the level where food can exert its limiting effect.

The complexity of predator-prey interaction can also be seen in a hypothetical example from birds, which probably take small percentages of any prey in spring when many prey-species are available but almost all in winter when there are fewer prey-species. Any food-effect on the bird-population, then, is exerted in winter. The numbers of the prey, such as spruce beetles, are limited by the birds' foraging success in winter. So strong seasonal effects are operating. As pressure is put on the birds they, in turn, put pressure on the beetles in winter. As a result, whereas depressions in numbers may coincide in the two species in the same area at the same time, they may be regulated by entirely different density-dependent mechanisms (here, food and predation).

In certain cases, density-dependent effects can alter their relative effects on numbers. Lack (1968) gives examples of insects, which are normally held in check by predators and parasites but which occasionally "overpower" these restraints and increase to their food barrier.

In our previous example of a decrease in prey numbers resulting in the starving of predators or in their switching to different food sources, there lies the essence of another important law of nature: a predator does not eliminate its prey. There are stories, in the annals of recent histories, of introduced species wiping out their prey. For example, the mongoose, introduced onto the island is locally given credit for the absence of poisonous snakes in Puerto Rico, and the introduction of the wild boar is said to be responsible for the annihilation of reptiles on Belle Isle in the Detroit River. Such accounts are almost always anecdotal in nature and, unless such circumstances involved a defenseless, exposed, and available prey which was attacked by predators sufficient in number to decimate the prey in a very short period of time, probably no such event ever occurred

There are certain characteristics which function importantly in determining whether any species is a candidate for limitation by predators. Some prey animals are more dangerous, cryptic, elusive, or aware than others, and this may discourage predators from relying too heavily on them. They may constitute a meager, but relatively constant part of a predator's diet, however, and therefore figure importantly in maintaining predator numbers. More available prey may, by their very availability, be quickly removed as an important part of the predator's diet.

The degree of reduction in predator numbers as its prey dwindles depends on certain characteristics of the predator. For example, a predator which forages in a rigid or stereotyped manner is more likely to be influenced by its prey's numbers than one which is more flexible. Switches in prey are made more easily by some species than by others, depending on several factors including what sorts of prey are around, the predators' innate restraints (see Chapter 3) and their abilities to learn and to utilize insight.

Certain types of predators tend to exert more pressure on their prey than others as a function of their hunting technique. A predator can be characterized, for example, according to whether it hunts by olfaction or vision. Visual hunters might be expected to take more of their prey when that prey reaches low numbers (Holling 1959). To show the importance of predator characteristics on prey limitation one might consider the entirely different results predicted by two opposing theories which assume differences in appetite and prey-finding abilities of predators (Thompson 1939; Nicholson 1933).

In Slobodkin's "How to be a Predator" (1968), he suggests that in an optimal system a predator would take primarily those animals which were about to die anyway so as to alter the natural pattern of mortality as little as possible. Thus the optimal prey would be old ones—or young ones which have not yet reproduced. Young should only be taken, of course, if they are subject to high mortality and would probably have died anyway. Such an idea is supported by Errington's (1956) theory that predators take those in excess of the carrying capacity of the environment (the ones that would probably succumb even in the absence of predators).

Errington describes two entirely different types of predation: *compensatory* and *noncompensatory*. The former refers to situations in which predators take a heavy toll of certain segments of a population when the prey density exceeds a certain level. Compensatory predation could function in those cases in which a limited number of hiding places or nest holes are available so that, when the population of prey rises above a certain threshold level, some individuals are forced into less optimal and more exposed areas where they are more likely to fall prey. The concept is important to the discussion of the regulatory function of territoriality in this chapter.

Noncompensatory predation operates when no segment of the prey population is more available than others. Such behavior may be visualized in the interaction of wolves and deer. The wolves apparently *search out* deer in an intelligent, selective manner. There are probably differences in the learning abilities of animals which specialize in each of the two types of predation.

It has been mentioned that predator populations do not rise and fall in synchrony with their major prey populations. According to the classical theories of Lotka (1925), Volterra (1926), Gause (1934), and Nicholson and Bailey (1935), in undisturbed conditions, prey numbers rise steadily

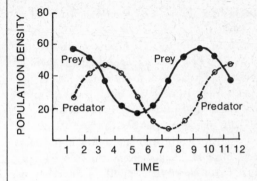

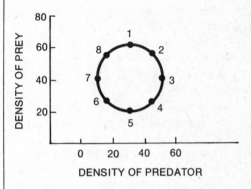

Figure 7.3 The theoretical relationships of predator and prey numbers according to the classical Lotka-Volterra oscillation. The top graph shows this plotted against time while the bottom graph shows it plotted against each other. (From G. F. Gause, *The Struggle for Existence*, Williams and Wilkins Co., Baltimore. © 1934.)

for several generations and then fall, while those of predators do the same but are a little behind in their timing (Figure 7.3). The generally accepted underlying principle seems sound and there is some evidence that such a pattern occurs in nature. As Varley (1947, 1953) interpreted the phenomenon, the death rate of the prey at any time varies with predator numbers and the latter is partly a function of the number of prey in the past. He described the phenomenon as a *delayed density-dependent effect*. The length of the delay in changes in the predator numbers, of course, is dependent to a degree upon the breeding characteristics of the predator. Fecund ferrets would be expected to show less delay than the slower breeding wolf.

It may be that population regulation, by whatever means, functions by "dampening" the oscillations rather than maintaining numbers within any particular range. The results may be similar, but the mechanisms are not. Such a dampening effect might conceivably occur in a number of ways. Let us consider one. The switching of predators to a different source for food when prey numbers are low functions as a dampening effect on fluctuation of prey numbers. When a variety of prey types is available, the number of each is likely to be more stable than if each were the primary food of a single predator. What happens to prey numbers when alternate prey is available, apparently, is that the numbers continue to fluctuate but not so widely. They do not reach the highs and lows that they would if they were a primary food supply of a predator and depended on the dwindling of predator numbers to reduce pressure on themselves. Obviously, predators which are able to switch food supplies would also tend to remain more stable in number since their food might never become severely reduced. As another example, Voûte (1946) found violent fluctuations in population numbers of insects in cultivated woods dominated by a single species of planted tree (see implications of simple habitats in Chapter 8). In mixed woods, where there was a greater abundance of alternate food for insectivores in the form of more species of insects, insect populations were more stable. There is a danger in wildly fluctuating populations that numbers might fall so low that the population might be unable to recover and extinction would result. It may be, then, that populations which have been around for some time are those which are subject to some dampening effect on their numbers.

Holling (1959) developed, by use of simulation models, four major tactics for population stability of both prey and predator. First, he theorized that an ideal predator is one which can alter its physiology so that at low prey densities reproduction does not fall off. One such predator (a pentatomid) lowered its metabolism when moved to a low diet, therefore more of its energies could be devoted to producing offspring.

Secondly, some predators are "wasters," killing all the prey at a single location. (A mink may destroy all the hens in a henhouse, but devour only one). Such animals normally hunt dispersed prey and have no innate inhibitor against wasting behavior. Others which normally hunt aggregated animals only kill one and, often, they return to the carcass until it is consumed (lions which hunt herds of ungulates are an example). It is apparent that stability will result only if each predator is primarily exposed only to its usual prey type.

The third concept is an interesting one and obvious when brought to light. If a primary predator (for example, a ferret) is, in turn, attacked by a secondary predator (for example, a hawk) the oscillations of predators and prey may become more stabilized.

And lastly, in cases of predators which do not attack randomly, increase in their numbers could result in multiple attacks on a single prey and help to stabilize prey oscillations. Random attack refers to an equal probability that any individual in the prey population will be attacked. If the probability is greater for some than others then the predator (or parasite for that matter) will have less overall effect on the prey numbers.

Parasitism

Because of the often more delicate relationship of parasites and hosts compared to that of predator and prey, we find an almost incredible array of specializations to maximize the benefits for the parasite while minimizing its effect on the host. Not only does the host sometimes serve as an ecological niche, as well as food (for example in the tapeworm), but in some cases the relationship has developed on a social basis which requires highly specific communication between the host and parasite (such as in ants and some of their insect parasites) as we shall see.

A parasite, of course, must have certain characteristics to qualify for the title. Basically, a parasite is a species which interacts with a host species and which derives benefit at the expense of its host. In other words, damage must be done. Since it is true that, usually, the host must remain alive in order to be of use to the parasite, it might seem that parasites would have little effect on population numbers. It is certainly true that in some cases little damage is incurred to the parasitized individual. Some small worms living in the intestines of mammals take nourishment from their host, but their needs are so small that the host is at no great disadvantage. The two species may live together for long periods with no apparent serious damage occurring. In other species, however, the parasite may directly or indirectly bring about the death of the host or the host's offspring. Parasites may weaken their host so that reproduction is decreased (resulting in fewer hosts for the next generation); or the weakened host may fall to predators (e.g., Cowan 1946). In either of the latter two cases the parasite loses as well as the host. In those situations in which the reproduction or vigor of the host is impaired, it may be assumed that the parasite is probably a relative newcomer to the host's world and has not yet completely adapted to the host's characteristics and that the host has not yet built up effective defenses against the parasite.

An example will point up the disastrous results which can occur when parasite and host are not well adapted to each other. In 1904, the sac fungus, *Endothia parasitica,* was accidentally introduced into North America. In China, from whence it came, it is held in check by a variety of control mechanisms which are not operating in North America. Sadly, the majestic American chestnut proved defenseless to the fungus, and by the late 1940s, the tree which had dominated our Appalachian forests was virtually extinct (Kormondy 1970). Americans are now witnessing the same sort of "devastation rather than regulation" as our elms are falling to the newly introduced Dutch elm disease.

Newly introduced predators are much less likely to cause the extinction of their prey, although their attacks are geared to result in death of the prey, because of the stronger operation of density-dependent effects when the attacker doesn't live within or on the attacked. There are certain other differences in the operation of predators and parasites. It is true that both are seeking out another animal and are, therefore, subject to some of the same influences of prey distribution and number. However, the securing of food for the predator often immediately ensures only its own success, while food for a parasite in many cases more directly functions in providing food for its progeny, usually in the formation of eggs. Also, the life history of the parasite probably must be more strongly coordinated with the habits of its host. Figure 7.4 illustrates the highly complex nature of the life history of one parasite and shows how the various components of the cycle (the aquatic species and the bird) must be in proper relation to each other in order for the offspring to mature successfully.

In our discussion of parasites we are primarily concerned with their effect on the numbers of their hosts. However, an interesting illustration may be taken from parasite populations themselves. Whereas a bird may lay only the number of eggs it should be able to hatch and rear successfully, the parasitic worms are not thus restricted.

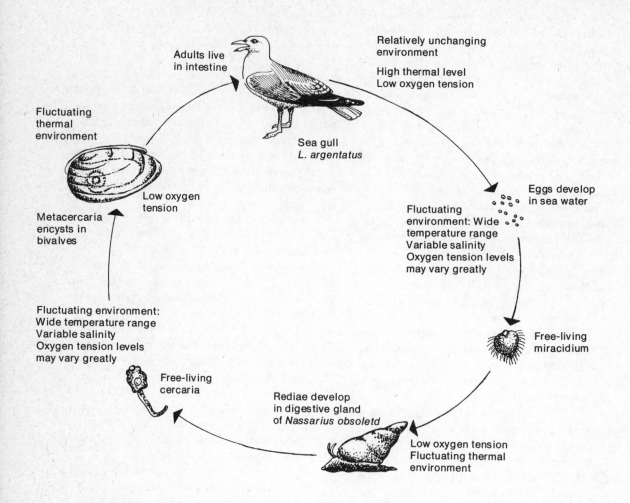

Figure 7.4 The complex life cycle of the trematode, *Himasthla quissentensis*.
Such complexity is not rare in the life histories of parasites. It is apparent that
each phase in the cycle has its own particular risks and that very few individuals
reach maturity. The reproductive solution to the high mortality rate in such species
is increased fecundity-maximizing egg laying. (From *The Animal and the Environment* by F. John Vernberg and Winona B. Vernberg. Copyright © 1970 by Holt,
rinehart and Winston, Inc. Reprinted by permission of Holt, Rinehart and Winston,
Inc.)

In order for a few eggs to hatch and the offspring to make it through the various types of environments (see Figure 7.4) thousands of eggs must be laid in a biotic game of chance. At different stages in the life cycle, the primary population regulator may be different. For example, small fish probably prey on the various intermediate aquatic stages of many parasites which are regulated at this point by laws of density dependence, while the egg which passes out with the bird feces is, very likely, subject to density-independent effects such as drying by the hot sun.

Host species, of course, are continually developing defenses against their parasites through natural selection (see Osche 1962, 1966). As examples, grass frogs, toads, and Alpine salamanders free themselves of leeches by sitting in the sun, the heat of which the leeches cannot tolerate (Eibl-Eibesfeldt 1970). The amphibians are probably not too fond of the sun either, but those individuals that fail to sunbathe remain parasite infested and, therefore, probably sicken or die sooner than their fellows, and their non-sunbathing genes are therefore less likely to be represented in the next generation.

In leaf-cutting ants, *Atta cephalotes*, the larger ants cut circles of leaves and carry them back to the nest for use there. While the worker is involved in leaf cutting and carrying, it is vulnerable to attack from small parasitic flies of the *Phoridae* group, so representatives of the smaller minima caste "ride shotgun" on the leaf and snap at flies which draw too near (Figure 7.5).

Other species allow themselves to be cleaned by "cleaners." We have mentioned the rhinoceros and its tickbirds, and there is the fascinating example of the cleaner wrasses, small fish which maintain cleaner stations or "barber shops" in the sea. Normally hostile species gather at these stations and peacefully wait their turn to be cleaned of parasites.

In some cases the answer to parasitism might be increased specificity of recognition signals. An example of parasitic behavior permited by a

[A]

[B]

Figure 7.5 Defense against a parasitic fly, *Phoridae,* by a member of the caste of minima workers in the leafcutting ant, *Atta cephalotes.* In A, as a larger caste member cuts the leaf, the minima chases away a fly. As the carrier transports the leaf, B, the minima acts as a guard. (From I. Eibl-Eibesfeldt, 1967. "Concepts of Ethology and Their Significance for the Study of Human Behavior" in *Early Behavior: Comparative and Developmental Approaches.* Edited by H. W. Stevenson. Wiley. New York. pp. 127-146.)

lack of specificity in communication is found in the slave-making ants. The fertilized queen of the red ant, *Formica rufa*, may enter the nest of the related *F. fusca* if she can't find a nest of her own species. The *fusca* ants are unable to distinguish her from one of their own species and, if no other queen is present, she will be adopted and cared for as their queen. All her eggs are her own species so the nest is soon entirely *F. rufa* (Eibl-Eibesfeldt 1970).

The fertilized queen of *F. sanquinea* has a more bizarre method of parasitizing her cousins. She is given to entering the nest of *F. fusca* and kidnapping a few of the larva. She defends the larva against recapture by the hosts and raises them herself. When they mature, they care for her as she lays eggs of her own species. For some reason, the host queen is later killed by her own offspring, but in any case, eventually the entire nest becomes *F. sanquinea*. The close evolutionary relationship of these species of ants probably has resulted in similar signaling devices and thus accounts for the fact that the queens are not attacked immediately when they enter foreign nests.

Finally, to illustrate the variety of population-altering interactions that can occur between parasites and hosts we consider the *brood parasite*. Brood parasites are species of birds which lay their eggs in the nests of other species and leave them to be cared for entirely (in most species) by the hosts. There are about 80 species of brood parasites and each has its own special methods of operation (Figure 7.6).

As fascinating examples of adaptive specialization in brood parasites, consider the parasitic cuckoos (as described by Lack 1968). When a female finds a nest at the proper stage of development she quickly lays one egg in the nest and flies away. (The cuckoo is a relatively large bird and one cuckoo chick is about all the host parents

Figure 7.6 Some examples of brood parasites and their hosts. (From Lack, *Biological Adaptations for Breeding in Birds*, Associated Book Publishers Ltd. 1968.)

Figure 7.7 A newly hatched and blind honeyguide, *Indicator indicator*, kills a barbet, *Lybius bidentatus*, the host nestling with special mandibular hooks on its bill.

can raise.) A syndrome of specializations for a parasitic life have arisen in the cuckoo, for example, in vocal communication. Cuckoos have a loud song, the advantage of which is related to their scarcity, and therefore, the sound must carry well. The sound is simple because the young cannot learn it from their own parents (innate patterns may lack embellishment). The song is also distinctive for species recognition where more than one species of cuckoo may be present.

At least one cuckoo species will destroy any nest that is too advanced for it to lay its eggs in. The result is that the parents begin a new nest. The cuckoo can then watch and wait until the nest is at the proper stage. When both parents are gone the cuckoo moves in. The females are able to lay eggs very quickly so that they can enter a nest, lay the egg, and leave before the parents return. Even hole-nesting species can be parasitized because the female cuckoo has an extensible cloaca and can therefore lay her heavy-shelled eggs into openings which she cannot enter.

Most cuckoo hosts will leave a nest in which an egg appears which is different from their own, or they may throw out the strange egg. Stephen Rothstein (1970) has described several behavioral, morphological, and ecological factors correlated with such rejection behavior. As a response to the hosts rejection, some cuckoos have evolved mimetic eggs. Even within a single cuckoo species, mimicking of different types of eggs may occur. One female of a given species may always lay eggs of one appearance, while another female consistently lays eggs of a different appearance. It is difficult to understand how such specializations could have arisen unless females imprint on a nest type or habitat type, and return to such nests or areas with some degree of persistence, so that distinct evolutionary lines can occur. Lack believes such a system could only be maintained by the male having no influence on the egg's appearance since, if he did, he might carry genes for mimicking a different type of egg and the system would break down. No matter what the appearance of the egg, it has a short incubation period and therefore usually hatches first, before the host's eggs. The young cuckoo is therefore stronger than its nest mates and is likely to direct more of its "parents'" attention to itself by its very vigor. In certain species, the brood parasite may attack the host nestlings or push them out of the nest (Figure 7.7).

It is interesting and not entirely unexpected, that young cuckoos often bear a striking resemblance to the young of their hosts (Figure 7.8) even to exhibiting special feeding releasers.

There are obvious differences in the effects of brood parasites and other types of parasites which derive their benefits directly at the expense of the parasitized animal. For example, brood parasites may kill their fellow nestlings whereas direct slaughter is unusual among the world of parasites. Brood parasitism represents an interesting example of an influence on populations, not through the effect on the host's immediate well-being, but through the adverse effects on its fitness. Here, the adult hosts suffer no individual or personal disadvantage (unless, perhaps, through the parasites' need for more care than their normal offspring required). They suffer instead through reduced fitness by failure to pass along their own genes.

There are a host of other behavioral characters which might get to influence population numbers. One of the more important is territoriality, as we shall see.

TERRITORIALITY

The first inklings that animals possessed anything like territorial behavior appeared in the writings of man hundreds of years ago, but were more or less neglected as a topic of scientific concern until, in 1920, Eliot Howard wrote his book *Territory in Bird Life*. After watching birds expel each other from certain areas, and trying to understand why they behaved in such a way, Howard gave two major functions of the phenomenon as (1) a requirement for pair formation and maintenance, and (2) a population density regulator which ensured food for the young. The vigorous and continuing debate over the function, and even over the definition, of territory is testimony to the depth of the problem (or to our ineptitude in such matters). The appearance of territorial behavior in widely diverse animal species and the variety of ecological and social contexts in which it is found indicates a high general adaptiveness of the phenomenon and suggests that no easy answers will be forthcoming. Territoriality is a common pattern among reptiles, birds, and mammals and it occurs occasionally in amphibians and fish and

Figure 7.8 The fledgling of the brood parasite *Eudynamis scolopacea* have plumage which resembles that of *Corvus splendors,* (center) the species in whose nest they are hatched. (After Lack 1968.)

even among some invertebrates. The phenomenon has been most extensively investigated in fish, in the laboratory, and in birds, in the field.

We will define a territory in the usual broad sense by calling it *any defended area* without attributing to it any special properties that might prejudice our discussion of its effects. Territoriality has also been described as "space-associated intolerance" (Eibl-Eibesfeldt 1970), and it will become apparent that the intolerance is directed most strongly toward the most direct competitors. The high degree of similarity in territorial behavior of some vastly different species is surprising, but it encourages searching across species lines for general underlying adaptive themes. It should be pointed out, however, that the study is, at the same time, made more difficult by the appearance of very different territorial behavior in very similar animals. For example, the Norway rat, *Rattus norvegicus*, chases strange rats only on special paths which he has marked. On the other hand the brown rat, *Rattus rattus*, defends the entire area that is crossed by his paths (Telle 1966).

Let us examine a few of the basic characteristics of territories and territorial behavior. First, territories are rather specific areas and do not, as a rule, include all the places where an animal may wander. Even in highly territorial species the animals do not always defend all the area which they might visit. The area in which an animal might be found at any given time is called its *home range*. Home ranges may overlap and animals meeting within home ranges (but outside territories) do not fight. The hamster, *Cricetus cricetus*, defends its den and the area around it, but will retreat from other hamsters it may encounter out in the fields; baboons defend their "sleeping trees" and feeding grounds, but they meet peacefully with other troops at watering holes. Interestingly, the territory is not a geographically defined area for every species. Some animals carry their territories with them—"individual distances"—which other animals must not violate (discussed below).

In species which form pairs, and live apart from others of the species, the territories are usually defended by the male against other males. The female however may aid the male in the defense. In many species, she shows a special intolerance for other females (toward which the male may appear more amenable). At certain times, such as in winter, the sexes of some species may hold separate territories, each defending its own, but in spring they lower such hostility and come together for purposes of reproduction.

In some species, pairs may join together and defend a mutual territory in a community effort against members of other groups; in other species, the pairs live close together and defend small areas around their nests from other pairs; in yet other species the animals come together during the breeding season to form small temporary territories on a communal display ground. So territorial behavior includes a wide variety of observable phenomena.

The selective mechanisms for territoriality in species with various social patterns may be much the same. Brown (1964) counters arguments that the evolutionary origins are different in each case. He maintains that territorial aggression will be employed to defend commodities when they are dependable (available and accessible) and within certain cost limits (in terms of time and energy). So the underlying theme, then, would be one of economics. As Brown points out, natural selection would probably not favor territoriality when commodities are not accessible. For instance, when a food supply of a species cannot be defended because of its mobility or its transient nature, no territorial system is evolved to defend it, and any territory that develops in that species is likely to be restricted to the nest site. Certain species of birds such as colonial seabirds, nomadic and social feeding songbirds, and aerial feeders seem to lend credence to this explanation. In short, defendability figures importantly among determinants of territorial systems and defendability should be defined in terms of the time and energy budgets of the individual as well as the physical description of the habitat.

Before going into the evidence for the adaptiveness of territories, we should first consider a few general hypotheses which have been proposed. The functions which have been attributed to territoriality include (1) limitation of population and the insurance of space; (2) protection against predators, disease, and parasitism; (3) selection of the most vigorous to breed; (4) division of resources between dominant and subordinate individuals; (5) stimulation of breeding behavior; (6) reduction of fighting and stress; (7) increasing inbreeding (population selection) within groups; (8) regulation of group size; (9) ensurance of a food supply; (10) a means of signaling potential mates and rivals; (11) provision of a mating and nesting place; (12) a means of reducing time spent in aggression; and (13) increasing efficiency of habitat utilization of a familiar area. Already the enormity of the problem becomes apparent.

Of course, we must remember that just because territoriality originally developed on one basis is no reason to exclude the addition of other advantages, or the possibility that its adaptiveness may change. We must also keep in mind that the advantage it bestows on one species may not be assumed to be equally adaptive for all species, so, in effect, territoriality should be perused with an unprejudiced eye for each species. Apparently, territoriality offers similar advantages for many species; however, such similarity cannot be assumed. Klopfer (1969) also warns that the appearance of any activity of obvious advantage within a territory does not mean it appears as a *function* of territoriality.

It may seem at this point that the vagaries and complexities of territoriality are too overwhelming to be considered competently in any brief synopsis, and that, in fact, is the case. However, our goals are modest. We will consider only a few environmental factors which may influence territories and territory holders, how territories may be demarcated, and, most importantly, how territories may influence populations.

Where, When, and How

First, it must be pointed out that territories are rather flexible entities and may be influenced in their formation and their size by a variety of ecological and evolutionary factors. For example, the structure of the habitat may determine territorial boundaries through *landmark influence*. A pair of nesting Puerto Rican woodpeckers claimed an entire wooded area which was surrounded by cultivated fields.

In some cases, as landmarks change, so may territories. A newly planted row of *Elodea* will be accepted by a cichlid fish as its territorial boundary even if it results in a decrease in size of his previous territory (Eibl-Eibesfeldt 1970). Saunders and Smith (1962) found that a population of brook trout could be almost doubled by adding physical structures to their habitat that provided extra territorial stations. Also, Watson (1964) found partridges have smaller territories in hillocky areas and larger ones in open flat ground (although the difference here may relate to food—see below).

Territories are rather evolutionarily labile entities. They are apparently easily changed or lost altogether by shifts in selective pressure. As evidence, recall the differences in the territories of the closely-related brown and Norway rats; or consider the scrub jay, which is aggressively territorial, and the closely-related Mexican jay, which maintains weakly-defended territories (Brown 1963). Whereas the morphologies and some social patterns of related species remain similar for long generations after the populations divide, territorial behavior may become quite distinct in the same period. *Site influence*, in its simplest sense, refers to the appearance of territorial behavior only at certain places, such as around the nests of some birds but not within the home range. Such influence operates in more subtle ways as well. Birds, for example, increase their aggressiveness as they near the specific area of the nest. Another example of this sort of influence may be seen in large wading birds, such as herons and egrets, which have both nesting and feeding territories. The nests are located near each other just out of the effective pecking range of the next pair. When the birds move to their feeding areas along streams, their aggression increases and the space between them widens (Festetics 1959). Site influences are graphically clear in some species which show unmistakably that their interests are focused on the site and not on its contents. For example, in some seal species territories are necessary to attract females. The male does not defend the female or hinder her from leaving, however, but he guards his territory zealously. In some gulls, their mates, young, and nest can be changed around without causing undue distress to the parent. Parental attachment and interest seems, rather, to be directed toward the area of the nest. Of course, such behavior would be totally unadaptive were it not for the fact that under normal conditions the odds are that the territory will hold commodities, mates, nests or aid in acquiring them.

Another type of lability may be due to *competitive influence*. Due to its operation, members of certain populations maintain small territories and high densities in some years, and are more sparsely distributed with larger territories in other years. Even in the same season an animal may decrease its territory size in response to the appearance of a particularly aggressive newcomer or increase it at the death of a neighbor. The term "competitive influence" actually encompasses several phenomena and through its broadness it sacrifices real utility. What is actually referred to here is the relationship between territory size and the number of competitors. As competition for territory increases, territories tend to become compressed. The number of competitors at any time, of course, is related to the food supply, present and past, and these considerations are the subject of much of the following discussion.

Time also figures importantly in territories. Many species which are territorial at one season may be gregarious at other times. Pairs of Puerto Rican woodpeckers maintain strongly defined territories in spring and in winter they move in flocks through the forested mountains. *Time influence* is critical in any concept of territory. Any area may be valueless at certain periods and the appearance of territoriality must coincide in time with the area's increase in worth.

In some species, territories may be maintained at times other than the breeding season and in some cases, territories are held year round. They may also vary in their nature over the year (such as when sexes hold separate territories in winter and joint ones in spring). In Costa Rica, hummingbirds solve certain time problems in an interesting manner. During the dry season they feed primarily on insects (a transient and mobile food of low "dependability") and do not hold territories. When the various flowers begin to bloom, each for a short time in the breeding season, the birds show short-term territoriality around whatever species of plants are flowering that month. Wolf (1970) concludes the hummingbirds entered the ecosystem secondarily and were forced into their territorial adaptations rather than having evolved with it. (He draws certain comparisons with the short-term territories which have been reported for North American hummingbirds during migration.)

Leyhausen (1965) observed that cats maintain temporally defined territories. Many male cats can use the same area but at different, well-defined times. There is a sequential ownership so that the owner at the time is retreated from and only those areas with old markings are considered safe to enter.

Short-term territories are unusual in the animal world but we will refer to one more rather rare example of an interesting time factor. In Costa Rica, three species of hummingbirds came to a certain species of tree every morning and moved about freely, showing no territoriality. As the day wore on, however, territorial behavior began to emerge, with each species maintaining a certain dominance-subordination relationship with the others, and about mid-afternoon, all species would abandon their territories and leave (Stiles and Wolf 1970). Such behavior is a good example of time-influenced territoriality since the value or position of the area has not changed; only time has.

We should also consider winter territories although these are relatively unusual. In the European robin, for example, individual territories are maintained in autumn and early winter. These areas are held primarily by males. The few females that hold such territories abandon them when pairs are formed (Lack 1943a). Similar types of territories are held by other species which often exclude species other than their own (Rooke 1947; Lack 1968; Hartley 1949; Simons 1951). Lack (1968) points out that some species may defend winter territories, not for their immediate value, but to ensure their ownership in the breeding season later on.

Of course, if territoriality is to function with any degree of efficiency, the defended areas must be marked somehow so that other individuals will be aware of the ownership. We discussed many such "announcements" in Chapter 6. As we saw, territories may be marked in a number of ways including visually, acoustically, and chemically. Let us review a few examples of communication used directly in territory advertisement.

One of the commonest forms of territorial display involves visual advertisement which includes posturing, movement, and aerial displays (in flying animals). Visual territorial displays often involve threat patterns since the recipient must be close enough to see the signaler and, therefore, such displays have a high competitive value.

Sound furnishes another medium through which territory ownership can be advertised. We are familiar with the song elicited in territorial male birds by other males. Other territorial sounds include the growl of the toadfish, the roar of the bull alligator, and the chirp of the male cricket (Moulton 1956; McIhenney 1935; Alexander 1957; Haskell 1957). Some animals make their territorial sounds in the absence of such stimuli as the appearance of a competitor or the onset of a di-

urnal period. Many birds, for example, sing without sighting another male. The reason could be because they are not obvious types of animals as they occupy their territories and cannot rely on being easily detected by other animals. They are also mobile animals, and a transient male might suddenly appear in a territory and increase the likelihood of a fight unless the territory is continually advertised.

Several species—mostly mammals with their well-developed sense of smell—mark territories with special scents (see Burkhardt et al. 1967). The badger, marten, and mongoose deposit gland secretions from the base of their tails; some ungulates (cloven-hoofed mammals) utilize hoof glands, and some rabbits use both chin and anal glands. The giant galago, a primate, urinates on the palms of its hands and rubs it into the soles of its feet and walks about on its territory. The brown bear urinates near its boundary, rolls in the urine, and then rubs against trees. The little Madagascan tanrec hedgehog spits on the place it wants to mark, wets a paw in it, scratches itself on the rump and rubs its scent on the object (which may be its keeper!). Territorial dogs may register their size by urinating on some object as high as they can. If a strange dog can't urinate as high as the previous dog he may leave the area. (If only man could solve his disputes with even this degree of elegance.)

Some mammals may even mark their mates as their property. The male tree porcupine, *Erethizontidae*, rushes toward his female on his hind legs and unceremoniously drenches her in urine. Short-headed flying phalangers, *Petaurus breviceps,* mark their territories with urine, but graciously use special glands to mark their mates. The sexes of clans or tribes may mark each other so that an odor-spectrum specific to the group develops in which the odor of strong males predominates.

Scent-marking may act also as a means of reassuring the owner of an object or territory, thus imparting a certain home-related confidence. A frightened badger in a strange environment can be calmed by letting it sniff a previously marked object (Eibl-Eibesfeldt 1970). The smell of a strange mark elicits hostile behavior in males of several species of mammals and probably has a repelling effect on intruders.

Territorial signals may be closely associated with mating behavior. In some birds, courtship is often interspersed with attacks as the male oversteps the fine line separating the two patterns. Males which overstep too often, of course, drive the female away and so do not contribute as greatly to the next generation as those males able to properly channel their aggression. The two types of signals, territorial and mating, are not identical in all species. For example, closely related species living in the same area may utilize common territorial signals since they are strong competitors, but different mating signals since hybridizing is usually unadaptive. As an example, the red-bellied woodpecker, *Centurus carolinus*, and the golden-fronted woodpecker, *C. aurifrons*, are very similar in appearance and vocalization, and where they come together along narrow bands in the Southwest, they maintain mutually exclusive territories, but they do not interbreed, so the two types of signals must be separate and distinguishable.

The Effects of Territory on Numbers

Now that we have some idea of the nature of territoriality, let us consider the role of the phenomenon in the regulation of population numbers. The problem is a difficult one, in large part because of the diversity of territorial behavior, some examples of which are described by Lack (1968).

Territoriality, as mentioned, must have a high adaptiveness because it occurs so widely and because it persists in spite of some of its serious drawbacks. It probably results in higher risk of predation for the territory holder through his conspicuousness in advertising. Time and energy is required to maintain a territory and therefore less time can be allotted for other pursuits of life such as courting, grooming, and resting. In sum, the cost of territoriality places the individual at certain disadvantages which can be expected to lower the population numbers to some degree. However, we are not overly interested in population *numbers* since for many ecological purposes the actual numbers have little relevance; we are concerned with population *density*, or the number of individuals per unit area. In a system of limited resources, it is important to consider how many organisms are utilizing those resources and how that number is reached.

The argument over the role of territoriality in population density is far from over. For recent reports on birds which purport to show such a role, see Jenkins, Watson, and Miller (1963) on grouse and ptarmigan; Delius (1965) on skylarks; Tompa (1964) on song sparrows; and Patterson (1965), and Coulson (1968) on colonial seabirds. Lack (1954, 1966, 1970) seems to be increasingly willing to accept the role of territory in population regulation; on the other hand, Brown (1969) critically assesses the available data and concludes there is no justification for some of the sweeping generalizations which have been made regarding the population-regulating effect of territoriality; Watson and Moss (1970) believe that territoriality is important in population limitation, but they stress that the evidence is, so far, circumstantial, indirect and inconclusive.

Probably no one believes that any single factor regulates population size. It is apparent that any such regulation by territoriality must operate with a number of other factors including food supply, avoidance behavior, weather, and habitat structure. In this discussion we are concerned with the role and relative importance of territorial behavior in this complex, but it must be admitted that more information is sorely needed before comprehensive statements can be made.

One of the first questions to be asked is whether territorial behavior acts to *disperse* populations thereby resulting in a spacing out of animals. It is true that in some cases once territories have been established there is "no room" for additional animals. After a certain number of territories were established by sticklebacks in a tank, no other males experimentally added could get territories (Van den Assem 1967). Kalleborg (1958) found that, at high densities, some male trout and salmon were unable to obtain territories and were constantly chased by territory holders. Studies of several species (Crook 1970) indicate that territories may cause nonbreeders (those unable to get a territory) to move to less optimal areas. The result of such movement is to lower population density as individuals move out of territories and, as a result, to lower the population number. The latter may occur for two reasons. First, some animals are kept from breeding. Second, territories are preferred sites and nonterritory holders must therefore occupy suboptimal sites; this means they may find less food or suffer higher predation because of a lack of hiding places. Watson and Moss (1970) give an extensive bibliography of work which shows that for a number of species population may be regulated by dispersal or by dispersal and mortality combined.

In some species, the unsuccessful bidders for territory do not move into suboptimal areas, but remain in the area to compete with the landowners surreptitiously and to be able to move into a territory should a vacancy occur. In such a system, territoriality might have a reduced effect on population regulation since the optimal area is shared rather than having some members exiled to inferior habitats. On the other hand regulation might operate through the territory owners' finding less food due to heavy competition with nonbreeders, therefore attempting fewer offspring, and through the continued inability of nonterritorial birds to breed. It has been shown (by Stewart and Aldrich 1951 and by Hensley and Cope 1951) that in birds when territory holders were shot, new males immediately moved in, took over the territories, and began to breed. They were previously unable to breed although food was abundant. So we see emerging three possible population-regulative effects of territorial behavior: populations might be limited by high death rates because some individuals are forced into a suboptimal habitat; because a certain part of the population is prohibited from breeding; and because of a reduced fecundity of territory holders due to time and energy spent in territorial pursuits. But the picture is not yet entirely clear because there is little hard evidence. Much of the earlier data purporting to show such regulation has been imprecise and misinterpreted.

Chitty (1967) suggests a genetic basis for population regulation which has been widely discussed, but for which there is, as yet, little real evidence. His explanation is that population declines are caused by genetic selection for aggressive individuals which are at an advantage in crowded populations, but are generally less viable in other ways. This is balanced at low densities by selection for less aggressive, but more fecund, individuals.

Brown (1969), in trying to make some sense of the tremendous amount of often sketchy information available, has defined territoriality in birds at three levels based on relative population densities. He figures that at low densities, territory sizes are not limited by competition and no birds are prevented from nesting in good habitats. At middle densities, some birds are excluded from preferred habitats, but may utilize poorer habitats. In such cases a *buffer effect* may be operating. Kluijver and Tinbergen (1953) described the effect in titmice in mixed woods where food is abundant. These birds held territories of rather stable sizes year after year and drove other titmice into adjacent woods where food was less abundant. In the pine woods the territory sizes varied widely from year to year as a function of the population numbers. When population numbers were high, territories in the pine woods were necessarily small. The pines are considered unbuffered areas while the mixed woods are buffered. It must be pointed out that the buffer principle has not yet been widely demonstrated.

At high densities, some birds are prevented from breeding anywhere, and they set up a breeding surplus or reserve which exists in and around territories or on separate ground. It is under such conditions that the elimination of territorial birds is followed by immediate occupancy of the territory, as was discussed. This sort of data has been used as support for the theory that territoriality limits the size of the breeding population since, apparently, there are prospective territory holders lurking in the vicinity which have been kept from breeding.

The degree to which failure of some males to breed affects population numbers depends on the social structure of the species. For example, among the great reed warblers, *Acrocephalus arundinaceus*, males driven out of the optimal areas may set up territories in suboptimal regions where it is impossible for any females they might attract to build nests. Rather than attempt to breed with these unsuccessful males, the females return to the optimal areas and mate with an already mated male who has a suitable territory (Kluijver 1951). So we see that the key to population regulation lies in how many *females* are excluded from breeding. The females cannot always choose an already-mated male, however. In many species established females eject newcomers (see Bustard 1970 for a report on an "intermediate" condition). Also, it wouldn't work if the welfare of the young depended upon assistance from the male parent. The fitness of all would be reduced if he attempted to spread himself too thin.

The individuals, usually males, which for some reason are excluded from breeding, comprise a "surplus" population, or a breeding reserve. Some of these are able to take their place in the breeding population at some later time and their addition to the reproductive community is termed *recruitment*. Recruitment is, in a more general sense, simply the addition of new breeding adults into the population. It is related to the number of young that survive to the breeding season and social phenomena such as hierarchy or territor-

iality which often dictate which individuals will be allowed to breed.

In some species the breeding surplus is hard to find. We have mentioned the rapid replacement of songbirds in their territories by males which were not apparent until the original owners had been shot. In other species the surplus is more easily defined. For example, when the nesting ground is limited in size, such as occurs for some colonial seabirds, those of lower rank may be forced to occupy nearby areas where they are not able to breed.

In some species of seals, such as those slaughtered in Pribilofs each year for fashion's sake, nonterritorial males group together in bachelor herds. These are usually young males which have not been able to obtain a territory and are therefore relatively unscarred until they die beneath the club. A young male which survives the yearly kill may be able to join the breeding population by aggressively displacing an aging bull through combat. The old bull may then join the surplus population where he is likely to remain until his death.

The alternative to "floating" among territories or establishing bachelor groups has already been mentioned. The unsuccessful bidder for an optimal territory may, perhaps, find a territory in another area. This recourse is common for those species in which permanent residents hold their territories so that the land is not "up for grabs" each year, and in those species in which status is reflected by the position as well as the possession of a territory, and in those which hold winter territories (Brown 1969). Lower ranked individuals thus increase their likelihood of survival by moving to areas with fewer pressures from superiors. Mass movements of such lower-ranked individuals are called *irruptions*. It seems apparent that the new areas which they find are not likely to be as desirable as the ones they left in terms of food abundance or predator danger, so many of these itinerant animals quickly meet their fate. Jenkins (1963) even found that surplus red grouse, *Lago-*

pus scoticus, in marginal areas suffered a higher incidence of parasitism. They gambled and lost, but their odds were better than if they had stayed to compete with dominant individuals.

Let us consider further the ecological implications of surplus populations. Gelada baboons, *Therophithecus gelada,* sleep on the bare cliffs on Ethiopian canyons. During the day they roam in harems (one-male reproductive groups) or groups of harems mixed with all-male groups. In the bountiful rainy season they move slowly in great herds over rich food sources. When the dry season approaches they break up into small groups of either single harems or all-male troops and spend most of the day foraging. The all-male troops tend to move away from the canyons and, apparently, they thus reduce competition with the harems for food. Since it is likely that canyons provide the best source of food and secure resting places, the all-male troops, during this period, suffer higher mortality than the reproducing groups. Crook (1970) believes such a system would permit an optimum allocation of sources to reproductive females. However, without attributing altruism to these bachelor males it is difficult to account for the mechanism which would select for such behavior unless we invoke kinship selection. Another possible explanation is that if the males stayed in the cliffs they would be excluded from many of the commodities by the dominant breeding group and would suffer even higher mortality than they do in the less optimal areas where any existing food is at least available to them.

A similar situation is described in one-male reproductive units along the Kariba River by Jarman (1968). In the dry season when food is at a minimum, the one-male reproductive groups occupy richer river areas whereas the excess males are displaced inland where there is less food and they are subject to higher predation. (The relationship of food to territory is discussed below.)

The breeding surplus factor varies among species. For example, in Old World tit populations there is no breeding surplus each spring, appar-

ently as a result of high winter mortality and because the territories can be compressed (see below) to accomodate the number which does survive. In other species, surplus animals survive the winter well enough to constitute a sizable part of the population the following spring (Brown 1969) and, in such cases, territoriality exerts a reduced effect on population numbers.

If there is a large breeding surplus contributing to a strong likelihood that any individual will fail to breed, the fitness of breeding individuals may be reduced in the sense that their offpsring are likely to end up in the surplus. So certain adaptations to a persistent breeding surplus are to be expected. Delayed maturation may be such an adaptation, if not to the surplus itself then to the conditions which brought it about. Selander (1965) explained that a large breeding surplus in birds decreases the probability that an inexperienced first-year male can successfully breed; therefore it is advantageous for him to not make the attempt until a later time. An older male, conversely, is likely to be more successful due to his greater strength and size and through the increased benefits of learning. Brown (1969) points out that adaptation to a surplus through delayed maturation is more likely in species having a high rate of survival. In those with a high mortality rate, the emphasis could be expected to be toward an all out attempt to breed as soon as possible.

In some resident species of birds, first-year males may remain in their parents' territories and help in nest building, defense, and care of young (Skutch 1961). Brown (1969) theorizes the system could have arisen thus: As the density of competitors increases, the likelihood of a young bird being able to acquire territory decreases. At the same time, a territorial male must spend an inordinate amount of time and energy in maintaining the territory. Subordinate young, which would normally be excluded at maturation, might then be allowed to stay and participate in all family affairs —except breeding. They might exert an intimidating effect on intruders by the strength of their numbers. The offspring of territorial birds or non-related subordinates willing to play the role, might, by remaining, increase the likelihood of their taking over the territory when the dominant bird dies, as has been reported by Rowley (1965) for the superb blue wren, *Malurus cyaneus*. Rowley found that groups with "helper" males produced 1.9 fledglings annually as opposed to 1.2 for those without helpers. For those interested in evolution, the selective mechanism here is different than that which accounts for grouping in colonial species or "lodge-builders" (Crook 1965, Hatch 1966).

The presence of nonbreeding adults without adequate territories constitutes a strong argument for the population regulatory ability of territorial behavior as has been pointed out. The question arises, however, whether any limits of population densities through territoriality are a function of some external factor such as the relative food abundance (discussed next) or some internal quality such as an innately centered spatial intolerance which operates no matter what the immediate conditions. In a study of birds of Bermuda, Crowell (1962) found that an increasing population density did not alter the size of territories, but simply crowded the territories closer together so that an increasing number of boundaries were shared between neighbors. In such a case it is important to realize that the size of the separated territories were most likely not dictated by environmental influences but, apparently, by some "inner" control, albeit undoubtedly ultimately arrived at through evolutionary adaptation to environmental factors such as food.

We have already seen too many influencing factors on territorial size to believe that an innate center directs the territory size independently of external factors. What we have learned though, does not preclude the existence of relatively fixed territory sizes, more or less influenced by immediate conditions or of an inherent *minimal* size. Huxley (1934) postulated a "rubber disc" model for territories, illustrating that territories could be compressed—but only so far (see Lack's

1966:260 criticism). It seems that there is a tendency for territory holders to give up parts of their areas as newcomers seek to become established. The result, of course, is smaller territories. However, for most species there must be a minimal size which, when reached, would lose the territory's usefulness if further reduced. If minimal territory sizes are governed more or less by specific and inherent tolerance levels, then territory could function on this basis in limiting populations (see Tompa 1962).

Territory and Food

If territory is important in population regulation, then we may ask upon what basis the resulting spacing out is adaptive. Intuitively, we can see the advantage to territory holders of expelling other individuals that would otherwise share their commodities. Let us consider the most obvious commodity: food.

It has been shown that some types of territories include a food supply at least during some part of the year (cf. Holmes 1970). Many observers believe that territorial behavior appeared through evolution primarily in response to a need to defend food supply, but the evidence, at present, is not conclusive by any means (cf. Brown 1964; Murray 1971); much of it is deductive, negative, or full of exceptions. Even the best evidence has serious argumentative shortcomings. Lack (1966) notes the rarity of species which actually feed within their territories. He also mentions that of those species which do feed within their territories, many do not protect the food there. The European robin, he states, prevents other robins from singing and breeding in his territory, but does not interfere with their feeding there. Klopfer (1969) points out that some bird species allow intruders to feed within their territories but not to display there (also see Jenkens 1963; Brown 1964; and Keenleyside and Yamamoto 1962). What is needed is a careful comparison of foraging success in animals with territories and those without. The apparent simplicity of such a study is deceptive. However, again, in the absence of any conclusive information we forge ahead.

It is fun to hypothesize safe in the knowledge that no concrete contradictory evidence is ever likely to appear. Let us now indulge ourselves in speculation as to how territorial behavior may have developed, but with one premise—one which places even less demand on our theorizing. If we acknowledge that any adaptiveness exhibited in territorial behavior at present does not necessarily reflect the original advantage of the pattern, then we can ignore the myriad variations of the behavior which we find about us. We begin by noting that there are indications that territory may protect food and that male holders of good territories are often "preferred" by females.

We might first ask how territory holders came to be preferred as mates by females unless the territories held food for the offspring or unless the ability to acquire a territory indicated the general vigor of the male. If the territory was considered a yardstick of his vigor, then we may ask how it came to be that the males began to defend territories in the first place. Successfully fighting for food has much more immediate advantage than fighting for other commodities, such as nest sites, and could, therefore, through its strong reinforcing effect, come to be established in the behavioral repertoire rather quickly. (Fighting for females might be less effective in general because, for example, of its seasonality or periodic advantage, and fighting for space per se is unimaginable.) Once males came to associate an area with food through learning, a general site-related belligerence might be expected. Females, smaller than males, would in some cases become dependent to a degree on the food which the male had secured. The male might allow females into the area of his food for purposes of copulation or mating. He would also increase his own fitness through allowing his reproductive partner to avail herself of his food. Aggressiveness in males would be then selected for through the generations until they even become intolerant of other males in

their proximity, at least at certain periods, such as in times of low food supply. Once the system became well established, patterns could become ritualized or altered as competitive conditions changed. The limited value of so general a hypothesis is apparent, but in any such widespread and diverse phenomenon as territoriality, its development must be explained in as broad terms as possible.

Observation of the timing of territoriality provides certain clues regarding the food-value theories. Territoriality in most species occurs only at certain times of the year. In North America, for example, birds are generally territorial in early spring prior to and including the breeding season. Such timing would be appropriate if territories were related primarily either to mate attraction (although we have seen that the benefits of mate attraction could have appeared secondarily) or to protecting a food supply. There are persuasive arguments in favor of the latter since after a long winter, food reserves would be low, and the approaching breeding season would place additional demands on the supply since females require additional food for egg formation and later on new mouths must be fed. Also, whereas territories appear at the time of the greatest demand on the food supply, territories, for many species, are relinquished at times of lower demand on a food supply such as in late spring and summer.

Territoriality cannot always be directly correlated with the *appearance* of a food supply. Some species become territorial in autumn, a period of high food abundance. It is apparent that in such cases increasing belligerence does not coincide with a building level of food. The winter is the period of lowest food abundance and the acquiring of territories in the fall is apparently an adjustment to an *impending* food shortage. A few important studies illustrate other ways the timing of territoriality can respond to the pressures of competition. Kluyver (1951) found that the great tit, *Parus major*, became territorial in fall, and the displaced birds suffered higher mortality as winter drew on. When winter came, the previously territorial birds gave up their territorial activities and devoted their time to foraging. In spring, pairs reformed and briefly resumed their territorial behavior, but when nestlings appeared the birds again relinquished their territories. Brown (1969) used marked birds and found those lacking territories suffered a higher mortality rate in the nonbreeding season. Jenkins et al. (1964) suggested that the number of red grouse dying during the winter was predetermined by territorial behavior in autumn, a time when food was in excess. Territoriality may function, then, in depressing populations partly through limiting access to food in the nonbreeding seasons, summer, autumn, or winter and by preventing some members from breeding in spring. The higher rate of survival of territory holders could be due to relegating unsuccessful birds to inferior habitat types, to dominance over nonterritorial "floaters" at food sites within the territory, or to an increased foraging efficiency in spring as a result of being more familiar with the territory through exploratory learning over the winter.

It may seem paradoxical that, generally, territorial behavior appears in spring, just at the time that food is increasing. At the times of lowest food supply, such as in winter or in dry seasons, many species of birds flock together and show little aggression. If territories are based, even partly, on the protection of a food supply, why do they often appear just as food increases and not when it is at its lowest level? The onset of territorial behavior coincides with, and may be part of, reproductive behavior. Natural selection has resulted in offspring appearing at the time of year when food abundance is high so that the new mouths may be fed. But even as the food level is high, so are the demands placed upon it at this time of year. Increasing demands on a growing food supply can be expected to reduce the net benefits of that growth. In other words, until some population regulating mechanism acts to reduce the numbers of the offspring, competition for food may remain

high or even increase in spring. Also, in the breeding season the foraging location becomes more restricted. Flocks of birds may cover wide areas in winter, but in the breeding season there is probably a tendency to remain in one place, partly due to a growing reluctance to leave the area which is associated with the nest and young (but see Kluyver 1951). It is probably generally adaptive for the parents to be able to forage in the area of the nest for reasons of nest protection; thus, in order to find enough food in a restricted area they might be expected to reduce the number of sharers of that food by excluding competitors from the area. These possibilities simply indicate the adaptiveness of territories at a particular time of year. It must be remembered that processes probably similar to ritualization have resulted in territories per se being a part of the male's releasing effect of reproductive behavior in females, and thus immediate environmental changes may have little effect on timing.

Special types of territories exist which undoubtedly function in protecting a food supply but which are relatively unusual and, hence, alone, do not lend enough weight to formulate a general rule. The red-headed woodpeckers, *Melanerpes erythrocephalus*, are attracted to oak woods in winter where they gather acorns and store them in cracks and crevices of trees. They protect their caches by hammering and molding soft rotted wood into place over each store (Kilham 1958). The birds drive away all other woodpeckers from their cache with the notable exception of one species which is not likely to exploit the hidden store, the yellow-bellied sapsucker, *Sphyrapicus varius*.

Red squirrels, *Sciurus hudsonicus*, defend winter food caches, but abandon them in summer. Interestingly, they defend other areas (called prime territories) year-round, and the distribution of such territories has been found to coincide with the presence of seed conifers, a year-round food supply (Kemp and Keith 1970).

One of the main divisions of current opinion

centers over whether spacing behavior limits breeding populations in vertebrates, or whether breeding populations are limited some other way (such as through starvation) before the animals arrange themselves spatially. The limited available evidence suggests that dominance and spacing behavior are usually affected by a change in the level of nutrition before starvation actually occurs.

In considering territoriality as a factor in the regulation of populations, it is, of course, important to discover the role of food in determining territory size. Generally both territorial and non-territorial species have denser populations and smaller feeding areas where the food supply is better (cf. Brown 1964; Kluyver 1951; Stenger 1958). The evidence that territory size is influenced by food abundance is weak and generally based on the inverse relationship that usually appears between them (see Schoener 1968 and Holmes 1970). Also, we must remember that the factors which influence territorial size are not necessarily those which influence the animal to take a territory in the first place. The establishment of territory is doubtless generally an innate pattern subject to those internal and external environmental influences which function in its release. On the other hand, territorial size, as indicated by its very flexibility, may be much more subject to learning in many species. There are limits as to the degree territorial size may vary, as we have seen. Some species show a tendency toward maintaining their usual territory size no matter what the environmental conditions, and in other species there is at least a minimum size for territories. However, if territories are related to preserving food supplies, territory size should generally reflect food levels to some degree. What evidence is there of such relationships and what mechanisms might be operating? First, as we have learned, food-related physiological conditions may influence a general aggressiveness in animals and thus help to determine the limits of territory size. Watson and Moss (1970)

suggest the animal might adjust its territory by assessing the food available, either visually or through somehow registering food accessibility after a brief period of foraging. If such assessment indeed occurs the investigation of the neural chain of events would be particularly interesting. It is unlikely that the animal thinks, "Since I see a lot of food and have had no difficulty getting it I will take only a small territory and save myself a lot of time and trouble." It is more likely that good nutrition reduces aggressiveness through a neurophysiological mechanism, or that an animal tends to remain in an area in which he has found good food, unaware that the level may be high elsewhere as well, and that this reduced roaming results in fewer hostile encounters.

It has been found that very large territories occur only in species which utilize them for foraging and that such territories are usually held by certain animal types. A solitary hunter, such as a lynx or a hawk, forages in such a way that the presence of other individuals would disturb it and reduce its success. So foraging patterns may influence territory size. Other types of species may adjust their foraging pattern after responding to other influences on territorial size. The European wrens hold large territories and by spacing themselves out presumably avoid attracting predators. So because of high predation they feed solitarily, close to thick cover.

In general, predators hold larger territories than herbivores or omnivores presumably because of their more sparsely distributed food. Also, large predators hold disproportionately larger territories than smaller predators probably because there is less food available per unit area for large animals than for small ones (Schoener 1968).

There is some very interesting evidence that territorial size for members of any generation may be affected by the food available to their *parents*. Cowley (1970) showed that protein-poor diets given to rats resulted in a reduced exploratory drive in their offspring. Calhoun (1963) had earlier demonstrated that exploratory drive was associated with aggression and spacing behavior in some rodents. So, during perennial periods of low food abundance, the tendency in these species might be toward smaller territories. If such is the case, it seems that preservation of food might play little part in the territorial nature of the animals. These species are, of course, social animals so, possibly, in times of low food abundance intragroup fighting, with its time and energy expenses, might be reduced.

The opposite situation is found in some birds. The quality of food eaten by the wild red grouse, *Lagopus scoticus*, affects levels of aggression and, therefore, territoriality in the next generation. It seems that with good food, the eggs will be more likely to produce healthy cocks which, when grown, will take *smaller* territories (Watson and Moss 1970). Jenkins (1963) stated that territorial behavior limited population density in red grouse breeding grounds in Scotland, but found that breeding density varied widely (14 to 34 birds per hectare) in different years. Apparently, the territorial behavior was being influenced by some environmental factor, such as food abundance. If territories are important in protecting a food supply, in times of food abundance smaller territories could be expected since adequate supplies would be preserved without exposing the holder to the increased dangers of establishing a large territory. Thus, it is emphasized that the population regulatory function of territoriality is complex and may vary from one species to the next.

Of course, the biological world can always be counted on to provide us with exceptions and so there are a few known cases where territory size is not related to a food supply. Certain species of mustelid weasels apparently hold a stable number of territories over their range despite fivefold increases in the numbers of their main food, a rodent (Lockie 1966). It is suggested that they and a few other species, such as tawny owls and golden eagles, hold territories as large as they can so that food is always available except under the most extreme conditions. It may be that the food supply of certain predatory species which seek elusive prey is difficult to assess before territorial size is established, or that certain prey species are given to fluctuations in number and therefore cannot be predicted by the predator. In such cases, selection for territories as large as possible would be expected. So stability of territory size is not necessarily an indication that the size was not related ultimately to food supply.

Interspecific Territoriality

One of the arguments against the food-value theory of territory is that the areas are not usually defended against other species with similar food requirements (cf. Hinde 1956). There are many examples of interspecific territoriality however, and these must be considered in the search for the adaptiveness of territoriality.

In some cases species may be so similar in morphology and behavior that where they occur together hostility between them could be expected simply as a result of mistaken identity. The red-bellied woodpecker, *Centurus carolinus*, and the golden-fronted woodpecker, *C. aurifrons*, are so similar that they are difficult to distinguish where their ranges overlap, at least for the casual observer. These species exclude each other from their territories, but they are much more tolerant toward the distinctly different red-headed woodpecker, *Melanerpes erythrocephalus*, in their territories (except perhaps around nest holes).

It should be pointed out that other species often encounter a lower level of aggression where interspecific territoriality occurs than do members of the same species. For example, fiddler crabs, of the genus *Uca*, live in large communities along the shores of the Indo-Pacific and America. Where there are several species occupying the same stretch of beach, males tolerate the burrows of other species closer to them rather than those of their own species.

In some cases the aggressiveness of territory holders toward members of other species may change with the passage of time. It was noted that in redwing blackbirds, *Agelaius phoeniceus,* the males gradually showed an increased tolerance toward specific members of other species, presumably as the result of habituation (Nice 1943). Such habituation could only occur, of course, if the advantages of protecting the territory were outweighed by the disadvantage of expending time and energy excluding the other species. The advantage of protecting the territory is reduced if the intruder is not a strong competitor, such as a member of the same species would be, so such habituation might be expected more often in interspecific than intraspecific interactions.

It may be difficult to separate "tolerance" from an imbalanced time-and-energy-expense factor. Redwing blackbirds exclude tricolor blackbirds, *A. tricolor,* which appear on their territories in late spring. The redwings are at first highly aggressive, but their task becomes insurmountable as more and more tricolors appear. As one tricolor is being excluded, another moves in from behind. The redwings finally must give up trying to hold territories or leave the area. So much time and energy must be spent in trying to repel intruders that it is simply no longer economical to attack them (Orians and Collier 1963).

The time and energy spent in territorial defense during the nesting season may reduce the attention that can be shown to the young through what is termed "aggressive neglect." It has even been suggested that interspecific aggression may cause the *dominant* species to reduce its brood size as an adaptation to the reduction in time available for nesting duties (Ripley 1961).

There are those who suggest that no useful purpose can be served by studying interspecific behavior in the search for the primary adaptiveness of territoriality. Perhaps interspecific territoriality is a misdirected intraspecific territoriality and is, in fact, unadaptive, but persists under certain conditions (such as along the edge of a geographic range). Most authors disagree with this assessment but Wynne-Edwards (1962) and

W. D. Hamilton (1964) point out that mutual interspecific competition contradicts the hallowed competitive-exclusion principle (discussed in Chapter 8).

Habitat complexity (see Chapter 8) may influence interspecific territoriality. Strong interspecific territoriality may be expected in complex habitats between competing species that are highly specialized in food getting, such as 1) those species which hunt large ground-dwelling arthropods by flying down from perches; 2) ground-foraging species; 3) large raptors which feed on ground-foraging rodents; and 4) species which forage on tree bark (Orians and Willson 1964).

Lester Short, an ornithologist, found that in three species of woodpeckers (specialized feeders) of Baja California, interspecific territoriality occurs in simpler habitats (such as those with only a few species of trees, relatively little variation in tree height, and with limited altitudinal variation). He found them coexisting peacefully in complex and diverse mountain areas where they divided themselves into the strata provided by the vegetation. Thus, in complex areas, competitors may overlap geographically by occupying different parts of the habitat; theoretically it is only when they are forced into the same parts of the habitat (or the same "niches") that they become territorial toward each other. The concept is discussed more fully in Chapter 8.

Finally, the territorial behavior of any species toward any other species is partly dependent upon the historical appearance of that species within an ecosystem. An example will illustrate the point. In Europe as many as six species of titmice may be found in the same area. They forage in mixed parties outside the breeding season and, when nesting, the territories overlap. In North America, no more than two species can be found together, but these exist with heavy competition from warblers and vireos, and the two titmice are mutually territorial. Apparently tits evolved in Europe, but when they reached North America the competitive situation was so severe that they were forced into interspecific territoriality to maintain themselves (Orians and Willson 1964).

HIERARCHIES

The Relationship of Territorial To Hierarchical Systems

With regard to the myriad social systems of animals, it might be suggested that territorial behavior is but one end of a social continuum. At the other end is the hierarchy, where individuals are recognized and related to according to their rank. The two systems might be considered part of the same social spectrum because there may be no sharp separation of the two systems and because in some cases they operate as different means achieving the same adaptive end. For example, they both decrease the likelihood of hostile interaction which takes time and which could be dangerous. We will now explore a few cases which indicate that perhaps linear dominance, or hierarchical arrangement, is a more organized or sophisticated result of the same selective advantages which produce territoriality.

Probably due to shortcomings in the observer, the nature of territoriality in some animals is so seemingly haphazard and its appearance so random that it is not possible to describe it. But such species serve to show the phylogenetic flexibility of the phenomenon. House mice, *Mus musculus*, for example, *may* develop territoriality, but there is no regular pattern to its occurrence. Rats, *Rattus norvegicus*, also show striking irregularity in territorial behavior. For example, some populations of rats defend the territory around the mouth of a burrow whereas others show dominance hierarchies but no territorial defense. The only regularly occurring territoriality is nest defense by the female rats (Scott 1966).

Southwick (1970) discusses work showing that the appearance of territoriality in some populations of house mice is at least partly a function of population density. It appears that these mice are territorial at low population density, but, as conditions become crowded, the system breaks down and is replaced by a hierarchical system in which all the animals share the area. The same phenomenon has been noted in salmon.

Just as increasing density moves populations toward hierarchies within a generation, there is some evidence that the same pressure may set the stage for hierarchies on an evolutionary basis. The Hispaniolan woodpecker, *Centurus striatus*, undoubtedly descended from territorial birds of North America, is unusual among woodpeckers in that the birds nest colonially. Each pair defends a small area around a nest hole, but several pairs may occupy a single tree. The birds have extremely high population densities in large parts of the island, and N. T. Ashmole (1967) theorizes that as the population density of the birds increased because of high food abundance, they finally reached a point where a territory holder was at a disadvantage because of the disproportionate amount of time spent in defending the area from so many potential interlopers. Reduced aggressiveness then was selected for and territories were given up; the birds then came together to nest colonially (for reasons discussed in Chapter 10). There is as yet no direct evidence of hierarchies, but it could be expected that those birds which exhibit the upper limits of aggressive behavior while not sacrificing excessive time or energy could be expected to be dominant at feeding stations. It is important to see from these examples the influence of environment upon social patterns.

Interestingly, territoriality itself may be the basis for congregating in some animals. Armstrong (1947) describes male Allen hummingbirds, *Selasphorus sasin*, which are highly aggressive and solitary by nature, but whose great spirit of belligerency causes them to take territories next to other males for the sake of combat. We immediately see certain implications here regarding the questions of the innateness of aggression (Chapter 8) and the concept of "drive."

Territories and hierarchies may exist simultaneously. Prairie dogs, *Cynomys ludovicianus*, as described by King (1955) inhabit territories that are divided into family holdings. Each family excludes members of other groups and, within each family, the membership is arranged hierarchically. In such complex social systems we may ask how the social patterns arise. What is the relative importance of instinct and learning? It is believed that in prairie dogs the young *learn* the limits of the family territory, either through communication of the information by the elders as Klopfer (1962) suggests, or through being thrashed upon violating the territory of another family. Selander (1970) found that interfamilial borders in house mice inhabiting barns are so strongly maintained through hostile behavior that gene frequencies may vary between families only a few feet apart.

The Welder turkey of Texas, *Meleagris gallopavo*, establishes hierarchical rank through fighting by first-year males. After males of a family or "sibling group" establish their intrafamilial rank, the members of each group fight with males of other groups to establish a "group hierarchy" as well. The larger groups usually win. Then the dominant males of the dominant groups do almost all the breeding. The dominant males of a subordinate group only breed in the absence of the dominant group (Watts and Stokes 1971). So here we see territorial and hierarchical systems operating simultaneously and resulting in the same reproductive advantages.

Certain new ideas regarding the relationship of habitat to social structure are emerging from studies such as that of Watts and Stokes. For example, we are becoming increasingly aware that the habitat can influence mating systems. When a species is readily able to find food or has precocial young, the male may not be needed to aid in rearing the young. He may then devote his time to attracting females, and polygamy may result. In turkeys the polygamous mating system can be of the lek type (where males come together to display on a common arena and females choose from among them), such as that shown by Welder turkeys, or of the harem type (where males fight for and "own" females), as in the Eastern wild turkeys, and the system may be dictated by the environment. For example, in Texas the climate is dry and severe, and when rain occurs food appears only briefly; females must, therefore, be brought to a breeding state quickly, and groups of displaying males on a lek may achieve this.

Crook, in his weaverbird study, found that those populations which live in woods form small social units, setting the stage for hostile—or territorial—interactions between groups. In woodlands, the food supply is widely dispersed and available year-round and could thus best be exploited by such groups. In grasslands, with their seasonal and localized food supplies, the birds flock together in large social units. In the latter case there would be little opportunity for territoriality to develop, but some hierarchical or "role" system might be expected (see below). So, again, we see the strong influence of the environment on social structure.

An interesting social system is found in bullhead catfish, genus *Ameiurus,* as reported by Todd (1971). At high densities, bullheads form dense communities where no territories are held and all members move freely and peacefully through the area. At lower densities, a "territorial hierarchy" is developed. In this system the dominant fish takes the largest and most protected territory and those of lower status take smaller and more exposed areas. Dominance is established by fighting and the accrued status is apparently reflected chemically. When a dominant bullhead was removed from his territory, subjected to a thrashing from a "hatchet man," and returned to his territory, his subordinates no longer fled. Apparently the change in him was chemical. (The importance of chemical communication in this fish is shown by the fact that territorial fish cease their aggression if water from a communal aggregation is pumped in.)

The relationship between dominant and subordinate is more than a system of partitioning the territories. The boss bullhead may act in some ways as a defender of the group. (The same pattern appears in some mammals.) If a strange fish approaches the group, the subordinates rush into the territory of the dominant male. The boss then engages the stranger in combat. After the fight the boss allows the subordinates to remain in his territory for a time before driving them back to their own areas.

There are certain ramifications for population regulation in such fighting. The loser of a bullhead fight often survives, but fails to grow normally thereafter even if placed alone under optimal conditions. His size is, therefore, not a result

of being excluded from adequate commodities. The fighting could thus be a means of magnifying the differences between the stronger and frailer individuals. In times of stress, then, the population might quickly be reduced to viable limits without placing undue stress on all its members. Some physical correlates of rank have also been noted in mammals (Figure 7.9).

It is difficult to know the importance of hierarchical systems in the regulation of populations because hierarchies demand a sustained and high level of complex social interaction, a requisite which is not always met. We have considered the

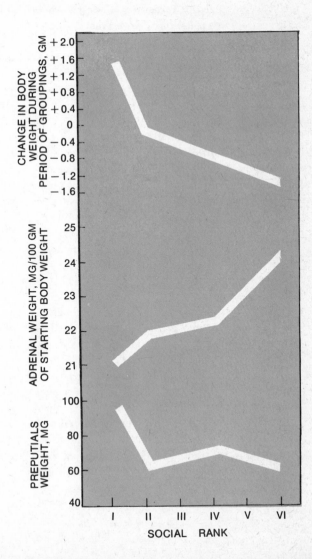

Figure 7.9 Changes in the social rank are correlated with changes in adrenal, body and preputial weights for wild stock house mice. I is the highest rank, VI the lowest. The study is based on 14 populations of 6 mice each. (Modified from Christian 1961.)

population-regulating effect of territoriality. The role of hierarchies in the regulation of population should also be stressed. For an excellent review of our current knowledge in this area the reader is referred to Crook (1970 a, c).

Lack (1968) notes that the higher ranking individual of a peck order (as hierarchies are sometimes called because of studies with chickens) increases his survival likelihood by taking food with little fighting, and subordinates likewise benefit by not wasting time in fights, which would have been lost anyway, and by going elsewhere to look for food. He notes that measurements of foods eaten and foods available in some species, such as the coal tit, *Parus ater*, and the wood pigeon, *Columba palumbus,* showed that the number of individuals surviving each winter was proportional to the remaining food supplies. Any such relationship, Lack points out, was most likely brought about through competition for food and the existence of a peck order functioning by individual recognition.

We have already noted the selective effect of environmental stress operating through hierarchical systems in bullheads. Such effects of dominance in the wild has not been proven yet but Wynne-Edwards (1962) and Lack (1966) suggest that hierarchies may act as "social guillotines" when food becomes scarce by causing the elimination of certain, usually less vigorous, segments of the population and ensuring the food supply of those at the top of the order.

Such a selective system of population control could only be expected to work when commodities such as food became *gradually* scarce and thus whittled away at the population. At times, however, the environment may exert a sudden and full effect and the hierarchical system may fail. Murton et al. (1964) showed that in wood pigeon populations, those forced to the front of a moving flock received less food by being pushed and hustled by those behind and, as a result, they suffered the greatest mortality in times of food shortage. One year, however, heavy snowfalls put all the pigeons into strenuous conflict for the few *Brassica* plants which were available as food and the whole population suffered a drastic weight reduction at the same time. As Crook (1970b) points out, the effectiveness of social factors in limiting mortality in populations must depend on certain critical environmental factors such as weather. Other considerations include habitat type, and the type of dispersion shown by the group.

It should be clearly understood that neither territoriality nor hierarchy depresses populations by *ensuring* the deaths of certain individuals or segments of the population. If those individuals unable to secure territories, or those at the lowest levels of hierarchies, were assured of death or of never reproducing because of having lost, it would be to their advantage to fight to the death to achieve higher status. However, such is not the case. Subordinate or nonterritorial individuals generally increase their likelihood of surviving and reproducing by temporarily assuming the consequences of their low status. Displaced animals or those of low status are at a disadvantage, but their chances are better than if they had continued to fight. By maximizing the probability of their survival they may be able to change their status at a later time.

Hierarchies and Roles

The ethological approach to social behavior has traditionally been confined to descriptions of pair interaction and their classifications. The sum of such classifications, of course, virtually defines the ethogram and this is about as far as we have gotten toward integrating the separate components. Crook (1970a) points out that, at least in advanced mammals, such a description is woefully inadequate. As he says, the approach is about as effective as discovering the nature of the game of football by compiling a list of all the observed moves of each individual player. Part of the problem in gaining a fuller understanding of animal social behavior lies in the difficulty human observers have in determining dominance ranking. The usual methods of determining rank are especially inadequate when dealing with higher animals. Social structure can be expected to be highly complex in species in which learning functions importantly in behavior, in those which are able to utilize subtle and graded communication methods and are gregarious. For a discussion of the effects of learning on baboon social systems see Rowell (1966).

Dominance concepts have now largely been replaced by the concept of *roles* (Bernstein and Sharp 1966; Rowell 1966; Gartlan 1968; Crook 1970). Roles are defined as the relative frequencies (percentages of occurrence) with which individuals perform certain *sequences*. When the "behavior set" of an animal is determined, it is said to reflect a role. For example, Bernstein (1966) described the role of "control animal" in a group of capuchin monkeys, *Cebus capucinus*, a species which shows no definite hierarchical system. The control is the one most likely to confront external dangers and to end intragroup frictions. Such an animal may not be the leader of the group, however, in terms of determining group movement.

Crook (1970a) points out that, in primate groups, it is one thing to say an animal has a role and quite another to define that role. He suggests describing individuals in terms of the group. Each individual shows certain responses in relation to older animals, dominant animals, subordinates, peers, etc., so that it can be described in terms of the sum of its reactions and this, he suggests, is its role.

Consider roles in macaque monkeys, genus *Macaca*. There is the control male, the central subgroup male (competitive with others in his group but dominant to peripheral males), peripheral males, isolate males, and central and peripheral females. Such roles are not fixed and immutable, and the rising and falling of an individual in the role hierarchy results in changes in its behavior. It is interesting that males may shift their roles many times in a lifetime, but females

are far more stable socially. Their stability thus gives them a certain importance in determining the roles of males of the group (Crook 1970a).

In baboons and macaques two conflicting social pressures contribute to role changing in males: (1) the ever-increasing freedom sought by the dominants, which constrains subordinates, and (2) the efforts of the subordinates to keep from being constrained.

Certain roles, as would be expected, are characteristic of some species and not of others. For example, the harem "overlord" occurs in hamadryas, *Papio hamadrias*, patas, *Erythrocebus patas*, gelada baboons, *Theropithecus gelada*, but not in other baboons or macaques.

Rowell (1966) found that rank is a function of the behavior of the subordinate. In some higher primates, at least, he found that subordinates almost always choose to leave any commodity to a dominant who wishes to compete for it. This is expected, since the subordinate would almost surely lose a fight should it occur. The subordinate, in order to avoid such situations, simply avoids dominant animals. Such "avoidance learning" means that the subordinate will often not even attempt activities which he *could* have accomplished, and so the dominant gains even more freedom. In competitive situations, the subordinates are likely to be deprived of the commodity, and in social interactions the stress produced may cause behavioral abnormality. Either of these two results is likely to have a depressing effect on the numbers of subordinate individuals and therefore function in regulating population. (For a discussion of aggression in primates, see Hall 1964.)

Subordinate males are left few options. They can become solitary and later take over a small branch group; they can affiliate with another male and rise in rank, and, lastly, they can act as "aunts" or "uncles" to infants of high-status adults and so affiliate with their superiors. Adult male macaques attach themselves to one-year-old animals when the mothers are entering new birth season and the young are being ignored. These males sit with the infants and hug and groom them, accompany them on the move and offer them protection. These are usually middle-class males which show low hostilities and are oriented toward high-caste animals (Itani 1959). By caring for high-caste children, subordinate males are tolerated by the parents and so may gradually become affiliated. Male care was not found in all troops by Itani so it may be that the phenomenon is a cultural one which may have an additional adaptiveness in kinship selection since the offspring are likely to be related (as most animals in a troop are probably related) to their protector.

Any "liberating effect" of changing roles, as Crook (1970c) points out, would be ecologically important. In times of food shortage a "freer" male would increase his likelihood of survival through gaining more commodities and being subject to less psychological stress.

INDIVIDUAL DISTANCE AND DISPERSION

The tendency of individuals of many species of animals to maintain certain minimal distances between themselves and their conspecifics (or, in some cases, members of other species) can have certain regulatory effects on population. Foremost, the effect is to reduce population density in any area, and, perhaps secondarily, to reduce population numbers by higher mortality of individuals which "prefer" to occupy suboptimal habitats rather than crowd themselves into already occupied areas. Any mechanism which disperses competing members of a population must function in reducing competition.

The simplest methods of dispersion, of course, involve passive movements in which the individuals drift aimlessly about, as do the medusae of some marine coelenterates, or the larvae of starfish and crabs. Other animals deliberately maintain a certain distance between themselves, and these are our primary concern here. Under a given set of environmental and physiological conditions that distance may be rather specific and inflexible for the species. Of course the distance may vary according to environmental or social conditions or the physiological state of the animal. Even the most solitary of mammals must, at times, permit a member of the opposite sex to draw near for purposes of mating.

Most species whether solitary or gregarious maintain a certain *individual distance,* which is usually defined as a defended area which moves with the individual (cf. Hediger 1955). The highly social starling, *Sturnus vulgaris,* will sit peacefully with his comrades on a telephone line as long as no other bird infringes on his individual distance, a matter of inches. Such an infraction usually results in an immediate threat by the established bird. In other cases, the distance is much greater and, therefore, ecologically more important. Birds seeking territories will often avoid those areas where they hear another of their species singing. (So territories may be maintained by two behavioral phenomena: aggressive expulsion of the intruder by the owner and avoidance behavior on the part of the newcomer.)

An interesting phenomenon which is associated with individual distance but which is probably less important ecologically is *flight distance.* Flight distance is that distance maintained by an animal which, when encroached upon, results in the withdrawal of the animal. Such distances are not species specific, but may be strongly influenced by learning. You may have noticed that you cannot approach too closely to English sparrows on the street. The same species may be seen around zoos hopping in and out of cages filching food from caged animals, where they may be approached much more closely and where they even seem to ignore zoo visitors. Flight distance can only be correctly determined in those animals which have no particular attachment for an area (such as an animal on a nest which might permit an intruder to draw much nearer than would be possible in, say, a communal feeding area). Flight distances may vary according to the other protective devices of the animal. For example, small animals often flee sooner. Larger cryptically-marked or dangerous animals have a shorter flight distance and some do not flee at all.

It is noteworthy that many animals on oceanic islands show no fear of man, a newcomer to their environment. They may be approached closely and even touched. Of course such trust has resulted in the slaughter and even extermination of many species.

Overcrowding may occur in some species when the young reach maturity and begin to circulate as adults or, at least, at a higher level of competition with adults. Then, mass emigrations or irruptions from an area may occur. Depending on the species, the animals may be the young or the old but in any case they leave and thereby the species is constantly invading new areas, successfully or unsuccessfully. The dispersing animals may continue to move until they have removed themselves from strong competition with the parent population by having responded to a tendency to maintain a certain distance from others. Swarming bees leaving an overcrowded hive, for example, reject any new hive within a couple of hundred yards of the old hive.

The dispersion of some animals is brought about, not so much by the presence, as the activities of other animals although these activities may not be hostile at all. Tinbergen has mentioned that in certain species of ducks, a male which has established a territory and already has a nesting female will greet any new female with rough attempts at mating without any of the normal courtship behavior. The new female, turned off by such crass behavior, of course withdraws. The male's behavior is probably adaptive in keeping the new female from disrupting the nesting behavior of his mate, and results in an increased likelihood of the female finding an available mate, but the immediate result is a reduced population density.

The importance of the distance between animals is reflected in studies of the selection of nest sites of birds. Lack (1970) lists some species which maintain territories in which they build their nests, but which forage in groups even at the height of the territorial season. It is believed that in such cases the birds maintain widely separated nesting sites to avoid attracting predators to the activity which occurs around nests. Nesting dispersion could, then, be expected in species with certain ecological histories such as those which suffer high predator risk. Nesting dispersion, it should be added, may be a rather labile character. Tinbergen (1952) found that undisturbed herring gulls, *Larus argentatus*, usually nested a certain distance from each other, but after the nesting grounds had been raided by a prowling dog or fox, the birds increased the distance between nests. Lack (1970) mentions that on Bear Island, the nonterritorial eider ducks, *Somateria*, nest close together; but on the mainland, where foxes can reach the nests, they nest solitarily.

Solitary or cryptic nest sites in weaverbirds are not advertised by song, presumably so as not to attract predators. However, colonial weaverbirds usually nest in protected sites, and here nests are blatantly advertised over long distances (Crook 1969). Gregariousness itself may act to reduce predator efficiency as discussed in Chapters 2 and 10.

Tinbergen et al. (1967) found that even in camouflaged species predation is higher on those that nest close together. They laid out artificially camouflaged hen's eggs in plots of different densities and attracted wild carrion crows by placing a conspicuous egg in the area. The crows searched longer among the more dispersed eggs but found fewer.

The spacing of concealed nests in birds is paralleled in other species of animals which have not, as yet, been as extensively observed. It is known for example that females of the poplar hawkmoth, *Loathoe populi*, and the eyed hawkmoth, *Smerinthus ocellata*, lay each egg some distance from the rest, presumably to reduce the chances of predation (Lack 1970).

DENSITY AND ABERRANT BEHAVIOR

There is evidence that overcrowding may result in behavioral abnormalities which reduce the population size. One result of high density may be a reduction in reproductive success. The phenomenon has been noted in a wide range of animals. At high densities, for example, mammals show such depression (Christian 1963) and, whereas the effect is probably rare in birds, Lack (1958, 1966) found reduced clutch sizes at higher breeding densities in the great, blue, and coal tits. Kluyver (1963) found fewer females of tits attempting second broods in high-density years. Others have reported similar findings for other species.

It may be argued that fewer reproductive attempts simply reflect an adaptation to a reduced food supply brought about by the severe competition which exists at higher density. However, appearing with such changes in reproductive success (and, sometimes, possibly appearing without a change in reproductive patterns) are certain interesting physiological changes and some obviously unadaptive responses. It has been noticed that population "crashes" in voles, *Microtus agrestis*, are not related to food, predators, or any other component of the environment, but actually to the number of voles themselves (Chitty 1952, 1957). Voles from large or declining populations reared fewer offspring than normal and the young suffered higher mortality from the usual hazards encountered by voles. At high population densities, the voles fought more frequently and were found to have enlarged spleens (a characteristic often associated with hemolytic anemia).

Chitty found that at times when the population was undergoing such a crisis, even *isolated* individuals showed increased sizes in the spleens. This was surprising. It was then suggested that perhaps the crashes are due to periodic changes in the frequency of some gene or genes, and are regulated by a biological clock rather than en-

vironmental conditions. The idea has not yet been adequately tested, but if it is true, then the biological timing mechanism undoubtedly arose as a response to historical waxing and waning of their numbers which were, obviously, reflections of some environmental factor. A genetically controlled periodic increase in ferociousness could act to ensure commodities during a simultaneous increase in crowding. The physiological effects (or side effects), such as the enlarged spleen, would be less detrimental than attempting to get along when population numbers are too high.

Some animals become more sensitive to their numbers at certain times of the year. Muskrats, *Ondatra zibethica*, seem to be more conscious of the presence of others during the breeding season, and when a certain level of crowding is reached the "fiercer or more determined" individuals drive out or kill the others. Those who are driven out suffer high mortality from, for example, predatory mink, *Mustela vison* (Errington 1943).

Another widely held hypothesis states that overcrowding causes increases in strife and aggression, but that the major physiological changes occur in the *losers* of conflicts. In confined animals, it is true that pathological changes may occur in the endocrine systems of subordinate individuals and their young (Christian 1968), but little data is available on wild populations. The effects of social stimuli upon gonad development has been shown for several species of birds (cf. Phillips 1964). Kendeigh (1941) found that at high densities, an increase in destructive behavior of the male house wren appeared. These aggressive wrens entered nesting boxes and actually threw out the eggs and young of other pairs. In chickens it was found that subordinate status depressed gonad development (Flickinger 1966). It must be stressed that high density does not always depress reproduction and that much of the above evidence is only circumstantially related to population density so that, at this point, such behavioral effects cannot be unequivocally shown to be primary factors in the control of reproduction.

Certain behavioral patterns may appear in response to crowding which are not directly related to reproduction, but which might affect population. Crowded animals may be subjected to such stress that they behave in ways detrimental to themselves. Toads, *Bufo bufo,* survive for years in captivity if left alone, but suffer high mortality if crowded. At such times they may starve to death in the presence of food (Elkin 1960). According to our definition of fitness (Chapter 6), such behavior must be considered as unadaptive and not as a self-sacrifice for the good of the population.

For results of a preliminary study on rats, from which some observers have drawn some alarming conclusions for man, see Calhoun (1963). In one experiment, eight mice were placed in a situation where food and water was abundant and where they were kept healthy and free from disease. They were allowed to multiply to over 2200 in two years. As they reached their peak number, their social structure began to fall apart. They were unable to complete acts of fighting or mating. They continued to ramble about, eating and drinking, but were unable to perform social acts. There may be implications here for studies of increasingly antisocial behavior of people in large cities. (This idea is expanded in Chapter 8.)

It may be that density per se should not be considered as the primary factor in bringing about the sort of stress to which we have been referring. Such stress may not even be due to the increase in competition which arises from crowding. Rather the crucial factor may be simply the increase in interaction with members of the group. If the level of interaction itself is critical, then the physical structure of the environment becomes increasingly important. A complex and heterogeneous environment affords increased protection or seclusion for an animal, and so, in complex habitats with abundant hiding places, the animals would be likely to interact less often and therefore be subject to less stress. Where food was unlimited, but space and cover were restricted, Brown (1953) and Southwick (1955) found high litter mortality in rats because of excessive fighting in adults. Calhoun (1963) showed that for the brown rat, when nests were small and cover was poor, fighting increased and reproduction decreased although food was abundant. Saunders and Smith (1962) found that a population of brook trout could be almost doubled by adding physical structures to their habitat, and Jenkins (1961) found that the home ranges of partridges were generally larger in fields with poor ground cover. So, in some cases, population density might be increased without detrimental effect by reducing the amount of interaction with others. The unwillingness of people to become involved with others under conditions of high population density may be the result of an adaptive mechanism which permits them to exist under crowded conditions. In order to avoid developing a severe antisocial reaction, the presence of so many others would simply not be "acknowledged."

8

COMPETITION

"Nature, red in tooth and claw" has too often been the image of competition operating in the wild. Remembrances of fictional violent conflicts between a leopard and a python simply confuse the picture of what competition really means. As Lorenz (1963) points out, there is nothing for a python or a leopard to gain in such a fight—unless one intends to eat the other. Neither is competition completely portrayed by two wolves fighting for a prey carcass, although the advantages of winning in this case are more apparent. Perhaps competition is better pictured by two plants of slightly different types growing side by side on a sun-warmed slope of an Alpine meadow. One is slightly taller, the other has somewhat broader leaves. As it happens, the taller plant tends to shade the broad-leaved plant just a bit when they occur near each other. The result is a slight increase in the taller plant's food production over that of the broad-leafed one. The taller, as a result, leaves a few more seeds, each giving rise to a new taller plant. Time goes by and the seasons come and go until, one day, a careful observer can see that the taller plants are present in abundance, and not a single broad-leaved plant is to be found. Interestingly enough, the presence of the taller plant seems to have had little effect on the number or types of bushes, trees, or grasses in the area, none of which it resembles much at all. (Plants were chosen in this example to emphasize the idea that competition is usually not violent.)

Let us return momentarily to our leopard-python fight. If the leopard attacked the python with the intention of eating it, then we are no longer talking about competition. Predator-prey relationships are quite different from competitive ones. For example, it is usually to an animal's advantage to eliminate its competitors, but certainly not its prey. When the vigorous and intelligent dingo was introduced to Australia it did not kill off its primitive marsupial prey, but its hunting prowess was so superior to its competitors, the Tasmanian devil and the Tasmanian wolf, that these animals disappeared from the Australian continent and, today, are found only on islands to which the dingo has not been introduced.

In this chapter, we will concern ourselves with how animals compete, what they compete for, and some of the results of competition. It will become apparent that there is some disagreement about these matters and, in fact, about whether competition is an important influence in nature at all. The answers to many of the questions we will consider will seem to be intuitively apparent and one might wonder since the answer is so obvious, why the question arose at all. According to George Bernard Shaw, the inspired guess comes first and the data which are supposed to verify it is only a dodge to knock it into the thick heads of uninspired numskulls. The scientific world may be full of uninspired numskulls with reasonably thick heads, but, nonetheless, time and again, cold hard data have burst many a theoretical balloon, even those which seemed eminently logical—except that they just couldn't be made to fit measurements from the real world. Even when intuition was upheld by experiment the results often proved more fruitful then anticipated (see Lack [1968:309] discussion of one of Tinbergen's "obvious" experiments).

We will see that for such a complex and encompassing subject as competition no well-defined and succinct description of its operation can be gleaned from the massive amount of information available. Apparent discrepancies only serve to point out that we haven't yet entirely deciphered the nature of competition—nor possibly even its true definition. However, in spite of some contrary arguments given below, it will become apparent that competition exerts powerful influences on interactions between living things. It can be argued on an intuitive basis that perhaps every other sort of interaction operates ultimately to increase the likelihood of success in competitive conflict.

We will set forth our topic in terms of Birch's (1957) definition: Competition occurs where animals utilize common resources in short supply or when animals harm each other while seeking resources which may not be limited. Instances described in the latter part of the definition are probably much rarer in nature. Conflicts over commodities not in short supply should, for now, be considered as (1) evolutionary hangovers from times when commodities were in short supply or (2) the result of a mechanism to keep aggression at a high level to increase success in seasonal periods of short supply.

It is true, as Andrewartha (1961) maintains, that competition is often used as an explanation for an observation when the term itself *explains* nothing. But rather than toss out the phrase (along with, for example, phlogiston and entelechy) we will simply remind ourselves it is a broad term which encompasses a variety of observed phenomena in the natural world. It will become apparent that the evidence presented to show the importance of competition as a factor in natural selection is, when carefully examined, inconclusive. It may seem that the concept of competition is derived largely from circumstantial evidence, a measure of faith, and a lack of a better explanation for what we see.

THE NICHE

All living things have their place in nature. Their surrounding—the place where they are found—is referred to as their *habitat*. The habitat can be defined several ways. For example, an animal may live in a desert habitat, or specifically in a briny pool in that desert. Furthermore, it may live in a certain part of the pool, its microhabitat. No matter where an organism lives however, it is forced to interact with its surroundings including other forms of life which it may contact directly or indirectly. The sum of all such reactions along with the organism's requirements is the *niche*. Eugene Odum, one of our more imaginative ecologists, refers to the niche of an organism as its "profession." Again we encounter an operational term which is mainly useful only in concept and which furnishes much raw material for scientific haggling over its precise definition and implication. For material relating to more detailed descriptions and operational models of the niche see Hutchinson (1957) and Levins (1968).

The description of the niche of a species at a particular place cannot be used to define the species as some have suggested, because of the high adaptability or tolerance in many species. A species may occupy a very diverse niche, as is demonstrated by its appearance in a variety of habitats, and thus render any attempt to describe it by its niche useless. The pitch pine, *Pinus rigida*, in the eastern United States, occurs on steep, rocky, dry, south-facing slopes at middle elevations in the southern part of its range; on level, sandy, coasted plains in the northern part of its range; and in different habitat types in still other areas (Whittaker 1970).

The habitat figures importantly in the dimensions of any niche. A group of closely related species of warblers living in the same woods would seem, at first, to be occupying the same niche. However, MacArthur (1959) showed statistically that the various species in his study had actually subdivided the habitat and, therefore, occupied different niches. One species foraged primarily in the lower areas of the trees, one primarily near the tops, and another in the outer branches. The birds, then, were actually occupying different niches, each taking food from a restricted area the location of which was undoubtedly in part dictated by the presence of other species. It is clear that such separation through specialization could only be accomplished in a heterogeneous environment which offered the opportunity for separation.

There are many examples of species occupying the same areas but different niches. Even an inexperienced observer may notice that the distinctly different species of shorebirds darting in and out of the edge of waves to take food are behaving differently. They may be assumed to be taking different food from the same area at the same time.

The most obvious way species can separate themselves into different niches is to occupy different geographic areas. The Alaskan ravens and the crows of Oklahoma are very similar in morphology and behavior. However, they are certainly occupying different niches simply because the commodities available to them are so dissimilar. Also, the animals with which they must share their habitat are vastly different. One might argue that either species is occupying the approximate niche that the other species would occupy were it there. It might also be argued that the dingo occupies the same niche in Australia that the wolf does in North America. Such reasoning, however, neglects to take into account the multitudes of ways living organisms interact with their surroundings. The sum of the differences of these interactions of two animals which are only roughly similar, and who live in habitats which may be vastly different, is undoubtedly too great to permit a prudent observer to maintain they are occupying the same niche in different places.

Just as animals may separate themselves spatially and behaviorally, they may also separate themselves in time. The same area may be occupied by different species as seasons change. The robin is considered to be an American bird, but people in certain parts of South America may wonder where it goes when it leaves home each spring. The area that the robin leaves each fall comes to be occupied by more northern species retreating from yet more severe winters. The robin's absence from South America each spring must change, to some degree, the complexion of the competitive situation there.

Time may influence niches in another way. Animals of the same species may occupy different niches in the same habitat by dividing commodities by age. Ward (1965) found significant differences between the diets of young and old birds in his study of the black-faced dioch, *Quelea quelea*, in Africa.

Ward also found another type of separation

operating within a single population. At certain times, males were taking different food from the food taken by females. We will have more to say about the ecological separation of sexes later in this chapter.

The concept of niche division is an important one since it is a classical ecological theory that no niche can be occupied by two species simultaneously. The *principle of competitive exclusion* (Hardin 1960)—also called Gause's law, the Volterra-Gause principle, or Grinnell's axiom—states that such a situation cannot last. No two species interact with their environment in identical ways, therefore, one will have a net advantage,

no matter how slight. Current theory has it that, in time, the species with the advantage will replace the other species at least in their zones of overlap (Figure 8.1) as was illustrated in the example of the Alpine plants.

TWO GEOGRAPHIC CONSIDERATIONS

Temperate and Tropical Zones

No attempt will be made here to describe habitat or ecosystem types as such topics are treated in general ecology textbooks. However, we will concern ourselves with aspects of two geographical

[A]

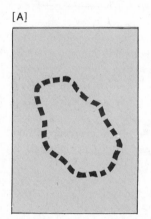

[B]

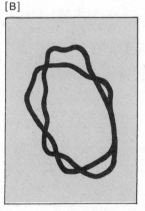

[C]

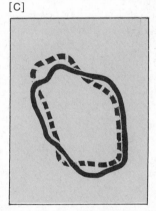

[D]

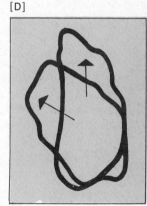

Figure 8.1 Theoretical results of competition for an ecological niche. The background represents all the possible environmental factors such as temperature, other species, oxygen, cover, food and so forth as projected on a plane. An ecological niche then would be any unique set of these factors such as in theoretical niche A.

In B, two niches are similar but not identical. They are each occupied by a different species. These species hold most, but not all, of the niche in common with the other species. Because each animal's niche includes so many factors which are identical to those held by the other species, it is logical to assume that they largely occupy the same habitat. The information here however, says nothing about how closely the animals are related.

In C, it becomes apparent that the two ecological niches held too many traits in common in order for each to remain filled. Gause's law states that two species cannot maintain the same niche indefinitely but that one species will come to replace the other through competitive interaction. The broken line indicates the niche of the successful competitor.

In D, a different situation from B arises. In this case, the unshared parts of each niche are sufficient to maintain each species for a longer time. If the species are not constrained (by other competitors, environmental barriers and so forth) from expanding into new areas, the species will reduce competition between them by exploiting still other facets of the environment. The result is a divergence of life-styles. See the discussion of adaptive radiation in this chapter. (From Bruce Wallace and Adrian M. Srb, *Adaptation,* © 1961, Prentice-Hall, Inc., p. 53.)

phenomena which graphically bring into relief certain principles of behavioral ecology.

First, it has been noticed that there are pronounced differences in the biological components of temperate and tropical areas. One of the most apparent differences in the two zones is in the degree of seasonal change in each. In spring and summer, in temperate zones, life flourishes and food abounds; but, in winter, life is harsh for temperate species. The winter landscape is one of bleakness and, at such times, most species are likely to find little food.

One implication of such seasonality is that both the food supply and the animal populations fluctuate widely. It is likely that the rises and falls in numbers of a population do not parallel those of its food supply as shown in Figure 8.2a. The reason for such a difference, if indeed it can be proven to exist, may be that in winter density-independent effects, such as cold temperature, are reinforced by a density-dependent reduced supply of food, the result being a severe depression of populations. In spring and summer, populations may be largely controlled by density-dependent effects, for example, food supply; and so, under reduced pressure, populations can rise toward the carrying capacity of the environment. Local population densities of some species, especially birds, may change because of their migratory habits. However, here we are primarily concerned with the overall sum of interactions between animals of an area and their environment, a figure probably not greatly affected by the coming and going of a small percentage of species.

Seasonal change in the tropics is much less pronounced. It is true that the winter dry spell can cause ecologically important modifications in the tropical wilderness, but the effects of such changes cannot approach those of temperate winters. So tropical niches are much more stable.

The stability of the weather is responsible for other ecological phenomena. As an example, the reproductive, or fruit-bearing, period of each type of producer (plant) may be seasonal, but different types of plants reach maximum productivity at different times; so for many tropical species food is available year round.

It may be, then, that in the tropics population numbers are stable and high and, therefore, populations maintain levels near the carrying capacity of the environment, so that food is actually in short supply throughout the year (Figure 8.2b).

In temperate zones animals must be geared for the seasons of low food supply when competition would be at its maximum. They can do this by drastically altering their behavior with the approach of winter, such as by changing diets or entering a resting phase. However, in some cases,

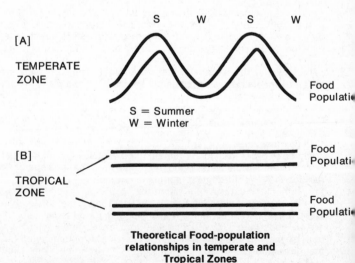

[A]

TEMPERATE ZONE

S = Summer
W = Winter

Food
Population

[B]

TROPICAL ZONE

Food
Population

Food
Population

Theoretical Food-population relationships in temperate and Tropical Zones

Figure 8.2 The theoretical relationship of population numbers to their food supply in temperate and tropical habitats. See the text for an explanation.

such flexibility would place a great behavioral load on temperate animals, some of whom are rather stereotyped in behavior. The problem could also be met by temperate species maintain strong ecological separation, with some degree of flexibility, even in periods of food abundance. It could be expected then that resident temperate-zone animals might show stronger separation of niches than their tropical counterparts throughout the year as a means of reducing competition in periods of low food supply. In fact, Klopfer (1969) and Klopfer and MacArthur (1961), in noting the great number of bird species in the tropics, point out that the phenomenon is probably due to increased tolerances for niche overlap as well as the ability to occupy marginal habitats. The constancy of conditions in the tropics assures the relative stability of food and other commodities and permits increased stereotypy in foraging and other activities. The stereotypy would appear as a result of relying on the same food and cover throughout the year. More stereotyped feeders might be expected to take a larger percentage of their food due to more practice in searching for only a few food types.

The increased number of species in the tropics itself is a contributing factor to the stability of the area. It is a basic premise of ecological theory that diversity increases stability in an ecosystem. Stability may be further increased by the behavioral stereotypy of the animals. For example, the large number of trees found in lowland tropical forests may be partly the result of highly efficient predation of animals on seeds and seedlings so that no species of tree can become dominant (Janzen 1971).

Increased species diversity in an area means that increased *habitat selectivity* is operating for each species. This does not mean that tropical diversity is high *because* of an innate tendency toward narrow and stereotyped behavior of each species that, in turn, permits crowding together. The species are, rather, probably *forced* into their narrow niches by strong competition which is not regularly reduced by seasonal hardship. The bananaquit, a small tropical bird, is restricted to a narrow niche, but in the absence of competitors it is capable of immediately broadening its niche and occupying new areas (Klopfer 1969).

In ecological terms, certain problems arise if tropical and temperate zones are defined by their proximity to the equator. In reality, strong differences exist between ecosystems of the temperate northern hemisphere and those of comparable distances from the equator but to the south. Darwin, and recently Moynihan (1971), as well as other biologists, have been struck by the appearance of ibises, flamingos, caracaras, parrots, hummingbirds and other "tropical" species amid the frozen sleet of Tierra del Fuego at the tip of South America. Moynihan believes that *constancy of environmental conditions* should be a primary criterion in the definition of tropics. Thus the constancy of what has been called the south temperate zone would permit the area to be reclassified as tropical. The north temperate zone remains biologically distinct from both due to the unique qualities and quantities of its life.

For a recent discussion of differences in the biota of the tropics and temperate zones see Kiester (1971).

Islands and Continents

A second type of geographical influence is reflected in differences in populations living on islands and those on continents. As we will see these differences may arise through peculiarities of the competitive picture in each of the two habitat types.

Important ecological differences between islands and continents exist and these have provided valuable insight into the nature of the niche and the effects of competition upon it. Islands differ from continents, not only in their insularity, but in other ways as well, such as in age and size, continents generally being larger and older than their nearest islands. (Certain islands such as Australia merit special consideration and will not be considered for now.)

Whereas each continent boasts a wide variety of habitat types (with the possible exception of Antarctica) great variability in complexity may be shown from island to island. Some islands are nothing more than flat stretches of sand barely rising above sea level that, at times, may even be submerged, such as the islands of the Chagos Archipelago of the Indian Ocean. Others are great bodies with tall mountains and lush valleys, as we see in the southeast Alaskan chain. It is therefore difficult to generalize regarding island habitats or niches; instead, we will focus our attention on general rules which may help predict the biota of any island.

The distance of islands from the nearest mainland and their size are critical factors in the types of niches they offer. Lack (1969) points out that smaller, more distant islands are usually low lying and therefore have fewer vertical transition zones. Size, it seems, would generally affect the complexity of islands by increasing the opportunity for variance in the habitat. Environmental complexity has special implications for competition as we have seen. The reader is referred to MacArthur and Wilson (1963) for a discussion of factors affecting island colonization.

The distance between islands and continents affects niche dimensions in several ways. Remember niches are defined by biological interaction as well as physical structure, so we may ask what biological factors are likely to be operating on an island. The first problem involved in colonizing an island is getting there, and the probability of any two different types of species reaching an island is not equal. No one is surprised to find birds on islands. Birds are good travelers (some better than others). They may discover islands while in migration, or resident birds may be blown out to sea by storms. So any animal reaching an island is likely to confront birds. That animal does not necessarily have to put up with snakes, however. Reptiles are poorer travelers and even if they may drift about on log rafts they would confront spe-

cial physiological problems in being continually wetted with seawater. A walk through a forested island of the West Indies is enhanced by the presence of many species of colorful birds and the knowledge that no poisonous snakes are about. The effects of island distance is inversely related to the traveling ability of any species. In other words, both good and poor travelers may colonize nearby islands, but more distant islands, especially the more recent ones, will be inhabited primarily by good travelers. Older islands have an increased probability of being reached by unlikely colonizers of course.

Islands generally have fewer species than the nearest mainland wherever they occur. This condition would not be unexpected, of course, since some species have particular problems in reaching islands. Besides problems of distance, the potential colonizer may not find a suitable habitat once he reaches an island. One reason is simply due to the difference in the size of the areas involved. All the habitats found on a continent are not likely to be represented on the smaller islands. However, other factors act to depress species numbers on islands. Even considering size, islands have still fewer species than would be expected. The point is this: fewer species are found per available habitat on islands than on continents.

One reason for this paucity is the high rate of extinction of the island species. Islands are likely to offer simple habitats, as we have seen, and in the biological world simpler systems are more unstable; thus, any biological component of a simple system has an increased probability of becoming extinct. There are other reasons as well for the reduced number of species on islands. Any species adapted for continental living is not likely to be concomitantly well adapted for island niches; fortuitously, some species are able, by their nature, to fit into the island niche they have discovered well enough to maintain their presence until they can adapt more finely to their new habitat. Such "preadaptation" does not necessarily ensure their success. To use an example by Klopfer (1969), a continental grassland species may require ½ acre per bird. Upon reaching an island it may find that only ¼ acre is available. So some of the birds may move into adjacent woodlands (assuming that niche is vacant). The grassland species may then, in time, begin to adapt to its new habitat. However, if a woodland species should appear on the island, the grassland species occupying the woods may become extinct, unable to compete successfully with the newcomer. On the other hand, the woodland species may encounter a strong competitor in a firmly ensconced grassland species and may become extinct itself. (There generally seems to be an advantage in "being there first"—but see Morse (1971) for an account of an exception.) No matter which species becomes extinct, however, the result is a simpler biological situation than that which exists on the continent from whence the species came.

Mac Arthur and Wilson (1963) have summed up the relationship of colonization and extinction to island distance and size: (1) Islands farther from the mainland have lower colonization rates. (2) Smaller islands have higher extinction rates than larger islands. (3) Increased size of distant islands has a greater effect on increasing the number of species than does increased size of islands nearer to mainlands. (In other words increased island size heightens the likelihood of colonization as the distance from the mainland increases.)

Since animals must rely on other organisms for their sustenance, we may ask, "but what about food?" Whether an animal is plant eating or flesh eating, if it exists on an island, it is dependent upon food species which have their own problems of colonization. Lack (1969) points out that the fewer species of birds on smaller outer islands is not due to the dispersability of the birds, but to lack of food. It follows from what we have learned that any island-colonizing animal will have fewer food sources at its disposal and will be likely to be forced to change its diet quantitatively if not qualitatively.

A change in diet does not necessarily mean a change in foraging behavior. For example, it has been found that certain species of birds on Bermuda take food from a wide spectrum of habitat types which, on the American continent, are occupied by other species. The Bermuda birds, however, have not changed their foraging patterns either quantitatively or qualitatively.

So now we are brought to the question of flexibility of behavior of successful island colonizers. The Bermuda birds were behaviorally labile enough to move into new areas, but apparently rather inflexible regarding their foraging patterns. Since colonizers are likely to be confronted with novel situations, their degree of behavioral flexibility would seem to be an important determiner of their success. There are, as yet, no experiments to yield quantified information, but certain tendencies of colonizers are apparent to field observers. Mayr (1965), in his long studies of island birds, finds these characteristics in the most successful island colonizers: plant-eating habits (the advantages of being herbivorous are discussed below), social tendencies (he indicates that solitary birds are the most easily stopped by geographical barriers), traveling ability, behavioral flexibility, and a tendency toward what is, in effect, exploratory (or latent) learning. (Also see Mac-Arthur and Wilson [1967].)

Morse (1971) discusses an interesting relationship between island colonization and interspecific dominance relationships. It might be expected that the more subordinate species among a group of competitors would show a greater behavioral flexibility as an adaptation to being pushed into suboptimal habitats. Morse found that where certain warblers are sympatric, the dominant species attain high density but are less flexible in behavior. Subordinate species then, with their greater plasticity, might be better candidates for the colonization of small islands where the sort of ecological conditions which they confronted on the mainland do not exist.

We can see, then, that because of problems of travel, habitat dimensions, and competition there are likely to be fewer species on an island than on a nearby continent. However, as a result, those species which make the journey to a hospitable island are likely to be benefited by the lack of competitors there. In classical theory, faunistically impoverished or "depauperate" islands offer more opportunity to an invader because of the presence of empty niches into which it may expand.

Any successful colonizer has its effect on other species which attempt to establish themselves. The influence is reflected in the fact that two closely related species do not often occur on one island. It is unlikely that the presence of a woodpecker would much affect the establishment of a wren, but other species of woodpeckers might be quickly excluded from the island—through competitive failure. Even if the woodpeckers occupied different but adjacent niches when they were together on the continent, they still are not likely to be able to coinhabit the island. The reason is, apparently, because the first colonizer would be likely to have expanded his niche to include that occupied by his former continental competitor. In other words the first colonizer would probably have had time to adapt to the characteristics of the island.

The time factor is probably very important for some species in that, under certain conditions, low flexibility could be overcome by an extended period of exposure to a new situation (given low competitive pressures). Behaviorally, flexible organisms would be expected to adapt more quickly on an individual basis through learning. Those species showing more stereotyped behavior may, under certain conditions such as an abundance of "non-preferred" but acceptable commodities, best adapt in time through "evolutionary learning" (modification in the instinctive repertoire).

By saying that a colonizing species moves into unoccupied niches on islands we are not saying that it adds other niche-units to its own. It is simplistic to refer to niches in terms of well-defined ecological slots. We are actually saying that that

species may have available to them larger niches on islands than they had on continents. An island colonizer is able to incorporate parts of its new environment into its own niche, parts which were unavailable to it on the continent because they were occupied by other species.

We may assume that a recent colonizer moves into a part of the island habitat which is most similar to the habitat it just left. For example, a grassland species from the continent could be expected to first inhabit the grassland areas of islands. The species would only later spread into unoccupied woodlands. But then what pressures does it face which impel it to move into woodland areas at all? We have already referred to species being forced into their niches. Such a concept implies, as well as those pressures which determine the *limits* of a niche, those forces which move the species into certain positions, or niches, in an ecosystem. On continents species may be kept from expanding their niche by competitive pressure, but on islands the same pressure may *force* them to expand. To understand such an apparent anomaly we must keep in mind the ways competition can develop. Strong interspecific competition keeps animals on continents in their place, but on islands, with low competitive pressures, population numbers may increase to the point that intraspecific competition forces expansion of the niche. Let us examine more closely how such a situation could arise.

First, as has been mentioned, islands usually present simpler biological situations than continents in terms of habitat structure as well as the competitive situation. Also, fewer species of any single adaptive type are present on islands than on continents. The result is a change in the dimensions of the food spectrum available to any animal which colonizes an island. If the animal is one that catches flying insects, for example, it may find fewer species of each prey-type available to it. Grant (1966a, 1966b, 1968, 1969, 1971) describes food resources for birds as being less varied on islands. Simberloff (1970, 1971), on the other hand, states that he finds an *increased* number of insect species per genus on islands, which he attributes to the similarity of congeners in their ecological requirements and dispersal ability. The bulk of the evidence seems to lie at this point with Grant and others (e.g., Moreau 1966). Let us consider an example which illustrates this viewpoint. Suppose an island colonizer is of a type which feeds primarily in the cracks and crevices of tree bark, such as a species of woodpecker. On the ecologically complex continent from whence it came, the woodpecker may find several species of ants on the bark of trees as it flits through mixed woods. It may also find several species of grubs and a number of kinds of caterpillars, spiders, and other crawling things. Since many kinds of larvae and insects appear seasonally, the woodpecker can usually find some sort of prey except, possibly, in severe winter conditions. The woodpecker is highly successful in capturing these food types because of special adaptations of the legs, feet, neck, tail, and especially tongue and bill.

Any species of woodpecker is very limited, however, in its foraging places on North America. One of the reasons for this is the presence of close competitors. The red-bellied woodpecker, *Centurus carolinus*, rarely, if ever, forages on the ground. One probable reason is that the flicker, *Colaptes auratus*, is frequently found there. The red-bellied woodpecker also does not usually fly up into the air to catch insects on the wing. It may share its woods with flycatchers, though, which are quite proficient at this means of catching food. So within the dimensions described by its particular foraging ability the continental woodpecker has available to it a variety of species of foods of relatively few adaptive types. (Bark-dwellers are available but not ground-dwellers or fliers.) The range of food types available to it is emphatically restricted due to competition from other species.

Woodpeckers on islands face a different type of competitive situation, as reflected by the fact that the Jamaican woodpecker, *Centurus radio-*

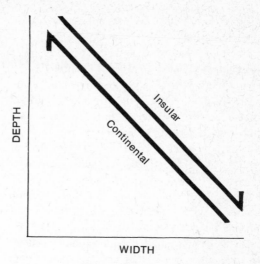

Niche Parameters In Continental and Insular Situations

Figure 8.3 Niche parameters in continental and insular situation. See the text for an explanation.

latus, often flycatches, and the Hispaniolan woodpecker, *C. striatus*, is not restrained from foraging on the ground. We can assume that the dimensions of their food spectrum differ from those of continental species, but how? We have learned there are likely to be fewer food species available to it, so it is not likely to find as many species of ants, grubs, or other prey. We have also learned that new food sources may be available to it through its niche expansion—incorporating unoccupied ecological areas.

We have referred to niche "dimension" for a reason. Niche parameters on islands and continents, as has been suggested, *are* different and the difference may be demonstrated in a model utilizing a two-dimensional concept of depth and width (Figure 8.3). Let us consider depth to be the *amount* of food of a certain type which is available such as the weight or mass of all tree-dwelling ants. Width, then, could describe the *range* of available food types, for example, if referring to size, from small to large prey. We see that continental species have deep and narrow food sources and island species the opposite. The model might help to explain why island species move so rapidly into unoccupied niches; they quickly begin to compete among themselves for a shallow food supply and are forced to expand outward.

In the biological world, insular conditions can exist in places other than on islands. Any relatively isolated species may be considered insular. Alpine species which can only exist at certain high altitudes may be restricted in their movement from one mountaintop to another since they are unable to pass through the inhospitable valleys. Strong isolation of populations may permit them to diverge in their evolutionary directions and one result, of course, might be a finer adaptation to the specific habitat of each population. We will consider other ecological effects of insularity in the section on sexual dimorphism.

Van Valen (1965) described certain relationships of morphology to niche width in his *niche-variation hypothesis*. He noted that animal populations living in wider niches show greater variation from individual to individual, especially in trophic (foraging) appendages. Conversely, in narrow niches, the measurements of individual animals could be expected to fall more closely to the population average or mean for that measurement. In other words, on islands, greater variation in some body parts could be expected as an adaptation to exploit wider niches.

Such a relationship should not be surprising, since morphologies would be strongly influenced by competition from neighbors of similar adaptive types. For example, any continental woodpecker of unusually small size with a small bill might fall into strong competition with the little nuthatches —so woodpeckers sympatric with nuthatches are kept from becoming too small. Any large woodpecker would also be at a disadvantage if he came into too strong competition with the large flickers. On islands, however, woodpeckers might not have

to compete with flickers or nuthatches and, while body size may not change much in island woodpeckers, structures associated directly with foraging, such as the bill, may be highly variable. The changes that occur in island species may also be directional. For example, Watson (1962) and Grant (1965) suggest that on islands birds develop longer bills and tarsi for exploitation of a wider range of resources. In other words, these body parts have shifted in a certain direction, toward greater size and the types of food the birds can take are thus increased.

There has been argument, of course, some of it recent, regarding the niche-variation model. Those interested in arguments may wish to refer to Van Valen (1965); Soulé and Stewart (1970); Van Valen and Grant (1970); Soulé (1970); and Rothstein (in press, Amer. Nat.).

It should now be apparent that the relationship between morphology and behavior is such that no student of ecology could attempt to interpret either without referring to the other. For example, after noting high variability in trophic appendages of any species, the observer should be able to make tentative assumptions regarding foraging patterns of that species and also formulate some idea of what competitive pressures may be operating.

More will be said about island species and the effects of competition upon them later in this chapter. For further discussions regarding island colonization the reader is referred to MacArthur and Wilson (1963); Carlquist (1965); Baker and Stebbins (1965); Grant (1968); Schoener (1970); and Lewontin (1965).

INTERSPECIFIC COMPETITION

We have learned that, in general, the level of competition that exists between two sympatric species varies with their ecological similarity. Since "ecological similarity" implies certain similarities in food preference, nest site, morphology, and behavior, we know that the highest level of competition must exist between members of the same species. It follows, then, that interspecific competition, when it occurs, may generally be considered highest in those species of similar types which occupy the same area at the same time. But there are exceptions, as we shall see.

Much of the evidence of competitive interaction is circumstantial. We have noted redwing blackbirds attempting to exclude tricolor blackbirds from their nesting area. Such aggression is demanding and would have been "selected out" of the behavioral repertoire were it not beneficial, at least at some time in their histories, for the redwings to make such attempts. The advantage is apparently in excluding similar types which might offer severe competition. Of course the redwing does not size up the tricolor and then attack what he fears may be a competitor. Rather, the tricolor, highly similar to the redwing, probably merely presents a certain configuration or pattern that releases aggressive behavior in the redwings. The sight of a wading bird, adapted to an entirely different ecological niche, would present a different appearance and release no hostilities. Tendencies which permit instances of mistaken identity (aggressive behavior toward similar species) are very likely *maintained* in the behavioral repertoire of the redwings and are not simply unadaptive and incidental patterns. Strong hostility of the redwings toward competitive tricolors undoubtedly reduces the numbers of the latter to some degree where the species overlap.

In addition to sympatric species reducing competition by occupying different parts of the same habitat, they may exploit virtually the same areas of a common habitat, as they separate in other ways (although these instances are probably rare). Moynihan (1962) describes four types of honeycreepers, *Diglossa lafresnayer lafresnayer, D. carbonaria atterina, D. cyanea cyanea,* and *Conirostrum cinereum fraseri,* which inhabit the same areas and the same parts of the habitat and exploit identical ranges of foods. They differ in the degree to which they utilize each food type however. Also, although they are found in the same

habitats, each species seems to prefer a certain area more than the others do. Individuals avoid members of other species so little interspecific hostility is shown; however, individuals frequently dispute with birds of their own species. Such behavior is not unexpected considering the general interest exhibited by most animals toward others of their species. Each species actively avoids competing species of honeycreepers since no "attraction" need be maintained for social or reproductive reasons. It is doubtless more advantageous for each species simply to avoid interaction with other honeycreepers and to forage elsewhere than to assume the disadvantages of attacking them.

Hartley's (1953) study of titmice buttresses the argument for the existence of strong competition between similar species. He found that although five sympatric species of titmice separated according to tree species foraging height and preference for parts of trees, the degree of separation changed with the season. In fact, the ecological separations sometimes disappeared. Such times, it was found, coincided with periods of superabundance of food when competition would be lowest.

An observation of T. H. Hamilton (1962) should be noted here. He reported that by a combination of differences in foraging levels and habitat preferences certain vireos have been able to occupy the same geographic area. He suggested that the species-specific differences which reduce competition also inhibit doomed attempts at interspecific matings and therefore function in reproductive as well as ecological isolation. Dobzhansky (1937) proposed the term "isolating mechanisms" for any of several processes or situations which act as barriers to gene interchange (the ecological importance of which was discussed in Chapter 6; also see Lack 1971). Those readers interested in genetics will wish to review subsequent revisions of the concept such as those by Mayr (1942) and Dobzhansky (1951).

We have primarily considered competition between species of similar types. However, in some cases competition exists between very different kinds of animals (see the discussion of allelochemics for examples from plants). The tiny mouselike Australian phalanger, *Tarsipes spenserae*, climbs among flowering bushes and, with its long protrusible tongue, sucks up nectar from the flowers. The basic plant-animal relationship, then, is much like the one occurring between flowers and bees (Von Frisch 1964). Lake birds such as grebes, *Colymbas*, and large fish such as pike, *Esox*, both feed on small perch; but their foraging patterns are so vastly different that any competition which exists between them must be of an indirect sort and, as Wynne-Edwards (1962) says, "buffered" in a variety of ways so that no true rivalry is ever likely to be exhibited. Wynne-Edwards believes that such indirect competition is probably common in nature.

A very direct sort of competition exists between some species of seabirds. In the Galápagos Islands, the frigate birds, *Fregata magnificens*, have specialized in taking food away from other predatory seabirds through piracy. A frigate circles high until it sees a booby or other seabird take a fish. Then it swoops down and pecks at it until it regurgitates its prey which the frigate bird then skillfully catches in midair. Eibl-Eibesfeldt (1970) reports seeing a tropic bird killed by a frigate bird in such an attack. He believes that several peculiarities of Galápagos seabirds are a result of their interaction with the frigate birds. For example, the swallow-tailed gull, *Creagrus furcatus*, hunts only at night and the dusky gull, *Larus fuliginosus*, has cryptic grey feathers. Eibl-Eibesfeldt suggests that since these species are after the same prey, this is a most direct sort of competition. Wynne-Edwards (1962) holds that the attackers in such cases must be regarded as semipredators, or parasites, since they are dependent upon the "victim's" presence. Strict competition between the attacker and the victim might be the attacker's undoing if it were strongly dependent upon its ill-gotten gains and, therefore, its activities might have no serious depressing effect on the numbers of the victims.

Allopatry and Sympatry

Competition is most effectively reduced when the geographic ranges of species do not overlap. Such a condition is known as *allopatry*. One might ask why allopatric species should even be considered then in a discussion of competition. To begin with, there is always the possibility that allopatric species may somehow be joined. Such union has occurred many times in nature as well as by the hand of man. The results have often been fascinating and, upon occasion, disastrous. The occurrence of ecologically similar species in different habitats could occur in a variety of ways. Any population which is divided by the appearance of some geographical barrier will form subpopulations which, in time, may become distinct species through *evolutionary divergence*, but which will continue to occupy very similar niches. Examples are seen in the differences in certain small mammals whose parent population was divided by the formation of the Grand Canyon. Such species, because of their close relationship, could be expected to be strong competitors if they are ever rejoined.

Distantly related species, under separate but similar environmental conditions, may respond to their environments by taking adaptive pathways. The result is *evolutionary convergence*, the development of similar characteristics in widely separated species (Figure 8.4). The isolated marsupials of Australia came to occupy similar niches to those held by placental animals on other continents. Thus the Tasmanian wolf occupies a niche roughly similar to that held by the very distantly related wolf of America. The virtual extinction of the Tasmanian wolf of Australia after the introduction of the dingo attests to the similarity of the niche type of these two species.

So we see that allopatric populations may come to have special importance in the consideration of competition. Also, in a practical vein, we can see the importance of carefully considering the niche requirements of any species before introducing it to a new habitat in order to prevent the extinction of desirable resident species as well as to ensure the establishment of the introduced species.

Sympatric populations are those which occupy the same geographical area. Each species, however, is not necessarily sympatric with the same groups of species throughout its range, so the competitive situation for a species may change from one part of its range to another. Except in simple and strongly demarcated ecological areas any species would probably be free of any given competitor at least in some part of its range.

The condition of occupying adjoining areas with no significant overlap is known as *parapatry*, but the situation is probably unusual in nature. Parapatric populations probably only exist where two ecotypes are sharply demarcated. Powerful influences would be needed to maintain discrete but adjoining populations so any ecological separation probably would be reinforced by behavioral activity through mutual exclusion (Figure 8.5).

Character Displacement

It should be apparent that the ecological niche of a species will be reflected in its morphology. Even an untrained observer viewing a heron and an owl side by side could tell which one was a wading bird. (I hesitate to be overly confident however, since after once leaving a group of students to identify the skeleton of a large pig, I returned to find that after careful consideration, they had concluded it was a leopard!)

Given the strong relationship between the niche and the morphology of its inhabitants it should also be apparent that even in sympatric and closely related groups of animals morphological differences will exist. For example, we might expect differences in the morphologies of MacArthur's sympatric species of warblers. The differences, of course, would be adaptations for specific foraging manners. Certain parameters of body size would

PLACENTALS

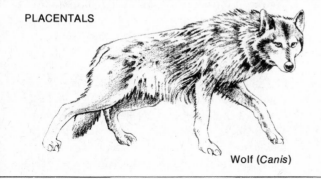

Wolf (*Canis*)

Anteater (*Myrmecophaga*)

MARSUPIALS

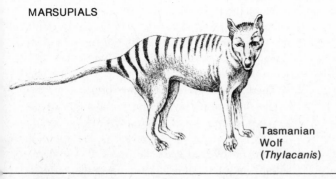

Tasmanian Wolf (*Thylacanis*)

Anteater (*Myrmecobius*)

Figure 8.4 The results of convergent evolution of some placental mammals and Australian marsupial mammals. Note the similarities in each pair of species.

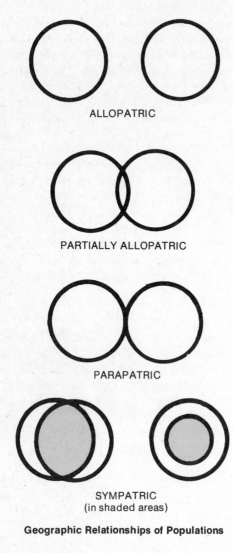

ALLOPATRIC

PARTIALLY ALLOPATRIC

PARAPATRIC

SYMPATRIC
(in shaded areas)

Geographic Relationships of Populations

Figure 8.5 Graphic relationships of populations. See the text for an explanation.

probably be affected more than others. For example, on the basis of their different foraging habits, we might expect the greatest differences in the trophic appendages (those body parts directly associated with foraging—for example, the bill). Body size and wing length might be less affected. We are reminded that differences in foraging behavior, habitat, and bill shape between sympatric and closely related species are believed to be adaptations for reducing competition for food (cf. Lack 1954:144; Mayr 1963; Selander 1966).

One of the primary forces that causes a species to occupy a special type of niche and to assume a particular morphology for that type of niche is, as we have seen, competing species. There are examples of such competing species which overlap in only part of their ranges, and the results provide evidence of the strong evolutionary effect of a species upon its competitor. In species which are sympatric over only part of their ranges, the strongest morphological and behavioral differences appear in the zones of overlap. To illustrate, consider Figure 8.6. Species 1 and 2 overlap in only part of their ranges. Note that they diverge in bill size to a much greater degree where they are sympatric (B) than when they are allopatric (A).

The phenomenon has been widely reported and is called *character displacement*. The general theory of character displacement was advanced by Brown and Wilson (1956), and since that time many such cases have been described. Unfortunately, the concept has been invoked rather uncritically in many cases where differences in species or populations may be due to some other adaptive effect. The result has been a growing question whether character displacement is an important influence in nature at all. However, let us consider some of the evidence.

There is believed to be selective pressure on sympatric or partially sympatric populations to diverge in morphology in their areas of overlap and thereby, presumably, to reduce competition. In areas of nonoverlap, the members of the two populations may be found to be more similar in mor-

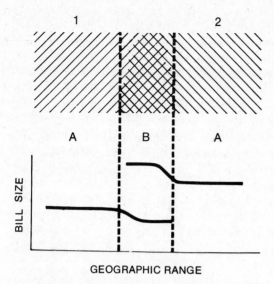

Figure 8.6 Theoretical model of character displacement. See the text for an explanation.

phology and behavior. The selective mechanism is apparently one which eliminates those members of either sympatric population which tend toward similarity with the other species. Such similarity would, of course, increase the level of interspecific competitive interaction and place these individuals at a disadvantage.

Character displacement has been demonstrated in island species. Grant (1968) shows that similar species diverge in bill length (an evolutionarily labile character) even more on islands than continents. Such a trend would not be unexpected in light of what we know about differences in continental and island niches. Two species of Darwin's finches on the Galápagos archipelago have similar bill lengths where they occur on separate islands (10.5 mm and 10.8 mm). On a third island, where they are sympatric, the difference increases— one species having a bill length of 8.5 mm and the other 11.2 mm (Brown and Wilson 1956).

It is interesting that the morphologies of two competing populations may not be displaced to equal degrees. One reason may be the operation of a dominance factor. Schoener (1970) found that where two species of unequal size overlapped, the divergence more often resulted in the smaller one becoming even smaller. The larger one usually changed little (and, if it did, it changed in either direction). The same dominance factor may be operating between sexes on islands as is described in the section on sexual dimorphism in this chapter.

Behavioral patterns other than those directly relating to foraging may also be displaced. Blair's (1963) study of frog calls provides a clear example of displacement in vocalization. He showed the difference between the calls of two species of *Microhyla* is much greater in the overlapping parts of their ranges. Alexander (1962) found that the development of complex calls in crickets was favored by the presence of closely related species of crickets. Increased complexity, of course, would make for increased divergence in sound through greater specificity as was discussed in Chapter 6. Behavioral characters strongly associated with mate selection might be important in maintaining other population differences once they began to appear.

It should be remembered that song is not *always* displaced in zones of sympatry, as we learned regarding birds in Chapter 6. This stability may be due to certain conservative properties in the song of some species as noted by Lanyon (1960).

Character Convergence

Sympatric competitors may reduce their competition in ways other than by increasing the differences between them. They may become more similar. Dixon (1961) described increased similarities in voice between species of *Parus* where they overlapped. He noted that they also held mutually exclusive territories in these areas. We are reminded that interspecific territoriality would be expected between species which are most similar in feeding ecology (see Cody and Brown 1970).

In cases where interspecific territoriality would be adaptive, a divergence of species characters might not be as effective as strong similarity. As Marler and Hamilton (1966:461) state, "Wherever two species compete actively for some commodity, it is possible that selection for a high degree of species specificity will be held in check in those signals which are used in competitive encounters." In other words, in certain situations it may be better for two species to be unable to tell each other apart. Such "mistakes" would be expected as sympatric species developed similarity in certain characters. The phenomenon is called *character convergence* (Cody 1969).

In situations involving interspecific competition it would be advantageous for either species to be able to recognize the other's threat signals. Stokes (1962a and b) found that four sympatric species of tits responded to each other's signals. If the aggressive bird raised its wings, its opponent of another species would flee. If he fluffed his feathers, the opponent often attacked. Of course any such closely related species could be expected to use some of the same signalling devices especially if threat postures are evolutionarily conservative features as Stokes maintains. We are not concerned, however, with differences or similarities due to "vestigial" patterns which are on their way out. We are interested in whether these similarities are being maintained or increased through natural selection.

So far, examples of character convergence have only been described for species which show interspecific territoriality. If two sympatric species are morphologically and behaviorally similar (suggesting strong competition) then mutual exclusion from territories would be adaptive. Cody (1959) argues that general physical similarities could permit rapid development of those specific clues which prompt territorial behavior. Suppose a mutation in a male of one territorial species results in a change in color plumage that shifts his appearance toward that of males of a competing species. If the change put him within a certain critical range of appearance so that he now releases aggressive behavior in the other species he will be ejected from the territories of males of that species. He will thus be forced into areas where he does not share his food resources with his competitor. Since he continues to eject members of his own species from his new territory, his food resources may be increased. In time, due to his foraging advantage as a result of being excluded from the territories of competitors, he might leave more offspring, and his characters would come to predominate in the population.

It is not necessary that this species react in the same way to its competitor, at least at first. In time, however, the appearance of the competitor could likewise be altered so that he would elicit aggression on the part of the first species whereby the resources of the area could be yet more finely divided.

There are certain restrictions upon convergence regarding which characters may be altered. For example, those characters (or sign stimuli) which function in mating behavior must remain distinct. Since in many cases the sexual releasers also function in territorial behavior, the complexity of the phenomenon becomes evident.

It would not be surprising to find, as more evidence comes in, that there are various environmental influences operating on the strength of the selective mechanism for convergence. For example, simpler habitats could be expected to push competing species more strongly toward convergence—all other things being equal. In fact, in the Greater Antilles a tendency toward convergence in body size of birds has been found to be operating in simpler habitats (Schoener 1970).

Moynihan (1968) discusses another implication of character convergence, "social mimicry" which is considered in Chapter 9.

ADAPTIVE RADIATION

A population of frogs may be interbreeding over the entire area of an expansive bog. At the onset of a dry spell, however, dry areas appear and begin to divide the frogs into isolated pockets of the deeper waters of the bog. The dry areas between the pools constitute ecological barriers to the subpopulations of the frogs. If the dry spell is prolonged, the genetic or behavioral characteristics of each breeding unit may diverge from those of the other units. Such divergence can be due to "genetic drift," which is the sum of random mutations accumulated in any population, neither harming nor benefiting it particularly, but altering it nonetheless. If the ponds, once divided, offer different environments, thus placing different selective pressures on their inhabitants, then the changes in the frogs may be primarily due to natural selection and may proceed much faster. Should the rains return after a long time, and the subpopulations be reunited, interbreeding between members of the once separated groups may not be successful. Interbreeding may be unsuccessful due to changes in morphology or behavior which appeared during the period of separation. Possibly, as examples, releasers, IRM's, or other communication mechanisms have changed or, perhaps, changes in morphologies no longer permit easy grasping of the female by the male during egg fertilization.

The reproductive barrier may also be genetic so that even after successful fertilization the offspring may not live or may not be able to reproduce. If the members of the former subpopulations have adapted to different sorts of habitats, then even "successful" offspring may be selected against because they may be of intermediate types, not well adapted to either habitat (see Bogert 1960).

Failure of two groups of animals to interbreed successfully where they come together is usually considered an indication that they are separate species. So in the case of the frogs, speciation can be said to have occurred. The splitting up of a group into species with different ways of life is called *adaptive radiation*.

The classical example of adaptive radiation appears in a group of birds usually referred to as Darwin's finches which inhabit the Galápagos Islands. The birds attracted Darwin's attention when he explored the islands during the voyage of the Beagle and what he saw served as an early impetus to his development of the theory of evolution.

The birds are four to eight inches in length and both sexes are drably colored in browns and greys. Species are easily distinguished on the basis of their bill structure. In one species the bill is heavy and finchlike for seed eating. In another it is long and downward curved for gathering nectar from cactus flowers. Others have parrotlike, chickadeelike, or warblerlike bills and each is a special adaptation for a particular way to gather food (Figure 8.7a). One species, the woodpecker finch, *Cactospiza pallida*, has a bill which is specialized for excavating wood. The bird lacks the long bill and protrusible tongue of woodpeckers, however, and it compensates with a behavioral pattern. A cactus spine is held in the beak and used as a tool to probe insects from cracks and crevices (Figure 8.7b).

Apparently the various species are descended from a common ancestor, a finchlike species which colonized the Galápagos from South America. As the species became established on one island, some members of the population made it to the other islands. On each island the birds, more or less isolated from populations on other islands, followed their own lines of evolution. Each species adapted to the specific requirements of its own island. Each group finally reached a point where its appearance, feeding patterns and mating system were distinct from all the others. Some of these new species were rejoined later and their differences increased through character displacement. Today there are 14 species in all (Lack 1947). Each of the principal islands has at least 3 species and some as many as 10.

For another example of adaptive radiation see discussions of the honeycreepers, *Drepanididae*, in which a nectar-feeding colonizer eventually produced up to 22 species of which 9 are now extinct (Amadon 1950, Baldwin 1953).

SEXUAL DIMORPHISM

Although adaptive radiation usually refers to divergence in populations the principle may also apply to a divergence in morphology and behavior of the sexes. First let us examine the phenomenon

Figure 8.7A These three Darwin finches have different bill shapes yet they all come from Indefatigable Island in the Galapagos. The small ground finch, *Geospiza fuliginosa,* top left and the medium ground finch, *Geospiza fortis,* top right feed mainly on seeds. Note the shape of their bills. This shows bill morphologies specialized for this kind of feeding behavior. The cactus ground finch, *Cactospiza scandens,* bottom center feeds on both the cactus and its fruit. For this, it needs a longer and sharper bill than the small or medium ground finches. All three share the same habitat. These bill changes are examples of adaptive radiation. (After Eibl-Eibesfeldt 1970.)

Figure 8.7B The woodpecker finch, *Cactospiza pallida,* uses a tool to help it feed. The bird uses cactus spines in much the same way continental woodpeckers use their long bills. The cactus spine may be used to probe deep into crevices to extract prey from their burrows. (After Eibl-Eibesfeldt 1970.)

of sexual dimorphism and then consider its behavioral and ecological implications.

We (most of us) have been aware for years of the differences in the sexes. Boys are not usually hard to tell from girls, and male dogs look different from bitches. In certain other species sexual differences are much more pronounced (Figure 8.8). On the other hand, we may have trouble determining the sex of our kitten. Experts are needed to sex baby chicks, and very few are able to sex black ducks on the basis of external appearance. So we see that levels of sexual dimorphism may vary widely.

Darwin, in 1871, set forth the idea that differences in the sexes are due to a particular type of evolutionary pressure called sexual selection, as opposed to natural selection. He said, "Sexual selection depends on the success of certain individuals over those of the same sex, in relation to the propagation of the species; while natural selection depends on the success of both sexes, at all ages, in relation to the general conditions of life." As an example, the cryptic color of the female pheasant is the result of natural selection, whereas the garish aspects of the male certainly were not developed on an ecological basis, but through sexual selection, as a mechanism to attract females and thus increase his reproductive success. A careful reading of Darwin shows there is probably less argument between him and his recent critics than it would at first appear (e.g., Wynne-Edwards 1965). For a discussion of sexual selection the reader is referred to Chapter 6.

Animals may be sexually dimorphic in a variety of ways. First, sexes may differ in size. It is generally, but not always, true among vertebrates that when the sexes are dimorphic in size the males are larger than the females. The difference is sometimes pronounced. For example, fur-seal males may be ten times larger than females. The tendency also appears in humans, although to a lesser degree.

Sexual dimorphism may also be expressed in fighting accoutrements. In some species males possess special fighting weapons, lacking in females. For example, consider the antlers of bucks or the enlarged canine teeth of male baboons. Birds do not usually show sexual dimorphism of weapons, but there are exceptions such as is seen in the long spurs of roosters.

Thirdly, sexual dimorphism may appear in display apparatus, such as in coloration, markings, or appendages. We have already considered the development of the bold markings and coloration of the male peacock. Behavioral specializations also appear which function in the effective display of such apparatus. Under certain conditions, the peacock tends to strut about with his tail feathers spread—a behavioral trait lacking in females. Finally, sexes may differ behaviorally. In some species of birds the sexes are similar or identical in appearance, but are dimorphic in behavior. The males of some "monomorphic" passerine species sing loudly or make themselves conspicuous in other ways. The appearance of sexual differences in behavior indicates a possible dimorphism in the nervous systems. Arguments are made that the nervous systems of the sexes are identical in these cases, and that behavioral differences appear because of differences in hormones circulating in the blood which activate only particular parts of the nervous system. Such may be the case for some species, but there is also an argument to be made for

Figure 8.8 Female deep-sea fish with male fused to her head. This is one of the more extreme examples of sexual dimorphism in animals. (From von Frisch 1964.)

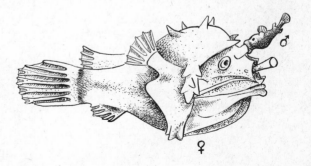

the "dimorphic nervous systems" theory. For example, fighting behavior of the males and females of wild rats and mice is vastly different, and the greater aggressiveness shown by males has been believed due to the level of male hormones in the blood. However, injections of male hormones into females and into castrated males produced two different results—indicating that the nervous system is essentially different in the two sexes (Scott 1966).

The observer of animal behavior should not seek to explain a single morphological or behavioral factor without considering the population's overall ecology. In explaining an observation, several factors may have to be considered at once. As examples of the interrelationships of morphology to behavior and ecology consider the following: In baboons the males are twice as large and heavy as the females and have well-developed canine teeth. The males are also highly aggressive and defend the young from predators. They have been seen to repel cheetahs and even, in a group, to tease lions. In patas, another primate, sexual dimorphism is also pronounced, but in this group the males are lean and very fast. Usually one male in a group is distinctive for its conspicuous size and coloring. This conspicuous male apparently functions to draw the attention of predators to himself. He doesn't often fight, but, instead, uses his speed to escape. His markings and behavior may also function to enable the troop to follow him to new foraging places through tall savannah grass by his conspicuousness as he sits in some tree (Hall 1964).

Amadon (1959) postulated that in most birds in which the male is larger, the female is probably of optimal size in terms of the ecological demands of the niche. The male has exceeded this size in response to evolutionary pressures of intrasexual competition (sexual selection) for both commodities and mates. In other words, the female best reflects the ecological dimensions of the niche. The male then may be at some disadvantage as he increases in size. His large size may enable him to win con-

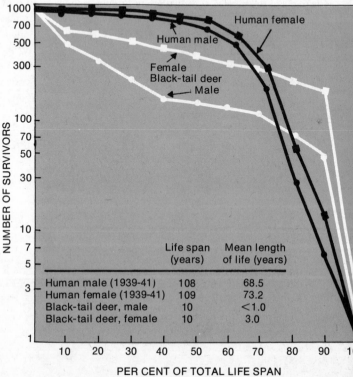

Figure 8.9 Different survival rates between the male and the female in humans and in the black-tail deer. It is interesting that in most mammalian species the male has a higher mortality rate. (From Edward J. Kormondy, *Concepts of Ecology,* © 1969, Prentice-Hall, Inc., p. 77.)

	Life span (years)	Mean length of life (years)
Human male (1939-41)	108	68.5
Human female (1939-41)	109	73.2
Black-tail deer, male	10	<1.0
Black-tail deer, female	10	3.0

Figure 8.10 In the red-necked phalarope the male is smaller and less highly colored than the female. He has less red on his throat and a less conspicuous white stripe over the eye. In this species the female courts the male by rising up in the water, fluttering her wings and calling loudly. After mating, the male builds a nest on the shore and incubates the eggs by himself. He conceals himself by pulling the tall grass over his nest. (From W. Etkin, *Social Behavior From Fish to Man,* © 1964, University of Chicago.)

flicts over commodities and mates, but, in some species including man, a net disadvantage is reflected in his shorter life span (Figure 8.9). Of course there is a limit to which males can diverge from optimum size in order to win conflicts and attract and defend mates. At some point, his fitness must decrease due to the increased hazards of conspicuousness. Also, any increase in size beyond that appropriate to the successful exploitation of the available food would be selected against. The evolutionary and physiological aspects of larger size of males were discussed earlier.

We have seen that there are notable examples of "reversed" sexual dimorphism where the females are larger than the males. In the red-necked phalarope, the male is smaller and colored more dully than the female. The brightly colored female courts the male with elaborate displays. The male builds the nest and, after the female lays the eggs, the male assumes all incubating responsibilities (Figure 8.10). Jehl (1970) reports that in species of sandpipers which show reversed dimorphism in size, the more successful pairings are between the largest females and the smallest males. The large ratio is apparently necessary to keep the proper dominance-subordination relationship between them, and it thus strengthens the pair bond. Reversed sexual dimorphism in vertebrates is the exception among dimorphic species rather than the rule. While such exceptions cannot be ignored, the trend must be considered as of prime importance

when discussing evolutionary phenomena, and larger size in males is by far the more common occurrence in dimorphic species.

There is no question that in many species sexual dimorphism promotes mating success as was postulated by Darwin in 1896. Lack (1968) believes that the large size in males is probably associated with sexual selection because it is so often found in promiscuous or polygymous species (see later). However, Selander (1966) and others believe that sexual dimorphism did not necessarily arise on such an adaptive basis, but, instead, that size difference may have functioned primarily in reducing competition between the sexes for food.

Sexual dimorphism in size may have important effects on foraging differences in the sexes. For example, consider the birds of prey. Storer (1952) found strong reversed sexual dimorphism in body size in several species of birds of prey. Selander (1966) maintained that the difference is probably related to separation in foraging and Schoener (1965:189) stated that, "For many birds of prey body size is probably a better indicator of the size of food preferred than bill size." Mueller and Berger (1970) found a difference in the food preferences of male and female hawks based upon their strikes at sparrows and starlings. Most of the studies of the relationship of sexual dimorphism to foraging behavior in other types of birds have involved measurements of bill size (cf. Amadon 1950, Selander 1966).

In the context of ecological theory it is apparent that dimorphic species exist only under special competitive situations. We know, rather we believe we know, that sexes are unlikely to diverge in a species occupying a narrow niche because of stiff competitive pressures. It is suggested, then, that since certain species have diverged they may be occupying a rather wide niche as a result of low levels of interspecific competition. Among owls, the insectivorous (insect eating) species show much less sexual dimorphism than those which prey on vertebrates. The probable explanation is that insects fall within a narrow size range and vertebrates do not (Earhart and Johnson 1970). A wide niche thus exists for vertebrate-eaters according to our previous definition of niche parameters. The shallowness of the niche is indicated by the paucity of vertebrates in comparison to insects over most area; thus the criterion for a niche which permits divergence of the sexes is met.

Although we may expect sexual dimorphism in species which hunt variable and relatively sparse prey under conditions of reduced competition, in some cases sexual dimorphism may be related to insularity which may, in turn, affect the level of competition. Two species of *Dendrocopus* woodpeckers provide evidence to this effect. *Dendrocopus arizonae* is found in somewhat insular situations among mountains of the west. These insular populations are sexually dimorphic in bill size and the sexes show differences in foraging patterns. The males probe and hammer more and the females are more likely to peel bark. On the other hand the relatively monomorphic and wider ranging *D. borealis*, a close relative, does not diverge in foraging pattern to such a degree (Ligon 1968).

Short (1970) describes the Magellanic woodpecker of South America as dimorphic in bill length where it occurs in the Fuegian forests. He also describes the depauperate forests of Tierra del Feugo as rather "insular" situations. The foraging patterns of the birds have not been studied, but sexual differences may be expected. Such assumptions

are made on the basis of the several studies mentioned in this chapter in which size of trophic appendages has been related to a particular foraging mode. Sexual differences in trophic appendages may have arisen on an ecological basis or through sexual selection, but no matter what their origin they can be expected to result in foraging differences (but for arguments see Willson 1971; and MacArthur and Levins 1964).

Considering the niche dimensions which are associated with sexual dimorphism of trophic appendages we might expect to find sexual dimorphic species on islands and, in fact, the best examples of sexual dimorphism in trophic appendages of vertebrates occur on islands (cf. Amadon 1950; Selander 1966; Schoener 1970). We will again depend on our friend the woodpecker, this time to provide us with an example of the relationship of sexual dimorphism to competition and social behavior.

The larger islands of the West Indies (and a few of the smaller ones) have been colonized by woodpeckers which apparently came from the North American continent. Hispaniola (comprised of the Dominican Republic and Haiti) provided highly suitable conditions for its colonizers and today the birds are found in abundance there. The Hispaniolan woodpecker may be seen darting about in the coconut plantations of the lowlands and in what remains of the hardwood forests of the mountains. They are noisy, not particularly shy, and may be easily observed.

This species is sexually dimorphic in bill size, as is shown in Figure 8.11, (Selander 1966, Wallace 1969) to such an extent that an observer can "sex" the birds by silhouette alone (young birds of both sexes present a problem, however, since their bill sizes are similar to females). Sexual differences are also found in the number of barb groups on the tongue (Selander 1966) and the supporting bones of the tongue, and the jaw muscles (Wallace 1969).

It is interesting that in bill length the sexes of the Hispaniolan woodpecker have diverged from the presumed continental progenitor in different directions. In other words the males of the Hispaniolan woodpecker have larger bills than males of either the red-bellied or golden-fronted, their nearest continental relatives. The insular female, on the other hand, has a smaller bill than the continental representative. Furthermore the insular female's bill is displaced more than the male's. Put another way, the bill of the Hispaniolan male is not very much larger than those of the continental males while the bill of the insular female is quite a bit smaller than the continental female's.

The greater displacement of the bill of the female may have occurred through a dominance relationship with the male. Such a relationship is demonstrated in numerous ways. A female quietly feeding on a tree limb may suddenly be "supplanted" by a male. The more aggressive male simply swoops directly at the female and the female must move to avoid being jostled. Kilham (1970) found that in another woodpecker species the males tended to drive the females farther down the tree by their attacks. The male takes pretty much whatever place he wants on the tree and the female is forced into other areas. Thus the greater morphological change in the females of insular species is not sur-

prising as they adapted to the new, previously unoccupied, parts of the niche into which they were driven. Ward (1965) showed that in weaverbirds, the females dropped in weight in periods of low food supply when males were actually increasing in number. He attributed this to the practice of the dominant males of pushing the females into less productive areas where they died off. Such evidence indicates that dominance relationships may have much greater importance to foraging ecology than has yet been realized.

Field studies of the Hispaniolan woodpecker show sexual differences in foraging behavior. Both sexes take food primarily by hammering to excavate burrowed food, probing into crevices with the bill and tongue, gleaning food from the surface of a limb. However, the sexes differ in the degree to which they employ each technique. Males hammer and probe more with their larger and stronger bills. Females tend to glean more often.

Sympatric species of similar adaptive types differ in the size of trophic appendages by a factor of 1.2 to 1.4 taken as the ratio of the larger to the smaller. The average of such difference has been

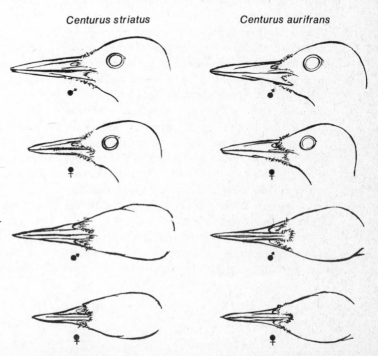

Centurus striatus   *Centurus aurifrans*

Figure 8.11 Two species of *Centurus* woodpeckers, showing the lateral and dorsal view in both the male and the female. Note the greater difference in bill size between the sexes in *C. striatus*. (From Selander 1966.)

found to be about 1.28 (Hutchinson 1959). This figure has been taken as an indication of the level of difference in trophic appendage that must exist in order for species to overlap in habitat (but see Willson's 1971 argument). In the Hispaniolan woodpecker however, the *sexes* diverged to an extent even exceeding this figure (Wallace 1969). The implication, then, is that the *sexes* of the Hispaniolan woodpecker may have divided their niche to the point where the overlap is no greater than occurs between different *species* on continents.

It was found that several environmental factors greatly influence the foraging behavior of the Hispaniolan woodpecker. For example, the population of the Dominican Republic at one end of the island foraged differently than that of Haiti at the other end, especially during the dry winter months when food was scarce. In the bountiful spring months the differences between the two populations disappeared. It seems, then, that in periods of low food supply the foraging pattern is more stongly influenced by local environmental conditions.

There were also seasonal differences in degree of separation of the sexes. In spring, the sexes overlapped much more in foraging technique than during the lean winter months when each sex was forced to use its particular morphology to maximum advantage.

Also, the degree of sexual separation could be influenced by habitat complexity. One group of birds foraged both in coconut groves and in wooded areas with small trees and shrubs on a nearby hillside in the Dominican Republic. Among the coconut trees, most of the foraging was done on the long trunks. In the wooded area, the birds were able to take food not only from the trunks but from the limbs, twigs, and leaves of the canopy. When the foraging data from the two areas were analyzed and compared it was found that the sexes separated more in their foraging patterns in the simpler coconut area.

Lewontin (1965) pointed out that whereas recent colonizers may at first be in strong competition with other species, they later meet increased

intraspecific competition as their numbers grow. This intraspecific competition is apparently an important pressure behind the niche expansion of the species. Whereas interspecific competition forces a species toward its optimal habitats, that is, the "adaptive peak" of the species, strong intraspecific competition may cause the expansion of the species into suboptimal habitats (Svärdson 1949) to which it may adapt, thus effectively widening its niche.

Since the sexes are able to separate and thus utilize different parts of their habitat, it may be assumed that they have increased the net commodities available to the species. Thus the Hispaniolan woodpecker increased its food supply by the fact that the sexes take food in different ways and, presumably, of different types. With such an increase in food supply it is not surprising to find an increase in population and, in fact, the Hispaniolan woodpecker is nothing if not abundant. By their sheer increase in numbers they have increased their levels of social interaction and competition, and the results have illustrated important relationships in behavior and ecology.

One of the peculiarities of the social system of this species is that it nests colonially. Most species of woodpeckers are belligerent and territorial, but as many as 26 pairs of the Hispaniolan woodpecker have been found nesting in a single tree. By no means do they always nest colonially, however. In many cases, a pair will nest entirely out of sight of other pairs and, in coconut groves, only one pair usually nests under the fronds of each tree. Such trees are often closely spaced, but the birds inhabiting them do not show territorial behavior (except around nest holes). Those trees harboring more than one pair are usually large dicotyledenous ones such as are used for shade in the cacao plantations. The factors governing the group size are not known; nonetheless, the gregarious tendency is well represented in the species.

Various theories have been proposed to account for the high level of sociality in this species. Ashmole (1967) postulated an interaction of sociality and population density. It is assumed that the colonizers from the continent were territorial when they reached the island. Then, once the species became established, sexual separation in foraging patterns permitted an increase in population through an expanded food supply (see Van Valen 1965). As population density increased, so did social interactions, including territorial encounters. Finally, the population reached such numbers that those individuals trying to maintain territories were at a disadvantage because they spent so much of their time confronting growing numbers of usurpers. Territoriality, then, became selected against on the basis of its distortion of the time-energy budget. Less aggressive and nonterritorial birds were then at a selective advantage. Once territoriality had been abandoned, the species could move toward the advantages of gregariousness and coloniality which are discussed in Chapter 10.

Kilham (1965) suggested that sexually dimorphic species of woodpeckers take different foods and so are able to forage closer together, thus facilitating social behavior. There is preliminary evidence that such a system may exist in the Hispaniolan woodpecker. In this species, the median measurements in bill size for the sexes fall farther apart than the mean measurement. The result is skewness of the curves (representing the two sexes), but in different directions (Figure 8.12, curves B and C). There are few individuals with bills of the sizes shown at the left tail of curve B and the right tail

of curve C because of competition from theoretical populations A and D. In other words, there is selection against birds of B and C with bills of those sizes (shown by arrows 1 and 3). However, it will be noticed that there is even stronger selection against birds having bills of the size shown at 2. The number of individuals at 1 and 3 are depressed by interspecific competitive pressures. At 2 there are reduced numbers due to intraspecific (intersexual) competition. The numbers at 2 may also be depressed by other factors which are not operating at 1 and 3. For example, sexual selection may operate at 2. If each sex recognizes the other, even partially, on the basis of bill size, there will be selection against those individuals whose bill size lies within the range of that of the opposite sex.

Finally, selection against individuals of both sexes with intermediate bill sizes may operate on an ecological basis to facilitate social interaction. To illustrate, if the bill sizes of the sexes are different, then the sexes may forage together in the same area, without competing too strongly, by taking food of different types or sizes. Thus the sexes may, through increased proximity, maintain stronger pair bonds. The test, of course, is whether sexually dimorphic species, in fact, do forage closer together than monomorphic species. In a comparison of four species of woodpeckers of differing morphologies and foraging modes, it was found that such a relationship does exist. The woodpeckers are *Centurus radiolatus* (Cr) of Jamaica,

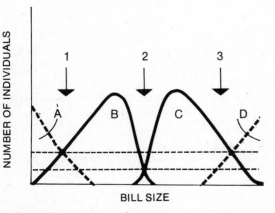

Figure 8.12 A theoretical social influence on variation. See text for an explanation.

C. carolinus (Cc) of central Texas, *C. striatus* (Cs) of Hispaniola, and *Melanerpes portoricensis* (Mp) of Puerto Rico. The degree to which the sexes differ in bill size is related to their foraging proximity as determined by the height at which they search for food in trees (Figure 8.13).

So we see that sexual dimorphism may have special implications for population density and social behavior and that the difference between sexes in size of trophic appendages may even be stronger than that between species because of a need for social interaction.

MONOGAMY, POLYGAMY, AND POLYANDRY

Mating patterns among animals vary widely and may be described according to the nature of the bond that forms between the sexes. Bonds may be categorized according to their duration and the number of mates an individual maintains at one time. Sexual dimorphism, as we learned in Chapter 6, is related to the type of pair bond that is formed, whether that bond is brief or sustained. Brief pair bonds are those which form only long enough for fertilization or copulation to take place. Sustained pair bonds may form well before fertilization occurs and may continue for varying periods of time. For example, in some birds which have sustained pair bonds, the bond is dissolved early after the nest is completed. In others it may continue for years or until the death of one of the pair.

An individual may form pair bonds with one or several mates. Those individuals which form bonds with several members of the opposite sex may do so "simultaneously," so that bonds exist with several mates at one time, or sequentially, by dissolving one pair bond before initiating the formation of the next. It may be argued that no pair bond at all forms in those species which meet only briefly for copulation, but at such times the intense mutual interest shown between partners and the repelling of mating competitors indicate that the relationship does hold important characteristics in common with sustained bonds.

For purposes of illustration we will consider examples of monogamous birds—those taking one mate. Such pairings occur in about 90 percent of bird species. We are reminded that in species which must feed their young the clutch size probably has been evolved according to the number of young which can be fed. Since more food can be brought by two parents than by one, each adult will tend to leave more offspring per union if it has only one mate, provided the sex ratio of breeding adults is about at equality. Then both can help to feed the brood. If a bird has more than one mate then, generally, only one parent is available to feed the

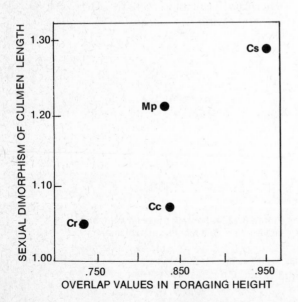

Figure 8.13 A social effect of sexual dimorphism. See text for an explanation.

young since the other may be off seeking another partner. The principle is discussed in Chapter 6.

Monogamy may also result if the numbers of the sexes are unequal. We have considered the weaver-bird in which males force females into suboptimal foraging areas in times of food shortage and thus, in many cases, cause their death. The result is a chronic shortage of females. Therefore the males are monogamous, since there would be little advantage to leaving one female to rear fewer eggs while seeking out another of the scarce females. Here, presumably, monogamy has risen as a result of socially induced mortality.

We know that, as a rule, monogamous species are sexually monomorphic (Chapter 6). Many of the examples of bird species which immediately may come to mind are sexually dimorphic in coloration or morphology so it may be surprising to find that in the greater number of species by far, the sexes are monomorphic (Lack 1968). Under certain conditions, such as that of high predator risk, the sexes may both be cryptic; in species which are able to flee, defend themselves, or in which little danger from predators exists both sexes may be conspicuous. In either case, however, an individual is likely to have only one mate at a time.

Polygamy is the condition in which a pair bond exists between one male and several females, either simultaneously or sequentially (see Lack 1968; Lanyon 1963). In these species the males are often garish, conspicuous, and relatively short-lived. In altricial birds the condition usually can only exist if food is abundant enough for females working alone to be able to gather sufficient amounts for herself and a small brood. Lack points out that among closely related species, grassland seed eaters, which usually suffer no food shortage, are more commonly polygamous than are forest-dwelling insect eaters which seek comparatively sparse food. Polygamy, for some species then, can be considered an adaptation to the food surplus when the sex ratio is about equal. Polygamy may also arise in populations where some males are forced into suboptimal habitats through territorial behavior of dominant males. It has been found that for some species a female can leave more offspring by mating with an already mated male in a good territory than with an unmated male in a poor territory. Shortage of nest space, strong differences in the suitability of territories for breeding, and "patchiness" in food distribution all select for polygamy in females and hence increase the numbers of surplus males (Brown 1969).

The relationship of food levels to breeding systems does not hold for all species. Lack (1968) reports that in some species which live amid abundant food the males are monogamous and, by helping the females, they raise even larger broods than the females could alone.

Polyandry presents special problems to behavioral ecologists. In such a system the female plays the dominant role in courtship and she may take several mates each season. She may be morphologically or behaviorally more conspicuous than the male and, after laying the eggs, she leaves the male to tend to them unaided. His responsibility restricts the number of matings he is able to effect each season. Polyandry is rare in animals and there is, as yet, no ecological clue as to how or why the condition develops but it may be a source of satisfaction to feminists.

In a discussion of wife-sharing in the Tasmanian hen (Smith and Ridpath 1972) it was reported that mating groups of one female and two males (usually brothers) were able to rear more offspring than simple pairs. In these cases, polyandry was simultaneous rather than sequential and the basic scheme of rearing offspring was much the same in triangles as in pairs.

Among the more fascinating types of animal behavior is that involving aggressive interaction—when one animal belligerently moves against another one. The result is often a redistribution of resources, and its impetus may involve competition. It should be made clear at the start, however, that by no means are all aggressive encounters the result of competition, nor does all competition involve aggression.

Aggression, and especially one of its specific expressions, fighting, has captured the interest of men for centuries. Only in recent years has the phenomenon been critically analyzed in an effort to discover its ecological importance. Probably a remarkable paper by Collias, in 1944, was instrumental in spurring discussions of the subject and his report remains a landmark in that it predates what are often regarded as current findings. Much of the recent interest in the subject involves efforts to discover the basis of the highly aggressive behavior of man, especially as his technical ability seems to increasingly outstrip his wisdom.

As we peruse the animal kingdom, we may notice that aggressive behavior exists at several levels. Some species are highly aggressive and others are not aggressive at all. Even among relatively closely related species of similar adaptive types there can be great differences in agressive behavior. Patas, for example, show almost no real aggression. These primates live in a woodland-savannah habitat in Africa in groups of about fifteen animals each. Such groups are strictly territorial and, while males of different groups may threaten each other, they apparently never fight, and within groups no aggressive behavior has ever been seen (Hall 1965). Baboons, on the other hand, live in a similar type of habitat and may engage in frequent and violent aggressive behavior, especially in areas of high population density (DeVore and Hall 1965).

It has been suggested that the more "successful" species are the more aggressive ones; Southwick (1970) maintains that it is more than coincidental that some of the world's most successful animals are characteristically aggressive and adaptable. In other words they may be described as both behaviorally and ecologically aggressive. "Ecological aggressiveness" refers to their ability to invade and colonize new areas. Behavioral aggressiveness may enable them to survive in competitive situations. If the word "aggressive" is to be used in an ecological context it should probably be applied to the more adaptable species showing high levels of exploratory behavior. In any case, we are primarily concerned here with what Southwick terms "behavioral aggressiveness."

Why is one species aggressive and another not? Why are members of a species more aggressive at one time than another? Why do normally placid individuals suddenly display violently aggressive behavior? Why are some individuals in a population much more aggressive than others? The solutions to such questions must be synthesized through a consideration of social structure, environment, and evolution and, regrettably, our level of information, or our synthetic abilities, at this time are not sufficient to yield unqualified answers.

INTRASPECIFIC AGGRESSION

Aggression, in most cases, can be expected to be directed toward competitors—the higher the level of competition the greater the likelihood of aggressive interaction. Therefore aggression can be expected to occur predominantly between members of the same species. We have already discussed the ecological implications of territoriality, hierarchies, and individual distance, all of which may result in a division of commodities. Such interactions, of course, are most often parts of intraspecific social systems. That aggression is often directed toward the strongest competitor is indicated by descriptions of aggressive encounters within a population. In experiments with rhesus monkeys, Southwick (1970) found that when food was in short supply, a strange animal introduced to the group was attacked by those with whom it would compete most directly. Juve-

niles attacked introduced juveniles and females attacked females, etc., seemingly in the operation of a type of social template. (Sexes are sometimes recognized on the basis of apparently insignificant characters. In the flicker the male has a "moustache" at the corner of the mouth which is lacking in the female as we see in Figure 9.1. If the female of a pair is captured and a moustache painted on her, she will be attacked by her own mate.)

Adults are generally inhibited from attacking

Figure 9.1 In the American flicker, the sexes are recognized on the basis of a "moustache" which is present on males. If a moustache is painted on the female, she will be treated as a male by the other flickers. (After Noble 1936.)

Figure 9.2 From bottom to top: first year, second year and adult herring gulls. The adult plumage does not appear until the third year. Whereas subadult birds are not likely to be able to breed successfully, they are also not attacked by adults in the breeding season. (Photo: Van Rackages, New York.)

subadults. The young of many species of birds do not grow adult plumage until they are sexually mature (Figures 9.2 and 9.3). The result of the absence of such coloration is the failure of the young to release the adults' aggressive behavior until they are no longer dependent upon adults for their food and can respond to attacks by defending themselves or fleeing. Thus they gain the aggression-releasing adult plumage at a time when they begin to compete directly with the older birds.

As another example of intraspecific competition consider the interaction around the nest sites of weaverbirds (Collias and Collias 1962, 1964). The nests are arranged communally, several in one tree. The male builds the outer shell and attracts females to it by hanging at the entrance and singing. A female accepts by entering the nest (or by copulating), and then she finishes the nest. When a female in a tree is about to enter a nest, competition becomes fast and furious and neighboring males may swoop in and knock the female away from another male's nest entrance. The female suffers the buffeting, but the aggression is actually directed against the male nest builder.

Female weaverbirds also compete for nests although they are much less aggressive than males. If one female hesitates at a nest entrance, another may dart past and enter the nest herself. Younger females take longer to choose a nest, vacillate more, and are likely to pause before entering. They are thus often displaced by older females darting past them. In such cases it may be assumed that learning has influenced the level of aggressive behavior between competitors.

Sometimes a male continues to display at the entrance after a female has accepted the nest. In one case, the female inside reached out and grabbed the displaying male's head feathers and held on while he tried to free himself. After that he stopped his displaying at her doorstep.

Unchecked intraspecific aggression would result in havoc, of course. In the maintenance of aggression as a response to competition it is important that the aggression occur only to certain levels and within certain contexts so that the delicate balances of the social system are not upset.

INTERSPECIFIC AGGRESSION

Aggressive interactions may occur between animals of different species. On the basis of what we know about the advantages of aggression, we can assume that in most cases interspecific aggression is directly related to competition for commodities. For example, the pugnacious starling, *Sturnus vulgaris,* may eject woodpeckers from a hole after the woodpecker pair has laboriously excavated the nest site. The tree holds no special interest for the starlings until the hole is made; then they show aggressive behavior toward the woodpeckers and actual fighting may occur. A review of the discussions of interspecific threat signals in Chapters 6 and 7 will show that in most of these cases the signals were developed as a response to competition.

Normally, the behavior of a predator toward its prey probably does not involve aggression. The lion about to spring for its prey shows no more aggressive signs than a man does toward his dinner. The prey's reaction toward its predator may involve real aggression however. A terrified wild pig, cornered by a young lion which has not been able to kill it on the first attempt, may charge the lion with all signs of true hostile aggression —tail high, ears back, and squealing loudly. Obviously here is an angry animal. At this point the young lion may show what is an integral part of the aggressive pattern but at the opposite end of the spectrum—fear.

It is important to recognize that fear may be a component in all aggressive behavior. Aggressiveness in animals is not simple encounters between two hostile individuals, as Tinbergen (1968) points out. Aggressiveness may be tempered by, and in some cases may change to, fear. The components can be seen manifesting themselves sep-

Figure 9.3 Northern boat-billed herons, *Cochlearius c. zeledoni.* On the left is a juvenile male, on the right an adult male. Notice the lighter color and more distinct markings of the adult. In this species the juveniles are sometimes able to breed before they develop adult plumage. (Photo: Van Rackages, New York.)

arately in territorial encounters between birds holding adjacent territories. The territory owner shows aggression in chasing an intruding neighbor back into his own territory; but once in the intruder's territory, aggressiveness diminishes and fear mounts in the first bird and he encounters rising aggression in the bird he had earlier been chasing.

CROWDING

The effects of overcrowding on levels of aggression can be demonstrated quite simply by a visit to New York City or a morning drive on a Los Angeles freeway, but such behavioral reactions to crowding are not exclusively man's. We have already referred to experiments on the effects of overcrowding in animals which were begun by John Calhoun in 1947 and which were to continue for several years. In one experiment, he placed five pregnant Norway rats into a quarter-acre outdoor pen. The rats had unlimited amounts of food and water and did not suffer from predation. They were allowed to interact freely and, over the next 28 months, the population never exceeded 200, and stabilized at 150. Considering the biotic potential of rats, the population could have reached 50,000 in that span of time. Calhoun estimated that 50,000 rats can be accommodated in 10,000 square feet of space and remain healthy if they are kept in small cages 8 inches square. So why did the population level off at 150 in the "wild" state? The answer seems to be that, at high density, aggressive behavior increases to the point where normal behavior patterns, including reproduction, are disrupted. Such stress may result in pregnant females not coming to term or in nesting behavior so disrupted that the young cannot be cared for properly. The aggressively dominant males continued to exhibit normal behavior, but the subordinates either (1) avoided both fighting and sex; (2) became sexually hyperactive, constantly following females, but breaking the normal sequence of events and showing abnormal copulatory behavior; (3) became

pansexual, mounting anything male or female, young or old, receptive and nonreceptive; or (4) withdrew from all social activities and roamed about chiefly when other rats slept. Male rats often engaged in unprovoked fighting. Those hardest hit by the high level of aggression were females and young, and their numbers were reduced disproportionately (Calhoun 1962a and b).

Southwick (1970) describes experiments he conducted at the University of Wisconsin with mouse populations. He found that as crowding increased, social disintegration occurred. The mice spent increasing amounts of time and energy in fighting. They became wounded, their health deteriorated, parasitic infections increased, and they frequently cannibalized their young. For further information on such behavior the reader is referred to Myers (1966), Burns (1968), and Stokes (1969). It has also been noticed in other species that as density increases so does aggression. Baboons fight more frequently in larger groups and in areas of high population density. Rhesus monkeys in India normally show a high level of aggression, but hostile encounters are much more frequent in cities, towns, and temple grounds where they are crowded and can easily see each other than in the forest areas where population density is lower and cover reduces the level of interaction (Southwick 1970).

The implications of such findings for man are alarming when we realize that Manhattan now harbors 75,000 people per square mile (Ehrlich and Ehrlich 1968) and the entire greater New York area (now at 12 million) is expected to increase to 30 million by 1985 according to urban architect Ian McHarg. Also, it seems that in spite of small depressions in rate of population increase here and there, the world's population is expected to double in 30 or 35 years and then again every few years after that. It may be argued that our population will be brought under control by "natural means" before such a situation occurs. That may be true, and that is precisely what we should try to avoid (see Chapter 7).

IS AGGRESSION INSTINCTIVE?

Although aggressive behavior is common among animals, including man, the nature of its neural seat is the subject of vigorous argument. There are those who believe that it is basically innate and subject to all the laws of true instinctive patterns. The opposing camp is comprised of those who maintain that aggression is learned, and others believe that both learning and instinct are necessary for the successful expression of aggression.

It has been demonstrated in a variety of species that aggressive behavior can be strongly affected by experience (Scott 1960; Kahn 1951; Kuo 1960, 1961; and Ulrich 1938). However, it should be apparent that because some factor can sway the expression of aggression does not mean that factor is the underlying basis of the phenomenon. Those who propose that aggression is based solely in individual experience offer a number of possible explanations for the formation of the trait. Scott, for example, holds that aggressive behavior is gradually learned early in life through pain encountered in competing for food and in play-fighting. Other researchers (cf. Dollard et al. 1939; Berkowitz 1962; Montagu 1962) believe that aggression is the result of frustration (any impediment to reaching a goal). Some proponents of the experience argument maintain that if aggression were instinctive, there would appetitive behavior for fighting and that no such behavior can be demonstrated (Craig 1928). (Although there is contrary evidence which demonstrates an appetitive phase, as will be pointed out.)

Marler's (1957) position represents an important step toward a theory of endogenous control. He agrees that aggression must be a reaction to environmental influences, but he admits to endogenous influences, such as hormones, which render an animal susceptible to specific stimuli.

The proponents of the theory of instinctive aggression include two prominent ethologists, from whom much of this discussion was taken: Konrad Lorenz and Irenaus Eibl-Eibesfeldt. In general agreement are other important figures who approach the problem somewhat differently, such as Freud and Mitscherlich. Let us examine some of the evidence indicating that aggression is based in instinct, which, to this author, is the stronger case.

An unusually clear demonstration that aggression is innately controlled has been described by Lorenz (1963) and Rasa (1969). In the highly aggressive chichlid fish, *Etroplus maculatus* and *Geophagus brasiliensis*, the males *must* fight before they can successfully pair with females. If no other male is around they will attack and kill the female. There is apparently a damming up of a "drive" (action-specific energy) which must be released before the next pattern (involving mating) in the sequence can be carried out. The fighting urge is quickly fatigued, and aggression stops well before the male is physically fatigued. We can see here certain important similarities with instinctive patterns as they are discussed in Chapter 2. It is certainly true that many aggressive patterns can be shown to operate through a system involving fixed action patterns, IRM's, and releasers. Consider the sticklebacks, which react in precise ways to simple decoys with red undersides. Such behavior alone stands as evidence of a close relationship between aggression and instinct.

As other evidence indicating an instinctive center of aggression, it has been found that rats will learn mazes to be able to kill mice, and thus, it is presumed, to perform consummatory behavior. (It may be argued that this is simply predation since rats sometimes eat mice.) Squirrel monkeys, after being infuriated by a painful shock, would learn a task in order to be able to attack a ball (Azrin, et al. 1965). It can be argued here that aggression in this case is *learned* as a result of painful experience; nevertheless the response does show the classical symptoms of the presence of an appetitive behavior for aggression. Provocation apparently elicits an aggressive urge which, when it is discharged, is followed by a reduction in tension.

To dispute the idea that animals primarily learn aggressive behavior, rats and mice have been reared in isolation so that no opportunity for such learning existed. When conspecifics were introduced to their cages, the isolated animal attacked, showing all the normal fighting and threat patterns (Eibl-Eibesfeldt 1963). Kruijt (1964) reared jungle fowl (the type used in cockfights) in isolation and found they were *more* aggressive than "socialized" animals. If left in isolation they would even attack their own tails. (We are reminded of the lowering of the threshold for courting behavior in caged doves as discussed in Chapter 2.)

Eibl-Eibesfeldt (1970) points out that the existence of species-specific patterns of fighting in isolates is not an entirely satisfactory indicator of the innateness of aggression since fighting or threat behavior may be derived from other types of patterns—such as feeding—which are instinctive.

Lorenz argues that since fighting is instinctive, if it has not been released for a long time it will go off "in vacuo" through a buildup of its action-specific energy. The implications for man are readily apparent. The view has been challenged by R. A. Hinde who maintains that fighting is derived principally from the situation and adds there is no reason to postulate causes that are purely internal to the aggressor.

Tinbergen has emphasized that the disagreement is purely semantic since the ethological instinct theory fully accounts for the interaction of internal and external variables. Lorenz's reference to the "spontaneity of aggression" must be predicated upon the existence of a certain set of environmental conditions. Tinbergen refers to the male stickleback, which does not always react to an approaching male the same way under all conditions. His response may vary widely, from none at all to a full attack. His response is, as we know, related to his internal state and that, in turn, is strongly dependent upon the environment.

Lorenz has maintained that a redirected attack exhausts the aggressive urge. Tinbergen (1968) does not entirely agree. He states that from animal work (and even from soccer matches, since after one match, *war* was declared by the two participating countries), we can infer that aggressive behavior has two simultaneous and opposite effects: a waning effect and one of self-inflammation. The latter may have the effect, when full-blown, of developing mass hysteria in large groups of people.

The appearance of a behavioral pattern is not evidence of a neural "center" for its control. If aggression is instinctive, however, such a center (IRM) must exist. There is some experimental evidence for the existence of such centers. For example, the electrical stimulation of specific areas of the central nervous system can elicit aggression in a number of species (see a review by Kaada 1967). However, it has been argued that the existence of an internal physiological mechanism, which needs only to be stimulated to induce fighting, does not prove the existence of a "fighting instinct."

IS MAN INSTINCTIVELY AGGRESSIVE?

An argument that may be as critical as any science has approached is centered over whether man possesses an instinct for aggression. Any successful action taken by man to inhibit the initiation of war must ultimately incorporate the answer since systems of control based on the two prevailing theories would be vastly different. Also, the theories are important in respect to such every-day matters as violence in the streets, sports, and television programming. Is aggression, for example, being *learned* or *released* through watching violent scenes on the screen?

The argument over whether man harbors an aggressive spirit which is deeply seated in instinct has been going on for years. Recently, several books have taken up the controversy and pushed it to some degree into the public consciousness. Many psychologists, sociologists, and anthropologists have concentrated almost exclusively on the cultural determinants of human behavior. The result has been a tacit, and sometimes vehement, denial of man's biological heritage. It seems that the notion of an instinctive aggressive spirit in man toward his own species is an unpopular idea. It is more pleasant to believe that man is a gentle spirit, driven by outside forces to commit acts of aggression. The result has been an effort to manipulate the environment, institutionally or culturally, in an effort to decrease the level of aggression among us.

Undeniably, in so brainy and social a creature as the human animal there is a strong culturally based component of behavior. To assume the existence of innate patterns or tendencies in man is not to deny that these can be modified culturally. We rarely see couples copulating wildly in romantic little restaurants no matter what their mood. Nor does the discovery of a peaceful tribe in some mountain refuge refute the existence of an aggressive instinct in man in general. Who knows to what degree the members of this tribe have learned to control themselves? There is another point to be made here. Even if it could be shown that they, in fact, harbored no aggressive urges, their condition might be explained on the basis of strong selection for pacifism in an isolated group. We are not particularly interested here in the behavioral extremes of our species, but in the prevailing condition for the group in general. Let us examine some of the evidence.

An interesting experiment by Hokanson and Shetler (1961) demonstrated that violence could be provoked in children, which when discharged, caused a measure of relief. First an experimenter was able to induce anger in a group of students, an increasingly simple task, with the result that they showed an increase in blood pressures. The group was then divided, and one group was given a chance to observe this experimenter in a series of tasks and to administer electrical shocks whenever he made an error. The other group could only inform him of an error by flashing a light. Those who believed they were administering painful shocks showed a rapid decrease in blood pressure while those who were not so released did not. In other experiments it was found that verbal insults also served to discharge aggressive urges. The release of tension was of short duration as is the case in other types of instinctive patterns.

If one wishes to debate whether aggression in man is innate, then he must also ponder the existence of *inhibitors*. Remember the jackdaw that abandoned his attack and began preening his intended victim when the latter turned his head and exposed his silver nape feathers? and the dominant wolf that was unable to attack a subordinate who purposefully exposed his vulnerable neck? Can aggression in man also be blocked or inhibited by signals on the part of the attacked? Certainly if they exist they are very weak, as is demonstrated by the frequent occurrence of what is termed "unnecessary" violence in robberies often against helpless or pleading victims. Eibl-Eibesfeldt points out that familiarization acts as an inhibitor, and one is less likely to attack someone he knows. Criminologists, on the other hand, indicate that most murders are carried out by persons who knew the victim—but this may be a function of an increased level of contact.

Early investigators of Australian aborigines found that adults often brought children with them when meeting strangers in the belief that no one would harm a child. We know that among dogs, puppies are rarely attacked or bitten, and young birds do not elicit aggression from older birds until they gain adult plumage. Among humans, childkilling is often considered outrageous —even by "civilized" man at war. Does the sight of a child inhibit aggression in man? We know that soldiers have been able to kill children purposively at close range, but the action is rarely applauded and, in fact, is often condemned by the citizenry. Still, there is no real evidence of man's being inhibited from killing children.

If any system of inhibitors does appear in man,

to *any* degree, our technology has brought us past the point where it could operate effectively. The long-range gunner or bombardier is certainly unable to see the pleading faces of the people, or to see their babies, so there can be little opportunity for the activity to be inhibited. In fact, those soldiers may only be filling breeches or pushing buttons with no feeling of aggression at all. The aggressive decision may have been made miles from the carnage by men moving pins on maps. I remember a discussion with a very properly accoutered co-ed at a large university. She informed me in the course of the conversation that she was a regular churchgoer, loved children, had small brothers and sisters, loved her parents very much, and that they were proud of her. Our conversation began because of a sign which she was carrying which said, "Bomb the Hell out of Hanoi." Perhaps it is true that some forms of aggression could be inhibited if the victim could somehow be personalized.

Man has developed certain signals which do not serve as inhibitors but which act to deter aggression by giving the potential aggressor certain information. For example, open-handed greetings, including handshakes, show that no weapon is being carried. Bowing places a man at a distinct disadvantage and therefore indicates peacefulness as well as a measure of trust. These must be considered learned patterns, but they are nevertheless generally effective in dissuading aggression. It is interesting that the most exaggerated and intricate forms of "polite" behavior have developed in countries which have the highest population densities, such as in Japan, where social protocol is of great importance.

A study of the maturation of instinct in nonhuman primates was reported by Deets and Harlow (1971). The findings have important implications for the study of aggression in man. They found that aggression is innate in certain primates and suggested that it is a solid component of the biological heritage of man. In their experiments, they deprived rhesus monkeys, *Macacus indicus*,

of the opportunity for social learning at various periods of their lives by isolating individuals in cells where they were unable to interact with any other individual.

In one set of experiments, infants were placed in isolation only a few hours after birth. These individuals had no opportunity to learn aggression, therefore if aggression were a learned trait they should never have exhibited this characteristic. However, this was not the case. At the period in their lives when they would normally have begun to show aggression, they began to react in new ways to stimuli. When a glove was drawn across the cage of one of the isolates at this time, it would respond by threatening the keeper. Just as often it would attack. However, there was never an object upon which the aggression could be released, with the result that the monkeys attacked their own bodies. They bit themselves so ferociously that in some cases they seriously wounded themselves, and one individual even blinded itself!

Just as these animals "suddenly" develop aggression at some point in their lives, they also, rather spontaneously, begin to show the desire to affiliate with members of their group (affection) and fear different stimuli. Each of these behavioral characteristics appears at rather predictable times in the individual's history. The sequence of their appearances is very important. During the course of their development, the animals first show a tendency to affiliate with members of their own species. During the early weeks, they do not fear the others nor do they show any aggression toward them. After a few months, however, they begin to show fear reactions, not only toward other animals, but toward novel inanimate objects as well. They develop fear reactions whether or not they have ever been exposed to threatening situations. The isolates, however, tend to develop the pattern a little later than their normally reared counterparts.

In another set of experiments (Sackett 1966), infants were separated from their mothers almost immediately after birth. The infants were placed in total isolation, with sounds masked by white noise. There was no physical or visual contact with other monkeys. Slides of other monkeys engaged in various activities, including threatening ones, were shown on a screen in the isolates' cells. In the early weeks of life, the infants showed no reaction to the pictures, but at about three months, there was an abrupt change in their responses. When the threat pictures were shown, the infants displayed fear and distress. It seems that some innate mechanism, one that produces fear under threatening conditions, had suddenly matured.

It is not until the end of the first year, according to Deets and Harlow, that aggression becomes part of the behavioral repertoire. At about this time the young primates engage in vigorous play which includes biting, threatening, and hair-pulling. Occasionally the roughhousing gets out of hand and breaks into brief episodes of barking, threatening and physical abuse. When the victim cries out in pain, the attack stops. As aggression is making its appearance, a dominance hierarchy is emerging which will render actual fighting unnecessary in later life. It seems that aggression, just as fear, must mature within the individual before it is expressed.

Deets and Harlow devised several experiments wherein monkeys were isolated during critical periods of their lives when one or another of the behavioral responses was maturing. They found that if the monkey is isolated from other monkeys during the time that the innate tendency to affiliate and the fear of the unfamiliar stimuli are maturing, the monkey becomes fearful of social contact. The aversion is rather permanent. The infant in such a case shows no affection for other monkeys and does not learn to control his fear of other monkeys. Later on, as aggression matures, the isolate's fears may temporarily suppress any expression of his aggression. But, not for long. The isolate proves to be hyperaggressive during later contact with other monkeys.

If a monkey is not isolated until the fear response has matured but before aggression has reached fruition, a different social pattern emerges. The developing infant will have learned to control fear of other monkeys, but will not have learned to control his aggression toward them. In the experiment, such isolates showed little fear of their peers but they were very aggressive and came to dominate the control monkeys. These isolate infants differed from the first group in their reduced level of behavior and in their ability to show some degree of affiliation.

In monkeys which were not isolated until maturation of fear and aggression were established, there was little behavioral abnormality after eight months of solitary confinement (except for a brief period of heightened social activity when first returned to the group).

If the patterns of affection, fear, and aggression are indeed innate characters, genetically seated in the constitution of the animal, then the importance of learning becomes apparent. Affection, fear and aggression seem to swell within each animal at a certain time, no matter what its experience. However, in order for these innate patterns to be of benefit, they must be tempered and moderated through the molding effects of experience. Primates are "learning animals" with extended parental care and there is therefore facility and time for experience to have its effect.

The timing of the appearance of the patterns of fear, aggression and affection is important to their general adaptiveness. For example, if fear developed before affection it might be difficult for the individual to form bonds. However, affiliation appears first. A monkey growing up in the wild stays close to the group and they protect him from danger. He may be reckless and foolhardy in the early weeks of his life, but later on, fear emerges and the infant begins to avoid many dangers on his own. Interestingly, in those first few months, the mother's protective responses wane as the fear pattern develops in the infant (Hansen 1966). The fear response is not generally elicited from the individual the infant has been associated with earlier.

While the advantages of fear and affection are intuitively apparent, we may have more trouble seeing how aggression can be useful in animals which are highly social. It must be remembered that most nonhuman primates live in groups and intraspecific aggression might be expected to be incompatible with such a system. However, the importance of dominance hierarchies has already been discussed and aggression would function in the development of the group structure. In fact, group living might not be possible in the absence of aggression.

We might ask why aggression would not disappear within the individual once his rank was established. However, the question neglects the complexity of social groups as well as the possible other advantages which might be accrued to the maintenance of aggression. For instance, the possibility of gaining leadership or changing positions exists for members of any group and such changes would be facilitated by aggressiveness in some types of systems.

In addition to in-group aggression, there may be out-group aggression as well. Primates are not usually territorial animals in the strict sense, but groups do usually avoid each other where their ranges may overlap. When groups encounter each other there may be vigorous threats or even fighting. In many species it is extremely difficult for a strange individual to be accepted into the group.

The adaptiveness of the out-group aggression may be in dispersing groups so that the resources of the area may be most efficiently exploited. Also, such aggression may be based in kin-selection if we are willing to assume that cooperation within the group has value such as in greater foraging efficiency or increased protection. Since groups are cohesive units, there is a strong likelihood that the individuals are related to one degree or another. Under such conditions, there is a fitness advantage to cooperative behavior. Any altruism may result not only in ecological advantages but may increase the likelihood of the performer's genes being continued via relatives. In order to increase the possibility of cooperative behavior, then, it is best if the individuals in a group exclude others who are not related.

The idea of "getting at" man's behavior by examining other animals is rife with dessention. It should be made clear that there is no intention here to say that because monkeys show a certain developmental scheme, man does too. On the other hand, *if* we are going to extrapolate from the behavior of other animals to man, it is probably better to choose those species which have the greatest similarity to us. The controlled study of other animals, which is not often possible with man, may give us certain insight clues to our behavior which we can then look for, or at least test in other ways.

In Deets and Harlow, they cite evidence which indicates that the same maturational sequence of affection, fear and aggression occurs in humans as in the primates they studied. In the human baby any adult is accepted with equal enthusiasm at first. By the second month, any face readily elicits smiling from the infant. Later, the infant becomes more discriminating and smiles only at familiar persons. By the sixth or seventh month, attachment to specific individuals is apparent. They baby is distressed when removed from them and generally cannot be quieted by strangers. In another month, the infant begins to show overt fear of strangers. Thus, normally affiliation and attachments are evidenced in the human before fear reactions develop. Aggression, according to the primate data, should appear in the first four or five years of human life but there is as yet no verifying information. Psychologists have concentrated on learning processes and correcting behavior in older children and have almost ignored the innate development of human behavioral patterns.

In one of the few studies available, it was found that aggression is established early and is relatively stable, particularly in boys. The level of aggressiveness in pre-school years appears to indicate the level of such behavior through early adolescence in females and through adulthood in males (Kagan and Moss 1962).

There is also dismaying evidence that children who have spent their early years in socially sterile institutions show an impaired ability to form social relationships. They also show an impairment in the capacity to control aggression (Yarrow 1964). Even in the face of such evidence however, psychologists have continued to ignore the ontogeny of behavior. It is reasonable to predict that in ensuing years there will be increasing attention to the biological heritage of man in the search for solutions to his social problems.

FIGHTING

Fighting is one expression of the aggressive mood. It is potentially the most dangerous to the participants and, in some cases, has become one of the most highly structured forms of interaction. The widespread occurrence of fighting in the animal world, and the existence of ritualized or "tournament" fighting, paradoxically indicates a strong selection for a dangerous behavior. Since fighting is dangerous it would have been selected out long ago if it were not highly adaptive. Instead, it is maintained in a wide variety of animals, and formalized and incredibly complex displays and rituals have developed to keep its risk at a minimum.

Some species do not fight at all and others may fight to the death. One of the more bizarre cases of high aggression occurs in certain sharks. In these species the eggs hatch in the uterus and the shark pups are thus born alive. However, the first young shark to hatch within the uterus cannibalizes his brothers and sisters as they emerge from their eggs (Kenney 1968). Such behavior may have elements seated in predation as well as aggression, but it is a most direct means of reducing the numbers of potential competitors.

Elephants are normally peaceful enough with their own, but occasionally serious fights do oc-

cur. Southwick cites Carrington's (1958) description of such conflicts: "They fight head to head, either attempting to push one another backwards with their foreheads, or intertwining their trunks and engaging in a titanic tug of war, so that one animal is drawn into the other's tusks. The struggle may continue until one of the contestants is killed. This usually happens through the weaker elephant breaking away, thereby exposing his unprotected flank to the tusks of his opponent. When thus caught at a disadvantage an elephant can be disembowelled with a quick lunge of the head. The bodies of elephants are sometimes found with their heads battered in, their abdomens ripped open, and great holes torn out of their sides, bearing witness to the ferocity of the struggle."

Such fighting is clearly unadaptive. Among the types of elephant behavior which cannot be so easily explained is that of "rogues"—solitary and ill-tempered bulls. Some rogues have been famous in their time, such as the rogue of Kankankote, a village 50 miles from Mysore in South India. In the 1870s, this rogue terrorized travelers on a road leading to the village, viciously attacking people, stomping them to death, and tearing them apart with his trunk and legs. Carrington (1958) states, "It seems that the typical rogue is either mad, like a homicidal maniac in our own species, or is berserk," although the distinctions are not made clear. The "madness" could be brought on by the pain of a toothache, overstrained tusks, disease, or a gunshot wound. If Carrington's analysis is correct, we must agree with Southwick (1970) that the behavior is aberrant and unadaptive—an evolutionary dead-end which must arise anew each time it occurs.

We are concerned here primarily with the adaptive aspects of the fight. Why does it occur? Where does it fit into the big picture?

One of the most obvious explanations of fighting is that it is a behavioral result of competitive interaction and therefore bestows the same advantages as successful competition. Put in simplistic terms, there is no need for an animal to try to "out-eat" his competitors if that animal can forcibly exclude his competitors from the food.

Fighting may actually function in reducing aggressive interaction. It need not occur every time there is a dispute over commodities or mates. Instead, fighting may be an effective means of establishing a hierarchy and thus avoiding much conflict. Once the hierarchical system is established, fighting might appear rarely within a group; it would probably occur mainly when an animal attempts to change rank, such as when a young animal achieves greater size and challenges his superiors. An animal of unestablished rank may be forced into frequent conflict for a time. For some species, the introduction of a strange animal to the hierarchy results in a round of fights until the position of the newcomer is established.

Fighting also plays an important part in the establishment of territories, as has been mentioned. Once territories are established fighting is greatly reduced. Such reduction could occur through a number of influences, such as the formation of nonbreeding groups which do not infringe on territories, "floaters" which do not challenge territory holders, habituation to nearby territory holders, and the increased level of aggressiveness in territory holders within their own areas which could lead to the quick expulsion of an intruder.

It is important that fighting occur as infrequently as possible because of the dangers involved. The danger is not only that posed by the

Figure 9.4 A quarrel between females of two different, but highly similar, species: a purple finch and a song sparrow. Such interspecific quarrels may develop when the appearance of an unrelated animal elicits aggressive responses which are adaptive on an intraspecific level. These species probably arrived at their similarity in markings through convergent selection for crypticity. In similar sympatric species, aggression may be minimized by differences in utilization of the habitat. (Photo: Robert Hermes from National Audubon Society.)

Figure 9.5 A highly "unlikely" fight. Here a hare attacks a raccoon. The raccoon had approached the hare in the darkness. The hare, apparently unable to get away, responded by thumping the earth. As the raccoon approached the hare leaped over it giving it a drubbing on the head with its hindleg after which the raccoon retreated. (Photo: Lynwood Chase from National Audubon Society.)

threat of bodily harm per se but to its aftermath as well. An injured animal is a weaker animal, and the results can be far-reaching. For example, a dominant squirrel monkey fell to the lowest status after suffering injuries from a "successful" heirarchy battle (Rosenbaum and Cooper 1968). Injured individuals might also suffer higher predation through being incapacitated, or injury could lead to interrupted or altered feeding patterns and place the animal at a competitive disadvantage.

Since fighting is usually a behavioral result of competition, we can expect to find it occurring most often between members of the same species. When fighting occurs between members of differ-

ent species, those species are usually in very direct competition, are very similar in appearance (Figure 9.4), or a prey animal has initiated an attack on its predator. In some cases, however, highly unlikely and unadaptive fighting may arise (Figure 9.5).

In cases of fighting between members of the same species there are distinct advantages to keeping physical harm to a minimum. In keeping with the concept of fitness it would be disadvantageous for an animal to harm a prospective mate, a sibling, or even other individuals that may share a significant number of gene types through kinship.

In point of fact, in most species fighting rarely

Figure 9.6 Two views of fighting male rattlesnakes, *Crotalus ruben.* The fighting is done primarily with the heads as each tries to push the other to the ground but the deadly poisonous snakes never bite each other. (After Eibl-Eibesfeldt 1970 from C. E. Shaw 1948.)

leads to real injury. All-out fighting, when it occurs, occurs usually in relatively harmless species. The dangerous ones, as Eibl-Eibesfeldt points out, are usually those which can also run fast and get away and those which utilize aggressive inhibitors. Among dangerous animals, when one realizes it is beaten in a fight it stops the attack on it through submissive signals (a wolf exposes his neck). Hamsters, *Cricetus*, have no inhibitions against fighting to the death, but this rarely occurs because after a few bites are exchanged one animal usually flees. Apparently, the ability of members of a species to retreat quickly can compensate for the lack of killing inhibitions. It is not known whether fleetness is a very effective protection against the willingness of East African lions, *Felis leo*, to kill members of other prides (Schenkel 1966).

Fighting may be rendered less dangerous by the use of ritual or ceremonial fighting (see Chapters 2 and 6). Such "tournament" fighting may take the form of vocalizations, displays, or "pushing" contests in which the stronger animal is decided with no injuries incurred.

There are many examples of tournament fighting in dangerous animals. Rattlesnakes can kill each other with their poison, but they never bite. Instead, they move side by side, heads raised and try to push each other to the ground. When one is pinned to the ground he is let go and he retreats (Figure 9.6).

Eibl-Eibesfeldt (1970) has described lava lizards which fight each other with the tail. In one fight, a tailless lizard didn't seem to notice his disadvantage and flailed away with the stub. After continually losing after several days of territorial conflict, it seemed to become fed up with always losing and bit an opponent on the tail, thus winning the fight. Such behavior indicates a degree of flexibility in tournament fighting in this species. In the marine iguanas, *Amblyrhynhus cistatus*, of the Galápagos Islands, males defend territories by head-to-head pushing contests (Figure 9.7). When one drops to the ground the fight is over. Rarely, one may bite the other on the back of the neck. Females may engage in damaging fights, however, as they compete for scarce egg-laying sites. In females of some species inhibitions against inflicting injury are not as strong as in males, but in the case of this iguanid the more serious fighting may be the result of increased levels of competition in females.

In some species there are special morphological adaptations for tournament fighting. For example, in fiddler crabs, which begin fights by butting each other with slightly opened claws, small protuberances on the front of the claws keep them from slipping off so that relative strength can be measured more easily. When the fighting increases in intensity the crabs may hold on with their claws, but here again, special structures ensure that the animals grasp each other just so, and no serious damage usually results (Crane 1966).

Horned mammals have provided important information regarding how damage may be avoided

Figure 9.7 Like many other animals, the male marine iguana, *Amblyrhynchus cristatus*, of the Galapagos Islands will defend its territory against intruding males. In A, when the intruder approaches, the occupant of the territory nods his head and struts. He then lunges at the intruder and they push against each other head-on as in B. When one iguana feels he cannot win, he drops to his belly as in C. (From "The Fighting Behavior Of Animals" by Eibl-Eibesfeldt. Copyright © 1961 by *Scientific American, Inc.* All rights reserved.)

in fights. First of all, horn size may give direct information regarding fighting ability (Geist 1966) and the fight may therefore be avoided entirely. When intraspecific fighting does occur the horns are rarely used to inflict injury. The oryx antelope, *Oryx gazella beisa*, uses its long rapierlike horns to impale attacking lions, but in intraspecific fighting the antelopes only spar with the tips. The horns also provide purchase for pushing contests (Figure 9.8).

A belligerent oryx will not attack the vulnerable flank of an opponent even when he has the chance. Instead he will wait until the opponent is facing him before initiating an attack (Walther 1958). Of course the attacker is not disuaded from injuring his opponent through any spirit of benevolence. The attacker is *unable* to pierce the flank of his opponent. When the system works, the male oryx could no more gore an opponent than fly! Remember, this same oryx would wreak havoc on an attacking lion who was unfortunate enough to expose a flank. Fighting a competitor and fighting an attacking predator have been shown to be controlled by different parts of the central nervous system (Kaada 1967). Eibl-Eibesfeldt, by the way, correctly points out that Ardrey, in his popular book *African Genesis* (1962) failed to recognize that there is no necessary connection between the aggressive nature of man and his predatory past. Plant eaters are no more peaceful among themselves than carnivores or hunters.

It is interesting that hornless females show no compunction against butting each other in the flank (Figure 9.9), but of course such attacks are harmless. In those species in which both sexes are horned, there is usually no attack to vulnerable areas by either sex.

In some species of horned animals, the horns or antlers play little part in interspecific fighting. Probably the most effective weapons in deer are the slashing hooves. These weapons are so effective that deer have even been able to repel attacking mountain lions.

A quick overview of African ungulates reveals a wide variety of horn types, although the animals often have common predators. If the horns were subject to selection on the basis of predator defense, one would expect to find a tendency toward similarly due to convergence. The strong differences shown between species tend to support the idea that perhaps horns were developed for intraspecific fighting rather than for predator defense (Eibl-Eibesfeldt 1970).

Since horns are not, then, primarily used to inflict injury, at least in some species, it might be expected that they could assume forms which reduce their effectiveness in battle. Such may be the case in bighorn sheep. The horns are strongly

Figure 9.8 Two fighting bulls, *Oryx gazella beisa,* use their horns as weapons, but only the upper third portion. Later in the fight head-to-head pushing may occur, but in such fights the horns are not directly employed. (After Walther 1958.)

Figure 9.9 The hornless females of the Nilgau antelope fight by butting against their opponent's flanks 50 percent of the time. However, horn-bearing males or females in other species rarely attack in such a manner. (After F. Walther 1961.)

curved and they are not used in repelling predators; instead, a mountain lion faces dazzling and powerful thrusts of the hooves. When engaging in intraspecific fighting, however, the large horns provide strong surfaces for relatively harmless butting and pushing contests.

Another explanation for the development of elaborate head weapons involves sexual selection. The bizarre and exaggerated horns could function in releasing mating behavior in females. Eibl-Eibesfeldt (1970) points out that in such a case, no matter what the original function of the horns, if predation is low enough and if females came to identify males on the basis of their horns, the situation could easily get out of hand. Larger and more elaborate horns could develop which might be almost useless in predator defense, but which could increase fitness in the males through increased likelihood of mating. (Remember, the effect of any releaser can be heightened as was demonstrated in the discussion of supernormal releasers.)

Social influences on fighting behavior have best been demonstrated in laboratory animals. Mice and rats have been used for several types of experiments on fighting behavior although these species are not representative of most social animals. For example, they show little inhibition against serious biting. In fact, each fight usually ends with the loser being bitten. A strange mouse introduced to a group may be inspected for hours, but will eventually be attacked and killed. Rats and mice both seem to lack the inborn system of aggressive inhibitors or appeasement gestures. Scott (1970) maintains they also lack threat signals and tournament fighting, but such behavior has been observed by other researchers. Eibl-Eibesfeldt (1963) describes Norway rats which threaten and approach their opponents broadside; the rats may then enter a phase of boxing and wrestling in true tournament style until one animal falls over. If that animal doesn't retreat, serious biting may result. The switch to real fighting after tournament fighting is not unusual among many species of animals. Rats and mice are unusual in that there is only one dominant and uninjured animal in any group and no status among the rest.

Laboratory experiments on social animals have indicated that socialization may be important in fighting behavior. Generally, exposure to other animals decreases the likelihood of fighting. Kahn (1951) found that animals which had been isolated after weaning attack more often and retreat less often than "socialized" animals. It may be, as Scott (1966) maintains, that socialized animals fight less often from the operation of *active inhibition* (reduced probability of fighting after being bitten in a fight). The phenomenon can also be explained by *passive inhibition* (not fighting as a habit developed by simply not fighting).

Fighting within a species may occur, not only as conflict between individuals, but between groups as well. We have learned of ant colonies which attack strangers on the basis of their scent. Rats and mice may show the same sort of social intolerance. Southwick (1970) describes groups of whitefooted mice which are peaceable as long as they have grown up together, but which react to members of other groups by killing them. One group may also engage another in combat. Rhesus monkeys happening abruptly upon another group may engage in fierce intergroup fighting. Troops of baboons may also attack other troops. Howler monkeys show intergroup hostility but avoid injury by merely howling and shrieking in an intimidating manner.

ALLELOCHEMICS

One of those rare papers which is both important and delightful is a review by Whittaker and Feeney (1971) on the concept of *allelochemics*. We will review and comment upon a few of their more pertinent findings regarding competition.

It has been found that many patterns of attack and defense involve, not only physical force, but chemical agents as well. These agents may operate between plants, between animals, or between plants and animals. Allelochemistry involves the study of the chemical interactions by which one species affects the growth, health, behavior, or population biology of another species.

Such effects are found, for example, in the suppression of the growth—or even the very appearance—of some higher plants by chemicals released from another higher plant, a phenomenon called *allelopathy*. One type of shurb was the hard chaparral studied by C. H. Muller in the hills around Santa Barbara, California. The rain which falls on the plant washes a variety of poisons into the surrounding soil. These poisons, mostly phenolic compounds, inhibit the germination and growth of herb seeds present in the soil. The effectiveness of the inhibitors can be seen after a fire because the destruction of the shrubs re-leases the herb seeds from inhibition. The ground begins to bloom with a profusion of annual herbs for a few years until the regrowth of the shrubs subjects the herbs to new inhibition.

In such a case, the similarities with fighting behavior of animals should be apparent. The shrubs do not compete with herbs by simply trying to catch more sunlight or acquire more water, but by directly excluding the herbs. Of course aggressiveness per se is not involved unless the plants may be called "ecologically aggressive." However, the development of such a competition-reducing mechanism may have occurred on the same adaptive basis as exclusion-through-fighting in animals.

Just as fighting in animals has its undesirable consequences, so are inhibitory chemicals dangerous to the plant forming them. (The term "dangerous" implies only a potential—as Gandalf described his own dangerousness in Tolkien's *Lord of the Rings*.) The chemicals may be especially poisonous to their producers in certain "successional" species (see Odum 1971). Successional species, though, are "vagabond" populations that dominate a community for only a short time at any given place, and then they are gone anyway; so imbuing an area with a poison to which competitors might have lower tolerance than the producer could have immediate advantages. Allelopathic compounds may also be chemically bound in the producer-plant so that their effect is diminished until they are released into the environment. The maintenance of such compounds, and the means necessary to reduce their effect on the producer, place a heavy "metabolic load" on that producer. Substances which could be used for growth and repair are diverted into the manufacture of the poison-systems. The development of the system in the face of such strong disadvantages is testimony to its high adaptability.

The curious naturalist, to which Whittaker and Feeny allude, may wonder why green plants continue to dominate the earth's surface in the face of so many animal consumers. One reason, as we have seen, may be because herbivore numbers are not limited by their food, but by predators and, therefore, they do not increase until their food is consumed. Another reason may be because some plants are able to repel herbivorous animals mechanically, as with thorns, or chemically, through allelochemicals.

The toxins may act directly, by causing convulsions and death in the animal ingesting them. Thus the storybook picture of a cow contentedly chewing a buttercup is misleading, since buttercups, *Ranunculus* spp., are distasteful and can cause death in cattle; cattle on western ranges frequently fall victim to larkspurs, *Delphinium* spp.; sterioids in foxglove, *Digitalis purpurea*, can cause heart attacks in vertebrates; and a single leaf of oleander, *Nerium oleander*, may be lethal to man.

The actions of plant toxins are sometimes less direct, in fact sometimes startlingly subtle and devious. Tannins make proteins in plants indigestible for vertebrates. Tannins also function as growth inhibitors for other plants, and for fungus and virus transmission, thus providing certain plants with a broad-spectrum defense against both animal and microbial enemies.

Several plant species, mostly gymnosperms, even contain important insect hormones which function in molting. If certain critical doses are exceeded by the insect, its metamorphosis is fatally accelerated. Juvenile hormone is also present in some plants. A chemical called the "paper factor," present in these very pages, has been isolated from the balsam fir. Applied to bugs of the family *Pyrrhocoridae*, the substance stops development at an immature stage and prevents the formation of a normal adult.

The forces of mutation and natural selection are operating in animals too, of course, so we can expect chemical defenses of plants, in some cases, to be overcome. Hypericin is a red secretion of plants of the genus *Hypericum*. Hypericin somehow causes extreme sensitivity to light, skin irritation, and blindness in animals which eat these plants. Some beetles, though, have evolved a mechanism for detoxifying hypericin and thus they have a food supply almost untouched by other herbivores. At least one species uses the repellent as a cue to locate the plant!

The field of chemical ecology is rapidly attracting the interest of increasing numbers of researchers. The potential subtleties and possible interactions made possible by the specific nature of chemicals promises to pose new and complex questions. The problems may be great but so are the possibilities.

10

COOPERATION AND SOCIALITY

We have all encountered intriguing tales of social behavior among animals. In some cases the truth is stranger than the fiction, and it may be precisely this fact which has given license to the development of numerous stories of animal cooperation, love, and self-sacrifice. Some such stories are patently fiction, never intended for literal acceptance, but they have found their way even into certain levels of scientific circles. Others are, paradoxically, based in fact, but often given the fisheye by the same men. For example, who could be blamed for refusing to believe that some ants (tailor ants, *Oecophylla snaragdina*) actually sew leaves together by passing a silk-spinning larva back and forth between them as a shuttle (Figure 10.1)? Other seemingly unlikely cases of animal interaction may involve one species "tending" another one. Do some ants keep fungus gardens? Do others tend "cattle"? And what about those fascinating stories which tell of one animal risking—or even sacrificing—its life for another? American youths grow up with stories of valiant dogs, Lassies, which race onrushing trains to save baby chickens. Although the Lassie stories may be dismissed out of hand, other anecdotes persist, sometimes cross-culturally, and may make even the more critical among us wonder what their basis could have been. Do porpoises sometimes push men through shark-infested waters to the safety of shore? Do antelopes rely on baboons to chase away cheetahs? Somehow, it seems easier for us to accept competition among animals than cooperation, especially at any complex or coordinated level. However, as we shall see, some animals do undertake highly coordinated cooperative efforts and some do risk their personal well-being to protect others.

It may seem that after discussing competition and aggression among animals, we are now considering the other end of the behavioral spectrum—that we have gone, in a sense, from "hate" to "love." However, it will become apparent that we have done no such thing. The type of behavior we will consider now is simply another way of *increasing individual fitness.* "Cooperation . . . seems often to be a subterfuge whereby an individual is enabled to gain or maintain that degree of social control of others at which his or her own behavior is relatively unconstrained" (Crook, 1970a).

It should be made clear that the same mechanisms that select for success in competitive encounters do not necessarily operate in the development of cooperation. In fact, Crook (1970a) points out that cooperative tendencies may be complicated by the *"problem of the male."* His more intense aggressiveness, so adaptive in competitive encounters, could easily be a disruptive influence on the harmony of an animal group, with detrimental consequences resulting in unsuccessful bearing or rearing of offspring.

Since probably no area of behavioral studies is so rife with anecdote and misinterpretation as that relating to social behavior, cooperation, and self-sacrifice among animals, we should review, at this point, a few general problems in interpreting animal behavior. First of all, the appearance of any pattern does not necessarily mean that pattern is adaptive. It may, rather, be a not-too-detrimental side effect of another, adaptive, behavioral characteristic. For example, we have learned that the highly adaptive aggressive behavior of some male animals may result in the release of that behavior against prospective mates, thus reducing its overall advantage; but still, in sum, it is adaptive. It is therefore naïve to assume an adaptiveness exists for any observed pattern, even if it appears repeatedly. Also, when a behavioral pattern of an individual directly benefits another, even of a different species, the advantage bestowed may be inadvertent. A bird taking flight to avoid a predator may alarm other species in the area, or a parent's alarm call to its offspring may be acted upon by other nearby animals which are also in danger. So there are many factors which might be operating which could account for any observed pattern, and the most apparent explanation may not be valid.

It seems that the search for the adaptiveness of any pattern is simplified if the animal being considered is one of relatively stereotyped behavior. In cases of advanced mammals, a pattern may have developed through learning and may even be, to one degree or another, a function of insight. If the insight of the man and the animal are at variance, the problems of explaining a pattern are increased. There are those who say that porpoises push *anything* afloat ashore, perhaps to clear their water of obstructions, and that men are simply considered flotsam. Others, in explaining the recurring tales of such assistance believe that, if it indeed occurs, it may be a conscious effort on the part of the porpoise to help. It *is* known, for example, that they will help a wounded comrade reach the surface so it can breathe (Figure 10.2).

Figure 10.1 An example of highly coordinated cooperative behavior in the weaver ant, *Oecophylla longinoda*. A group of worker ants pull the two leaves close so that the other group may sew them together. The sewing is accomplished by pressing the spinning glands of their larvae against the edges and weaving back and forth with them. (After F. Doflein 1905 from Eibl-Eibesfeldt 1970.)

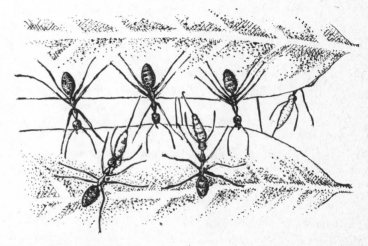

Figure 10.2 An injured porpoise being carried to the surface by its comrades. (After Siebenaler and Caldwell 1956.)

GROUPING BEHAVIOR

Some animals are usually found in groups—groups which may be composed of one or many species. One of the more obvious, and deceptively simple, questions is, "Why do animals come together at all?" The answers are varied. Animals may be brought together passively by physical factors, such as movement of wind or water. Chaim Kropach, a herpetologist, believes the great rifts of deadly sea snakes which have been reported in drift lines in the Pacific Ocean, are simply due to current convergence which brings these surface swimmers together.

Also, animals may aggregate in certain areas through the operation of some form of taxis, or simply as a result of a common search for favorable conditions. In other words, a number of animals may be attracted to the same place, but not necessarily to each other, as insects are attracted to a light. The different scents of various species of pine trees function in attracting the parasitic fly, *Drino bohemica*, to particular species of larvae upon which they lay their eggs (Monteith 1958). Often, specific chemical stimuli attract parasites to their hosts. The odor of humans attracts the louse, *Pediculus* (Wigglesworth 1953). Carbon dioxide, an animal by-product, and other factors, attract female mosquitoes to areas where animals may be (Laarman 1960). Animals may also come together for hibernation, breeding, or migration, but these cases will not be considered here except perhaps as side effects of other patterns.

Basically we will concern ourselves in this chapter with social groups which are formed as a result of individuals being held together by a mutual attraction. Animals may be classified, according to Eibl-Eibesfeldt (1970), as to whether they are *solitary,* such as the puma or mountain lion (a species in which individuals live alone except when mating or caring for offspring), or *gregarious.* Generally, the term gregarious includes all nonhostile, nonpredatory reactions between two or more individuals, excluding sexual or parent-offspring interactions. Moynihan (1960) defines the term more rigidly as the tendency actively to come together. (See Moynihan's paper for an extended bibliography on early work relating to the subject.) As an aid to background reading, perhaps it should be pointed out here that "social" to students of insects usually refers to communities in which there is more than one female, one or more being sterile which care for the young. The definition does not apply to vertebrate social organization as we shall see.

Gregariousness may not indicate the level of social interaction of a species. For some purposes of description perhaps a "social index" should be employed. Such an index might reflect the relationship between group size and the frequency of the dyad interaction of Lorenz. For example, three tomcats living in the same neighborhood might have a higher social index than would an anonymous flock of a thousand starlings, but a lower figure than a dominant clique of three highly interactive baboons.

Among gregarious or social animals we may distinguish between *distance animals* such as starlings, which appear in great flocks but which maintain discrete individual distances, and *con-*

tact animals. An example of the latter is the gold-crest, *Regulus regulus*, which keeps together as a family even after the young are fledged, and which huddles together through the cold nights during which they would otherwise be apt to freeze. Contact animals show a definite appetitive behavior for contact (Eibl-Eibesfeldt also speaks of a "drive"). Chimpanzees, gorillas, and other primates in zoos need to be touched and scratched by their keepers; otherwise they seem to deteriorate in their relations with their keeper. One may observe primates as well as humans sitting with their arms around each other; and, among apes, higher ranking animals reassure subordinates by clasping them.

Many contact animals show *grooming behavior*—for example, Norway rats, agoutis, house mice, and many primates such as vervet monkeys and chimpanzees. The effect of such behavior is twofold. It frees the "groomee" of parasites, hardened skin secretions, and debris in the skin and it enables the animals to touch and be touched. Grooming confers some degree of satisfaction to the participants and, as Eibl-Eibesfeldt (1970) maintains, it may facilitate group ties via the reinforcement mechanism. Jane van Lawick-Goodall has noted that wild chimpanzee mothers are almost always in contact with their very young offspring and frequently touch them as the young gain their independence.

Harry F. Harlow (1959), working at the University of Wisconsin, described love in infant monkeys as being derived, not from the satisfaction of feeding, but from close bodily contact. Anthropologists have described very primitive tribes, such as the recently discovered stone-age forest men of the Phillipines, who almost constantly hold or touch their small children. In such cases, the young are sometimes described as radiating an unusual degree of self-assurance.

In any group of animals that interacts socially, there is the problem of coordination of activities. The problem may actually be considered an aspect of the greater area of communication. Dim-

ond (1970) lists some ways coordination through communication could take place: (1) social feeding or trophallaxis (see Schneirla 1952)—as seen, for example, in insects which transfer hormone-containing food between them in a form of chemical communication; (2) social facilitation—the activity of one animal increasing the probability of another animal performing the same act (see later); (3) tradition learning (see Chapter 3); and (4) through a chain of command or hierarchy. Any observer must keep in mind that there is the likelihood that animals react similarly but independently to common environmental stimuli, such as the appearance of a predator, and thus give the semblance of coordinated behavior.

Exceedingly complex and elaborate social systems may develop within, and in some cases between, species. It will become more apparent as we continue that there exist incredibly complex and highly coordinated social systems in animals ranging from insects to primates. In fact, in a sense, we are only now beginning to see the extent of the ecological importance of social behavior, and what we see has caused us to reconsider certain ideas and to redefine many of our terms.

Before embarking on the study of higher animals, especially birds and mammals, we should first take a glimpse at the astounding complexity of social systems as they appear in the hymenopteran insects and termites.

INSECTS

Some species of ants, bees, and termites show extreme levels of social development in terms of complexity and coordination. Regimentation may be enhanced by a caste system in which each individual acts out a carefully programmed series of roles and in which there is little variation in expression. Although behavioral variation within a caste is usually minimized, there are exceptions to the rule. For example, in winter, some ants dig a hibernation chamber over a yard deep where the temperature is about 10°C and the ants mass themselves into a great ball to conserve heat.

The workers show great variation in their resistance to low temperatures. When the temperature in the hive reaches about 57°F bees form a winter cluster. The entire colony forms a ball, with the queen in the center. They rotate their position so that the bees at the outside layer have a chance to warm up. Those most resistant to cold wander between the surface and the chamber all winter. If the day is relatively warm, they wander outside, catch a few rays, and go back down with the extra calories they have absorbed to add to the average heat of the chamber. As the weather warms in spring, other insects such as ants are activated by the heat and these, too, join into the "heat transport," until the entire population is activated (Chauvin 1963). Generally speaking however, great variation within any caste of social insects is probably selected against.

Among the most intensively studied of the social insects is the honeybee, *Apis mellifera*. In this group the queens lay eggs, but other duties are performed by the workers, which are sterile females. As a worker matures she changes jobs. Newly emerged workers prepare cells to receive eggs and food; after a day or so, their brood-food glands develop and they begin to feed larvae. After nursing duty, they begin to accept nectar from the field workers and pack pollen loads into cells. About this time their wax glands develop and they also begin to build combs. Toward the end of house duty, some become guards and continually patrol the hive. Lastly, they become foragers, and their brood-food glands atrophy; they then fly afield and begin to collect nectar, pollen, propolis, or water according to the immediate needs of the hive. Such needs may be communicated to the field workers by the "eagerness" with which different loads are accepted.

Under abnormal circumstances, such as the removal or death of a large number of bees with a particular duty, the normal sequence of duties can be altered. Young bees may shorten or omit house duties and go more quickly to foraging, or foragers may even redevelop their brood-food and wax glands and return to house duties.

The emphasis is on efficiency in these hives. After the queen has been fertilized, the rest of the drones are quickly killed by the workers in the more truly feminist species, where drones are largely treated as sex objects useful only in copulation. The females which remain live only to work. They tend the queen, rear the young, and maintain and defend the hive, and they literally wear themselves out in their service. When their wings are so torn and battered they can no longer fly, they die or are killed. But the hive goes on.

Immediately there may come to mind questions regarding the concept of fitness. Since fitness is related to reproductive success, how have these devoted but sterile workers been selected for? In spite of the fact that they cannot pass along their own genes, they can see to it that genes identical, or very similar, to their own do appear in the next generation and that larvae, very similar genetically to themselves, reach adulthood. These new adults, of course, must continue to care for the egg-laying machine which is the queen, and which is their sole hope for continuing their own genotype. The problem is discussed in more detail in the section on altruism.

Two other fascinating instances of social behavior among insects occur in the ants. Some ants, it seems, are shepherds and others, farmers. Certain ants of the genera *Formica* and *Larius* care for aphids, or plant lice, in the true sense of husbandry. The aphids are kept, not for their flesh, but for their "milk"—honeydew, a secretion high in sugar and amino acids. The honeydew is released when the aphids are stroked by the antennae of the ants. The ants tend their herds in a variety of ways. They drive away predators and they build sheds of earth, "paper," or silk for their aphids. Also, they may rush them to safety if danger threatens. In fall they may gather aphid eggs which are then kept over the winter. In spring, young aphids are placed back on the stems or roots of plants (Trager 1970).

Farmers are found among the attine ants. They grow a fungus underground, in the dark, in their nests as a primary if not sole source of food. The substrate (ground) for the fungus depends on the genus of the farmer. The "simpler" genera use insect feces and carcasses. The "intermediate" genera use plant debris and fragments cut from live plants. The most "advanced" genera culture their fungus almost entirely on leaves and flowers cut from large plants. The fungus gardens are fragile spongelike structures composed of small pieces of substrate held together by the fungus overgrowth. The fungus of the ants is a poor competitor easily overcome by many wild types unless tended by the ants. In sum, the fungus *depends* on the ants. It has been found that their fecal material which the ants use as fertilizer contains proteolytic enzymes which compensate for a deficiency of such enzymes in the fungus. Also, the nitrogenous components of the feces act as a true nitrogen fertilizer, facilitating the initial growth of the fungus. The complementary aspects of the system are typical of so many other symbiotic and parasitic associations in nature (Martin 1970).

In the preceding two examples, both the ants and their symbiotes benefited from the relationship and therefore the association may be labeled mutualistic. In the case of the ant-fungus relationship however, we can see that the definition may be somewhat strained, since the fungus is actually eaten. However, without the ants the fungus apparently would not survive at all.

Wilson (1971) is impressed with the functional similarity between insects and vertebrate societies. As evidence, he notes that both may occupy territories and communicate hunger, alarm, hostility, caste status or rank, and reproductive status by nonsyntactical signals. Also, he notes, that in both groups individuals are aware of the distinction between group mates and nonmembers; that kinship is important in group structure and is the probable ultimate force behind social-

ity. He reminds us that in some cases certain groups, in both insects and vertebrates, share the advantages of division of labor, and that both have been subject to evolutionary forces where fitness is increased through cooperative tendencies—at least between relatives. In spite of these similarities, however, there are important differences which do not lend themselves to generalizing from one case to the other, as we shall see.

HIGHER ANIMALS

We shall now consider what may be equally complex organizations, with perhaps subtler gradations between roles, in certain vertebrates. Most of the vertebrate research thus far has been related to birds and mammals. In these animals, cooperative behavior may occur in a number of ecological contexts, but especially in relation to food storage, territorial defense, predator defense, group hunting or foraging, parental care and kin care, and, at its most complex, the cooperative control of social interaction, which is best seen in some primate groups. The advantages of sociality will be considered primarily in terms of these groups because of the data available, and because a wide variety of social advantage is expressed within their range of behavior. The results are intended to give some idea of the variety of adaptive effects of sociality in higher animals. However, extrapolation of the adaptiveness of any pattern from one species to another may not be warranted since social patterns so easily reflect other facets of the animals' histories.

Protection

It is axiomatic that there is safety in numbers. The "safety" element may be due to the superior fighting strength of large numbers, the confusing effect of many individuals on predators, and the increased likelihood of another individual being between the predator and any potential prey individual. The protective benefits of groups are high and, in some cases, not surprisingly, dangers may increase for animals in too small groups

(Collias 1944). For example, members of guanay colonies below a certain size do not multiply. It has been suggested that in the smaller colonies the ratio of circumference to area is large and, therefore, the likelihood of predation is increased (Hutchinson and Dewey 1949). The basis of such reasoning is discussed in Chapter 7. Group size may also be important in ways other than as a passive factor. For example, herds composed of fewer than 15 antelopes are usually decimated by wolves since they are not numerous enough to fight off the predators (Leopold 1933).

In some cases, animals which find themselves temporarily isolated from their groups are unable to perform behavioral sequences in an adaptive manner. If a single bird in a group takes flight he provides strong stimulus for others to follow so that he rarely leaves alone. Moynihan and Hall (1953) noted that if a spice finch, *Lonchura punctulata,* left the flock in order to feed or drink, and no other birds followed, it would rush its activities, perform them in a disorganized manner, or abandon them altogether and return to the group.

Although some groups, such as flocks of birds, increase the likelihood of detecting, mobbing, confusing, or distracting predators (Tinbergen 1951, Kruuk 1964), they may also attract predators. Visual and auditory signals are necessary for maintaining flock cohesion through communication (Moynihan 1962) and therefore may make the group conspicuous to predators. The evolutionary aspects of the resulting compromise are discussed in the section on social mimicry in this chapter. So, whereas animals may in a sense show cooperation by spacing out, thereby making themselves inconspicuous to predators, they may also seek out each other's company for the protective effect of numbers.

The protection conferred may be rather "impersonal" such as when a flock of starlings closes ranks in the presence of a hawk (Tinbergen 1951), or when coots attacked by an eagle splash up the water with their wings and escape in the confusion they manufactured themselves (Bent 1926). We also find cooperative defense of a group territory (see, King 1955; Southwick, Beg, and Siddiqi 1965) where a group attacks a threatening interloper and the protective advantage is derived from what is apparently sheer multiples of individual territorial behavior—each thereby protecting his own interest in the territory. In other cases, the effort may be much more coordinated, such as in musk oxen which form a circle of outwardly facing adults with their massive heads lowered. Such behavior is effective in protecting the less powerful segment of the group inside the circle from wolves (but the hapless beasts tend to remain in this defensive position as they are felled one by one by the rifles of men).

Among the highest forms of cooperative protection is that exhibited by animals which attempt to rescue others of their group. For example, Lorenz (1935) found that his tame jackdaws would attack anyone holding a jackdaw, or even a pair of black bathing trunks, in his hand. Rhesus monkeys will attack their caretaker if he catches one of their number which then utters the alarm call (Eibl-Eibesfeldt 1970). Porpoises will circle a female which is giving birth and so protect her against sharks attracted by her labor (Siebenaler and Caldwell 1956).

There is no intent here in the separate considerations of advantages of groups to imply that groups are formed on any single adaptive basis. In fact, in some cases grouping may have such separate and distinct advantages that it is difficult to tell which one was the basis for its development and which was added secondarily. For example, in some birds, such as grouse, males display on small territories or arenas on grassland well within sight of each other, and the females choose among them (Figure 10.3). Lack (1968) figures that leks have been evolved separately nine times in birds, and his multiple-origin argument is supported by the marked diversity which exists among the various lek species. Males of some species display silently, for example, while others call or drum, and some males rely much more on colors and patterns than others. Although the leks must be conspicuous to attract females, risk of predation is reduced by such precautions as displaying only in the early morning or late afternoon when the cooled earth does not furnish upward drafts which could carry predatory birds. Also, most lek species use flat ground where mammals cannot approach undetected. Some remove fallen leaves from the area so that snakes cannot approach unseen, and some display in the tops of trees (see Lack 1968). Also, leks are formed on traditional sites which have proved safe in the past. Although precautions are taken to reduce predator risk while males are displaying for the benefit of females, there is also a strong positive effect of such groups regarding predator safeguards. It is likely that a group of displaying males might be expected to release reproductive behavior in females more quickly than a single male through a cumulative effect; but the advantage of a group in predator detection is considered by some (cf. Koivisto 1965) to be the basis of lek formation, and the reproductive advantage to be secondary. There may well be other advantages of leks in terms of predator detection. If predators are drawn to leks and are detected, at least

the birds can know the whereabouts of the local predators at the expense of the temporary disruption of the mating process. Also, the sight of so many conspicuous birds all at once may cause a predator to attempt a capture prematurely, thereby reducing his general efficiency.

Aspects of colonial nesting in birds were discussed in Chapter 8. It was mentioned that, in the absence of a positive motive for territoriality, birds could move toward the advantages of coloniality, including its protective benefits. Almost all seabirds are colonial, but the coloniality may have developed on different adaptive bases in the various species. The differences between them may allow us to explore the relative importance of protection in the development of their nesting behavior. First, in some seabirds, it might seem that nesting colonies are not necessarily the result of selection for grouping, but simply the result of a limited number of suitable nest sites for which the birds must compete. Although in some seabird nesting areas all the available space seems to be taken up by nests, thus supporting the idea that the basis of the coloniality in such cases is simply limited nesting space, in other nesting areas, nests may occupy part of a cliff while another part, perfectly suitable to

Figure 10.3 Males of the ruff, *Philomachus pugnax,* displaying on their lek. These birds are unusual in that there is high individual variation in the male plumage. (After Lack 1968.)

the human eye, is left vacant. In such cases, it seems that the birds are actively gregarious, seeking out each other's close company. It may also be that there is simply a "conservative" element operating in such cases which is expressed in first-year breeders tending to nest within the bounds of an established colony—which is safe or else it would not be there—and showing a reluctance to extend the borders of the colony. (For a discussion of how the tendency could be maintained through selection see the discussion of Coulson's work below.) Of course man's approval of a location as a suitable nest site is irrelevant since there could be qualities which go unnoticed by the human eye, but which are critical to the suitability of the area. In other words, an apparently adequate peripheral site actually may not be suitable at all. Also, the tendency toward a choice of peripheral or new areas may have been selectively reduced in some earlier period in the evolution of the birds when such expansion would have been more detrimental than it is at present.

All the offshore feeders, and some inshore feeders, nest in rather inaccessible places such as on sheer cliffs. The eggs and young of these birds may be conspicuous and there is no defense against predator by the parents, the reason being that predators are unlikely to be able to reach the nests. Inshore feeders, for the most part, nest in smaller and more accessible colonies which are defended against predators. The eggs and young are cryptic in these species and there is no competition for nest sites (Lack 1968). Colonially nesting species must be comparatively free from nest predators for reasons discussed in Chapter 7 and, of course, nests on sheer cliffs would be relatively safe from terrestrial prowlers.

Probably the strongest protective advantage of nesting colonially lies in the mobbing response of some seabirds. Terns and gulls are so effective in their mobbing that birds of other species have come to nest in terneries, apparently for the protection afforded. Eider ducks similarly nest in

Figure 10.4 The yawn of the young adult male chacma baboon, *Papio ursinus*. In this baboon, the yawn is not a sign of boredom but rather a threat. (From *Primate Behavior: Field Studies of Monkeys and Apes* edited by Irven DeVore. Copyright © 1965 by Holt, Rinehart and Winston, Inc. Reproduced by permission of Holt, Rinehart and Winston, Inc.)

colonies of herring and great black-backed gulls. It was found that predation of those ducks nesting in gulleries dropped from 43 percent to 13 percent (Lack 1970).

It is fortunate, and not entirely coincidental, that the bulk of the current knowledge on animal sociality is the result of studies of two groups. On the one hand are studies of birds with their relatively stereotyped behavior. Such strong stereotypy is probably related to exceedingly stringent selection operating through sometimes specialized food supply, predation, and strong competition. On the other hand are the primate studies involving intelligent and exploratory animals usually inhabiting tropical areas of relatively stable food supply and having the facility for exceedingly complex, subtle, and malleable social interaction.

In Barnett's (1971) survey of social behavior in primates, he describes several facets of group protection in baboons. A troop of hamadryas baboons, *Papio hamadryas*, of Ethiopia, usually contains only one adult male with several females and adolescents of both sexes suggesting a kinship breakdown of a male, his consorts, and their young. During the day they feed together, but remain apart from other groups. At night they may join other groups to sleep on steep and relatively safe cliffs. The slumber parties may number several hundred. Some of the possible advantages of such behavior were discussed in Chapter 7. There is no experimental evidence which tests any hypothesis, but Barnett suggests such patterns may spread out the population to best utilize certain types of food distribution, ensure regular mating (females are not allowed to stray from the group and wanderers are brought back by the dominant male), and best utilize the protection offered by the male. Baboons are prey for lions and leopards, but the cats go for isolated individuals and show an unwillingness to confront a formidable full-grown male (Figure 10.4).

Most baboons live in groups larger than the family unit just described. Even the closely related chacma baboon, *Papio ursinus*, lives in groups of 100 or more. There would seem to be no organization to the troop as it moves about but there is actually a rather specific arrangement of the troop (Figure 10.5). There is a central group of females and young, accompanied or surrounded by larger powerful males. At the periphery are adults of both sexes and subgroups of juveniles. Females in heat may be accompanied by a consort—a large male who does not interfere to a great extent with other males copulating with her, but who may be the greatest recipient of her favor simply as a result of proximity.

When a predator is spotted, a baboon gives a loud bark and the reaction of the troop is to move closer together. The alarm is usually sounded by a young male which "walks point" ahead of the rest. Chauvin (1963) reports that females may also give the alarm at times, but that the real sentinels are the big males that sit scanning the countryside as the troop passes. These males even ignore estrous females at such times. The quick barks given as the alarm cause a rather

Figure 10.5 The members of a troop of chacma baboon, *Papio ursinus,* appear to be randomly distributed. However, the pattern of such groups is rather structured. In the center are the dominant males, adult females and young. Others are arranged concentrically. Note the two estrus females (with dark hindquarters) and their consort males. (From *Primate Behavior: Filed Studies of Monkeys and Apes* edited by Irven DeVore. Copyright © 1965 by Holt, Rinehart and Winston, Inc. Reproduced by permission of Hold, Rinehart and Winston, Inc.)

vigorous hubbub within the troop as it prepares to flee or give chase. If the troop attacks, the pattern is carried out in a rather well-coordinated manner.

Not only does group structure protect animals from dangers such as predators, but in some cases also from each other. For example, among gorillas the large and formidable silver-backed males rarely fight, but if two females begin a conflict which may end up as screaming and wrestling the male has only to draw near and grunt to break it up (Barnett 1971). Thus the stability of the social system is maintained and the animals are protected from each other. In sheep (Geist 1966) and baboons (Hall and DeVore 1965) two or three males may join forces to occupy the top of the hierarchy (see Chapter 7). Schaller and Lowther (1969) describe lion prides in which several adult males join forces to maintain their area. In each case, as "authority" increases with the strength of numbers, the social system can be considered to be increasingly stabilized and secure.

In rhesus monkeys mutual support is important in dominance hierarchies. Young males tend to leave smaller breeding groups and to move into the all-male periphery of larger ones. When they seek to enter the all-male group, they will be attacked and driven away unless they can enlist the support of a male already established there. It is interesting that the newcomers are often protected by residents which are their relatives, brothers in some cases, who came from the small troop the newcomer just left (Crook 1970b).

Reproduction

In many species the density of the reproducing segment of the population is exceedingly critical. That density can, as we know, be influenced by the social structure of the species; it can also be influenced by more passive factors which simply affect aggregation.

The reproductive advantage of aggregation in some simpler animals may be as uncomplicated as merely increasing the likelihood of a chance union of male and female gametes. In sea urchins, for example, sperm released into the sea may not reach sparsely distributed eggs, and the fewer the reproductive individuals in an area the more remote is the possibility of fertilization occurring.

In other animals the reproductive advantage of proximity to others of the species may be physiological. Allee, probably the most responsible for recent interest in animal sociality, cited some important pilot studies in his 1958 discussion showing that even a lowly protozoan will reproduce (through dividing itself) more frequently when it is in the company of others of its species than when it is alone. The same effect has been noticed in higher animals. For instance, a sow's ovaries do not develop normally if she is prevented from hearing and smelling a boar (Chauvin 1963). A pair of mice alone may be unable to breed successfully; several breeders must normally be present, otherwise a female may start a gestation and then reabsorb the growing foetus. The physiological mechanisms of such behavior are not entirely understood.

There may also be physiological effects on animals converging into a breeding area such as a lek. The male ruffs or sage grouse, *Bonasa umbellus*, for example, display on their small territories for the benefit of females, but well within sight of other males. As a result, the males may stimulate the production of reproductive hormones on each other as well as on the hens who are about to choose from among the madly displaying cocks.

It should be mentioned that although we have already considered other species which engage in group advertising, such as some insects and frogs, the phenomenon is rare among higher vertebrates. If lek display is advantageous as a collective advertisement, then it stands as a rare example of the phenomenon even among birds. It must be admitted, however, that there are possibly other cases of group advertising in birds. For example, males of Layard's spot-backed weaverbirds build nest after nest for successive females. The males often display together, each one shrieking and fluttering his wings as he clings to the entrance of his newly completed nest. Just what mutual effect such simultaneous advertising might have is as yet not known.

Although the nest site and timing of reproductive patterns are basically determined by environmental influences, the breeding behavior of a pair of birds may be strongly affected by the behavior of other pairs. Just how this effect operates has been the subject of much theorizing. One type of possible influence has been labeled *social stimulation* or *facilitation* (see Chapter 3). Such an effect is said to exist when the performance of an act by some members of a group increases the tendency for others in the group to perform the same act; for example, an ant that works at an intermediate rate will slow down if placed with a slower worker, and vice versa. Social facilitation is assumed to lie behind the fact that chickens in a group eat more food than those kept singly; apparently chickens which are not hungry can be induced to eat by the sight of their fellows eating (cf. Harlow 1932). Other examples of such stimulation are given by Chauvin (1963): If a penguin raises its beak, stiffens "in ecstasy" and gives its rallying cry, hundreds of others will follow its example. The same phenomenon has been found in terns. A captive tern, isolated in a cage, will sit on imaginary eggs if it sees others outside the cage occupied in that way. A pair of Florida jays cannot continue to build their nest if they see a flock of their own species calling and flying over them; they put aside nesting activities until another time and fly off to join the flock. Also, Lorenz has noted that if a heron, after eating, strikes the typical well-fed and lethargic pose, some of his companions, though still hungry, will stop eating and strike the same pose.

Synchronization in groups of animals may occur through other means than that of one individual inadvertently influencing another to perform a pattern. For example, in some cases synchrony is achieved by signaling, vocally or visually, among members of a group (Evans and Patterson 1971).

Darling, in 1938, reported that larger colonies of seabirds showed earlier and more synchronous breeding than smaller ones, and he attributed this to the contagion of social stimuli which altered the birds in preparation for nesting. In fact, he proposed that the chief value of colonial nesting is mutual social stimulation of the sexual cycles of its members. His ideas were criticized and alternate explanations of the observation were proposed (Fischer 1954; Coulson and White 1960). Lack (1970) states simply that there is no reason to make the supposition that social facilitation is operating, based on Darling's observations, although he agrees that social facilitation may well exist in colonial species. Hailman (1964) delineated the possible hypotheses for the correlation of colony size and breeding synchrony: (1) it is a common reaction of all pairs to environmental cues; (2) it is a result of normal behavioral responses, such as the approach of an individual in reproductive condition to conspecifics; (3) it is increased recruitment of individuals to places occupied by birds in a similar reproductive condition; and (4) Darling's "contagion" hypothesis was correct.

What are the advantages of synchrony in reproduction? It is obviously advantageous for males to be in a reproductive state at the same time females are. Also, synchrony in a colony would reduce the time that chicks and eggs would be available to attract predators. Synchrony, if regulated by physical environmental conditions to some degree, might also effectively permit the exploitation of a seasonally limited food supply.

There are other examples of social facilitation (although the effect has not yet been widely demonstrated). For instance, Makkink (1942) observed that the highly pugnacious oystercatchers seem to more readily show sexual behavior within a flock than outside it because of the stimulating influence of other birds. Ashmole

(1963) attributes the synchronous breeding of some birds to possible social stimulation of nearby nesters and the contagious effect of mutual displays. Crook (1965) suggests that the ritual of magpie "marriage" may function in promoting the synchronization of reproduction in a population, thereby ensuring the appearance of young at a period of seasonal food abundance. Emlen and Lorenz (1942) showed that group display may accelerate the sexual development of a local population. In one experiment they implanted testosterone into two birds of the family phasianidae, *Lophostyx californica*, which led to copulatory behavior on the second day. Eight untreated birds reared with this pair began to show the same behavior within two weeks—two months before the normal date. Crook (1965) stressed that such an effect would be especially important for birds with relatively limited breeding seasons. Group behavior in ensuring synchronization has been found in studies by Orians (1961), Ashmole (1963), and Crook (1964). Simmons (1970), on the other hand, indicated that in the brown booby which is "loosely colonial" (densely aggregated only when nests are in short supply) any synchronization in reproductive behavior seems to result from the appearance of favorable conditions, such as the onset of a good food supply. So probably if social facilitation of reproductive behavior does exist in colonial birds, it does not occur with equal effect in all species.

In studies of social effects on weaverbirds (Collias, Brandman et al. 1971; Collias, Victoria et al. 1971) it was found that the effects of increased crowding on breeding behavior was largely dependent on the sex ratio of the group. When the relative number of birds of a sex was experimentally increased, the result was an increased stimulation of members of the opposite sex rather than the same sex. When relative numbers of the sexes were not altered, increased crowding resulted in increased singing of males to each other as well as to females. There was no increase in clutch size with added numbers, but there was

an extension of the breeding and nest-building seasons. The extension of these periods was considered to be favorable to establishing new colonies when conditions were crowded.

There are apparently advantages in nesting colonially which are not yet completely understood. Coulson, in 1968, published his observations of nesting in the kittiwake, *Rissa tridactyla*, in which he described some interesting behavioral patterns and thereby added a few more unknowns to the Great Puzzle. In the kittiwake, there is more intense competition for nests in the center of the colony than at the periphery. Birds removed from the center will be replaced by a member from the nonbreeding population (comprised of those individuals previously unable to secure a site). Should a vacancy at the periphery of a colony occur, however, it may not be filled. Annual mortality rates show higher death rates for males at the periphery, but not for females. The high death rate of course, might not be due to any effect of the peripheral area per se but to its inhabitation by inferior males—those unable to secure a central position—who might be expected to succumb more easily than the more vigorous centrally located males. Stress, Coulson maintains, is apparently not greater at the edge, but is, in fact, greater in the center. It would follow that since the center is occupied by competitively successful males, the level of aggression would be higher there. Coulson also found physical differences in the males of the two areas. The males at the periphery were slightly smaller and, he believes, differed also from the central males in the quality and quantity of certain body tissues. Finally, he found a larger mean clutch size, higher hatching success, and more young fledged per pair in the center of the colony.

Again it must be pointed out that higher reproductive success in the center of a colony may have little to do with the location itself, but may, rather, be a reflection of more vigorous parents that are better able to secure food for egg production in the female (thus larger clutch sizes) and for the young (thus more young are fledged). Chauvin (1963) notes that the young of centrally located birds in seabird colonies reach maturity quicker and here, again, we have a difference which might be accounted for on the basis of more vigorous parents. If there is no inherent advantage to securing a more centrally located nest site, then we are left with the questions of why competition for such a site is so intense and why some birds refuse to breed in peripheral areas. Coulson indicates that predation is not a problem, and since they are wide-ranging fish eaters, nest location can have nothing to do with the amount of food secured. So why are centrally located nests important?

In a study of the adaptive significance of colonial nesting in the bank swallow, *Riparia riparia*, Emlen (1971) found that the clumping was related to a shortage of suitable nest sites but that the birds, once together, interacted in a complex manner. He found reproductive synchrony within a colony but not between colonies, but, more importantly, he found that centrally located birds in a colony have higher reproductive success than those at the periphery. It was theorized that the difference was due to decreased social stimulation at the periphery (as demonstrated by a greater tendency to abandon nest sites) and not due to differential predation at the two locations.

Lack (1966) discusses three aspects of colonial nesting which need much more investigation. He mentions that in the tricolored redwing the size of the breeding colony is correlated with the food supply and that flocks *apparently* make exploratory flight prior to settling to breed—as if assessing the food potential in relation to their numbers. Secondly, he notes that kittiwakes raise more young in crowded than uncrowded colonies. The reason for this is not known. Lastly, he refers to N. P. Ashmole's suggestion that crowding at island colonies depletes the food supplies in adjoining waters thus making it hard for birds to raise young. The result of such depletion, if it exists, has been the evolution of smaller clutches

and deferred maturity. All of these suggestions provide excellent working hypotheses for future fieldwork.

A number of species of birds nest colonially and, in fact, show various levels of cooperation in their nesting activities. In several perching birds (and one parrot), several pairs may build a large common nest together in which each pair has its own chamber, in a system of *cooperative breeding* (Lack 1968). Cooperative breeding exists when more than one pair share in building a nest, lay eggs in a single nest, or help to feed one brood.

Since cooperative breeding occurs in several groups of not-too-distantly related species we may search for the ecological variables which could select for such behavior. Lack (1968) points out that diet seems to have had no influence on the evolution of cooperative breeding. Crook (1965) surmises that communal behavior involving cooperation in reproductive activities appears, in birds, to have evolved under two sorts of conditions. The first is where crowding into protected areas has reduced territorial sizes. Communal nesting could begin by one bird "extending" the nest of another—as long as the entrance of the first one is not infringed upon. In such cases agonistic behavior and territorialism around entrances are not lost. The second condition is where parent-young bonds extend into the adulthood of the offspring. The mechanism here would be kinship selection and increased likelihood of the young being in a position to breed later (see Chapter 7). In such cases group territoriality may appear. Lack (1968) notes that a high proportion of cooperative breeders occurs in Australia and he surmises that at higher latitudes migration might make it difficult for young to stay with their parents. As a result he suggests that cooperative breeding should primarily be looked for in the warmer regions.

Foraging and Hunting

The distribution, abundance, and periodicity of

available food for any species will strongly influence the social and reproductive structure of that species, as we have seen. For example, in richer savannahs the plentiful food is able to support large troops of baboons and macaques, which are then able to avail themselves of the protective and reproductive advantages of grouping. The smaller troops of hamadryas baboons utilize what is, most likely, a scattered or sparse food source, best exploited by smaller, wide-ranging groups. In the nonbreeding season, an abundant food supply may operate to bring birds together. Any casual observer has probably noticed that some birds which are territorial in spring may be seen in flocks in the winter. Such flocks may even be composed of mixed species, some species showing a greater tendency toward joining such groups than others; for example, in the nonbreeding season many finches form interspecific flocks. Apparently, localized and abundant food in the nonbreeding season minimizes competition and permits animals to join together for other reasons, such as mutual surveillance for predators (Marler and Hamilton 1966).

Gregariousness in birds is particularly characteristic of insectivorous species and those whose food (such as fish, carrion, or fruit) usually occurs in large irregularly scattered masses (Moynihan 1960). Although gregariousness is more often a social pattern of the nonbreeding season, we know that many species nest colonially. (In addition to seabirds, there are herons, swifts, weavers, hirundines and a few other species such as some crows and woodpeckers [Lack 1970].) Food must be abundant near any colony, of course, but food does not seem to be the primary cause of nesting groups except in a few species, such as the rosy pastor and wattled starling which breed alongside locust swarms (Schenk 1934, Roberts 1970, in Lack 1970).

There are instances also of animals not only associating because of food factors of the environment but actually working together to avail themselves more efficiently of that food. For example, certain group-living species of birds establish stores to tide them through periods of scarcity and these stores are then used by the community as a whole (Ritter 1938; Morris 1962). Such instances occur in primates as well but the storage may not be carried out in a coordinated manner (Crook 1966).

Hunting animals which live in groups may catch their prey by working together. Groups of predatory jackfish sometimes circle swarms of small prey species apparently to keep them contained as they make strikes into the midst of the swarms. Wolves chasing an intended victim may split up, some continuing to chase at the heels while others run ahead in an effort to head it off (Murie 1944).

In the same vein, an interesting case is presented in Cape hunting dogs, *Lycaon*, of South Africa. These dogs will rush as a group into a herd of gazelle, each taking the gazelle nearest it. The chances of catching a sprinting gazelle are probably not particularly good and a single dog may be too small to make such a kill singlehandedly. These disadvantages are somewhat reduced by each dog keeping an eye on how the others are doing. If a pack member seems to be gaining on his gazelle, the others will leave off their chase and join him (Kuhme 1965). Parenthetically it might be added here that Schaller and Lowther (1969) were unable to detect any hierarchy or any form of aggression whatever in these packs even though males outnumbered females. Eibl-Eibesfeldt (1970) believes that such amiability is secondarily derived (added relatively late in the evolution of the social system). He theorizes that possibly injuries are so frequent in these animals that it is advantageous for no animal to fall into a specific role. For example, if an animal filling a key role in the group were injured he might not be immediately replaced and perhaps hunting efficiency of the group might then be reduced.

Bartholomew, in 1942, made an important study of cooperative fishing in birds. It had long been observed that some species, such as certain pelicans, often fish together by swimming in a specific formation and diving in a rather coordinated manner. It was assumed that they caught more fish that way than by feeding alone, but the importance of group feeding was not really understood. Bartholomew added important evidence, albeit not as quantitative as some might wish, by studying the double-crested cormorants, *Phalacrocorax auritus*, of San Francisco Bay. He found that these fishing birds, after spending the night on the telephone wires of San Francisco, fly to the bay in small groups. The groups usually don't begin serious fishing immediately, but individuals make a few dives while other small flocks join the group on the water. When the group has grown to a certain size (which may ultimately reach several hundred) the birds line up side by side and begin to swim in the same direction. A few birds may follow the long line, but these individuals are usually not actively fishing. These large fishing parties primarily pursue schools of fish while smaller flocks may hunt individual prey. When a flock turns sharply it is apparently in response to a change in direction of the school. Birds in the flock splash a lot, apparently to discourage the fish from attempting to slip beneath the line while individual divers disappear beneath the water, the divers showing no synchronization or coordination with others in the flock. The flock appears much smaller than it really is because so many divers are beneath the surface at one time. Bartholomew maintains that, as a rule, fewer fish are caught by members of small flocks than by those of large flocks, probably because the former have to hunt for their prey individually, while the latter need merely to swim into a herded school and seize a fish.

In many cases, when fishing flocks form they are accompanied by individuals of other species. For example, gulls often follow large groups of fishing cormorants and retrieve any fish which happen to escape while the cormorants are arranging them into the "head-first" position for swallowing. They do not follow smaller groups, presumably because they catch so few that it is not worthwhile. Gulls, according to reports cited by Bartholomew, also often catch the small fish which the cormorants inadvertently squeeze from pregnant perch.

Paulson (1969) reported a group of grebes diving within a yard of a fishing scoter and following its dives within a second. He also reported an instance of four least grebes, *Podiceps dominicus*, following six mallards, *Anas platyrhynchos*, and diving among them as the mallards dabbled. The grebes dropped off sharply in the number of dives made when the mallards left. Although he refers to other instances of commensal feeding in grebes, any evidence that more food is gathered in this manner is circumstantial and can only be validated by direct means such as stomach analysis.

Leck (1971) reported a more coordinated type of group feeding between two species. He noted snowy egrets, *Leucophoyx thula*, and grebes, *Podilymbus podiceps*, foraging on small fish in a man-made canal. Apparently (again hard data are needed), the grebes diving in the center of the canal drove fish toward the egrets which remained near the edge. The egrets, for their part, kept the fish from hiding along the shallow banks and bottom. Significantly the grebes did not fish the other side of the canal where fish were undoubtedly hiding, but where no egrets stalked about. Of course it can be argued that each species was simply fishing where it was finding the most fish and was oblivious to the other species. It is not unreasonable to assume though that the other species was noticed and, in time, could have come to be associated with the fish reward so that a form of cooperation could be developed through association learning.

Sociophysiology

We have considered elsewhere certain physiological effects that one individual may have on another either simply by virtue of its presence or by some relationship actively entered into by the individuals. In some species, for example, the internal reproductive condition will not be reached unless an individual is in the company of the opposite sex. In other species a female will abort or reabsorb developing fetuses if she detects a strange male. In yet other species the presence of too many conspecifics can cause changes to occur in various organs of the body and behavioral abnormalities to appear. As an example of a coordinated physiological interaction refer to the discussion of heat-bearing ants at the beginning of this chapter. There are other examples of physiological effects of individuals upon other members of the species which indicate an area of study ripe with possibilities—an area which might be termed *sociophysiology*.

The simplest sort of physiological effects of groups are seen in animals which huddle together to conserve moisture or heat. Normally, solitary land isopods, in periods of dryness, bunch up into balls and conserve their moisture (Allee 1926). Many warm-blooded animals avail themselves of heat escaping from other animals. Pigs, in winter, may sleep in great restive heaps with continual squealing and confusion all night long as those on the perimeter attempt to move to the middle. I have been told by one in whom I have great confidence in such matters that among the itinerants who sleep under the bridges of Paris in the winter there is a strict hierarchy. As the men lay huddled side by side the dominant or more revered among them have the warmer central positions and newcomers must take their place at either end.

More elaborate forms of social thermoregulation may also exist. In Antarctic storms, penguins form large crowded groups which rotate slowly so that the birds walk in concentric circles. The great circles of birds move continuously leeward and thus the individuals are believed to conserve heat (Chauvin 1963).

Allee (1938) found that the small marine flatworm, *Procerodes*, swells and bursts due to osmotic effects if placed into fresh water by itself. However, if a group of worms are placed into the fresh water, most of them last longer. It was found though that the first worms in a group to die did so in about the same time as isolated worms. The benefit to the rest of the worms of the rupture of the first individuals, however, was greater than could be accounted for by changes in osmotic gradient alone. It was then found that the ruptured worms "conditioned" the water by releasing calcium into the medium and that calcium, for some reason, has a protective effect for animals placed into new osmotic conditions.

Later Allee and his students (1951) found that if aquatic animals, such as goldfish or flatworms, are grown in unfavorable waters (for example waters in which small amounts of harmful chemicals have been added), they do better in small groups than as individuals. As Etkin (1964) points out, the reasons may be due to body secretions neutralizing the harmful additives.

Newly hatched larvae of the sheep blowfly, *Lucilia sericata*, cannot survive on the skin of a sheep unless the relative humidity is above 90° for several hours until the maggot can penetrate the skin. In dry weather practically the only larvae which live are those from aggregations of several egg-masses laid together (Cragg 1955). Pearson (1947) measured oxygen consumption of mice at 26°C, a temperature at which much of the mouse's energy must go for maintaining the proper temperature. Pearson found that four mice when they were separated used 1.82 times as much oxygen as when they were huddled together.

In 1944, Collias made an interesting observation on quail, the implications of which have been largely ignored since that time. He found that the average covey size of quail is larger (12.5) in North-Central states than in Gulf states (10.5). He called this "a social application of Bergmann's rule" (1944:41) which states that warm-blooded animals attain a larger size in colder than in warmer regions. The "rule" is generally thought to be an adaptation for conserving heat since as size increases, the heat-radiating surface area decreases with respect to volume. Larger size of

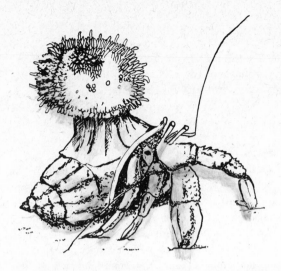

Figure 10.6 An example of mutualism shown between a sea anemone and a hermit crab. The anemone has attached itself to the crab's shell. The crab is protected by the anemone which has stinging tentacles and the anemone benefits by gathering bits of food from the crab's meals.

groups in colder areas, if the correlation can be demonstrated, may also be a mechanism for conserving heat if the animals pack together at certain times such as when sleeping.

Other physiological effects of animals upon each other have been observed and need explanation. As examples, there is an acceleration of body processes for many types of animals when they occur in groups. Cleavage of sea urchin eggs increases in frequency with density of individuals up to a point. On the other hand, when snakes are in groups, their metabolism decreases (Etkin 1964).

INTERSPECIFIC ASSOCIATIONS

We have considered many of the advantages inherent in members of a species grouping together, but interspecific, or mixed-species groups, are far from uncommon and adaptations for interspecific socializing provide often fascinating glimpses of the unexpected directions to which natural selection may lead. In America, symbiosis has come to refer to a number of types of interaction between species including parasitism, commensalism, and mutualism. In *parasitism*, as we know, one of the species is harmed in some way. Commensalism refers to the sort of interaction which results in one of the species being

benefited, and the other largely unharmed. Certain species of fish such as jackfish, *Caranx*, may follow a barracuda by swimming closely above its back where they are relatively safe from him and also protected from other predatory fish which avoid the barracuda. It should be noted that the barracuda may thus be more conspicuous because of its entourage and may, therefore, suffer some small disadvantage. So the difference between parasitism and commensalism may be a quantitative one. It has been suggested that perhaps both mutualism and parasitism usually begin with commensalism.

In *mutualism* both species derive some benefit from the association. We are all familiar with the hermit crab which lives in an empty snail shell and carries the shell about with it to protect its soft hindparts. Sea anemones often settle on the shells and are carried about by the crab (Figure 10.6). These animals have stinging cells and are avoided by many predators that would otherwise make a meal of the crab, shell or no. The anemone derives its benefit from the association by eating the scraps of food that fall from its companion's table. When the crab outgrows its shell it must find a new one. When it does this it often prods and pinches the anemone to induce it to detach itself and move to the new shell (Von Frisch 1964).

Other mutualistic animals are much less closely associated. Mixed groups of baboons and antelopes may largely ignore each other until danger threatens, then they may respond to each other's warning signals. Such a group is difficult, indeed, to approach. The keen noses of the antelope can smell danger and the sharp-eyed baboons can see it, therefore there is some form of complementation. Also, Chauvin (1963) states that antelope in a troop of baboons do not flee from a cheetah, but rely on the baboons to chase it away.

Often animal associations provide no clear indication of the basis of the association. In some cases it may even be a side effect of a misdirected gregarious tendency. The highly social springbok antelope, for example, readily joins up with members of many species—even ostriches. There seems to be no advantage in some such associations; however, it cannot be denied that any association may confer some as yet undetected benefit. Perhaps the springbok is able to react appropriately to a wide variety of warning systems. The inability to perceive the advantages of an association, of course, may be due to ignorance on the part of the observer regarding the myriad and subtle ways animals can interact.

There is one rather unusual interspecific reaction which involves man and deserves mentioning. The black-throated honeyguide, *Indicator indicator,* may attract humans or other mammals, such as the ratell or honey-badger, *Mellivora,* to beehives. It likes honey, but has problems reaching it. If it happens to find a beehive, it sets out to find help. When a man is found the bird flutters and darts around him in a most peculiar manner; then it flies away in the direction of the hive, calling loudly and darting back occasionally to be sure it is still being followed. When the man arrives at the hive the bird reaches a frenzy of excitement. After the man robs the nest there is always enough left to reward the bird. The bird eats the wax as well as the honey. It must be admitted that such a description involves perhaps unwarranted anthropomorphizing, but according to those who

have observed it, there is little room for doubt that the bird is purposefully leading. Such a system undoubtedly requires several facets of learning behavior as we understand it, and important questions arise regarding its ontogenetic and phylogenetic development.

Because of the incredible complexity of ecological systems and the level of our understanding regarding them, we are often forced to deal with the problem of cooperative interaction at very simplistic levels—usually by describing how some specific behavioral pattern results in some broad benefit to two species. New studies are now being attempted which seek to correlate a wide variety of ecological interaction at several levels simultaneously. While the new light often reveals more puzzles than answers, the new "systems" approaches show renewed promise of our ever knowing what sort of world we live in. As an example of how animals may interact, consider Bell's (1971) report of grazing animals on the African plains. Great herds move across the plains in waves, one species following another—in a certain sequence. The principal grazers are wildebeest, zebra, and Thompson's gazelle—and their movement is in response to annual shifts in rainfall. Each species is physiologically adapted to eat specific types of tissues of grasses and herbs (leaves, sheaths, or stems). As each species begins to run out of its preferred food it moves on —zebras first, then wildebeest, then Thompson's gazelle. The first species to enter a new area actually affects it in such a way as to prepare it for the species which follow. Therefore, a reduction in the numbers of one species is likely to reduce the numbers of other species.

There is another type of behavior in birds described by Moynihan (1963) which seems to be the antithesis of mutualism, but which, if the definition were sufficiently flexible, could be covered under the term. In this case, instead of the advantage being a result of coming together, the benefit lies in species actively and specifically avoiding each other to their apparent mutual advantage. In studying four types of honeycreepers in the Quito region of central Ecuador, Moynihan found that each species ignored other species of birds except those in the "complex" (three *Diglossa* species and one *Conirostrum*). Each species of the complex avoided every other species although they occupied the same area and even sang from the same perches (but not simultaneously). Normally some interspecific interest exists in birds —a fact which makes this avoidance behavior seem even more unusual. The birds of this complex showed almost no hostilities to others of the complex and within the complex there were no mutual appeasement gestures. Apparently, avoidance offers more benefits than aggression in this case. The social structure of the complex was found to be elaborate and stereotyped. Each species was belligerent toward its own species, and to a lesser degree, to all other species outside the complex. Members of the complex would not hesitate to sing when one of their own species was singing, but would fall silent at the song of another species of the complex. The song of other species which shared the habitat with these four were for the most part ignored.

Helpful Parasitism

The very word "parasite" immediately connotes images of harmful organisms and arouses disgust in many of us. Perhaps this reaction is unfortunate. Perhaps, even, parasitism can be "good." Linicone (1971:139) states, "Parasitism, one of life's great phenomena, possesses a quality of goodness that has been largely overlooked because man has been so possessed with the disease aspects of this association."

Linicone is primarily concerned with the beneficial physiological effects of parasites, but Neal Smith (1968) has presented interesting ecological data also expressing its benefits. Smith has found that under certain conditions among birds, it is advantageous for the host to accept the offspring of brood parasites. In fact, he reports that in one host-parasite interaction more host offspring reach breeding age in parasitized nests than in parasite-free nests. He studied colonies of oropendolas and caciques which were parasitized by the giant cowbird *Scaphidura oryzivora*. In some colonies the host species would throw out the eggs of the nest parasite, in other colonies the cowbird egg was allowed to remain. It was found that in some cases the hosts built their nests around huge bee or wasp nests. The birds' nests were placed at the tips of branches and were therefore protected from vertebrate predators. Instead, the chief source of mortality was a parasitic botfly which deposited eggs on the chicks' bodies. The hatched larvae later bored into the chicks' bodies and caused high mortality. In colonies with no bees and wasps the birds were heavily parasitized by the botfly, a situation which did not exist in the presence of the stinging insects. However, if the nest were parasitized by the cowbird then no botflies occurred. It was found that the cowbird young preened their nestmates thus removing the eggs and larvae of the botfly. Colonies lacking bees and wasps, it was found, were the ones which did not discriminate against cowbirds.

Mixed Species Flocks

The careful and extensive field studies of mixed flocks have furnished many clear and unusual examples of a number of phenomena we have discussed elsewhere dealing with adaptive characters related to competition, communication, population density, and social behavior. Such studies have also revealed fascinating new facets of these phenomena.

Flocks of birds composed of more than one species have been reported for some time (Chapin 1932; Davis 1946; Murphy 1936; Odum 1942; Wing 1946). They occur in both temperate and tropical areas, but are more prevalent in the latter. In the tropics, most mixed flocks are composed of passerine species. Such flocks may be composed of anywhere from two to about twelve species. The flocks may be transitory or semipermanent and may be dissolved and reformed at intervals. Such flocks may have tight or loosely knit social structures. Overall, more species occur in mixed flocks than in single-species flocks, although in temperate climates single-species flocks appear more frequently.

As might be expected, mixed flocks are more likely to appear in winter when many birds demonstrate an increased tendency toward gregariousness. In northern Europe, tits of several species travel with tree creepers, nuthatches, and certain woodpeckers through the winter woodland.

Moynihan (1960) was unable to show that the more gregarious species are less belligerent than solitary ones. He theorized, however, regarding the nature and degree of hostile interaction in gregarious species that perhaps gregarious species are less likely to actually fight or attack each other physically, relying instead more on threat and appeasement gestures. In the moderately gregarious green honeycreeper much supplanting occurs, indicating a belligerent spirit, but contact of any sort is very rare. It must be realised that aggressiveness may vary between species in a mixed flock and the levels of such aggression may very well help to determine the composition of the flock (Moynihan 1960, Wiley 1971).

Certain of the advantages of mixed-species flocks are readily apparent and, in fact, may be the same as for single-species flocks. There is, of course, the simple safety factor in numbers. Predators might be confused by a mixed group just as by a single-species group. (There may be less of such advantage in mixed flocks since it is possible that a predator would be less distracted by the sight of several individuals of different types than he would by several individuals of a type for which he had formed a "search image.") In addition, there remains the possiblity that a predator might be intimidated by a large flock.

Also, many watchful eyes are better than a few. If the birds in a mixed flock were "tuned in" to each other's warning signals, the efficiency of predator detection would be increased. Such alarm recognition could be specific, such as when one species correctly interprets the specific warn-

ing cry of another. (Remember, there may be marked convergence of such signals due to need for crypticity of sound.) The alarm recognition could also function with less precise "attunement" of two species. For example, the sight of a bird taking off in flight might be expected to alert any individual, even if of another species, and possibly induce a following reaction.

The protective advantages of mixed flocks may also appear in rather unmistakable contexts. As an example, in some mixed flocks the species will join together to mob a common predator, such as an owl (Lack 1970). It must be pointed out, however, that there is little hard data as yet to show any protection from predators in flocking.

When any animals forage in the same area simultaneously, there arises the possibility of competition for food. If birds have grouped together primarily for protection from predators, the resulting competition for food could be reduced in a number of ways. In species of different adaptive types such as tits and woodpeckers, little foraging overlap would be expected. Some might be foraging on leaves and buds, others on twigs and bark, and others might be catching insects in flight. Even if the species take similar sorts of food (for example, insects) competition can be reduced by each species foraging in a particular way (Willis 1966; Vuilleumier 1967; Morse 1969). In this light it is not surprising that mixed flocks are more common in the tropics since many tropical species, as we know, have highly specialized foraging adaptations. Also, in the tropics, a single species may be represented by relatively few individuals thus favoring reduced competition. There remains the possibility that some displacement of foraging behavior could occur, at least temporarily, in mixed flocks of similar adaptive type.

For many species there is an actual foraging advantage in forming mixed flocks. Several observers have suggested that mixed flocks are primarily foraging associations that result in each bird getting more food than it would by foraging alone (Rand 1954; Short 1961; Brosset 1969;

Moynihan 1962). For insectivorous (insect-eating) birds the flock may serve as a "beater" to arouse insects causing them to stir about or to flee, thus revealing themselves to the birds. In flocks composed of insectivorous birds and those of other dietary specialization the main advantage of beating may be to the insect-eaters, with less food advantage being derived by the other species (Lack 1970).

Frugivorous (fruit-eating) or nectarivorous (nectar-eating) birds are forced to search for widely dispersed food sources such as fruit- or flower-bearing trees—trees which yield a rich supply once found. The probability of finding such irregularly dispersed food supplies may be increased by flocking behavior. Moynihan (1962) maintains that if the food is regularly dispersed and easy to locate there may be little "food advantage" in flocking and, therefore, any association under such conditions can be considered due to other advantages—such as protection.

Diamond and Terborgh (1967) showed that interspecific bonding, or mutual attraction of the species, at fruiting trees is weaker than the bonding that exists between members of mixed flocks moving through forests in search of food. Lack (1971) discusses the reasons for such differences and notes that species already at a stationary food source would, of course, not need assistance in locating food such as would those at a moving food source such as an insect swarm (Willis 1967); they also don't need help flushing prey, and once food is found they would all be likely to exploit the same food source, and thus a weakening of bonds might be expected, at least temporarily. For a discussion of the range and dispersability of flock-forming species, see Moynihan (1962).

In the light of what we know about interspecific social patterns which include territoriality, mutual avoidance, and the ignoring of other species (sometimes tempered with a slight general interest), we might ask, what is the behavioral basis of mixed-flock formation? The answer may be approached by a study of signals.

Mixed flocks may be comprised of rather similar species. For example, in the nonbreeding season, several species of finches may come together into one flock. In such flocks interspecific signaling would, of course, be adaptive. Marler (1957) found that in such times the vocalization of members of the flock are much less distinct than in the breeding season, a time when it would not be advantageous for signals of one species to become confused with those of another.

Coloration may play a more important part in mixed flock formation than vocalization. It is interesting that many species of birds which are gregarious, at least toward their own species, have developed conspicuous markings and color patterns. Many are all black, such as crows, blackbirds, starlings, anis, cormorants, and vultures; or all white, such as herons, spoonbills, swans, and geese; or pied, such as magpies, gulls, and terns (Moynihan 1960). The advantage is, apparently, that they can see each other more clearly, thus facilitating signaling and group action. Conspicuousness to predators, it is reasoned, is countered by the increased predator defense of groups. In some cases predation is reduced in other ways such as by cliff-nesting. Huxley (1938) termed such coloration "episematic." It has been pointed out that this kind of appearance, in many cases, is identical with aposematic, or warning, coloration and may serve both purposes simultaneously.

In certain types of mixed flocks there are some species that are drab and indistinct and others that are brightly colored, and it is believed that in some circumstances the "nucleus" of the flock may be the drab individuals. The dull plain-colored tanager, for example, forms the nucleus of certain mixed flocks in the tropics. Its drabness is believed to increase its attractiveness to other, brighter colored species. Dull plumage, it is believed, might well minimize aggressive signaling and so promote the formation of the mixed flocks (Hamilton and Barth 1962); the very neutrality of a drab species may add to its appeal. So, in a sense, although the tanagers may not turn on their brighter fellows, they don't turn them off either.

Moynihan (1960, 1962, 1963) noted that mixed flocks (especially in the tropics) tend to have similar plumage types. Others found that members of mixed flocks are similar in other ways. For example, Immelmann (1962) studied seven species of Australian ground finches which form mixed flocks and found each species associates only with other species of ground finches which have the same bill color. There are several routes by which similarity in associated species could develop of course, such as through common descent or common environmental pressures, but Moynihan (1968) theorized that perhaps in some cases it was due to a specific *social mimicry* where selection might move one species toward the appearance of another species. There would be certain restrictions on such selection. Selection would never permit any two species to become identical of course, because of the importance of species distinctiveness (Chapter 6). Also the types of species in which social mimicry might play an important role may be rather limited. Social mimicry, it seems, may be most likely to develop in species in which discrete sign stimuli (rather than gestalt perception) elicit and direct adaptive responses. Thus, the system could be expected to function best in species of rather stereotyped behavior—such as in birds. Social mimicry is certainly not associated with all species of relatively stereotyped behavior, such as crocodiles and sharks, since they seldom react in very complex ways with other animals on a social basis.

Social mimicry is hypothesized in a wide variety of bird species, from those of tropical forests to gulls. Of gulls Moynihan (1960:532) says, "The principal advantage may be that their resemblances encourage them to act as if they were all members of a single species in situations where joint action may be beneficial (and they certainly do act in this way during defense of the breeding colony as well as during feeding and resting)."

In some mixed flocks, similarity of signals based on social mimicry may act in ways other than flock formation or coordination. Dissimilar species may be discouraged from entering the flock. The large mixed flocks of small finches in Panama indicate such an exclusion. Social mimicry is highly developed in such flocks and the flocks are composed of very few, but very similar, species.

In theory, when related forms come into "secondary" contact (rejoining after division of a parent stock) any divergence caused by character displacement must be checked and reversed in order for social mimicry to occur, or character displacement and social mimicry must operate on different characteristics. For example, it might be possible that two bird species could converge in plumage while diverging in bill length, but such an evolutionary dichotomy has yet to be demonstrated. If social mimicry occurs through an arrest and reversal of character displacement, one might suspect that the ecological advantages of separation through displacement are far less than those of forming mixed groups, at least in some competitive situations. It seems, though, that in some cases the evolutionary problems inherent in moving toward social mimicry are less than those associated with character displacement. In tropical regions where adjacent niches are likely to be filled, character displacement might meet with immediate restrictions through competition, thus opening other evolutionary possibilities.

Obviously, social mimicry usually occurs between sympatric species. However, it may also occur between allopatric species when it is advantageous for them to elicit the same reactions in another species which is sympatric with both. For example, a warbler and a tanager are reported to be only partly sympatric but to resemble each other in voice and color. The resemblances apparently do not facilitate reactions between the two species, but rather elicit similar types of reactions in other species which overlap with both (other species that join and follow both the warbler and the tanager). In other cases, such similarity of characters in allopatric species could encourage common *avoidance* by other species as is described in at least one instance in tropical birds (Moynihan 1968).

Wiley (1971) described an interesting sort of association in three species of the antwren. Two were of the genus *Myrmotherula* and a third *Microrhopias*. Apparently, the dissimilarities in the species permit them to interact in a complementary manner. One species of the congeners was described as much more visually conspicuous, but the other could be much louder (usually, though, all vocalizations were relatively subdued). The loud species, *Myrmotherula fulviventris*, was the more visually cryptic and members of this species would immediately congregate around a human observer in the woods, setting up a raucous clamor. Although its alarm could be heard as it darted about the foliage, its plumage made it difficult to see. The male *M. axillaris* with bold plumage and quieter manners probably functioned, not in warning, but in keeping the flock together through visual communication. The call of this species was never loud and was difficult to locate. It is assumed that flock cohesion is better maintained by visual signals since loud calls might attract predators from afar. The third species probably had a less critical function in terms of group function. Both sexes of *Microrhopias* had bold plumage, but they frequented the densest foliage so their patterns functioned for shorter distances, perhaps primarily between mates.

THE DEVELOPMENT OF SOCIAL BEHAVIOR

The development of any behavioral character may be studied in terms of its evolutionary descent or its history within an individual group. The general problem of the evolution of behavior is discussed in Chapter 11 and, for now, it is only necessary to mention that certain forms of complex social interactions demand a reduction or redirection of aggressive behavior toward competitors. Given the prevalence of such countering

forces as aggression, avoidance, escape behavior, and individual distance among animals, in the relatively few cases where cooperation has reached a high level the magnitude of its adaptive value must be impressive.

We are able to discuss the ontogenetic, or individual, development of social patterns in a more meaningful light. It is possible to observe the development of social patterns in an individual, and this development thus readily lends itself to experimentation. It should be pointed out, however, that the picture revealed by experimentation is not, as yet, a clear one in terms of the adaptiveness of social behavior. Certain laboratory animals have been studied in great detail in experimental situations, but the experiment is often not geared toward understanding how a pattern operates in nature. As an example, much is known about the aberrant behavior shown by laboratory monkeys isolated at birth. But how important is such information for animals in which the condition is not likely to occur—at least when the young would survive? I know of only one field report related to such work, that of unusual social behavior in an orphaned chimpanzee which continued to live with the group (Goodall 1971). Perhaps laboratory investigations with more ecological importance are those which consider the ramifications of chimpanzee adolescence. This is a period of adjustment (with marked similarity to that in humans) which may have great importance to the animal's later status and, hence, to his access to certain commodities and his general success.

There are a variety of ways in which social patterns could develop in any species. We will now consider several of these. First, we know that some animals may associate because they are simply exploiting the same parts of an environment, such as is seen in insects responding independently to tactic influences. Animals may also group together on an anonymous and nondirected basis, such as schooling fish. However, we are not concerned here with such species; of greater interest are those which recognize each other and interact on a truly social basis. It must readily be admitted that more complex forms of social behavior could have their origin in association based on simple aggregation. Diamond (1970) argues that social aggregation comes about early in the lives of individuals of some species through mechanisms of perception and locomotion; thus the opportunity for the development of complex interaction is increased. Animals could associate incidentally, come to recognize each other, and then rely on each other—all through common utilization of parts of the habitat. Perhaps, for example, the sleeping parties of the gelada baboons, which develop when they congregate at safe sleeping sites, at least partly provide the association upon which the complex social structure has developed.

Other possible bases for social development may be related primarily to reproductive behavior in one sense or another. For many species, the basis of group development comes by way of an extension of sexual relations over greater portions of the life span (Allee 1958). In other words, animals may show affiliation as a result of pairing. The affiliation may be temporary (such as that extending through reproductive season or until the young become independent) or relatively permanent (such as the long-term mating of geese and wolves). In some cases, the real basis of a social group may be masked temporarily by the affiliation imposed by the demands of mating. For example, during the mating season a male deer may "lead" a harem. However, at an alarm when the buck may take off in one direction, the actual leadership of the herd is revealed as an old female leads the group in another direction. Obviously, the basis of the group is not as strongly rooted in mating affiliation as might at first be presumed.

Reproductive behavior may also influence social structure in ways other than specifically, through pair-formation. Grouping among primates, for example, may be due to the likelihood of the sexual receptivity of some females in the group at any time, since these animals do not show pronounced estrous seasons. Social structure may also be based on females seeking the protection of males (Hall 1965). Communal organizations in birds may appear where close physical association has resulted in cooperative nest building, or where several individuals participate together in reproductive activities with an absence of territorial antagonism (Crook 1965).

The nature of the pair bond—that "force" which holds mates together as a cooperating unit—is very little understood. Animals which come together only to copulate present no great conceptual problem. It is apparent why they are together —to us and to them. Animals which join as mates for longer periods, such as through the breeding season, might be held together by the fitness advantage of joint efforts to rear young. Those which form lifelong pairings, however, present interesting problems relating to the "mind" of the animals. What is the attraction between them outside the breeding (or sexual) season? The clues are meager. It has been theorized that perhaps personal bonds are somehow derived from the same motivation that results in aggressiveness. (Among humans, love is sometimes described as a love-hate relationship, the smile may be an intention movement to bite, and we know of the aggressiveness that the males of a number of species show toward their prospective mates when pairing and, sometimes, even after the pair is established.) It is apparent that the pair bond is not entirely a result of an expression of aggressiveness. Aggressive behavior increases and wanes with changes in reproductive behavior in some species in which pairs continue intact from one season to the next. Jane Goodall (1971) noted that when certain female chimpanzees became sexually receptive they tended to leave the group in the company of specific males. The pair would travel alone until the female lost her sexual swelling. Then the pair would return to the group. There was never any indication however of any feeling of "love" or even affection between them. When the mating period was over they seemed to lose interest in each other and returned to the group separately. It must be admitted that the attempt to look into the mind of animals is not a promising one. Who can say that the greatest expression of chimpanzee love is not to ignore each other?

Animal sociality may also be operationally based in parent-offspring relations. In some cases the critical relationship which serves as a base for group cohesiveness is between the mother and her offspring. Goodall noted that adult chimpanzees often showed great respect for their old mothers as expressed by their tendency to be near them and their general reluctance to enter into any conflict with them. A family unit in chimpanzees is comprised of a female and her young —the estrous female accepts a number of males and fatherhood can never be determined. A female may be followed by her juvenile, adolescent, and even young adult offspring and the social interaction among them is generally higher than for the group as a whole. (See Harlow, 1958, for an experimental analysis of love in infant monkeys.)

Lambs tend to follow their mothers closely. As a result, the oldest females emerge as the leaders of the flock, followed by their offspring which have appeared over time (Scott 1945). Red deer are matriarchal as a result of the association of the young with their mothers. The females usually stayed together the year round, are long-lived, and have a strong social system, with the old females leading. The yearling females pay close attention to the older females and thus learn herd traditions. Yearling males, on the other hand, are less attentive and they leave the group when they become adults. They form bachelor herds with a loose structure and no hierarchy. The males then separate from their fellows each rutting season to round up the hinds. Each male collects as many females as he is able. As harem-master he services all the females and defends his rights against other males. The demands of such duties are so rigorous that he is only able to last about

a week when he is replaced by a fresh male. The females make no effort to help any harem-master to defend the group from other males. At the end of the rutting season the males depart and the females continue on as a group. The leader females must direct the herd over their migratory route through the mountains and valleys as the temperature begins to change, a route they most likely learned when young by following an older leader (Etkin 1964). So here we see exhibited a flexible behavior in which learning plays an important role in the development of a social unit.

In other species, both parents may be involved in the formation of the "core" relationship with the young. A wolf pack is basically a family unit composed of a father, mother, and the offspring of several years. In some cases, however, two or more such packs may join forces for a time. Mating is apparently for life. When a female is pregnant and unable to hunt, her mate or other members of the pack may bring her food. Members of the pack also bring food to the wolf pups, either in chunks or by regurgitation. The wolf-type of socialization is exceptional in that a pack includes a dominant male which may carry out all the breeding. Dominance hierarchies exist, but little agonistic behavior appears since the structure is formed when the wolves are very young and it remains rather stable through life (Etkin 1964).

The importance of the association of wolf pups must be stressed as a factor in the development of the pack. The pups show a high level of interaction through their romping, licking, touching, play-fighting, and chasing. In fact, Scott (1945) indicates that in wolves and dogs the strongest social relationships are developed with littermates, not parents. He argues that the parents are likely to be off hunting during the period of socialization of the young. There is a current revival of interest in our diminishing populations of wolves which may yield important new evidence. Such studies are likely to bear out Scott's assessment and to indicate the importance of sibling interaction in other "litter-type" social animals of nonstereotyped behavior.

It was noted among wild chimpanzees that adult males show strong affiliation with each other. The tendency is expressed by all-male grooming sessions, sessions to which adolescent males are attracted, but which they are afraid to enter. No female is likely to even closely approach such a group. In general, Goodall implies a higher level of social interaction among males than among females. If females interacted with others it was usually with young or rather timorously, with adult males. Lionel Tiger (1969), the anthropologist, has attempted to answer questions about the tendency to form all-male groups in humans, and bases his findings partly on observations from the animal world—from primates in particular. He notes that men seem to prefer the company of their own sex more than do women and argues that the basis of the difference is not learned or cultural as is so often maintained, but soundly based in biological principle.

There has been some argument regarding whether social behavior is innate or largely acquired through learning. It is clear that differences may be due to species-specific characteristics. Bees, for example, certainly do not learn complex social patterns in their brief lifetimes. Social patterns may be largely learned in monkeys, however, as is demonstrated by the aberrant social behavior of isolates. If social behavior is not learned in some cases, then we may ask to what degree the patterns are based in instinct in the classical sense described in Chapter 2. Tinbergen (1951) thought that social "instinct" is the effect of the operation of other instincts and that there is no social instinct per se. Moynihan and Hall (1953) and Keenleyside (1955) seemed to disagree. However, the argument in the former paper was based on rather unrigorous observations of members of a species (the spice finch, *Lonchura punctulata)* wanting to be together, presumably in the appetitive sense. Keenleyside cited as evidence the species-specific nature of schooling in fish, but his argument was open to criticism based

on the possibility of learning in these animals. Moynihan (1960) said later that there is some evidence to indicate that at least a few of the most gregarious species of birds do have a general gregarious instinct which has become partly independent, in some sense, of all other instincts. Crook (1961) noted that there is important evidence indicating a social instinct, but warned against calling it instinctive in Tinbergen's sense. He prefers instead the term "social tendency."

There is indeed a need for social contact in gregarious animals. A fish separated from its group swims rapidly back and forth apparently seeking its group (Eibl-Eibesfeldt 1970). Gregarious mammals, if isolated, become apathetic and show clear signs of loneliness (Meyer-Holzapfel 1958). Lorenz (1931) reported that his tame jackdaws would not suffer members of the group to leave. In one case a large flock of migrating crows and jackdaws settled near his tame jackdaws, and it looked for a time as if much of Lorenz's flock would travel with the wild group when it took to the wing. However, two older birds of the tame flock went among the wild flock, rounded up the tame birds and headed them home, thus retrieving all but two in two hours. Of course the real basis of this retrieval behavior is unknown, but it could be the expression of a tendency to insure that the retrievers do not become isolated.

The problems of nullifying the effects of learning in any experimental situation designed to discover the innateness of social behavior and formidable. For example, there may be simply an innate tendency of species to associate with their own (Crook's "social tendency"); then once drawn together social patterns might be learned, as was discussed earlier.

The importance of inheritance in social behavior must be acknowledged. However it has in many cases been too long viewed as the overriding determinant of social interaction. Now it seems that the effects of tradition and other forms of learning have been underestimated. Crook (cf. 1970 a, b) has repeatedly emphasized the importance of learning as a determinant of social behavior. He has even referred to the habitat, physical and social, as "nature's Skinner box." As indirect evidence of the environmental shaping of behavioral patterns he cites the lability of social structures as they appear across a species' range, together with their local stability. Mosaic behavioral patterns across a species' range is considered to be an effect of local differences in the learning situation, whether that situation is a construct of environmental differences, local tradition, or a mixture of these factors.

THEORIES OF SOCIOBIOLOGY

Since Lorenz and Tinbergen first began to describe social behavior in animals there has been a divergence of opinion as to just how animal relationships should be regarded in operational terms. The question has great importance with reference to how any study of animal interaction should proceed. There are those who continue to describe animal interaction in terms of the classical dyad relationship; and, rather recently, a new school of thought has developed which more fully incorporates principles of ecology, population dynamics, and social behavior. The object of the new school is to attempt to establish unifying principles of social behavior through presenting social behavior as an ecological construct reflecting the net effect of environmental conditions, innate tendencies, and acquired behavior. The task is a formidable one since we can only broadly generalize regarding physical influences of an environment and we know even less about the predisposition and intelligence of wild animals. Much of the more recent evidence is based on field studies of primates (see the discussion of roles in Chapter 7), and its most articulate chronicler is probably John H. Crook of the University of Bristol.

Crook (1970a) calls the broader study "social ethology," and bases his approach on several points. First, he notes, there are important intraspecific variations in social structure and these, as well as interindividual relations, may be correlated to the ecologies of the subgroups within a species. Secondly, he continues, social structure is not subject to the same evolutionary pressures as morphological characters and cannot be dealt with on the same conceptual basis. Instead, social structures are much more dynamic and labile—within the behavioral limitations of the species. Thirdly, since individuals are dependent upon the group, they must conform to its norms or be selected out; for example, if a bird chooses to feed apart from the flock it may be taken by a predator; if it does not read the signals of its fellows, it may be attacked and killed by them. Fourthly, the problem, he maintains, should be studied at the level of the social process itself rather than by asking questions about sources (i.e., the relative significance of genetics, traditions, environmental programming, etc.). It is hoped such an approach will avoid the persistent nature-nurture controversy. And, lastly, he maintains that historical change in social structure appears as the net of changes occurring at different rates on various processes. Thus the environment may change a social structure quickly, but its indirect effect on tradition occurs slowly, and its effect on the genetics of a population more slowly still. Crook (1965) also made the important point that selection pressures should not be conceived as acting directly on social organization (a statement reminiscent of Tinbergen [1951] who argued that social behavior in the dyad sense is not the result of a social instinct). Rather, it acted upon other tendencies (nest-site selection, escape tendencies, sexual behavior, etc.) which then alter the social organization accordingly. So, whereas "social organization" may not be a subject of selection in and of itself, it reflects the sum of a series of other pressures and is useful in description and comparison.

It might be pointed out here that the group-selection hypothesis of Wynne-Edwards (1962), mentioned earlier (Chapter 8), promotes the idea of selection operating on populations. According to his idea, then, social organization might well be acted upon by natural selection.

Wilson (1971) reemphasized the importance of correlating concepts of evolutionary studies, ecology, and sociobiology in an effort to establish unifying principles. The need is for increasing our level of information regarding what sorts of environmental influences may be molding social systems. Already, limited field data indicate convergence of diverse species in the social systems which are subject to similar environmental pressures. Huxley (1959) used the term *grade* to describe characteristic life-styles of species adapted to a particular ecology. Crook (1970a) points out that species belonging to the same grade often show similar social organization (see below). For example, grassland sciurid and cricetid rodents living in comparable niches show similar social structure. Also, carnivores are often unsociable whether they are marsupial or placental (possible reasons are discussed in Chapter 7). Such correlations have also been demonstrated by Pitelka (1942); Orians (1961); Stonehouse (1960); Crook (1964, 1965, 1970a, b); Cullen (1960); Nelson (1967); and Tinbergen (1967). See Lack (1968) for a review.

Any valid comprehensive statement regarding the molders of social patterns certainly must reflect our knowledge of both heritable and acquired characteristics. Wilson (1971) reminds us that the principal goal of a general theory of sociobiology should be an ability to predict features of social organization from a knowledge of population parameters combined with information on the behavioral constraints imposed by the genetic constitution of the species.

We shall now attempt to summarize some of the findings which illustrate ecological effects on social patterns. The principle was discussed with a different emphasis in Chapter 7 and we will simply add to some of those findings and investigate the possibility of developing unitary rules.

Tinbergen's group (see the discussion of Cullen's 1960 work in Chapter 9) at Oxford demonstrated that many features of the behavior of the kittiwake (a gull) were related to features of the environment. Other work, primarily involving field studies of birds and mammals, followed which indicated a strong interrelationship between social systems and the environment. Social structures, it seemed, could be interpreted or described on the basis of their adaptive significance, a concept which had, until the 1960s, been largely ignored. Earlier in the study of social behavior, patterns were, logically enough, considered primarily or entirely the result of Darwinian natural selection and therefore innately determined. This idea persisted until certain studies indicated the importance of learning. Field studies of primates showed that there was marked intraspecific variation in primate social organizations, and that these could be correlated with the type of environment in which a group was found, a relationship which could most easily be explained by differential learning in the groups living in different types of environments.

But we're getting ahead of our story. Let us first review some of the evidence from field studies of birds. We have previously noted certain correlations of the environment and the social behavior of its denizens. For example, colonial nesting increases foraging efficiency and predator avoidance, but it is only likely to appear where there are suitable nesting sites surrounded by patchily (abundant in separated areas) distributed food. Crook's extensive studies of weaverbirds of the subfamily Ploceinae (1961, 1964) emphasized the principle that social systems are strongly correlated with ecology. He found, for example, that dispersed breeding, active pursuit in courtship, and monogamy could be correlated with insect eating and low light values in the forests of tropical Africa, while flocking, static courtship with visual advertisement of colonial nests, and polygamy were correlated with well-lit savannahs. Aerial advertisements, furthermore, were performed only in those birds which hid their nests in a dispersed manner in grassland. In order to clearly establish the adaptive effect of the behavioral correlates, one must keep in mind such variables as food dispersal and food depth (biomass per unit area) in terms both of its presence and its locatibility.

Solitary or territorial nesters are likely to have nests which are accessible to a predator should they be discovered. The birds avoid attracting attention to the nests by reducing the level of activity around them and by approaching them discreetly. A dispersed nesting pattern permits foraging without social interference and this advantage is only likely to be important if food is not abundant. You may recall the discussion in Chapter 7 which points out the smaller spatial needs of omnivorous and herbivorous birds as opposed to predatory species which hunt sparse or elusive prey (Schoener 1968). Patchiness of the food of herbivorous species may contribute to the fact that they are much more frequently colonial or gregarious than predatory birds, such as hawks. In a situation where food is patchy, grouping may increase the likelihood of finding food. If grouping results in colonial nesting, the nests are usually made inaccessible to predators since the activity around them makes them conspicuous. Also, Crook (1965) maintains there must be sufficient food around the colony for some recruitment to occur; that is, there must be enough food to support a nonbreeding population so that at some time they may take their place among the breeders.

We should also remember that the historical availability of food may strongly affect the sort of mating system that developed. Under conditions of low food abundance, monogamy (and sexual monomorphism) might appear as a mechanism to ensure enough food for the offspring through the cooperation of both parents. In birds, then, population dispersion and, to some degree, social systems are considered to be functions of (1) the preferred food, its abundance, accessibility and distribution, and (2) nest-site preference in relation to predation. Let us now examine some of the evidence from primates, where again we will

see the importance of food, predation, and habitat type as determinants of social systems.

We noted in earlier discussions the effects of environment upon the social structure of some primate species. For example, in savannah areas, which have seasonal periods of low food supply, certain species of baboons move about in one-male units with bachelor groups also in the area. Predation is generally low, so the added strength of numbers of males is not needed for protection and the food supply wouldn't support such a large group anyway. In ecologically more stable woodland type savannah and sparsely forested areas, there is less climatic fluctuation and a more dependable food supply. Here multimale groups may exist as a protection against higher predator risk. Less is known about species of heavy tropical and semitropical forests, but it seems that a number of types of social structures are correlated with such areas.

Jane Van Lawick-Goodall's (cf. 1971) remarkable and loving study of the chimpanzees of the Gombi Stream area of East Africa is the most complete account yet produced of the behavior of wild primates. She has described large and powerful males which move with smaller subordinate females through the deep forest. The size of the males apparently does not function in sexual selection since both sexes are highly promiscuous, the females even copulating with adolescent males. Size in males is probably more important in defense of the group, although the chimpanzees are not often threatened by any predator in an Africa being decimated of its large cats. These great predators are among the many species which continue to disappear from Africa to appear as status-symbols in the wardrobe of civilized man.

Goodall was able to discern specific loosely defined groups in the study area which ranged widely, sometimes converging or interchanging membership. The omnivorous primates probably never face severe food shortage, but they would converge at sites of preferred food, such as fruiting trees and termite mounds as well as Goodall's banana supply. In nature, the food sources of chimpanzees are likely to be patchily distributed; thus, the wide-ranging group structure would be the best means of exploiting such sources.

Aldrich-Blake (1970) compared several species of monkeys and found that an arboreal habitat imposes a certain uniformity on group size, population density, and home range for all the primate species living in that habitat. Others, perhaps with a touch of cynicism, have mentioned that influences of food, sleeping sites, and predation would be similar for any species living in the area so that the adaptive similarities are not unexpected. But this is precisely the point. Can we generalize regarding social systems if the ecological conditions are known? The answer can only be deduced from extensive fieldwork. It is often a "giant step" between armchair predictions and real proof acquired in the field and, in fact, the field data have time and time again shown a disconcerting lack of respect for hypothesis.

The high population density and small range size of forest monkeys is presumably related to the greater year-round productivity of forest as compared to savannah or grassland. Also, forests are "three dimensional" as opposed to the "two dimensional" open country. The added dimension increases the habitat complexity and therefore presumably the stability and environmental carrying capacity (a measure of the life it can support).

What are the other social differences that have so far been found between forest and open-area primates? Not only are home ranges of savannah primates usually larger than those of forest species, but the savannah groups are generally larger where they do exist (although more species may be encountered in the forests). It is thought that since in the woods monkeys may escape from terrestrial predators by running along small branches to another tree, or from eagles by dropping into the understory, there might be an effect on sexual dimorphism and group size. In grassland or sparsely forested areas primates are left with two alternatives: to fight (thus selection would favor multi-

male groups and large size in males) or run away (thus we see great speed in some species such as patas). The predation pressure can be expected to select for large size in males or multimale groups if the food supply permits, abundant food being a prerequisite for body growth and for the maintenance of large groups. Of course, once large males were selected for on any single basis a change in social structure might result as we learned in the last chapter.

Anyone who has attempted to observe animals in deep woodland has found problems in seeing clearly what an animal is doing, observing an individual for any extended period, and finding the animal to begin with. The heavy vegetation presents similar problems for its inhabitants. Thus, in deep forest, reduced levels of visual communication might select against large coordinated social units. Vocal communication would probably not often be selected for as a substitute because of the likelihood of attracting predators from long distances.

Because of the problems inherent in forest study many researchers have been discouraged from attempting field studies there. However, more data are sorely needed if we are to be able to make any valid generalizations regarding ecological effects on social structure. Aldrich-Blake (1970) has pointed up our lack of information by finding that social diversity among forest monkeys is as great as the differences between forest and open-country species. For example, he found that some forest species have the one-male groups formerly considered an adaptation to seasonally arid conditions of the savannah (also see Crook and Gartlan 1966). The question is whether the tendency toward one-male groups is adaptive or is a side effect of an adaptive response to a greater problem. Could the forest support the heavy demands of multimale groups if such groups should occur? The one-male structure in forest monkeys is apparently permitted by their being able to flee from predators through the complex habitat, thus alleviating much of the necessity for protective males. But is the system simply permitted or is it maintained at some cost? These are but a few of the problems and general observations regarding the correlations of ecology and social behavior.

Finally, with this background in mind, let us review one of the more important studies to date regarding a unifying theory of sociobiology in which Crook and Gartlan (1966) correlated environmental pressures with social patterns for several primate species (Table 10.1). Their object was to try to understand some of the selective pressures responsible for adaptive change in social structure and thereby to be able to construct

evolutionary hypotheses regarding the phyletic history of some animals. They theorized that the adaptive radiation of primates runs from forest-dwelling insectivores to larger open-country animals which are predominantly vegetarian. The table shows a shift from insectivorous, nocturnal, solitary forest animals with a population dispersal based on aggressive contacts, through leaf- and fruit-eating forms which move in small family groups or larger parties and which show a variety of types of territorial defense (but little intra-specific aggression, sexuality, or intermale competition), to, finally, vegetarian browsers of open country which live in well-structured groups, us-

Table 10.1. Adaptive Grades of Primates (see text)

Species, ecological and behavioral characteristics	Grade I	Grade II	Grade III	Grade IV	Grade V
Species	*Microcebus* sp. *Chierogaleus* sp. *Phaner* sp. *Daubentonia* sp. *Lepilemur* *Calago* *Aotus trivirgatus*	*Hapelemur griseus* *Indri* *Propithecus* sp. *Avahi* *Lemur* sp. *Callicebus moloch* *Hylobates* sp.	*Lemur macaca* *Alouatta palliata* *Saimiri sciureus* *Colobus* sp. *Cercopithecus ascanius* *Gorilla*	*Macaca mulatta*, etc. *Presbytis entellus* *Cercopithecus aethiops* *Papio cynocephalus* *Pan satyrus*	*Erythrocebus patas* *Papio hamadryas* *Theropithecus gelada*
Habitat	Forest	Forest	Forest—Forest fringe	Forest fringe, tree savannah	Grassland or arid savannah
Diet	Mostly insects	Fruit or leaves	Fruit or fruit and leaves, Stems, etc.	Vegetarian-omnivore Occasionally carnivorous in *Papio* and *Pan*	Vegetarian-omnivore *P. hamadryas* accasionally also carnivorous
Diurnal activity	Nocturnal	Crepuscular diurnal	Diurnal	Diurnal	Diurnal
Size of groups	Usually solitary	Very small groups	Small to occasionally large parties	Medium to large groups. *Pan* groups inconstant in size	Medium to large groups, variable size in *T. gelada* and probably *P. hamadryas*
Reproductive units	Pairs where known	Small family parties based on single male	Multi-male groups	Multi-male groups	One-male groups
Male motility between groups		Probably slight	Yes—where known	Yes in *M. fuscata* and *C. aethiops*, otherwise not observed	Not observed
Sex dimorphism and social role differentiation	Slight	Slight	Slight—Size and behavioral dimorphism marked in *Gorilla*. Colour contrasts in *Lemur*	Marked dimorphism and role differentiation in *Papio* and *Macaca*	Marked dimorphism. Social role differentiation
Population dispersion	Limited information suggests territories	Territories with display, marking, etc.	Territories known in *Aloutta*, *Lemur*. Home ranges in *Gorilla* with some group avoidance probable	Territories with display in *C. aethiops*. Home ranges with avoidance or group combat in others. Extensive group mixing in *Pan*	Home ranges in *E. patas*. *P. hamadryas* and *T. gelada* show much congregation in feeding and sleeping. *T. gelada* in poor feeding conditions shows group dispersal

ually within a home range, and which show much sexuality (often seasonal) and high intermale competition.

There are more arboreal species than open-country species. The reason is, very likely, because there are more niches in forests where populations have specialized in terms of diet, feeding area, daily rhythms, etc. The greater complexity of the forest should also make for increased stability, thus more species might be maintained there. Whereas the species-packed forests might increase the specialization of each species as it increases its efficiency in exploiting a narrow niche, the opposite tendency holds for the open-area species. The latter show very flexible behavior and great adaptability in exploiting a range of habitats in the relatively low competitive milieu.

Table 10.1 shows that coadaptations of Grade I primates are related to their nocturnal insect-hunting behavior (except for two leaf-eating forms). The switch to frugivorous and leaf-eating behavior in II and III is associated with diurnal activity and the formation of larger groups. One-male or multimale groups with territorial inclinations in II and III may not be able to reserve a specific territory, but such behavior at least serves to disperse the groups and therefore achieves one of the effects of successful territoriality.

Small size of the groups in many forest frugivores is probably related to a limited food supply which appears as a result of stable conditions in the tropical forest (see Chapter 8). Under such conditions populations of similar adaptive types may be maintained and thus increasingly efficient exploitation of a narrow niche might be expected. Recruitment in such groups may be difficult because of the strong competition which would limit the likelihood of ultimate reproductive success of members of nonbreeding groups. In small reproductive groups, nonseasonal breeding might be expected since they probably do not suffer periods of drastic food reduction.

Grades IV and V inhabit dry forest, savannah, and steppes where strong seasonal change occurs with harsh dry periods of food shortage. Probably these grades show high mortality rates in older and infirm animals. In the rainy season food is abundant and those animals which have survived the dry season embark on a program of vigorous breeding which results in a replenishment of the population. As with birds, it is not clear whether the timing of the breeding season is correlated with the demands of "child-bearing or "child-rearing."

Savannah primates are subject to harsh predation pressures and large groups probably provide a form of defense. Grouping, of course, is not possible under all food supply conditions. Some baboons (e.g., *Papio*) and other primates such as rhesus monkeys are allowed to group because they largely utilize patchy food sources which are not subject to overexploitation.

In the larger groups which occur in open country, marked competition exists between males for females and therefore the animals show the result of strong sexual selection (Chapter 8). Sexual dimorphism in size, appearance, and behavior in in these species is the result of a number of selective influences. First, the animals live in close proximity in open country and therefore can easily see and respond to each other. There is stronger seasonality in savannah areas than in forests and the females may all come into estrus at about the same time, thus increasing the level of intermale competition. It has been suggested that the sex ratio is such that there are even fewer males than females, thus further heightening competition, and that open-country females may be sexually attractive for longer periods than their forest-dwelling counterparts. All these factors could increase intermale competition and thus produce strong sexual dimorphism. The differential aggressive behavior (which is correlated with the increased size of the male) has an effect on the selectivity of the males involved in mating at any time in the estrous period. The estrous females of such groups are promiscuous until the time of their greatest receptivity when they are likely to

mate only with the troop leader. Crook and Gartlan believe that the sexual dimorphism arose as
a response to sexual selection, that size and aggressiveness in males did not develop directly
as a response to the need for troop defense, but
that this need played a direct role in the organization of the troop and the male cooperative tendencies.

Grade IV encompasses species of rather varied
habitats including, not only typical forest-fringe
and savannah-woodland species, but also a number of forest forms. These latter, in secondary
habitats provided by man's destruction of their
natural woodland home, show social organization
similar to that of the savannah and forest-fringe
species. All these species are characterized by a
marked adaptability and flexibility of behavior.
For example, the population of *Cercopithecus
aethiops* on the rich but small Lolui Island is territorial, but this species is not territorial where it
exists in more expansive but impoverished areas.
Such flexibility is undoubtedly highly adaptive
in the variable forest-fringe environments.

The change from Grade IV to Grade V is characterized by the shift in habitat to grassland or dry
savannah where food is even less abundant and,
at least seasonally, more sparsely distributed. In
such areas it would be best for groups to split up
into smaller more widely ranging parties to avoid
local overexploitation of food. There is no longer
a place for large males which function only in
mating and do not help rear the young. Such
males, however, do consume large amounts of
food, which then is not used in maintaining the
population. Instead, one male which can mate
with all the females and doesn't eat much is about
all the group can afford. In small groups the protective advantage of males is reduced anyway,
since even powerful males derive an important
advantage from numbers. One-male groups (males
with harems) necessitate the exclusion of other
males from the group, and thus the intermale
competition is intensified. The occurrence of
all-male groups indicates strong forces which are
able to exclude potentially reproductive individuals. In some species the strong sexual selection has resulted in such embellishments as
lengthened and strongly marked hair on the back,
forming dramatic capes which increase the visual
impact and apparent size of the animals without
great metabolic expense.

The differences in the coadapted characters of
the three species of baboons represented in Grade
V suggest the variability possible in interaction of
such environmental characters as food shortage,
predation, and habitat structure. Thus *Theropithecus gelada*, in the Ethiopian mountains, under
good conditions form herds which split up as
conditions become more rigorous. There is never
a shortage of sleeping sites on the cliffs no matter how large the group. *Papio hamadryas* forms
one-male groups, but shows less dispersal apparently because of a limited number of sleeping
sites which they must remain near. Such groups
may be forced to come together at night. The
patas of open savannah grassland form one-male
groups which keep well apart. There are no cliffs
to serve as sleeping sites and plenty of predators
are about. At night, the animals disperse into
separate trees and reassemble each morning.
The male does not defend members of his group,
but acts as a watchdog, sometimes risking himself as a diversion for predators. Such males show
a rather low level of aggression in other ways also;
for example, they do not show dominance over
other members of the group. It seems likely that
aggressiveness in these males would be strongly
selected against under the strong predation pressures.

For each grade the environmental pressures
such as food availability, predation and availability of sleeping sites have a different value. In other words, any environmental factor may be more
important or critical for one species than another.
Crook and Gartlan have prepared a general flow
chart (Figure 10.7) which relates these environmental characters to the adaptive response of
any of these grades. Crook and Gartlan's study is

an important one in that it indicates the importance of the interrelationship of social structure to environmental variables. Such studies, as they grow in number, should ultimately be useful to many disciplines including some areas of anthropology and psychology where there is too often a tendency to regard social structures of man as cultural and divorced from any environmental, ecological, or evolutionary effects.

ALTRUISM

If one wishes to approach the question of how social behavior may have evolved he eventually must deal with the prickly but intriguing problem of altruism. *Altruism* may be defined as that behavior which is detrimental to the individual performing it, but beneficial to another organism. Altruistic behavior appears in a variety of animal species from insects to primates and its expression and effects are correspondingly diverse.

We can account for a certain level of altruism according to our concept of fitness (Chapter 8). A pregnant mammal is at a disadvantage as she carries a fetus which drains her of energy and may increase the likelihood that she will be taken by a predator. However, the genes of animals which do not make this sacrifice are not represented in the next generation. Put another way, the species at any one time is composed of individuals whose mothers made that sacrifice. If the trait is inherited, the offspring are prone to make the same sacrifice. Males also may place themselves at a disadvantage for the sake of their offspring although there is probably more variety in the levels and design of their contributions. Among polygamous species a copulating male

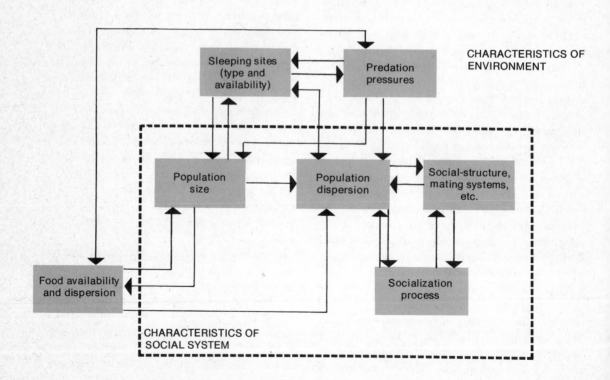

Figure 10.7 Diagram showing the theoretical relationship between habitat and specific social system through time in a given environment. The characteristics of the social system are shown inside the dotted lines. The arrows show the direction of influence of one factor upon another. (From J. H. Crook and J. S. Gartian 1966.)

may reduce his vigilance for predators—or for anything else—for a time. Males of monogamous species may spend their energy in bringing food and they may even defend their family to the death. But the net effect of such behavior within a species is to increase the number of offspring which live to adulthood, each of which carries the genes for altruism.

Altruistic behavior may appear in other forms which are not so easily explained. For example, why would an individual fight for a cousin? or why would an individual feed the offspring of another individual, even of another species? Answers have been formulated for such questions although sometimes they read, "We don't know," or, "The pattern is unadaptive." In some cases, however, there is evidence available, supported by mathematical models, which indicates the adaptiveness of such behavior. For reference refer to the work of W. D. Hamilton (1963, 1964a, 1964b).

Problems of explaining altruism arise when one tries to interpret observed behavior which cannot be accounted for by the classical view of natural selection in regard to fitness. It seems that unless one wishes to accept the idea of group selection (Lack 1966; Smith 1964) the fitness concept must be expanded. With very few exceptions, the only parts of the theory of natural selection which can be supported by mathematical models do not account for the possibility of the evolution of any characters which are disadvantageous to the bearer. If natural selection actually operated as depicted in the classical models, species would show no behavior any more social than mating behavior or parental care. The problem must be approached through describing the likelihood of a certain behavioral pattern resulting in an increase in frequency of a certain gene in a population. It must be kept in mind that the gene which is thus "benefited" need not be carried by the individual performing the act. The reader may wish to refer to the brief discussion of kinship selection in Chapter 8 since, primarily, we are concerned with altruism not related to parental care.

Haldane (1932) proposed a model by which altruism could be selected for if the starting gene frequency were high enough and the advantage to the group were high enough in comparison to the individual disadvantage. Hamilton expanded the idea to say that if the affected individual is a relative of the altruist, thereby increasing the likelihood of the benefited individual also carrying the gene for altruism, then, given Haldane's requirements, altruism would be selected for.

What must be the relative advantages and disadvantages of altruistic behavior in order for the gene for altruism to increase in a population? Hamilton has determined that the relationship depends on how closely the altruist and the benefitor are related. In other words the advantage must increase with the distance of the kinship or the behavior will disappear. To illustrate, altruism toward brothers and sisters will be selected for if the resulting gain is *more* than twice the loss, for half-brothers, four times the loss, etc. So the altruistic animal would sacrifice its life for more than two brothers, but not for less, for more than four half-brothers, but not for less. Therefore, we may deduce that a bird will give a warning cry when the chance of attracting attention to itself is not too great and when the average neighbor is not too distantly related.

Considering the fitness concept, Eibl-Eibesfeldt (1970) mentions that mutations for altruistic behavior could best prevail in closed groups such as families, demes, clans, and tribes, since individuals of such groups are most likely to be related. Hamilton (1964b) discusses the probability that individuals in colonies or clones are related. When the genetic structure of a group is not influenced by some constraint such as intrabreeding demes or common descent, the question of individual recognition (Chapter 6) may become more important. Animals might conceivably be more inclined to behave altruistically in the presence of individuals they recognize, since recognition might reflect a kinship. The recognition might be a simple correlate of altruistic behavior or, in higher animals, such behavior might be predicated upon recognition. As yet there is almost no data to support such theorizing, however.

Altruism might also be expected in "viscous" groups. Species which do not move about much or those which return to or frequent the same areas would likely be more related than those which randomly and freely disperse.

The hymenopteran insects and termites seem to present special cases of altruistic behavior. It seems that the reproductive specializations of these insects have rendered them distinct from most other animals to the extent that generalizing from their behavior to other animals may be invalid. In some of these insects, as we know, there may be large segments of the population in which individuals labor valiantly and defend the group with their lives, but they are not involved in reproduction. The development of such individuals may be an evolutionary result of deferred maturation (ecological implications are discussed in Chapter 7) resulting in permanently neotenous (sexually developed at immature stages) individuals. Among some of these social insects, such workers are strongly related as a result of all having come from a single mating of a queen. Under such conditions, the genes present in any individual are very likely present in the other individuals, so altruistic behavior may be expected. (Hamilton [1964b] also discusses cases where a queen may undergo multiple matings with different males.) The key lies in whether the queen carries genes for altruism so that a worker bee sacrificing herself for a queen (or a soldier termite sacrificing himself) ensures the transmission of genes for such behavior. It will be recalled that in higher organisms the benefitee must carry the altruistic gene expressed by the altruist.

Hamilton has provided us with an elegant description of how such a system could have arisen in the hymenoptera and termites. The problem of the evolution of altruism has puzzled scientists for decades and in the hymenoptera the system has apparently evolved independently no fewer than ten times. Why do these animals have such a propensity for the system? The answer is related to their unusual system of sex determination. Males are produced from unfertilized eggs and so they have half the number of chromosomes as the females; in other words, one of each type. The result is that all his sperm are identical. All the daughters then have 50 percent of their genes in common as a result of one parent producing only one type of gamete. Furthermore, on the average, the daughters share another 25 percent of their genes in common from their mother so that the total genetic affinity among daughters is 75 percent. Now, each daughter has only the normal 50 percent affinity with her mother, so hymenopteran sisters are more strongly related to each other than to their mother. In the context, then, of what we know about kin selection, we can see that it is more advantageous for each daughter to help rear her sisters than for her to have offspring of her own. Thus, we can appreciate the role of sex determination in the development of altruism in the hymenoptera.

Hamilton (1964b) discusses several other aspects of the phenomenon of altruism as related to insects. One such aspect involves the evolution of distastefulness. The concept is an important one since it involves not only the basis for warning coloration but also both Batesian and Mullerian mimicry. The evolution of warning coloration is not easy to conceptualize since, at every stage, the more conspicuous individuals would be selected out. Fisher (1930) suggested that nearby siblings would be most benefited and theorized that perhaps such warnings are correlated with gregariousness. If a warningly colored and noxious larva for example were taken by a bird there is a reduced probability that the bird would take another one. So, whereas the selective advantage of saving a brother is only half as great as if the individual itself were protected, the possibility of saving an entire brood increases the likelihood of conspicuousness developing. With the warningly colored moth it is best to continue to live at least through the egg-laying period of the species. Thus the number of noxious individuals is increased and the probability that any specific individual will be taken is reduced.

There is another way altruism can manifest itself—through the suicidal behavior of those individuals past their reproductive period. A postreproductive animal might be expected to be entirely altruistic. Any kinship at all with a neighbor would be sufficient to select for the trait. David Blest showed that the postreproductive period of certain moths is characterized by this selflessness. He argues that in cryptic species the discovery of any member by a predator increases the likelihood of others also being taken. (Recall the discussion of the formation of search images in Chapter 3.) The predator which captures a cryptic individual, in effect, will take a step toward recognizing the crypsis. This is opposite the adaptive effect for species with warning coloration where the discovery of any individual benefits the rest. Therefore, with the crytpic moth it is best to die directly after reproduction. Blest found that among the cryptic species these moths, after reproducing, show behavior which might be interpreted as an effort to destroy the cryptic pattern. In some cases they seem to fly randomly about to use up the remains of their vital reserves and to fray their wings beyond recognition. Hamilton points out that the selective forces operating on the postreproductive life span are doubtless weak and will generally be strongest where the relationship of neighbors is highest (e.g., in the more viscous populations).

Hamilton (1946b) points out that scattered throughout the literature are records of behavior which do not conform or are antithetical to the principles described. In some cases kinship is blatantly disregarded and in other cases harms and benefits are not accrued at all according to expectations. For example, how can one explain the behavior of birds feeding the young of other species (Summers-Smith 1963)? In this case the behavior is observed seldom enough that one can say it is undoubtedly unadaptive behavior—a mistake.

Other puzzling cases however are much more regularly reported. As examples, some bees pool their broods in a common nest, as do some birds; some Hymenoptera are unable to recognize their own nests; some birds are unable to recognize their own young in a group with other offspring; and penguins are able to leave their young with baby-sitters while they go off on fishing expeditions. Hamilton suspects in such regularly occurring cases that there is a strong likelihood of misinterpretation by the human observer or that there is some form of positive deception of their fellows going on by some animals.

For reviews of social behavior with extensive references to the literature see Eibl-Eibesfeldt (1970), Ewer (1968), Tinbergen (1953), Crook (1970a,b), and Allee (1938).

11

EVOLUTION

Not long ago Ernst Mayr wrote, "There are vast areas of modern biology, for instance . . . the study of behavior, in which the application of evolutionary principles is still in the most elemental stage" (1963:9). In the few years since that statement some notable advances in theory and technique have appeared, but these have not been consistent in their assumptions and the impact of their designers has thus been lessened. The result is a proliferation of schools of thought, each scrambling for a toehold in the conceptual world (which actually means in the minds of the "synthesizers," those who are able to take the available data and fit them into the big picture).

How do the assumptions vary? Some groups hold heartily to the idea of the inflexiblility of an instinctive pattern and find their greatest argument is in deciding which patterns to consider instinctive; others believe that almost all behavioral patterns are learned; some, that any innate pattern can be greatly affected by environmental input, or that only the propensity for performing a pattern is inherited. The result is a revival of the old nature-nurture controversy—although wrapped in new syntactical garb. The question, of course, centers around whether any behavior is, as we know morphology to be, inherited, variable within limits and subject to natural selection. If heritable, is it species specific? Can it be used to describe species and relationships between species? If these questions are valid, how can the problem be most fruitfully approached?

We know, from noting the stability of a pattern through time in a population, that behavior can somehow be transmitted through the generations. Such transmission could occur through innate mechanisms by being encoded in genes, by learning—common conditioning—and further behavioral stability in populations might appear through tradition.

Tradition learning could be an important means of continuing a behavioral pattern through the generations in certain groups such as mammalian carnivores or primates, animals which are relatively intelligent and which have extended parental care. Tradition learning, it must be pointed out, has also been demonstrated among the more flexible species of rather stereotyped orders. For example Hinde and Fisher's (1952) study of titmice which were able to open milk bottles indicated the behavior was transmitted through learning. In any case, learning as an important adaptive feature requires intelligence far beyond that of most animals. Therefore, Manning (1971) reasons, most behavior must evolve by the operation of natural selection upon inherited variations.

There are formidable problems inherent in the study of the inheritance of behavior. Some of these problems are similar to those confronting the study of evolution by the comparative anatomist. For example, some animals change rapidly, such as birds apparently have, while others, such as the horseshoe crab and the opossum, are virtually living fossils. Obviously any changes in these animals must be considered from different perspectives since the level of variation in ecological pressures on each is distinct. Also, there are characters which are more conservative than others. For example, the bones in the flipper of a porpoise are startlingly similar to the skeletal forelimb of a man, or bat. The bill size and shape of many species of birds, on the other hand, seem to be evolutionarily labile. Inherited behavioral characters must vary in their lability as well.

The problems and advantages of studying evolution through behavior and morphology are not entirely identical however. The student of the evolution of behavior confronts special problems. For example, behavior itself cannot be fossilized, and the fossil records of the results of specific behavioral patterns are scarce. Such clues are usually limited to footprints or tracks, burrows, wounds, and tooth marks. As special monuments there are examples of animals fossilized in the act of copulation. In even rarer cases the fossil record of a behavioral pattern indicates the development of the pattern. Fossil burrows of worm-like animals of the Cretaceous and Tertiary periods called *Zoophycos* show a change in movement and orientation which probably led to increased foraging efficiency. Basically, the change was from tunneling randomly through the mud to the excavation of one large food-laden area (Seilacher 1967).

As has been mentioned (for example in regard to the empid flies, in Chapter 2) one means of studying the evolution of behavior is through a comparison of living forms. Certain extant species of Hymenopteran insects (bees, wasps, ants) show different levels of social organization, for example, which when arranged from simple to complex indicate the evolutionary route taken was that (1) the female remained with the eggs; (2) the female built a communal shelter and remained with the larvae; (3) the female began to survive successive generations of her offspring; (4) female workers became sterile with a subsequent dependence on the group; and (5) distinct castes developed (Lindauer 1965). As another example, the Meliponi bees show important interspecific differences in their "dance." The differences are believed to indicate the sequence in the development of the dance (Johnsgard 1967).

One of the more fascinating accounts of the evolution of behavior as determined by a comparison of extant species was by Gilliard (1963) who described the evolution of bowerbirds by looking at all the birds with similar behavior—such as those with arena, or lek, behavior. He assumed that arena behavior in the various species is an advanced characteristic with a common sequence of development. Once the stage is set by the proper environmental conditions, there begins rapid evolution to the highly distinct and specialized behavior seen in all the far-flung arena species. The bowerbirds, he reasoned, are simply at the pinnacle of this evolution, substituting fancy houses and jewelry for personal coloration. The system of males and females sharing work loads is considered primitive—but very conservative and resistant to change. In arena birds the males

Figure 11.1 The satin bowerbird, *Ptilon-orhynchus violaceus,* is an "avenue builder." Avenues are passageways through the grass into which the female must be enticed before mating can occur. The female is attracted to the bower by trinkets placed in a cleared area near the opening of the avenue. In this species, most of the objects are blue in color. Another species, the duller colored crestless bowerbird, builds tent-like structures which may be surrounded by moss decorated with flowers. Generally the duller the males in appearance, the more spectacular their bower.

have been freed from these duties (arena behavior, it will be remembered, exists where males establish mating stations that have no connection with feeding or nesting). There is wide variation in the 24 species of birds of paradise which practice arena behavior. Some of these highly conspicuous birds clear arenas by picking up debris in their bills or by violently fanning with their wings. This clearing is the first step toward bowers. From here, it is a rather small step to decorating the arena. Gilliard proposed that the forces of sexual selection are transferred from the individual to external objects. Thus released from personal garishness, the individual could become more cryptic. In some species of bowerbirds, when the male approaches the female, he twists his head oddly as if to display a crest which is no longer there—so, perhaps, there once was a crest there which has disappeared, leaving the behavioral pattern. It is also theorized that such movements are simply displaced nest-building motions which cannot be easily discarded. The whole system of arenas and sexual dimorphism most likely results from a "shift in the work load" to the female. The freed males then may attract females through personal conspicuousness, as do peacocks and some birds of paradise, or through the decorated bower. In summary, arena behavior is the courtship behavior of emancipated males and is probably derived from nest-building behavior. The cleared arenas are the first step in building the gaudy bowers. Generally, the duller the appearance of a bowerbird, the more elaborate its bower. These dull-colored bowerbirds which build the most conspicuous, complex, and ornate bowers are probably at the leading edge of avian evolution according to Gilliard (Figure 11.1).

The theory of recapitulation has been applied to the problem of the evolution of behavior in the hope that the ontogeny of an organism might reveal clues as to its phylogeny. The recapitulation model is far too questionable concerning behavior to be applied in any but the most tentative of terms. Seilacher (1967), in his discussion of the evolutionary development of *Zoophycos,* says that the Tertiary (or advanced) forms built separate tunnels or lobes early in life and large excavations as adults. They were probably descended from the Cretaceous form which built separate lobes as adults. As another example, it will be recalled that some birds show primitive loco-motor behavior early in life and the more advanced method of getting about appears later. Some sparrows do not hop about; instead they employ the relatively advanced technique of walking, but at the nestling stage, they hop (Armstrong 1965). In all, recapitulation provides interesting clues but very little solid information regarding the development of behavior. We must rely on other sources.

When considering the evolutionary history of animals it is tempting to oversimplify, calling some animals primitive and others advanced. Lorenz (1950) warns us, however, that such classifying is naïve in that all animals show both primitive and advanced characters. Thus, some animals may have many advanced characters while possessing some very primitive ones. For example, the mouth and teeth of man are much more primitive than those of a "primitive" monotreme, the platypus. Such inequities in characters result because evolution proceeds not in a simple linear fashion but rather as a branching tree, some branches evolving faster than others. "Advanced" species are those showing rapid evolution in many characters, whereas "primitive" lines are those evolving rapidly in only a few characters.

Even when broad trends are considered, there are often disturbing exceptions or disjunctions as one proceeds along the developmental line. For example, there seems to be a tendency in some phylogenetic lines toward increasing the role of the higher brain centers at the expense of purely instinctive behavior. Zsolt Megai, an anthropologist, reminds me that there is evidence that humans must even be taught how to copulate. The tendency toward cerebration, or braininess, has been noted in vertebrates and especially in mammals. Even among primates the

primitive insectivores apparently rely much more on innately determined behavior than do the chimpanzees. In birds, the progression toward cerebration is evident in a few families, such as the crows and parrots. On the other hand, no insect group shows the tendency though insects comprise an evolutionary line with many advanced characters. There are important distinctions between the learning ability of insects even at about the same stage of phylogenetic development. Some hymenopteran insects show a remarkable facility for associative learning, whereas the other "advanced" order of insects, the diptera (two-winged flies), show very little of the ability.

There is an understandable tendency in ego-centric man to consider the characters he possesses as advanced, and even to asume that all animals are ever progressing toward the attainment of humanlike characters. There are pronounced vestiges of this tendency in behavioral scientists who attempt to study our own behavior through the analysis of other "lower" animals which are often, in a sense, regarded as cheaper, shorter-lived, simpler, and expendable men. This is a peculiar point of view, especially since there is actually reason to assume that other animals are more "successful," according to several indicators, than man is. For example, are our social systems more efficient than those of the hymenopteran insects? Perhaps bees do not agonize in guilt about their feminist societies, nor do they hold endless dialogues on the inequities within their system, but then, there are no bee slums.

One result of the increased application of ecological and evolutionary theory to the study of behavior should be an increased reticence to extrapolate from one animal species to another or from other animals to man. For example, the selective bases for social organizations of ants and men cannot be the same. Not only did vertebrates and insects separate early in their evolution (Figure 11.2), but their potentials and recent natural histories are vastly different. Likewise, birds and mammals diverged early from the reptilian stock (Figure 11.3). How valuable can experiments with artificially selected rats be in terms of expanding our knowledge of human learning? Even careful laboratory experiments on primates may not even reflect the characters of those species, let alone man. Jane Goodall, after years of close association with wild chimpanzees —the animals with learning abilities probably most similar to our own—tells us that the behavior of caged laboratory chimpanzees bears little resemblance to that of their wild brothers. We must seek to understand, not only innate tendencies, but variables which are now operating as well as those which were operating all along to produce the behavioral type we see today.

Let us very briefly review certain prevailing notions regarding the evolutionary development of mammals according to Romer (1970). The serious evolutionist might well argue with such generalized treatment; however, there may be readers unfamiliar with the precepts of biology, and certain fundamental information on the development,

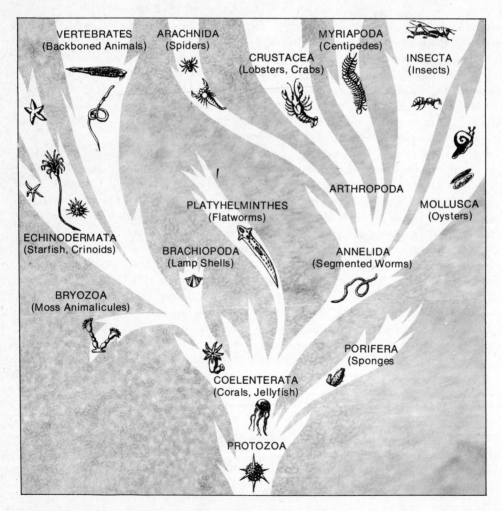

Figure 11.2 A simplified family tree of the animal kingdom. It shows the probable relationship of the vertebrates. (After Romer 1970).

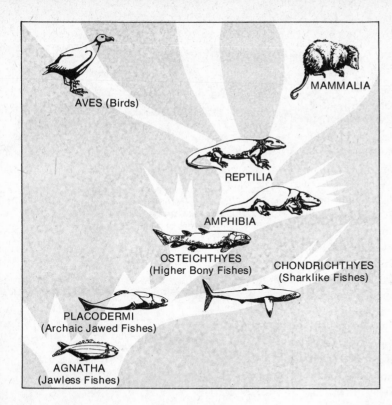

AVES (Birds)

MAMMALIA

REPTILIA

AMPHIBIA

OSTEICHTHYES
(Higher Bony Fishes)

CHONDRICHTHYES
(Sharklike Fishes)

PLACODERMI
(Archaic Jawed Fishes)

AGNATHA
(Jawless Fishes)

Figure 11.3 A simplified family tree showing the vertebrate classes. (From Romer 1941.)

and hence the relationships, within the group which includes man might be useful. We will consider specifically the sorts of evolutionary influences which might lead toward the pronounced development of the higher learning centers.

We begin by noting that the reptiles which gave rise to mammals diverged from the other reptiles before the end of the carboniferous period about 300 million years ago. The mammalian ancestors were the Synapsida—a more specialized member of this group being the Therapsida (Figure 11.4). The Therapsid skull suggests this animal had high olfactory powers and the skeleton is that of a swift-running animal. It probably rushed its prey like a dog rather than stalking it catlike. The brain was small, but it showed the beginnings of a mammal-like cortex (the part responsible for "higher" brain functions).

By the end of the Triassic period (about 200 million years ago) the mighty dinosaurs appeared. The Therapsids died out about this time except for a small form which continued to coexist with the dinosaurs. This form was able to survive and ultimately gave rise to the mammals. The period of coexistence with the dinosaurs—many of which were large, fleetfooted and carnivorous—very likely placed a high premium on intelligence and alertness in the small premammals. These early mammals were, by the way, a very insignificant part of a world dominated by the Ruling Reptiles. About this time, probably due to intense pressure from predators, the brains of the early mammals began to show signs of increasing size. Other changes were also occurring, such as homoiothermy (warm-bloodedness—where body temperature is maintained within rather narrow limits). Homoiothermy meant the mammal could function at a certain level in a wide range of temperatures. Hair probably developed about this time as an insulator of the body. The mammals were now able to incubate their eggs within their own bodies and the young were born alive rather than in eggs.

Nursing and care of the young could then begin. This care meant the young had time to develop complex nervous systems before they left on their own to enter a world dominated by the stupid but voracious dinosaurs. Even today, extended parental care is characteristically found in the more intelligent species, presumably to provide time for the development of learning and learning sets (Figure 11.5). The nursing habit also could have initiated family units. When the dinosaurs died out at the end of the Mesozoic (about 65 million years ago) the mammals, already equipped with well-developed brains born of existing under constant danger, began their rapid radiation over the earth.

Among mammals the most intelligent are the primates (Figure 11.6), most of which are tree dwellers. The results of tree living are varied: (1) a trend toward a herbivorous or mixed diet; (2) a necessity for agility with a concomitant development of the motor part of the cortex; (3) the development of the grasping hand; (4) a shift from nose to eyes as the most important source of environmental information; and (5) a trend toward increase in relative brain size (probably correlated with eye and hand development). For details see Romer (1958, 1970).

Later in this chapter references will be made to orders, classes, and families of animals as well as genera and species. These terms are simply the most convenient way of sorting the different types of organisms according to their characters to try to distinguish them from each other and to show relationships among them. For example, virtually all living things are placed into one of two categories, called kingdoms, according to whether they are considered plant or animal. Among animals, furthermore, those that show a number of characters in common are then placed in groups by themselves. Each of these groups may be more finely divided according to the distinguishing characteristics the members possess until, finally, in the smallest groups, the members have so many characteristics in common that they can inter-

Figure 11.4 A mammal-like reptile, *Lycaenops,* from the late Permian period of South Africa. Reptiles such as these are thought to be the forerunners of mammals. (After Colbert 1955.)

Figure 11.5 Olive baboon with young. Parental care in mammals provides time for the young to learn how to behave. In many such intelligent species, several years are required to reach maturity. (Photo: Leonard Lee Rue III from National Audubon Society.)

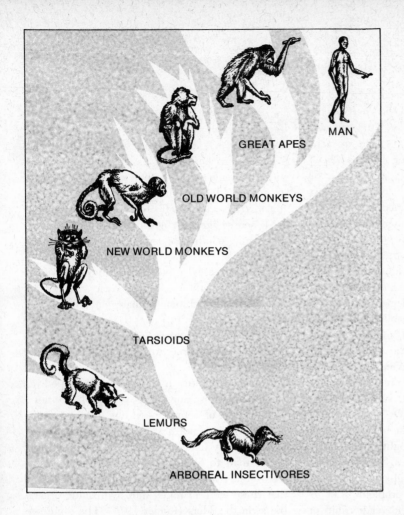

Figure 11.6 A simplified family tree of the primates. (From Romer 1970.)

breed successfully. These are species. From kingdom to species the divisions are:

Kingdom
  Phylum
    Class
      Order
        Family
          Genus
            Species

Of course, there are varieties within a species and super- and subgroups of the classifications, but these will not concern us here. We only wish to show that, for example, the genera of a family are considered to be more closely related to each other than to members of other families of the order.

BEHAVIOR AND MORPHOLOGY

The relationship of morphology to behavior is in some cases obvious, in other instances exceedingly subtle. If members of two populations or species of animals are constructed differently, it is logical to assume those differences may be due to adaptions to different conditions or niches, and behavioral differences related (as well as unrelated) to the observed morphological specialization may be expected. The concept is a simple one. The question involves "why" any animal has a certain appearance, structure, size, or morphology. How does it employ this specialization behaviorally? A related question centers over what nervous specializations must exist in order to utilize a particular structure as part of an overall adaptive pattern.

Such questions need not be restricted to differences in populations. We have seen (Chapter 9) that morphologies of sexes of a single species may be quite different. In humans men are generally larger, stronger, and swifter than women as measured by comparisons of either averages or upper limits. On the other hand, women appear better "constructed" as determined by their resistance to many sorts of stress and their greater longevity (females of many species live longer than males but it might be argued that this is because the roles are less demanding or because they are protected by males). Can we assume, on the basis of pronounced morphological differences, that the behavior (or anatomically, the neural complex) which utilizes the distinct advantages of each morph is specific to the sex? In other words, assuming a historical advantage for large size in males, can we not also assume the development of a particular mental set, such as aggressiveness, to go along with it? Or is it that size and strength are inherited, but the behavior which utilizes them is cultural or taught? Such questions are being asked, and perhaps studies of the evolutionary development of behavior can help to shed light on these vexing problems. Let us now explore certain facets of the relationship of behavior to morphology.

"Birds are so stupid because they can fly." This statement is attributed to Heinroth and it implies a great deal about how particular morphology might affect the development of behavior. The therapsids were forced to deal with the speedy, voracious, and formidable dinosaurs, and the result was the development of higher brain centers. The dinosaurs couldn't be outfought or outrun, so any animal that survived in their presence probably had to outthink them. Birds, on the other hand, developed lighter bones, air sacs, large pectoral muscles, and feathers. Thus equipped, they reduced the likelihood of having to deal seriously with terrestrial predators; they could fly away and leave most dangers. So while they never became

very smart, they did become very specialized. Such specialization arose as a result of their flying abilities (since rules of aerodynamics must impose rather severe strictures on those which became flyers) and their strong competition. Competition, both between and within species, might be expected to become an important factor in animals which are likely to increase to the food (or other) barrier by effective predator avoidance. In a sense, then, a morphological development may strongly influence certain behavioral developments.

In other cases a morphological pattern may act more directly in concert with a behavioral one. For example, some primates have ischial callosities—callouses on their rears—which enable them to sleep upright on limbs in trees that most predators are unable to climb (Washburn and Hamburg 1965).

Ischial callosities undoubtedly developed *de novo*. They arose anew and were probably not a modification of some preexisting external structure. But this is not always the case. Natural selection is very likely to remodel an existing entity rather than to form a new one. For example, it seems that the very earliest fish had lungs and that these were changed into hydrostatic organs, the swim bladders (Romer 1970). The same sort of "conservation" is seen in ritual patterns. Rather than develop whole new patterns, new uses are made of the old ones.

The morphology of an animal may often provide important clues as to what behavior we should expect from it. The idea is an obvious one. We don't expect to see housecats pecking grain. If on a walk in the woods we suddenly confront a large strange animal with long pointed canine teeth, we can rightly expect activation of the sympathetic nervous system. We are beginning to learn of other, less obvious, correlations of behavior and morphology. For example, the three-spined stickleback has longer spines than the ten-spined. It is theorized that this difference is responsible for the greater boldness of the three-spined because the longer spines provide greater defense against predators, reducing the need for hiding and crypticity.

It is often assumed that evolutionary changes in behavior involve changes in the brain or central nervous system (Sperry 1958). Since the brain controls behavior in many species to a large degree, any changes in behavior are strongly influenced by the rate at which the nervous system can change. On the other hand, Harlow (1958) has indicated that the brain is capable of much more complex activity than it is called upon to employ by existing morphological demands. Thus, behavioral changes may be possible without concomitant neural changes. For example, some worms can learn a T-maze the likes of which they would probably never encounter in nature. (The opposite but probably less important evolutionarily argument can also be made. Washburn and Avis in 1958 argued that the adoption of tools by early apelike creatures such as the australopithecines probably resulted in the development of brains which could better employ such tools.)

Scientists sometimes seem to assume that the application of Occam's razor to any theory will result in a better theory. While this is often the case in scientific explanations, it may be an invalid assumption in the study of evolution. The result may be a simplistic picture which does not correspond to the real world. Evolution should probably not be considered a parsimonious process. Nature has no reason here to stress economy, particularly in a variable and changing world. It is thus probably a mistake to look for a step by step progression from simple to complex, from primitive to advanced, or from good to better in evolutionary processes. We have pointed out that in recent vertebrates there is a general progression toward the "advanced" brain, but even in cases where the record is relatively complete, certain anomalies occur. Who would have guessed that the brain of *eohippus*, the "dawn horse," would show little similarity with primitive ungulate brains, but, instead, would have much more

in common with the opossum (Simpson 1958)?

Simpson (1958) notes that in the continuing study to associate behavioral patterns with their neural centers some have attempted to correlate early mammalian brains with stereotyped or instinctive behavior. It is then assumed that in the development of the brain the cerebrum was added secondarily. The argument implies that evolutionarily newer brain parts function in higher ways, such as in learning. Such a trend in morphology supports the position that vertebrate species are generally moving toward greater intelligence.

Behavior may also be correlated with morphology on another level. We have already noted the more recent physiological studies with electrodes implanted in different parts of the central nervous system which, when stimulated, elicit a behavioral response under the control of the area stimulated. Other interesting but preliminary work is being done which indicates the importance of naturally occurring chemicals in the blood, such as metabolic by-products or hormones, which influence behavior by acting on the nervous system. If it can be shown that certain normally occurring chemicals, such as lactates, influence a person's level of irritability or "mood," then perhaps altering the concentration of that chemical can produce a more desired mental effect. A result of such studies might be the reduction in the use of "unnatural" additives to the blood in an effort to change a mood or state of mind.

Since behavior is often directly correlated with a morphology or structure, we may ask which appeared first, the behavioral or morphological pattern. The "mutationists" of earlier days lent support to the idea that a mutation arises first which causes a morphological change and the animal then develops the behavior for employing it. Each case must be considered separately since no hard-and-fast rule can be formed which covers all cases. However, a general pattern does emerge which seems to include most cases. The behavior is usually older than the structure which it makes conspicuous—the structure which emphasizes or enhances the effect of a behavioral pattern. For example, many species of birds raise the feathers on the top of the head when excited or alarmed, but only a few, such as the bluejay, have developed crests which make the pattern obvious.

Lorenz (1937) and Tinbergen (1940) stated that in display (signaling) the ceremony is almost always older than the structure being displayed. In other words, a bird does not bow because it has a crest, but it has a crest because of its habit of bowing. Manning (1971) points out that the eyespots on the moth *Caligo* would have been ineffective if they had developed without the behavioral pattern (spreading the wings) which exposes them. The quick spreading of the wings, on the other hand, may have had some startling effect on predatory birds before the eyespots arose, so that the behavior could have developed before the structure. In some cases a structure may arise on one adaptive basis, but come to be employed in another context as well. For example, some birds are strongly sexually dimorphic in bill size as a mechanism to permit differential foraging. The bill could then be employed in sex recognition and take on new importance as a display.

In other cases, the structure may persist after the behavioral pattern has gone away. The Guira cuckoo, *Guira guira*, for example, raises its crest on being alarmed or when it hears the alarm note sounded. On the other hand, the smooth-billed ani, *Crotophaga ani*, has elongated crown feathers which are never erected (Davis 1942). Armstrong (1965) argues that when a structure or ornament is present with no ceremonial or display behavior associated with it, we may assume the structure is vestigial rather than a recently acquired character awaiting its behavioral pattern.

Tinbergen (1940) pointed out, in still other cases, that the structure may occasionally precede the behavior. The gravid three-spined stickleback positions her body so that her swollen belly is accented when she confronts the male (Figure 11.7). In this case it is apparent that the structure did not follow the display. Armstrong (1965) also argues that the display might not precede the structure in displacement patterns.

GENE ACTION

Can behavioral patterns, or more precisely, the potential for performing specific patterns, be inherited? If they can be, then behavior can be investigated at the level of the gene. The evidence for the heritability of behavior is varied and ranges from the appearance patterns which are performed in an adaptive manner, with no chance of their being learned (Chapter 2), to indications of behavioral changes as a result of certain mutations (changes in the gene or chromosome which are then passed along to the next generation).

Sometimes mutations produce altered behavior which is correlated with gross changes in morphology. One type of mutation, for example, may produce microcephaly in humans—the small head related to an almost total absence of brain tissue. A mutation also produces "waltzing mice," which spin when disturbed due to inner ear changes. The result of mutations on physical characters

Figure 11.7 Two views (A, side and B, front) of the female stickleback in which her swollen appearance is emphasized by a behavioral pattern. (From ter Pelkwijk and Tinbergen 1937.)

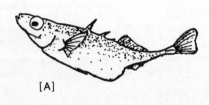

[A]

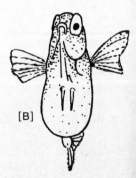

[B]

which are related to behavior may be much more subtle in its manifestation. For example, phenylketonuria is due to a metabolic change. The result is the accumulation of a chemical in the blood which produces gross defects in the biochemistry of the brain and which causes severe mental retardation. These examples all involve great changes in the organism, and any great change in finely adapted organisms is likely to be deleterious. We are more interested in small changes which may gradually accumulate through the generations thus enabling selective forces to operate with less vigorous results.

A serious problem in trying to study the evolution of behavior from a genetical standpoint is to determine just what constitutes a unit of behavior. Some patterns are performed in a variety of contexts, some patterns gradually change into others, and some are subject to various levels of learning influences. Therefore, it is difficult to determine when a given behavioral pattern has been observed. (Tinbergen [1959] described the usefulness of *displays* as behavioral units—as is discussed in the section on the homology of behavior in this chapter.) Then we have the problem of not knowing enough about animal behavior to be aware of the repertoire the animal might have at its disposal. Signals unrecognized by us may be used as modifiers of signals we do recognize, for example. Also, we must be thoroughly familiar with the natural history of an animal in order to be able to interpret what we see. The baring of teeth in various primates may have entirely different meanings. As a further complication of matters, the same behavioral change may be caused by a number of genetic alterations, thus making the search for the genetic control difficult. It is known that several single-gene mutations in *Drosophila* all result in a reduction of courtship patterns in males probably through acting in different ways (Manning 1971).

In some cases the problem of determining gene influences on behavior is made more difficult by the operation of "switch" genes. Here a single gene may turn a set of other genes on or off (see Rothenbuhler 1964a and b). Lorenz (1941) described a number of fixed action patterns (behavioral units which are genetically based) held in common by several closely related species of ducks. One of the fixed action patterns involved courtship behavior of the drakes. He found that when two species of these ducks were crossed, the offspring showed a courtship pattern not found in the repertoire of either parent species. It seems that the pattern is controlled by a "block" of genes which is, in turn, controlled by a switch gene. The block has undoubtedly descended intact through the generations because the genes comprising it lie in close proximity along the chromosome and have been present, but "turned off," by the switch gene in the parent species. In the hybrid offspring, apparently the effect of the switch has been reduced and the pattern, long hidden, emerges. Such information thus indicates the affinity of the parent species. It is unlikely, however, that hybrid studies will provide much information about the inheritance of behavior since closely related species must be used in the crosses and their behavioral repertoire is likely to be similar.

As another example of the behavioral effects of genes, consider the case of the honeybees. Some strains of honeybees are "hygienic"—that is, if a larva dies the workers uncap the cell and place the corpse outside. Nonhygienic bees do not show this behavior. Rothenbuhler (1964a and b) made the classical crosses and backcrosses of the two strains and found the pattern was, in fact, a discrete unit of behavior. The genes controlling the behavior were apparently switch genes which determine whether or not the fixed pattern is performed. Fuller and Thompson (1960) showed that crosses between related species or strains could result in a variety of behavioral changes such as in fixed action patterns, selective responsiveness, circadian rhythms, orientation, and learning ability.

For extensive reviews of the work on the genetics of behavior see Fuller and Thompson (1960)

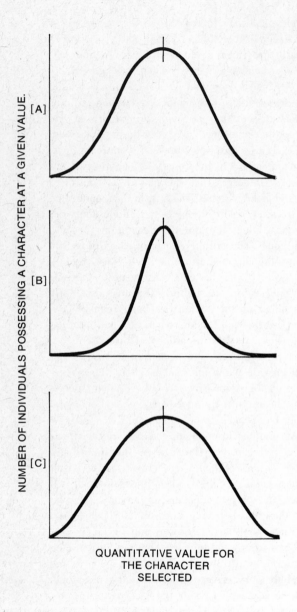

NUMBER OF INDIVIDUALS POSSESSING A CHARACTER AT A GIVEN VALUE.

[A]

[B]

[C]

QUANTITATIVE VALUE FOR
THE CHARACTER
SELECTED

Figure 11.8 Variation within populations.
See the text for an explanation.

and Hirsch (1967).

VARIATION

From an evolutionary point of view there are two important opposing tendencies operating in individuals of populations. One favors the behavior which is "optimum" for most individuals of the species at a given time and it therefore places a premium on uniformity of behavior throughout the group. The other favors variation between individuals as a means of preserving evolutionary flexibility. (Variation, it might be said, provides something for natural selection to work on.)

The uniformity of a species is probably best maintained through natural selection strongly favoring those members of a certain type. The more any individual differs from that optimal type the more it decreases its likelihood of reproductive success. On the other hand, genetic variation is probably maintained primarily through geographic and temporal variation, where different populations within a species are likely to have different optimal phenotypes due to adaptation to local conditions. Variation within some populations, then, may be accounted for by rather distinct subpopulations maintaining a certain level of gene flow between them (see Mayr 1958). Other factors may be operating as well which result in increased variation within populations.

The variation of any character within a population can be expressed graphically (Figure 11.8). If selection is strong as a result of, for example, a limited type of food or strong competition, variation will probably be lessened (Figure 11.8b). If selection is weak, as in Figure 11.8c, variation could be expected to increase.

It will be remembered that in some cases the norm may not be "optimal." For example, recall the effect of supernormal releasers. It is known that a black cardboard "bill" with a contrasting white dot elicits stronger begging responses in gull chicks than the normal red bill of the parents. So why does the normal bill of the gull retain its less effective color? It is possible that the red bill color has a number of uses and that the norm merely represents a compromise between its various adaptive demands. Perhaps the red bill is epigamic—functioning as a threat which results in territorial spacing out. Perhaps, also, it would be more useful as a threat if it were not necessary that it be utilized in feeding young as well.

Some species are highly variable. For example, mongrel dogs are usually immediately distinguishable even for humans comparing them for the first time. Individuals of highly selected breeds, especially those of a single color, may be more difficult to distinguish. The reason is simply that man has subjected these animals to severe artificial selection and, in most cases, increased selection results in decreased variability. (For an exception refer to selection for variability in starfish in Chapter 6.) Artificial breeding programs have also demonstrated that distinct behavioral characters can be developed in populations. As examples we find that different strains of bees communicate in different ways and different strains of laboratory rats show identifiable qualities (for example, some are wilder than others). Probably no one would deny the strong behavioral differences in domestic bulls and the famed "brave bulls" of Spain.

Humans are usually very easy to distinguish or recognize individually. We come in a variety of shapes and sizes and we vary greatly in our abilities. We need not all be able to judge the rate of a car's approach and then dart across the street with agility, slower or dimmer individuals being thus removed from the population through being struck by cars. We all simply wait for the light. Those among us who are unable to provide for themselves are often provided for to some degree, thus others than "good providers" remain in the population. In other words, we have altered our environmental situation and reduced the level of selection operating upon us. The result is a species with highly individualized members and a wide range of abilities, appearances and interests.

Variation in humans is also increased by our cosmopolitan dispersion. We occupy a wide range of habitats and adaptations to local conditions have resulted in strong differences across our range.

Among wild animals great variation also may exist, even to the human eye. We noted in Chapter 6 that in some bird species, such as gulls, where the members are indistinguishable to us, they are easily recognizable to each other. Among such birds the behavior also varies little from one individual to the next, at least to the human eye. Recognition is easier in less stereotyped animals. Jane Goodall was able to recognize her wild chimpanzees on the basis of their faces (Figure 11.9). They also differed greatly in their size, vigor, aggressiveness, sexuality, parental care, and ability

Figure 11.9 Different facial features in chimpanzees. Among learning animals, such variation may be important in individual recognition. Subtle changes in expression may also be used in communication.

to form friendships.

One might expect populations of learning animals such as chimpanzees to vary greatly. Such variation might be possible as a result of their ability to recognize special characters in each other. They may also vary as a result of variation in environmental input based on differences in experiences.

There is evidence that there may be great variation in more stereotyped species as well. The Peckhams, in 1898, wrote about their observations of the female wasp, *Ammophila urnaria:* "While one was beguiled from her hunting by every sorrel blossom she passed, another stuck to her work with indefatigable perserverance. While one stung her caterpillar so carelessly and made her nest in so shiftless a way that her young could only survive through some lucky chance, another devoted herself to these duties not only with conscientious thoroughness, but with an apparent craving after artistic perfection."

It was once assumed that variation was the price a species paid for genetic flexibility with which it could capitalize upon any change in the environment. The result of such variation was an increased number of individuals being different from those at the current optimum and therefore at an immediate disadvantage. These variant individuals, however, might come to be at an advantage should a change in the environment begin to favor individuals with their special qualities. As we know from our discussions of specializations of subgroups in a variable habitat, high variation may be adaptive in and of itself. Antonovics (1971) showed that seeds of the hawkweed, *Hieracium umbellatum,* taken from sea cliffs, from woodlands, and from sand dunes and grown experimentally, produced distinct types of plants (but all of the same species). The sea cliff and dune plant progeny were dwarf and the woodland plants tall. It seems that the constant wind of dunes and sea cliffs might select for plants which are short and less likely to be uprooted. (The reader may wish to refer to the population-recognition discussion in Chapter 6 for examples from animals.)

On the other side of the coin we may ask how much a character may vary from the optimum before it no longer imparts an advantage to the bearer. The eyespot on a moth's wing can be crude indeed and still maintain a degree of its startling effect on birds, but at some point in its divergence from the optimum it loses its net advantage to the moth. It should be apparent that the variation "permitted" in a character is dependent upon a number of factors including the type of organism and the nature and adaptiveness of the character in question.

SELECTION

Variation implies inequality. From a variable population, then, certain individuals are likely to be more reproductively successful than others. The characters which enhance their success are likely to continue in the succeeding generations and these are said to be selected *for.* Other individuals possess characters which reduce the reproductive success of the bearer. These characters, then, may be selected *out* of the population. The process is called natural selection.

It is sometimes assumed that sweeping changes in populations appear in a short time as species make great saltatory leaps from one form to another. However such is apparently not the situation. In most cases evolutionary change can be explained on the basis of the accumulation of small changes over long periods of time.

It might be asked that if behavioral patterns and the associated structures arose through a series of small steps, then what was the pressure behind them—the force pushing them along in these small steps? For example, why would a reptile begin to develop wings? Why would it place its evolutionary eggs in a new basket, so to speak? It seems any running reptile would have reaped more advantage from becoming a better runner rather than a poor flier—and the first flights must have been poor attempts indeed if the characters necessary for flight arose in small steps. Such questions cannot be answered in definite terms, but Alexander and Brown (1963) maintain that, in insects, wings were probably rather well developed as courtship organs before they were used for flight. A comparison of advanced living crickets with primitive living crickets suggests that sound production originated from wing lifting and vibration during courtship. The probable sequence began with a vibratory sign stimulus which incidentally produced sound. Once the sound had become associated with the courtship there followed an elaboration of auditory organs. Selection then improved both the producers and receptors of sound until, finally, sounds could have become differentiated into specific patterns carrying more precise information (see Alexander 1966). Perhaps in birds, also, the wings developed on some adaptive basis other than flight, such as for gliding—a characteristic that would accent the immediate advantage of a broader forelimb with its increased surface area possibly without detracting too much from running or climbing ability.

The argument, however, continues: although a character has value now, it couldn't have developed on the basis of its present adaptiveness; as an incipient character it would have been selected out when it first appeared in an imperfect form. There is some evidence, however, that even the imperfect forms of adaptive characters have a selective advantage. Blest (1957) showed that even very crude eyespots on moths had a repelling effect on birds. Even slightly twiglike caterpillars have an advantage over those who make no effort toward disguise. Tinbergen (1965) points out that our experimental technique is very crude and that usually a character would need to have great value before we could detect an advantage at all. For theoretical discussions of how minute selection advantage could produce evolutionary change, see Fisher (1930) and Haldane (1932).

There is a higher premium on some adaptive characters than others. Therefore we may speak of *adaptive value*. To illustrate, consider an oversimplified scheme in which a mutation is completely favorable (with no undesirable effects); its value would be designated as $+1$. A neutral change would be given 0. Neutral changes would be mutations which exerted no effect on the behavior or morphology of the organism. These are rare according to Simpson (1958), but a vigorous argument has developed (cf. Cain 1964). A -1 would designate those changes which are completely adverse or lethal. Now consider a gene with a selective value of 0.001, a very low figure which means for every 1000 individuals that survive each generation lacking the gene, 1 survives to carry it. Once a gene with this selective value appeared in 1 percent of the population, it would take 120,000 generations of selection for it to reach 100 percent (Manning 1971). Such predictions, of course, are predicated upon a stable environment which does not shift the selective value of a character. The time is described in generation time because of the vast differences in this period among animals. A population of flies could therefore be expected to alter gene frequencies faster than the same number of elephants. Changes in animals with long generation time is possible because of the great span involved in what is termed "geologic time."

Selective value can change; furthermore so can the direction of selection. An adaptive character can become less advantageous as time goes by or it can even become a detriment. The peppered moth, *Biston betularia,* of England flies at night and rests on the bark of trees during the day where it is vulnerable to predatory birds. For ages the population was comprised of speckled gray individuals that blended well with the lichen-covered bark on which they rested. An occasional dark form would arise as a result of a rare dominant mutation in a single gene. These individuals were conspicuous and quickly captured by the birds since their choice of a resting site did not change. (See Kettlewell 1956 for experimental evidence.) In the mid 1880s England began its conversion to an industrial economy and began burning soft coal in its factories. The greenery of the English countryside quietly submitted to its new cloak of soot. One result was that the gray lichen-covered bark of trees turned black. Now the rare melanic or dark moths were hidden against the darkened background. In the industrial areas around Manchester the dark form has almost completely replaced the light. In rural western England, however, the environment has not changed and the peppered moth still predominates.

Most shifts in gene frequencies within a population are not so clearly documented in terms of selective advantage. The hamster, *Cricetus cricetus*, in Russia produces a mutant black form in addition to the normal gray form. The animal is trapped for its fur in Russia and thus records are kept of the distribution of its various forms. Gershenson (1945) was able to trace the spread of the black form into the Ukraine. The selection coefficients were rather high indicating strong selection for these dark forms in certain regions (Dobzhansky 1951), but just what the adaptive advantage might be remains a mystery.

Artificial selection has also produced strong behavioral differences in strains of animals. It has been mentioned that certain strains of laboratory rats are demonstrably more aggressive than others. In other cases a species which varied normally for a specific character has, through selective breeding, been separated into subpopulations which differ strongly for that character (Figure 11.10).

In some cases, variation within a population is expressed in characters which fall neatly into one category or another. Such a case arises, for example, when a character is due to the presence or absence of a single gene, such as a switch gene or the dominant gene which gave rise to the dark form of the peppered moth. In other populations variation is not expressed as an either/or polymorphism but as a gradual change in the population from one extreme to the other and with most individuals being a type about midway between the extremes as in Figure 11.11a. The reduced number of individuals at either extreme can be regarded as due to stronger selection operating against those most different from the optimum. Under stable conditions the optimum can be expected to remain unchanged as *stabilizing selection* operates. However, as we know, the

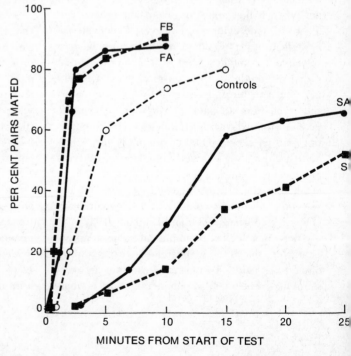

Figure 11.10 The results of selection for mating speed in the fruit fly, *Drosophila melanogaster*. The curves show the mating speed from two fast-mating lines, FA and FB, and two slow-mating lines, SA and SB, after the 18th selected generation. A comparison is made with unselected controls. About 80 percent of the fast lines have mated before the slow line has begun. (From Manning, *Effects of Artificial Selection for Mating Speed in Drosophila melanogaster*, "Animal Behavior" Vol. IX, Nos. 1 and 2, January-April 1961.)

Directional Selection

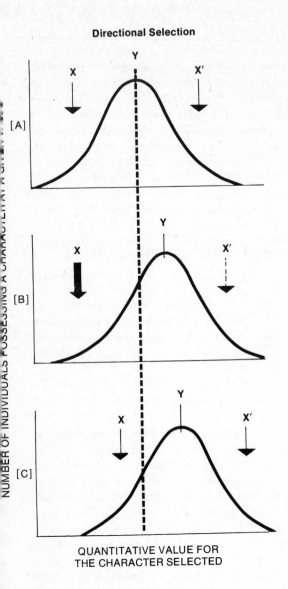

QUANTITATIVE VALUE FOR
THE CHARACTER SELECTED

Figure 11.11 As long as the selection
pressures (X and X[1]) remain stable the
population character for any parameter
are likely to remain stable. When the pressures of X and X[1] change, the optimum Y
may shift causing directional changes in
the population for the observed character.

optimum can shift as the environment changes.
In such a case those at one extremity might come
to be favored and the curve representing the
population might be shifted in one direction or
the other. The phenomenon is termed *directional*
selection (Figure 11.11 b and c).

The likelihood of selection ever operating on
any new character is largely dependent upon the
size of the population in which it appears. In
large populations any genetic changes (mutations)
which appear may be swamped by the other possible types of that gene in the group and therefore never really catch hold. If, on the other hand,
the population is too small, a new gene combination may be lost purely by chance, such as by the
death of the few members carrying it.

The most rapid evolution occurs when a large
population is divided into smaller ones—reproductively isolated from each other except for occasional cross-breeding. The frequency of any
gene in small temporarily rather isolated populations changes rapidly through mutation or through
immigration from larger populations. These new
combinations may take hold since the numbers
in the population are too small to produce a
swamping effect. The best examples of such rapidly evolving populations occur on islands, such
as the Galápagos and the West Indies (Chapter
8) and Australasia (Mayr 1963).

All changes in small populations, it must be
pointed out, may not be due to selection operating on variation. In small, permanently isolated
populations, the rate and direction of evolution
can be altered through the accumulation of random changes. The phenomenon, described by
Sewall Wright, is termed genetic drift. Often
characters which cannot be immediately explained in terms of adaptation are said to be
due to drift. Although the phenomenon may explain some evolutionary changes it is probably
invoked much to freely as Manning (1971) maintains. Under certain conditions drift could play
an important part in evolution. Changes which
appear in such a manner may not be acted upon

by selection under the environmental conditions which prevail at teh time. However, if the environment should change, selection might obfuscate or ameliorate the results of the drift; but then, again, it could act to enhance the newly adaptive characters.

ADAPTATION

Tinbergen (1965) objects to the free use of the concept of drift to explain what is apparently nonadaptive. He stresses two points: first, the search for the mechanism of survival value has to be made with respect to *all* the properties of behavior mechanisms, all the details of behavior control. Such consideration emphasizes the need for thorough understanding of the behavior of an animal in the context of the animal's natural history. We have actually approached such a level of information in few instances, such as Griffin's (1958) astonishingly detailed description of the intricacies of echolocation by bats. Also, we know much about communication in some animals (Lanyon and Tavolga 1960). On the other hand, adaptiveness of movement is less well understood. Komp (1954) showed, as an example of one such study, the manner in which a godwit, *Limosa*, walks—by lifting and folding its feet—is an adaptation for walking through tall grass. Our scant knowledge of locomotor activities in reference to the animal's environment must be greatly increased, however, if we are to understand much about the adaptiveness of variations and peculiarities in such patterns.

Secondly, Tinbergen points out that it is useless and even unscientific to make assumptions regarding the adaptiveness of any feature until one has tried to find out what the adaptiveness might be. DeRuiter (1955) has checked out Thayer's (1909) study, a work which is remarkable for its inclusion of worthless theorizing alongside important observations. In his paper, Thayer made the surprisingly naïve statement that red coloration in flamingos enable them to disappear into the sunset, and in the same paper he pointed out

the significance of countershading. (Countershading is the condition of animals having darker colors on the back than on the belly.) DeRuiter found that countershaded coloration was adaptive when employed with a certain behavioral set (correct position, scattering, and immobility). It seems that a countershaded animal is less likely to be detected since a view from the underside is likely to be against a lighted sky, and from the topside against a darker earth. For other examples of apparently unadaptive characters that were found to have advantages see Cain (1964).

Tinbergen and his group (1962), it will be recalled, demonstrated the high adaptive value of the black-headed gull's habit of removing empty egg shells from the nest. It was found that the peculiar habit made the nest less conspicuous to predators. It is believed that such experiments can indicate strongly the relationship between a pattern and its adaptiveness and can show what forces are presently acting on a species. Tinbergen admits, at the same time, that the findings can only suggest what selective pressures were operating in the past to mold the species to its present condition.

There is no intention here to imply that any observed character, when the data is in, will be found to be adaptive. There are undoubtedly unadaptive characters in any population. In some cases these are being selected out and we simply observe them on their way to oblivion. In other cases, though, unadaptive characters may be maintained in a population. One method of continuing such characters is through *pleiotropism*, multiple effects of a single genetic factor. As an example of a pleiotropic effect, a certain gene in mice which produces short ears also produces fewer ribs; a single genetic factor in *Drosophila* produces small wings, lowered fecundity, shorter life span and other changes. Unadaptive characters may also continue in a population through *linkage*. In such a case, an unadaptive gene may be located very close to a highly adaptive one on the chromosome so that when the genes undergo their continual "reshuffling" there is a high probability that the bad gene will be carried along on the coattails of the good one.

In the black-headed gull, the egg-shell removing behavior does not appear until after a delay in which the chicks become dry. It has been theorized that the delay is a pleiotropic and unadaptive effect of the removal behavior. Tinbergen warned however that such a statement is, in essence, a refusal to investigate. He developed an experiment to test for any adaptiveness of the time lapse. His results indicate that the delay is highly adaptive in that it gives the chick time to dry so that it will be hard to swallow and therefore the pattern decreases the likelihood of the chick's being attacked and eaten by neighbors while its parents are gone on their chores.

Because of the complex nature of relationships in the wild it can rarely, if ever, be said that any character is completely adaptive and without its drawbacks. As a species of tree places its energy for growth into increasing its height, it may increase its exposure to sunlight but, at the same time, its girth is reduced, thus increasing its susceptibility to high winds. Tinbergen (1965) has pointed out that in the black-headed gull colonial nesting is advantageous in promoting mobbing responses as a means of predator defense. Another result is that some birds lose their young to nearby cannibalistic neighbors. In sum, however, the advantages outweigh the disadvantages.

We will stress once again that natural selection is opportunistic. It takes advantage of existing conditions. As an example, many species of fresh-water fish build air-bubble nests which float at the surface among the vegetation. The male usually builds these nests by gulping mouthfulls of air and blowing out clusters of froth into which he puts the fertilized eggs after mating. It has been suggested that the building of air-bubble nests is an outgrowth of air breathing in these fish. Air breathing is a behavioral and physiological result of low oxygen content in the tepid waters of many tropical lakes and rivers (Manning 1967).

Opportunism of the mechanism, natural selection, can be described in terms of its object, the phenotypic or observable character. In other words, opportunism viewed at the level of the character may involve "preadaptation." When a character evolves in response to one set of selective forces and later turns out to have quite different evolutionary possibilities, we can say that that character represents a preadaptation. Behavioral flexibility, as we have seen, is often a prerequisite for successful island colonization. Certain mainland conditions, such as peripheral habitats or high seasonal variability, might select for flexibility so that animals with this characteristic might be generally better colonizers. There may also exist a more specific type of preadaptation— for a certain type of niche. If the invading species is not flexible enough to respond immediately in an adaptive manner to the new conditions it encounters, it may still survive if it is already adapted in another way to the island ecosystem through a compatible earlier phyletic history. If, for example, a flycatcher colonizes an island, it may not find the same range or type of insects there that existed on the mainland. But it might be expected to be highly successful (after perhaps a few modifications in its flycatching behavior) in capturing the types of flying insects that are found in its new home. The flycatcher may be said to be preadapted to finding a niche on the island.

Adaptation to the same environmental pressure may take entirely different forms in different animals. An animal may adapt physically by increasing the abundance of its fur as a response to cold or behaviorally by huddling together in groups. Some animals may also alter their environment to match their needs. Certain termites, for example, which are highly susceptible to desiccation are able to cross dry open areas by building covered corridors over their paths.

In some cases the adaptive response of an organism may set the stage for later responses. In other words, once an evolutionary direction is taken the adaptive alternatives open to the animal become increasingly restricted. The animal, in a sense, has placed its bet on a certain strategy and—as any gambler knows—some strategies are better than others. When the primitive and ancient fish, the Sarcopterygii, were faced with seasonal drought, one group apparently stayed in the mud and waited for the rains to return. These animals, in order to survive in their pools of mud, began to rely on oxygen from the air, and this is how the lungfish developed. Another group, however, left their drying pools and clambered about overland in search of water. These were the pretetrapods (von Wahlert 1965). The difference in the results of these two strategies may be seen as bipedal men stand gazing in wonder at lungfish in an aquarium.

Von Wahlert (1965) gives an interesting theoretical account of the development of the flatfish which stresses the ethological component of evolutionary influences. He maintains that the evolutionary origin of the flatfish was initiated and directed by a change in the role played by the ocean bottom in the lives of their ancestors. This role change was in effect a construct of a behavioral pattern. The progenitors of the flatfish, the argument goes, probably slept on their sides as do many modern fishes, such as wrasses and triggerfish. If, upon awakening, such early fishes tended to remain in the horizontal position for some reason, such as to escape predators in the area, the stage might thus be set for a horizontal existence Selection might then favor a shift of the eyes to the top together with the appropriate countershading. The flatfish could then, through adaptive radiation, come to use the bottom in different ways—as ambush sites for perch-flounders, hunting areas for flounders, or grazing sites for soles and tongues. In all cases, the morphological adaptations followed the shifts permitted by key ethological innovations. The ocean bottom didn't change—only the use to which it was put.

When we speak of adaptation we often are referring to an organism's adjustment to its physical environment. Since other forms of life with which an individual must react directly or indirectly are also part of that individual's environment, special problems arise in the adaptive picture for any animal. Many of the environmental factors to which an organism must adapt appear or change independently of that animal. The weather heeds not the presence, whereabouts, or activities of most animals, but exerts its effect independent of their influences. In the case of the biotic component of the environment, however, a different situation exists. Animals interact. As an example, among prey animals the slower are more likely to be caught. The result is a faster prey. None but the swiftest predators thus are able to catch the speedy prey so the faster predators are those which survive and reproduce. The result is to place even more premium on speed or evasiveness in the prey. So while either predator or prey may be adapted to a regularly varying but slowly changing climatic system, each may be much more quickly responding to the adaptable biotic component of its milieu.

The mutual adaptation of biota sharing a habitat may also be seen in competitive interaction. As was stressed in Chapter 8, the results are quite different from those of predator-prey interactions in which the pressures do not usually result in the extinction of one by the other. In competitive interactions there is probably an increased likelihood of one species excluding another from a habitat or a niche and thus forcing it to die out or to adapt to a different set of environmental conditions.

One notable study has been made of a change in habitat in a species of gull, the adaptive value of which may have been a reduction in the level of predation. The range of adaptive results of the change was startling. Most gulls, including the herring gull, nest in low-lying areas or on offshore islands (Figure 11.12a) and are therefore subject to some predation. As a result of such predation they build cryptic nests (Figure 11.12b) composed of bits of twigs and grass piled together

Figure 11.12A Above left. Nesting grounds of the herring gull. Such areas are subject to predation because of their accessibility. The gulls respond to such pressures by vigorously defending their nesting area through mobbing any prowler. (Photo: R. Wallace.)

Figure 11.12B Above right. Hidden herring gull nest. The nests are often located in clumps of grass in the nesting area. The advantage in such placement might be in hiding the nest or providing shade for the eggs. (Photo: Van Rackages, New York.)

Figure 11.12C Right. Cryptic eggs and young of the herring gull. The eggs and young are mottled and the young respond quickly to the warning calls of the parents by running to cover or "freezing." Such peculiarities are considered adaptations to nesting in vulnerable areas. (Photo: Grant Haist from National Audubon Society.)

Figure 11.13A Nesting area of the kittiwake. The development of nesting on sheer cliffs which are inaccessible to predators has resulted in behavioral changes in the kittiwake (see text). (Photo: Henry C. Kyllingstad from National Audubon Society.)

among clumps of shore-grasses. The eggs and young are also cryptic (Figure 11.12c). The young have certain behavioral characters which maximize their concealing patterns. At their parents' warning call, they quickly run under the nearest cover, and thus may escape any predator which has been attracted to the nest. Or they "freeze" and rely on their markings to render them less conspicuous. Esther Cullen (1957), one of Tinbergen's students, investigated a small gull called the Atlantic kittiwake, *Rissa tridactyla*, which nests on secure cliff ledges (Figure 11.13a). In addition to a peculiar nest site, the kittiwakes display a wide range of behavioral traits not found in other gulls. There is evidence that many of these patterns have developed as a direct result of the type of nest site.

If one simply compared the behavioral characters of the kittiwake and other gulls it would seem at first that the differences are great and that the species are only distantly related. The kittiwakes fight by grabbing each other's bills and twisting thus causing the opponent to fall off the ledge. Ground-nesting gulls usually try to get above and peck down or to pull at the body of the other. As a result of this change, the kittiwake has lost the "upright threat" posture from among its repertoire. Female kittiwakes sit down to copulate, thus reducing the risk of falling off their ledges, some as narrow as four inches. The kittiwake builds much tighter nests than ground nesters; the nests are also deeper to keep eggs from falling out since retrieval would not be possible (Figure 11.13b).

It is also interesting that when the kittiwake is on the nest one can almost reach out and touch the bird without eliciting an escape reaction; also, they show almost no antipredator defense of nests. Nests are undoubtedly considered safe places because of their inaccessibility. However, when kittiwakes are on land gathering nest material, they move about in groups and are extremely shy.

Later on, when they are nesting, conspicuous egg shells and droppings are left around the nest, a habit which in other gulls would attract predators. Young kittiwakes, of course, must remain in the nest until they can fly; therefore, all feeding is done at the nest. The young take the food directly from the parent so no partly digested matter is left lying around the nest as a potential source of disease. Ground nesters, on the other hand, feed their free-roaming young anywhere in the nesting area and they sometimes regurgitate food onto the ground near their young. Ground nesters must be able to recognize their wide-ranging young. The kittiwake, however, cannot recognize its young except by location—which is how the ground nesters recognize their *eggs*.

Also, the young of ground nesters practice flying by jumping high into the wind. The young kittiwakes never jump very high and they always face the cliff when they jump. There are other differences in the behavior of kittiwakes and ground-nesting gulls which can be related to the choice of nest sites, but these examples show the range of repercussions which may stem from a single behavioral change.

Cullen believes that the kittiwake originated from ground-nesting stock because of certain similarities of kittiwakes to ground nesters: (1) the eggs are partly cryptic, like those of ground nesters, although the habit of removing conspicuous shells and droppings has been lost, and (2) the kittiwake young can run—an unusual ability in species which nest in precarious habitats.

Other studies have supported Cullen's work. For example, Hailman (1965) investigated the Galápagos swallow-tailed gull, *Larus (Creagus) furcatus*, and found its nesting environment to be intermediate between the kittiwake and ground-nesting gulls. Its behavior was also intermediate between the two types. Also, see a paper by Cullen and Ashmole (1963) on the black noddy, *Anous tenuirostris*.

The most fruitful searches for the adaptiveness of characters, then, are likely to involve one of three basic approaches. First, we may make comparisons between species. Examples of such studies are those involving differences in cliff-nesting and ground-nesting gulls. As another example, Hoogland et al. (1957) compared the three-spined stickleback, *Gasteosteus aculeatus*, and unspined

Figure 11.13B The exposed nest of the kittiwake. (Photo: Allan D. Cruickshank from National Audubon Society.)

fish as prey species in order to determine the value of spines in predator defense. It was found that when a predatory perch or pike attacked a stickleback he usually spat it out and avoided the species thereafter. Unspined fish such as minnows, roach, and rudd were more often attacked. (Interestingly, and not unexpectedly, the three-spined stickleback is a bold fish which schools and nests in open habitat and has conspicuous nuptial colors.)

Secondly, we may make comparisons within a species such as was done in the studies of relative nesting success at the center and the edge of a colony of birds. And thirdly, we may carry out experiments such as Tinbergen did in his test of the advantage of egg-shell removal as a means of decreasing the conspicuousness of vulnerable nests.

Tinbergen (1965) delineates two operational approaches to the problem of adaptiveness. The first is to single out a particular environmental pressure, a "challenge to survival," and then to find out how the animal meets the challenge. As an example, he and his colleagues, H. Kruuk and I. J. Patterson, have attempted to find out how the black-headed gull meets the problem of predation. They found that egg-shell removal is part of the system and that patterns of habitat selection, diurnal rhythm, colony density, and synchronization of the breeding cycle are also involved. The diurnal rhythm of habitat selection was first described: All birds spend the night on their roosts, which are wide, open spaces such as are found along the lower part of a seashore, on open mud flats, or shallow lakes. Only at daylight do they move to the breeding grounds where they establish territories and continue in the pair formation behavior. Each night the birds return to the open flats until the eggs are laid. After the eggs are laid they continue to sit on them through the night. Tinbergen argues that the habit has (or had at one time) survival value. On the open flats predators are much easier to spot and few gulls are taken there by foxes—except on dark, stormy nights.

The density of the nests seems to be a compromise between grouping to enhance the mobbing effect and scattering to reduce the effectiveness of predators which are not deterred by mobbing, such as foxes. The advantage of synchrony in nesting was demonstrated by the high nestling mortality of those pairs which raised young out of phase with the peak nesting period of the group, the advantage apparently being due to the higher predation on nests at the beginning and end of the nesting season.

As a second general method Tinbergen suggests starting from the other end: describe an observable behavioral pattern and then find out what it does. For example, what is the advantage, if any, in the "fanning" behavior of the male three-spined stickleback? Fanning is done mainly when there are developing eggs in the nest. The pattern involves a particular movement of the pectoral fins and the tail which results in a flow of water around and through the nest. When the fanning was prevented or when a watchglass was placed over the eggs to shield them from the current, the eggs died. The eggs survived however in the absence of a male if they were aerated artificially. The tests showed that fanning is adaptive as a ventilation mechanism and that the rate of fanning is regulated so that the eggs are always adequately ventilated.

Perhaps a note would be appropriate at this point regarding the time involved in adaptive change and the importance of this knowledge for man. Small changes may take millions of years. The time involved must be made clear to those who would placidly view our modern environmental crises with an inner peace coming from confidence in man's great adaptability. It is true that man is adaptable. How could our distant forefathers have guessed that their descendants could live in population densities approaching 100,000 per square mile? Or that they would not strenuously object to breathing air so bad that daily reports are issued on its quality? Or that they would allow themselves to be subjected to the crush of other subway commuters amid the din of screeching wheels as they ride past highway construction designed to carry more cars into jammed cities? Or that they could live near a river without really interacting with that once-source-of-life because it was being poisoned upstream? Or that, in their own homes, they would interrupt conversations as huge airplanes screamed overhead spreading trails of poisonous gases? All this without serious complaint—at least not serious enough to cause great changes. It is true, man is adaptable and can devise stopgaps and philosophies for accepting almost anything. Almost. Philosophy or psychological tolerance has little effect on poisonous water, and physiological man has very definite limits. Our population is burgeoning, our pollution per capita is rising, our resources are dwindling, our limits are fixed, and our generation time is long.

THE HOMOLOGY OF BEHAVIOR

"Is it not possible that beneath all the variations of individual behavior there lies an inner structure of inherited behavior which characterizes all the members of a given species, genus, or larger taxonomic group—just as the skeleton of a primordial ancestor characterizes the form and structure of all mammals today?"

The question was asked by Lorenz in 1958. The concept, however, was born much earlier. Whitman (1899) laid the groundwork by stating that instinct and structure are to be studied from the common viewpoint of phyletic descent. Whitman was not at all bothered by the special difficulties in such a proposal such as in following the whole development of an instinct. Those who followed, however, met problems beyond those encountered by evolutionists who use the tools of anatomy and paleontology. For discussions of the critical nature of the lack of paleontological evidence see Blest (1961), Hinde and Tinbergen (1958), Mayr (1958), Simpson (1958), Tinbergen (1951), and Wickler (1961).

Forming Criteria and Other Problems

What is actually involved here is the question of the usefulness of behavioral description in the study of relationships between animals. In other words, can behavior be homologized? Simpson (1961) describes homology as resemblance due to inheritance from a common ancestry. To give an anatomical example, the bone structure of the flipper of a whale is more similar to that of the arm of a man than to the pectoral fin of a fish. The reason is assumed to be because the whale, once a land vertebrate which returned to the sea, is more closely related to the man; the dichotomy which separated the ancestors of whales and men occurred later than that which separated the fish from land animals. The homologizing of behavior is more likely to be attempted among ethologists than comparative psychologists at present and there is some argument over whether the attempt is valid at all (Atz 1970). It has been argued that the principle of homology is in some sense tautological in its reasoning: evolutionary relationships are based on homologies and homologies, in turn, are explained on the basis of phylogeny. The student of behavior can avoid the problem to a degree by studying animals already classified on some other basis, such as through the usual comparative morphological studies. Also, it seems that perhaps too often there is a tendency to label a behavioral character as homologous among species before such a judgment is warranted and to ignore contradictory evidence. Besides stressing the need for objectivity we hope here to describe the limits of studies of behavioral homologies and to discuss what criteria should be met before homology is indicated.

Atz (1970) summarizes Remane's (1961) criteria for determining morphological homology: (1) Position; homology results from structures occurring within comparable anatomical areas. (2) Special quality; similar characters can be homologized if they agree in several unusual characters. (3) Constancy; dissimilar forms may be homologized if intermediate connecting forms are found. (4) Distribution; the probability of homology increases with the frequency of its occurrence among related species and decreases with its appearance in unrelated forms. Generally, it may be said that the more continuously distributed and the more similar a display throughout a group of animals, the more probable its common origin. In terms of the homology of behavior, the consensus, as elucidated by Wickler (1961), is that in order to be homologous two patterns must be exhibited by two related forms and must have been present as a single behavior in their common ancestor. However, the criteria for morphological homology cannot be rigidly applied to behavior. For example, how could one determine "position" in a behavioral pattern? Such a criterion would demand precise knowledge of the location of the neural seat of the pattern and such information is, at present, not available.

The problem of behavioral homology is more difficult in some types of animals than others. For example, mammals present special problems because of the flexibility of their behavior and their great ability to learn and to alter their behavior on the basis of experience. The investigator must be sure that the differences between species he sees are based in genetic diversity and not in environmental dissimilarity. He must also have a good idea of how much learning has affected an innate pattern or what part of the entire adaptive pattern is due to learning (for example, an inexperienced ringdove must learn to walk up to its chicks in order to perform an instinctive pattern—feeding [Lehrman 1955]). Tinbergen (1951) maintained that only the "innate basis" of behavior could be homologized (see below); Wickler (1961) disagreed and argued that two patterns, one innate and one learned, could be homologized.

One reason sometimes given for homologizing learned patterns is that learning abilities of animals are inherited anyway. However, such an argument neglects the fact that under natural conditions animals may learn far less than is actually possible, and members of the same species living under different environmental conditions may learn different things; so learned behavior is probably not a valid subject for homology.

Some behavioral characters are considered divergent or labile in that they may change rapidly in evolution. Conservative characters are those which change little, maintaining a degree of constancy even through the evolutionary radiation of its bearers. Some characters are so conservative as to be useless in homologies, and others lose their value by their very lability; to cite morphological examples, consider the two eyes of vertebrates or the patterns of tricolored dogs respectively. In other cases, environmental pressures can easily alter a rather conservative character so that it loses its taxonomic value. For example, many types of animals are born with an escape reaction to fast-approaching objects. Habituation sometimes results in the nullifying of that tendency, as, for example, in the cases of skittering leaves or passing automobiles. So the ontogenetic lability of a pattern does not reflect its innateness. The tendency in some rats to hoard may be reduced or obliterated by certain treatments or experiences but this change does not negate the heritability of the pattern to begin with.

Some patterns stubbornly resist any environmental modification of their expression and show a large degree of independence from environmental stimuli. For example, dogs and birds both scratch their heads by reaching the scratching foot in front of the shoulder (Figure 11.14). So do almost all legged reptiles. In the case of the bird it would be much simpler to move its claw directly to the head without moving the wing at all. Lorenz (1958) interprets the necessity of the clumsier action as an indication of an inborn determinant. Heinroth (1930) interpreted the motion in birds as a relic of reptilian ancestry. Lorenz further suggests the value of such conservative patterns in evolutionary study. It must be admitted, however, that such an invariable pattern has little to recommend it beyond determining the relationship of classes of animals—in this case behavioral homology is a rather blunt instrument. In general, however, conservative factors are more useful than labile ones in the reconstruction of phylogenies (Mayr 1958).

Mayr also points out that even within an overall adaptive pattern, the components may vary in their evolutionary lability. For example, in birds the courtship movements seem much more conservative than the releasers which elicit them.

Hinde and Tinbergen (1958) stressed the importance of selecting the appropriate character in studies of the homology of behavior. They point out that markedly divergent or conservative characters are not suitable for studying relationships between closely related species, but that conservative characters gain in value as the relationship between the groups being compared decreases. For example, all species of tits in the genus *Parus* nest in holes and use moss for nests. The behavior differentiates them from others in the Paridae family but not from each other. (Probably, in general, nest building itself is not suitable for homology for reasons discussed below.) Threat postures and some courtship displays, on the other hand, are useful for studying relationships between genera or species, but these patterns are often too divergent to be used to distinguish between families (Hinde 1952). As another example, the precise "tail flicks" made by passerines when moving through the foliage are conservative within families and can help assign genera to families (Andrew 1956).

As with morphological characters, one cannot use behavioral comparisons to determine taxonomic relationships if the pattern is due to analogous development—similar characters acquired independently in "unrelated" groups. An example is the similarity of the high-pitched warning call in many species of birds. Such a call may have developed independently in several species because of its acoustic crypticity. It must be admitted that the risk of any character similarity being due to convergence is almost always present (thus the "special-quality" criterion of Remane). Lorenz once proposed that the display behavior was unlikely to show convergence, but this has been shown not to be the case (Marler 1957; Tinbergen 1959). For other discussions on the convergence of behavior see Blest (1961), Cullen (1959), Remane (1961), and Mayr (1958).

Social systems do not lend themselves to homology. We have seen in the discussion of grades the strong environmental effect on social struc-

Figure 11.14 A bird scratching. This pattern is a pattern that it has in common with many other birds, reptiles and mammals in that the scratching leg is brought up behind the forelimb. In birds, the pattern means that the wing must be brought forward. This is an awkward movement and is considered to be due to inheritance of the pattern from reptiles.

ture which could contribute toward analogy or convergence in animals living in similar habitats. Social systems may also be exceedingly labile. For example in times of high food supply a baboon troop may swell in numbers as nonbreeding males join breeding units. As food decreases, some males may move off in bachelor herds to forage separately. Descriptions of the social structure of these baboons would be partly a function of the time of year they were observed. We must also keep in mind the fact that natural selection may shift its emphasis when a population moves into a different habitat so that the entire range of behavior is altered. A species of primate moving from the forest environment into a new habitat type, such as the savannah, might suddenly find an advantage in larger males which could protect the group in their increased vulnerability. If larger males became selected for on such a basis, there could also be a shift in the reproductive strategies of the species in accordance with the principles discussed in Chapter 8. It might be suggested that since the social condition of a species has definite limits in its variability, perhaps the ranges or "potential" social structures of two species could be homologized. However, such theorizing neglects the incredible array of factors which might be subtly interacting in the formation of a social system. Better to choose something simpler and less susceptible to environmental feedback.

Since similarity between two species does not necessarily mean common descent, the student of evolution is forced to decide whether a certain pattern is due to homology or analogy. The decision between these two alternatives is more difficult for the behaviorist than the anatomist. The anatomist can always fall back on such rules as "Owen's criterion" of homology which stresses the usefulness of general anatomic position and relations to adjacent organs. There are those who would say that since the behaviorist lacks this knowledge, homologizing of patterns is beyond his realm; this, however, in the context of modern evolutionary and biological theory would appear to be an overly strict interpretation of what conditions must be met before such studies should be attempted.

One particular difficulty in assessing the systematic significance of behavioral patterns lies in their interdependence. For example, among passerines territoriality, song, sexual dimorphism, and aggressiveness in courtship may all be linked so that a change in one may shift the selective advantage of the others (Hinde and Tinbergen 1958).

Toward a More Rigorous Approach

We may ask, then, what criteria can a student use to establish homology? His method is essentially the same as those used by taxonomists even before Darwin. He must base his conclusions on the sum total of behavioral characters. Since the study of evolution by behavioral description faces so many special problems, any phylogeny should first be postulated on morphological grounds, at least until the data is found to be contradictory.

The use of behavioral homologies in the study of evolution is most likely to avoid the problems mentioned here if only fixed action patterns (Chapter 2) are compared. The idea is not new; in fact it was employed in some of the earlier work of Lorenz (1950) and Tinbergen (1942). Fixed action patterns, as we know, are considered little affected by learning or practice, but are genetically determined and relatively invariable within populations. Much earlier, both Heinroth and Whitman showed that fixed action patterns can be separated from the total adaptive motor pattern. A complex behavioral sequence such as is involved in nest building may be made up of a series of fixed action patterns. In some cases the performance of one pattern may serve to release the next so that the proper sequence is maintained. Learning could operate at several levels, but might function primarily in modifying the releasing effect of certain environmental components so that a specific fixed pattern might be more successfully employed. Learning could also operate, of course, to enhance the performance of a motor pattern. In any case, however, complex adaptive sequences are far too complex and too little understood to be the subject of homology. We must concentrate on a single, genetically fixed component of such a pattern. So, whereas nest building or other complex acts may not be-homologized, if we wish to utilize nest building we might direct particular attention to a fixed component—particularly one that could have no other use than as a very special nest building action. For example, we might wish to homologize a particular nest-building motion such as a peculiar sideways sweep of the head which is used to insert material into the fabric of a nest once the nest has reached a certain stage of completion. Quantitative or qualitative differences in such patterns or differences in the sequence that fixed patterns are employed, may, of course, result in nests of different types as will be pointed out below.

There may be problems in identifying fixed patterns of course, so one might wish to employ those patterns that appeared in out-of-context behavior in play in young animals or in "vacuum" situations.

A fixed action pattern, it must be remembered, is also composed of component parts (Chapter 2), and all the parts of a fixed action pattern must be rather rigidly controlled. Figure 11.15 shows the sequence, duration and strength of contraction of a set of specific muscles involved in the fixed pattern of swallowing in dogs. The characteristics of contraction of each muscle must be maintained within rather strict limits. A major change in the action of any one of these muscles would probably be strongly selected against since the swallowing "action profile" indicates a highly coordinated muscle interaction. In other words even a "simple" action may be maintained within set limits by the complexity of its component interactions. It doesn't matter whether such an

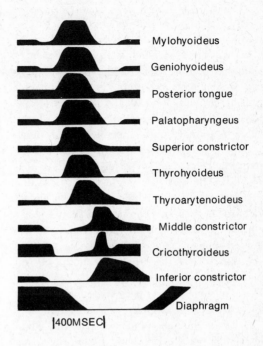

Figure 11.15 Diagrammatic summary of the sequence, timing and intensity of muscular contraction of swallowing in the dog. The height of the shaded area shows the strength of the contraction of each muscle involved. (From Doty and Bosma, *Journal of Neuro-physioliology* 19:44-60.)

action is under the neural control of one center or several, a great change in any component is likely to render the resulting pattern unadaptive and hence subject to "selecting out."

Ideally, one would wish to compare fixed action patterns in terms of the "action profile" demonstrated in the description of swallowing in dogs. Such descriptions would greatly increase the validity of comparisons of behavior, but the problems of such studies at present are vast. Field and laboratory studies might first furnish appropriate characters for comparison. Such studies require great knowledge of the natural histories of the animals, however, and few field workers are familiar enough with the behavior of any animal group. Then the laboratory experiments present technical problems as is apparent in the description of Doty and Bosma's (1956) procedure. The comparison of behavior at the level of the interaction of specific muscles, however, would help to close the vast gap between our knowledge of adaptive patterns and their neural control. The next step might be to determine the action of muscle bundles, the next largest component of muscles. The goal in such a study would be to determine the innervation of the motor components and then to locate and describe the seats of these patterns in the central nervous system.

If a group of related species is compared it is possible that the same fixed action pattern may be identified throughout. These patterns, Manning (1967) says, are truly homologous; they have descended to each species from a common ancestor. He points out, however, that the fixed action pattern may be modified by selection. Dif-ferences may arise in a number of ways. Such patterns may vary in their relative emphasis on different parts of the pattern (Figure 11.16). Also they may vary in the frequency with which the pattern is performed as is demonstrated in lizards which do display "pushups" at different rates (Figure 11.17). Such variation in frequency is a common difference between species. Tinbergen (1959) showed that a group of gulls may have the same behavioral repertoire with a characteristic probability for each species that any pattern will appear. Manning (1959) showed that in two fruit flies both show "scissoring" in which both wings are opened slowly together and "vibration" in which one wing is extended and vibrated rapidly in the vertical plane. Scissoring was found to be far more prevalent in one species, *Drosophila simulans*, and vibration appeared more frequently in *D. melanogaster*. In some cases, a pattern might become so infrequent as to disappear, thus effecting a qualitative change in the repertoire.

Changes in frequency of a pattern may reflect changes in the threshold for the stimulus of that

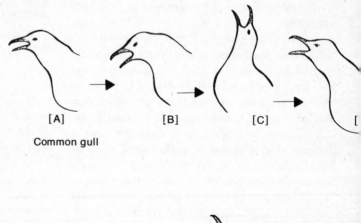

Figure 11.16 Sequence of the "oblique long call" in two species of gulls. Each call begins with the head in the oblique position (A). The emphasis in the sequence varies from one gull to the other. In A, the head is in the oblique position but is jerked down (lower in the herring gull) in B. The head is then thrown back and up as in C and the call continues. In D, the call dies away as the head is gradually lowered. Whereas the herring gull emphasizes the action in B, the common gull performs the action in C more vigorously. (From Tinbergen 1959.)

[A]   [B]   [C]   [

Common gull

[A]   [B]   [C]   [

Herring-gull

pattern (Manning 1967). It is possible that changes in threshold are responsible for a wide range of differences which may appear between related species. The control of such changes might be at various levels or sites and these centers might be the important target for genetic changes. The threshold changes could be brought about by differences in the sensory system, the motor system, the "motivational system," or any combination of these. Changes could also be brought about directly by genes acting on the nervous system itself or indirectly by genes affecting motor rate or hormone secretion, which in turn affect the motor system. Manning maintains that while proof is lacking, there are strong indications that the action is likely to be on the nervous system itself. Experiments on inbred lines of guinea pigs illustrate that the frequency differences in reproductive patterns of the two lines remain, even after injections of sex hormones or even thyroid hormones which increase the rate of metabolism. It seems probable from such experiments that the lines differ in the threshold properties of the sexual mechanisms in the brain.

Qualitative changes may also be explained on the basis of small changes in threshold. Each fixed action pattern must have a coordinating "center" in the central nervous system which is inherited. This center, when activated, produces a stereotyped pattern of neural signals to lower centers which control muscles and groups of muscles. The center activates each muscle group in order at the correct time and for the proper duration, thus effecting the fixed action pattern. The fixed action pattern may be completely stereotyped, as is probably the case in most swallowing patterns, or it may be altered from environmental feedback operating on the orientation component (recall the egg-retrieving experiment in a nesting goose or the variable orientation of a female duck in inciting behavior in Chapter 2). It is proposed (Manning 1971) that genetic changes affecting thresholds either within the coordinating center or one of the subordinate muscle groups will alter

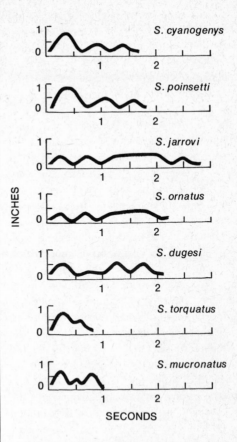

Figure 11.17 The head-bobbing patterns of some species of *Sceloporus* lizards. The height of the head movement is shown in the vertical axis. Variations in speed, amplitude and pattern of movement are also shown. Theoretically, each species could be identified on the basis of its head-bobbing movements alone. (From Hunsaker 1962.)

299

the fixed action pattern so that muscles might be brought into action sooner or later in the sequence, held for a longer or shorter time, or they might change the intensity and speed of their response as more or fewer motor fibers are activated.

Perhaps because of the various motor components (muscles) involved in any fixed action pattern, each with its own specific characteristics of behavior, changes in such patterns occur very slowly. In such a coordinated system any drastic change in a component is likely to be selected against very strongly, and it is unlikely that harmonious changes would occur in all parts at once. Threshold changes, however, occur more easily and, in fact, may be affected by the animal's early experience (see reviews in Hinde 1970; and Marler and Hamilton 1966). As an example, in male rats which are exposed to different rearing conditions, social experience, and handling early in life, the age at which sexual behavior can first be elicited varies widely, but the sexual behavior itself remains unchanged (Manning 1971).

It can be shown that some changes in the threshold for the elicitation of entire fixed action patterns is dependent upon other adaptive characteristics of the organism. For example, noxious moths with warning markings move at the slightest touch whereas palatable and cryptic species are much harder to budge, since it is to their advantage to remain unnoticed. As a different sort of case, consider the intention movements of birds. A bird about to fly crouches, raises its tail and wings, and withdraws its neck. In some cases this intention movement has become incorporated into display patterns. Most birds, because of their similar morphologies, must have very similar flight intention postures. As a signal of course, the posture might come to have different meanings for different groups, but the pattern is more likely to be used in some groups than others. Shy birds, which are more inclined to "take off," might be expected to be more familiar with the sight of movements associated with flight than

bolder birds. Some finches, for example, have large individual distances and the sexes often fear each other. Flight intention movements might be expected to appear with greater frequency in the mating behavior of such species (Hinde and Tinbergen 1958).

The fixity of any pattern may be strengthened, also, if the pattern is used in communication, especially as a display, to release an innate pattern in another individual. It doesn't matter whether the signal maintains its original adaptiveness (such as flight intention movements in birds, when the movement is reacted to by another individual but the bird is, in fact, still ready to take off). The pattern may also have been released from its original adaptiveness and have come to be employed only in signaling (such as the dancing with "veils" in empid flies discussed in Chapter 2). Once a fixed action pattern is used in communication it is subject not only to the restraints within the nervous system of its bearer, but also to those of the recipient of the signal. Any great change in such a pattern will not be recognized and the behavior would thus lose its adaptiveness in communication. It will be remembered, however, that constraints which are based on a releasing effect are more violable or labile than those which are due to the conservatism of the neural apparatus of the bearer.

Tinbergen (1959) advocates the "weighting" of characters when determining phylogenetic relationships. The procedure is sometimes not rigorously employed in morphological comparisons, but it is essential in behavioral studies. The weighting is done as follows: when species are believed related based on a number of similarities, the differences between them are first considered to be recently acquired and then are "peeled away" revealing the phylogenetically older "core." The core behavior of the species is then compared. If such cores are more similar between species than their total complex of characters, affinity is indicated. If the cores are more different than would be suggested by the total complex, then common descent of the species is doubtful. To illustrate, consider Cullen's work showing that the differences between the behavior of kittiwakes and ground-nesting gulls is largely due to differences in nesting habitat and that the differences were simply specific characters superimposed on a common adaptive theme. The core behavior of the two groups is similar; the differences are due to relatively recent evolutionary dictates. A detailed ethological study was able to show which behavior was to be "peeled away" and what parts were subject to valid comparison in evolutionary studies. When the kittiwake's peculiar mouth-open "choking" display is stripped of its mouth-open quality, the result is a display more similar, not less, to that of other gull species. Facing away or head flagging in black-headed gulls is more strongly oriented than in gulls with less distinctly marked heads. The more extreme turn of the head hides the mask which is used in aggressive displays; a similar behavior is seen in kittiwake chicks and is a corollary of their peculiar nesting habitat since they must appease neighbors nesting close-by. Once such morphological and ecological influences are understood, it becomes easier to see the strong homogeneity of the pattern throughout gulls as a group. So the "peeling off" of the obviously special adaptiveness of a pattern makes it easier to compare cores.

The necessity of stripping to reveal the core behavior becomes apparent when attempting to homologize ritualized behavior. Once a common pattern has been ritualized, it may be altered to such a degree that its original basis is no longer easily recognizable. Only careful comparison of a ritualized pattern throughout a group of species can reveal what the basic pattern of a ritualized behavior might be and which aspects of it have been added secondarily (Tinbergen 1962).

Ideally one would search for a "progression" of characters—slight differences appearing in the character from one species to the next—so that in proper sequence a trend or cline, becomes

evident. The criterion of continuity (Remane's third criterion) deemphasizes the stress on anatomical similarity. Structures which are undoubtedly homologous may differ greatly anatomically and histologically, such as the pineal eye of reptiles and mammals (De Beer 1938, 1958). Certain problems arise in the attempt to place a series of characters in their proper evolutionary order however. Lorenz (1952) shows how a "progression" of characters may be devised from rather unrelated forms if certain evidence is lacking (Figures 11.18a and 11.18b).

Homologous structures or functions need not have an ontogenetic similarity as well as phylogenetic continuity according to De Beer (1958). As the basis for the statement he maintains that: (1) homologous structures are not necessarily controlled by "identical" genes, and that characters controlled by such genes are not necessarily homologous; and (2) homologous characters do not necessarily arise from similar parts of the egg or embryo.

Hinde and Tinbergen (1958) review the procedure involved in homology studies and thereby give an indication of what information is necessary and what level of results might be expected. First, one should look for similarities between species in the character which has been chosen. Since the species are assumed to be related *on other grounds*, the suggestion is that the patterns are related through common descent. Secondly, the differences are related to possible causation and function. Hypotheses are then formed regarding which form is older. Third, hypotheses are developed regarding the probable evolutionary origins of the behavioral pattern. An effort might then be made to explain the differences between the original and present form. It could than be asked if the change is adaptive and therefore the result of natural selection rather than some other phenomenon such as drift. Here, experimental studies might be employed in order to determine the particular specializations in the character. Tinbergen (1959) added that the comparative

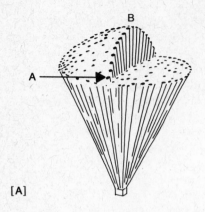

[A]

Figure 11.18A Diagram of an apparent "series" of animal forms (A and B) from simple to the more complex. A relationship is indicated when part of the lines of descent fall out of the record. In spite of the apparent sequence, no real phylogenetic series exists. (From Lorenz 1952.)

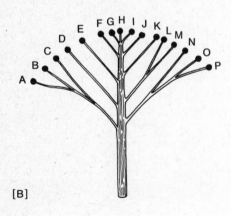

[B]

Figure 11.18B Diagram of the similarities of the recent animal forms which are based on true phylogenetic relationships. Here animals in row A-P owe their similarities to some degree to the part of the development pathway they hold in common. (From Lorenz 1952.)

method should be used in conjunction with motivational analysis (which indicates the origin of a pattern) and studies of function (which indicate the selection pressures) to show the adaptiveness of a character. The final result of a study such as has been described might be a tentative description of the descent of a behavioral pattern; this is about the most that can be expected from any comparative study.

There is a need for more quantified comparative ethological studies in order to understand more about which characters appear between species, which are variable, and to what degree. For examples of such studies on a wide range of animals which have been made to date, one might wish to refer to: Crane (1952, 1957) on mantids and fiddler crabs; Blest (1957) on moths; Spieth (1952) on fruit flies; Crook (1963, 1970) on weaverbirds and primates; Goss-Custard (1970) on wading birds; Aldrich-Blake (1970) on forest monkeys; Dilger (1960, 1962) on lovebirds; Lorenz (1941) and Johnsgard (1965) on ducks; and Tinbergen (1959) on gulls.

We will now consider some examples of behavior which have been considered homologous. In spite of the recent tendency to tighten the process of homologizing behavior by adding restrictions, some of the early work has remained unscathed. Whitman, 1919, found that while no distinguishing morphological character is peculiar to all pigeons and doves, they all drink water by sucking it up through pumping actions of the esophagus rather than by tilting the head back as other birds do. The sand grouse, Pterocletidae, has downy young which greatly resemble young grouse of the family Tetraonidae. For years the sand grouse was considered closely related to other grouse until it was found that they drink by pumping water up. Comparative anatomists had found some similarities allying the sand grouse with the pigeons, and the behavioral work reinforced the anatomical findings. The sand grouse was then placed into the order Columbiformes with other birds showing the peculiar drinking behavior. For another early study refer to Friedmann's (1929) study of cuckoo relationships.

Courtship displays or species-specific rituals are sometimes considered as valid behavioral characters for homologizing (Tinbergen 1959). Figure 11.19 shows, for example, the homologous "grunt-whistle" display in different species of birds. Lorenz (1939) looked at 16 courtship displays which appear in many species of ducks. By considering two of these—the chin lift, a pattern derived from drinking motions, and the over-the-shoulder inciting—he determined that the gadwall should be placed between the mallards and the wigeons. Later it was found that the mallard-wigeon hybrids showed the same mingling of the foxed action patterns of the parent species as appears in the gadwall. Thus the earlier work was supported.

Members of Tinbergen's group described gulls at many sites around the world and found that in spite of species differences the signaling systems were very similar. Morphological similarity suggested a common ancestry and Tinbergen (1959) employed behavioral studies, primarily "displays" (signals), to try to find out how the ancestral group divided into the 35 or so distinct species which now exist. He was able to distinguish between families on the basis of such behavior.

Display behavior has certain advantages to recommend it for homology studies. Since displays are basically signals, they must be obvious at least to conspecifics, and the likelihood is great that an observer will also detect them. The primary advantage is that such patterns are usually distinct and discrete. A displaying animal usually moves rapidly from one display to the next, diminishing the chance for confusing intermediate characters. Also, there is likely to be strong similarity of displays throughout a population.

All the large gulls, such as the herring gull, have similar signaling systems which were derived from adaptive patterns already in the gulls' repertoire. The displays of the hooded gulls are

[A]

Figure 11.19 These three examples (A, B and C) show drakes on the water exhibiting a homologous fixed-action pattern, the grunt whistle. The species are closely related. A is the mallard, *Anas platyrhynchos,* B the crested duck, *A.specularoides,* and C the gadwall, *A. strepera.* The timing and emphasis of each movement vary among each species. However, you can see that the gadwall and mallard show more emphasis on the sideways thrust of the head after the bill has been dipped into the water. Also, the gadwall and the crested duck start to rear up their body slightly after the mallard and the crested duck returns to the beginning position later than the other species. (From a film sequence after van der Wall 1963.)

[B]

[C]

Herring gull

Hart-laub's gull

Common gull

Figure 11.20 The similarity of the aggressive upright position in gulls. (From Tinbergen 1959.)

distinct from these, but similar to each other. Other species such as the kittiwake also have distinctive signaling systems. In spite of such diversity a current of similarity runs through the displays of all species (Figure 11.20).

Some displays, such as the aggressive upright, are simply postures preparatory to the act of pecking downward and are not ritualized. On the other hand, many signals appear to have been ritualized. For example the choking display is used by males to advertise a nest to passing females and to repel other males. It may have been derived, however, from the posture a gull assumes just before it settles on the eggs. The up and down movement in such patterns may be derived from displaced nest-building and regurgitation movements.

If should be apparent that the relationship of the behavioral model to the display derived from it could not be known without careful and extensive fieldwork of the type done by Tinbergen and his group. The value of such studies on display behavior is clearly demonstrated in the pecking-into-the-ground or "grass pulling" display (Figure 11.21). After assuming the aggressive upright behavior some gulls strike the ground hard and pull up bits of grass or sticks. Tinbergen believes this pattern is composed of two fixed components: redirected pecking followed by displacement behavior (picking up material as part of a nest-building pattern). Two of the species studied diverge in their behavior at this point. The herring gull tends to follow the displacement grass-pulling with a nest-building motion and the black-headed with a bill-wiping pattern.

There is a considerable variation in display, plumage, and fishing behavior in the families of pelicans, boobies, and cormorants. (Their families are Pelecanidae, Sulidae, and Phalacrocorcidae respectively, but they are all in the order Pelicaniformes.) There are similarities in behavior in the three families however, which indicate relationship. For example, all three families use similar forms of posturing—such as gaping (mouth open displays with no sound emitted—most pronounced in cormorants). The flying-up posture of the gannet is similar to the nest-relief ceremony of the brown pelican. It should be noted here that the displays may be homologous, but the environmental circumstances (or the releasers) which elicit the performance of such motor patterns may change.

The accepted view, based on morphology, that the pelicans are relatives of the ibises and the spoonbills (which are in the order Ciconiiformes and the family Threshkiornithidae) is bolstered by descriptions of flight patterns. They all fly by intermittently flapping and then planing over the surface of the water. Cormorants, also placed with gannets and pelicans in the order Pelicaniformes, sometimes glide, but rarely. They adopt the flap-glide rhythm of pelicans whenever they do fly together, thus showing the flight mannerism is held in common, but is more latent and harder to elicit in the cormorants.

The operation of environmental influences on the displays of certain of these seabirds was shown by Williams (1942). He found that while the shag, North Atlantic cormorant, and southern cormorant all exhibit a brilliant yellow-lined mouth by opening the mouth, the Pacific species—Brandt's cormorant—distends a blue gular (throat) pouch when advertising for a female. The general display pattern for all these species is about the same (Figure 11.22), but in Brandt's the mouth-open character is much less a prominent part of the display; the striking coloration in this species is external, on the neck. The Brandt's makes little sound in its displays, but Kortlandt (1940) has found the southern cormorant utters cries which are an important part of its signaling. Brandt's lives among rocks which are pounded by the large Pacific swells and it is theorized that any sounds it made would be drowned out. Since, then, vocalizations are not important in its displays, perhaps the mouth-open pattern which is necessary to make sounds never had a chance to become ritualized as part of a gaping display and neck coloration developed instead.

Ornithologists have not been able to subdivide the family of titmice Paridae on a morphological basis (Mayr 1948). Yet the nest-building habits of members of the family suggest that four, perhaps not closely related, groups of birds have been lumped together. The first includes the true titmice, the genus *Parus* and relatives, which always nest in hollow trees or other cavities. The second group includes the long-tailed tit, *Segithalos*, the bush tit, *Psaltriparus*, and related forms which build an oval nest with a lateral entrance; these are very social birds all with essentially the same call notes and habits. The third group consists of the penduline titmouse, *Remiz*, and its relatives, which build a peculiar retort-shaped nest consisting of plant material worked into a feltlike consistency. Lastly the bearded titmouse,

Figure 11.21 Certain behavior such as grass-pulling or pecking-into-the-ground may be complex and involve more than one fixed action pattern. (From Tinbergen 1959.)

Panurus, builds a stick nest with a lateral entrance which, along with certain other habits, unmasks the little bird as belonging to the babbler family *Timaliidae.* Mayr concludes that the behavioral study not only indicates that these four groups of genera are not very closely related but provides clues for placing them in their proper position. On the basis of restricting homology to fixed action patterns, nest building in the Paridae should probably be looked at again although it is probable that no changes would be merited since each type of nest undoubtedly requires highly specific and distinct fixed patterns. Such studies might, however, provide new insight into the development of the patterns.

As another case, consider a study of how grasshoppers clean their antennae. Jacobs (1953) used the behavior to justify the separation of various grasshoppers into families. Gryllidae, Tettigoniidae, and other groups with long antennae clean them with their maxillae mouthparts. The Acrididae step on one antenna and pull it through between the leg and the substrate. The Tetrigidae clean the antenna by stroking them with the legs and then clean the legs with the mouth.

In a study such as this, the behavior is undoubtedly a series of relatively simple fixed action patterns of a species not strongly affected by learning and therefore the validity of such comparisons is strengthened.

Behavioral characters have in some cases proven to be particularly useful in distinguishing morphologically similar species, the so-called "sibling" species (see Mayr 1948). As an example, consider the wasp genus *Ammophila.* Adriaanse (1947) noticed that some individuals in the species *A. campestris* has a peculiar behavior pattern (Table 11.1). Close examination revealed that these aberrant individuals were actually a new species. Sibling species have also been found in other behavioral studies (e.g., Barber 1951; and Evans 1953).

In spite of such demonstrations of the usefulness of behavior in systematics and evolution, there continues to be some argument over the validity of the studies. Basically the question of the validity of homologizing behavior centers over the sketchiness of our information regarding the relationship of morphological structures to behavioral patterns. G. G. Simpson had argued

[A]

[B]

Figure 11.22A Mating display of Brandt's cormorant, *Phalacrocorax penicillatus.* A shows the side view and B the front view. (After Williams 1942.)

Figure 11.22B Mating display of the southern cormorant, *P. carbo sinensis.* (From A. Adrea, 27:1-40, *Phalacrocorax carbo sinesis.* By permission of E. J. Brill 1938.)

Table 11. Separation of two groups of morphologically similar birds into different families based on behavior characteristics.

Character	Estrildidae	Ploceidae
1. Nest	A globular structure of small twigs or grass stems with lateral entrance.	Usually a finely woven structure, often hanging from twigs.
2. Pair bond	Tightly knit, often lasting through years.	Either no pair formation, or polygamy, or a pair bond of short duration.
3. Parenal care	Nest-building, incubation feeding of young jointly done by both parents.	Most parental duties performed by the female alone.
4. Tail movements	Lateral	Vertical
5. Courtship posture	Stiff upright, with wings pressed against body. Stereotyped repetition of song strophe.	Excited courtship dances with wing fluttering and occasional display flights. Noisy chatter.
6. Incubation	From first egg on; young hatch with daily intervals.	After completion of clutch; young hatch simultaneously.
7. Tongue, gape, and throat of nestlings	With peculiar species — or genus-specific pigment spots and papillae.	Without markings or papillae.
8. Feeding of nestlings	Take regurgitated food from the crop of the parent.	Normal food begging. Parents feed with the bill.
9. Begging of young	Without wing flutter.	With wing flutter.
10. Nest hygiene	Droppings of young not removed.	Droppings of young removed by parents.

From Adriaanse 1947.

some time ago that in order for a behavior to be called homologous, there must be also a homology of the morphological entity used to perform the pattern. He said the functions considered as abstractions, and without consideration for the structures that perform these functions, should not be spoken of as homologous. There are also arguments made for homologizing only that behavior related to morphological entities which are known to be homologous; the homology of claw-waving of fiddler crabs is an example of the proper application of the concept. Structural homology, of course, need not be as obvious as an appendage, but may be an enzyme, a hormone, part of the central nervous system, or any other character of the physical phenotype. Tinbergen (1962) agreed that movements employing homologous structures in a similar way may be considered homologous. On the other hand, Lehrman (1953) stated that nonhomologous behavior may be based on homologous structures, and Atz (1970) added that it is impossible for nonhomologous structures to have homologous functions. Atz also argued that although homologous structures are involved in a behavioral pattern and may *indicate* the patterns are homologous, such a relationship cannot be taken as proof. The anal fin of the males of some species of the guppy family Poeciliidae is modified into a gonopodium with which to fertilize the female. The anal fin and gonopodium are homologous, but the elaborate and specific motions of the latter cannot be homologized with the limited types of movements of the unmodified fin (Rosen and Gorden 1953). As an extension of the problem of morphology to behavior it is argued that behavioral homology cannot have definitive value until we are able to associate the behavior with its neural seat (Atz 1970). Thus, if we had information regarding the specific part of the nervous system that was responsible for each behavioral pattern, then we would probably choose to homologize the neural seats rather than the behavioral results of their activity. However, we do not have this information and herein, perhaps, lies the crux of the problem. Bullock (1965) has declared that our understanding of behavior and its physiological basis is the widest gap between disciplines in science. Atz pointed out that although homologous nuclear regions are known in the brains of animals as diverse as fish and mammals, this information has yielded nothing in terms of the homology of their behavior. Even if more were known about which nervous centers are related to a given behavior, still we might not be able to relate these correlates in evolutionary time. The problem lies in the uncertainty of being unable to be sure any behavior has been continuously associated with any particular condition of the central nervous system.

There is no question that the homology of behavior presents more fundamental problems than such treatment of morphological characters. However, it has been demonstrated in certain cases that behavioral studies if carefully designed may be used to indicate descent. In spite of the inherent problems in method and certain important questions regarding the value of the results, our best approach is probably to utilize primarily fixed action patterns to describe these in terms of their action profiles and to attempt to relate these to their neural centers. Until the time that our level of information, particularly regarding the nature of neural "seats" of behavior, increases to the point that such an approach might justify real expectations, we should continue to phrase our findings in tentative terms. More confidence would be merited of course when any anatomical or physiological studies are preceded by careful and extended fieldwork across the ranges of the species in question.

BIBLIOGRAPHY

Adler, H.E. 1963. Psychophysical limits of celestial navigation hypotheses. *Ergbn. Biol.*, 26: 235-252. (also in *Animal Behavior*, 11:566-577.)

Adriaanse, A. 1947. *Ammophila campestris* Ltr. und *Ammophila adriaansei* Wilcke: Ein Beitrag zur vergleichenden Verhaltensforschung. *Behaviour*, 1:1–34.

Albrecht, H. 1966. Zur Stammesgeschichte einiger Bewegungsweisen bei Fischen, untersucht am Verhalten von Haplochronis (Pisces, Chichlidae). *Zeitschrift für Tierpsychologie*, 23: 270–301.

Aldrich-Blake, F.P.G. 1970. Problems of social structure in forest monkeys. In *Social Behaviour in Birds and Mammals*, ed. by J.H. Crook. Academic Press, New York, pp. 79–99.

Alexander, R.D. 1960a. Sound communication in orthoptera and cicadidae. In *Vertebrate Speciation*, ed. by W.F. Blair, University of Texas Press, Austin.

Alexander, R.D. 1960b. Sound communication in Orthoptera and Cicadidae. In *Animal Sounds and Communication*, ed. by W.E. Lanyon and W.E. Tavolga, AIBS, Washington, D.C., pp. 38–92.

———. 1966. The evolution of cricket chirps. *Natural History*, 75:26–31.

——— and W.L. Brown, Jr. 1963. Mating behavior and the origin of insect wings. Occasional Papers of Museum of Zoology of the University of Michigan. No. 628., pp. 1–16.

Allee, W.C. 1926. Studies in animal aggregations: causes and effects of bunching in land isopods. *Journal of Experimental Zoology*, 45:255–277.

———. 1938, reprinted 1951. *The social life of animals*. Beacon Press, Boston.

Amadon, D. 1950. The Hawaiian Honeycreepers. (Aves, Drepaniidae). *Bulletin of the American Museum of Natural History*, 95:151–262.

———. 1959. The significance of sexual differences in size among birds. Proceedings of the American Philosophic Society, 103:531–536.

Andrew, R.J. 1956. Intention movements of flight in certain passerines, and their use in systematics. *Behaviour*, 10:179–204.

Andrewartha, N.G. 1961. *Introduction to the study of animal populations*. University of Chicago Press, Chicago.

Antonovics, J. 1971. The effects of a heterogeneous environment on the genetics of natural populations. *American Scientist*, 59:593–599.

Ardrey, R. 1962. *African genesis*. Collins, London.

Armstrong, E.A. 1965 (first published 1947). *Bird display and behavior*. Dover, New York.

Aschoff, J. 1963. Comparative physiology; diurnal rhythms. *Annual Review of Physiology*, 25:581–600.

———. 1965. *Circadian clocks*. North Holland Publishers, Amsterdam.

———. 1965. Circadian rhythms in man. *Science*, 148:1427–1432.

Ashmole, N.P. 1963a. The biology of the wideawake or sooty tern *Sterna fuscata* on Ascension Island. *Ibis*, 103b:297–364.

———. 1963b. The regulation of numbers of tropical oceanic birds. *Ibis*, 103b:458–473.

———. 1967. Sexual dimorphism and colonial breeding in the woodpecker, *Centurus striatus*. *American Naturalist*, 101:353–356.

Atz, J.W. 1970. The application of the idea of homology to behavior. In *Development and Evolution of Behavior,* ed. by I.R. Aronson, E. Tobach, D.S. Lehrman, J.S. Rosenblatt. W.H. Freeman, San Francisco.

Azrin, N.H., R.R. Hutchinson and R. McLaughlin. 1965. The opportunity for aggression as an operant reinforcer during aversive stimulation. *Journal of Experimental Animal Behavior,* 8:171–180.

Baerends, G.P. 1941. "Fortplanzungsverhalten und orientierung der Grabwespe, *Ammophila campestris. Tijdschrift voor de Entomologie,* 84:68–275.

————. 1950. Specializations in organs and movements with a releasing function. *Symposia of the Society for Experimental Biology,* 4:337–360.

Baker, H.G. and G.L. Stebbins (eds.) 1965. *The genetics of colonizing species.* Academic Press, New York.

Baldwin, P.H. 1953. Annual cycle. Environment and evolution in the Hawaiian Honeycreepers (Aves, Drepaniidae). *University of California Publications in Zoology,* 52:285–398.

Barber, H.S. 1951. North American fireflies of the genus *Photuris.* Smithsonian Institution's Miscellaneous Collection, 17:1–58.

Barnett, S.A. 1971. Apes and monkeys: social behavior. In *Topics in the Study of Life.* Harper and Row, New York.

Barth, R.H., Jr. 1961. Hormonal control of sex attractant production in the Cuban cockroach. *Science,* 133: 1598—1599.

————. 1962. The endocrine control of mating behavior in the cockroach *Byrsotria fumigate* (Guerin). *General Comparative Endocrinology,* 2:53–69.

Bartholomew, G.A., Jr. 1942. The fishing activities of double-crested cormorants on San Francisco Bay. *Condor,* 44:13–21.

Bastock, M. 1967. *Courtship, an ethological study.* Aldine, Chicago, 220 pp.

Beach, F.A. 1944. Responses of captive alligators to autitory stimulation. *American Naturalist,* 78:481–515.

————. 1945. Current concepts of play in animals. *American Naturalist* 79:523–541.

————. 1955. The descent of instinct. *Psychology Review,* 62:401–410.

Beer, G.R. de. 1938. Embryology and evolution. In *Evolution,* essays on *Aspects of Evolutionary Biology,* ed. by G.R. de Beer. Oxford University Press, London, pp. 57–78.

————. 1958. *Embryos and ancestors,* 3rd ed. Oxford University Press, London.

Benson, C.W. 1948. Geographical voice-variation in African birds. *Ibis,* 90–48–71.

Bent, A.C. 1926. Life histories of North American marsh birds. *U.S. National Museum Bulletin,* 142.

Berlyne, D.E. 1960. *Conflict, arousal and curiosity.* McGraw-Hill, New York.

Berkowitz, L. 1962. *Aggression. A social psychological analysis.* McGraw-Hill, New York.

Bernstein, I.S. 1966. Analysis of a key role in a capuchin (*Cebus albifrons*) group. *Tulane Studies in Zoology,* 13:49–54.

————. and L.G. Sharpe. 1966. Social roles in a rhesus monkey group. *Behaviour,* 26:91–104.

Billings, S.M. 1968. Homing in Leach's petrel. *Auk,* 85:36–43.

Birch, L.C. 1957. The meanings of competition. *American Naturalist,* 91:5–18.

Bitterman, M.E. 1965. The evolution of intelligence. *Scientific American.* (January), 212: 92–100.

Blair, W.F. 1963. Acoustic behavior of Amphibia. In *Acoustic Behavior of Animals,* ed. by R.B. Busnel, Elsevier Publishing Company, Amsterdam, pp. 694–708.

Blest, A.D. 1957. The evolution of protective displays in the Saturniodea and Sphingidae (Lepidoptera). *Behaviour,* 11:257–309.

————. 1961. The concept of 'ritualisation.' In *Current Problems in Animal Behaviour,* ed. by W.H. Thorpe and O.L. Zangwill. Cambridge University Press, New York, pp. 102–124.

Bogert, C.M. 1960. The influence of sound on the behavior of amphibians and reptiles. In *Animal sounds and communications,* ed. by W. E. Lanyon and W.N. Tavolga. American Institute of Biological Sciences, Publ. No. 7. Washington, D.C., pp. 137–320.

Borror, D.J. 1959. Variation in the songs of the

rufous-sided towhee. *Wilson Bulletin,* 71:54–72.

_____ . 1961. Intraspecific variation in passerine bird songs. *Wilson Bulletin,* 73:57–78.

Brand, A.R. and P.P. Kellogg. 1939. Auditory responses of starlings, English sparrows and domestic pigeons. *Wilson Bulletin,* 51:38–41.

Bronson, F.H. 1968. *Pheromonal influences on mammalian reproduction and sexual behavior,* ed. by M. Diamond. University of Indiana Press, Bloomington.

Brosset, A. 1969. La vie sociale des oiseaux dans une forêt equitoriale du Gabon. *Biologia Gabonica,* 5:29–69.

Brower, L.P. 1969. Ecological chemistry. *Scientific American,* 220:22–29.

Brown, F.A. 1970. In *The biological clock: two views,* by F.A. Brown, J.W. Hastings, J.D. Palmer. Academic Press, New York, pp. 15–59.

Brown, J.L. 1963. Social organization and behavior of the Mexican jay. *Condor,* 65:126–153.

_____ . 1965. The evolution of diversity in avian territorial systems. *Wilson Bulletin,* 76:160–169.

_____ . 1969. Territorial behavior and population regulation in birds. *Wilson Bulletin,* 81:293–329.

Brown, R.Z. 1953. Social behaviour, reproduction and population changes in the house mouse. *Ecological Monographs,* 23:217–40.

Brown, W.L. and E.O. Wilson. 1956. Character displacement. *Systematic Zoology,* 5:49–64.

Bullock, T.H. 1965. Physiological bases of behavior. In *Ideas in Modern Biology,* ed. by J.A. Moore. Natural History Press, Garden City, pp. 449–482.

Bunning, E. 1967. *The physiological Clock.* Revised 2nd edition. Springer, Berlin.

Burkhardt, D., and W. Schleidt, H. Altner. 1967. *Signals in the animal world.* McGraw-Hill, New York.

Burns, R.D. 1968. The role of agonistic behavior in regulation of density in Uinta ground squirrels, *Citellus armatus.* M.S. thesis, Utah State University.

Burrell, H. 1927. *The platypus.* Angus and Robertson, Ltd., Australia.

Bustard, R.H. 1970. The role of behavior in the natural regulation of numbers in the gekkonid lizard *Gehyra variegata. Ecology,* 51:724–728.

Cain, A.J. 1964. The perfection of animals, In *Viewpoints in biology,* ed. by J. Carthy and R. Duddington. Vol. 3. Butterworth, London, pp. 36–62.

Calhoun, J.B. 1962a. A behavioral sink. In *Roots of Behavior,* ed. by E.L. Bliss, Harper and Bros. New York.

_____ . 1962b. Population density and social pathology. *Scientific American,* 206:139–146.

_____ . 1963. The ecology and sociology of the Norway rat (cited in Watson and Moss 1970). Bethesda.

Carlquist, S. 1965. *Island life. A natural history of islands of the world.* Natural History Press, New York.

Carpenter, C.R. 1934. A field study of the behavior and social relations of howling monkeys (*Alouatta palliata*). *Comparative Psychology Monographs,* 10:1–168.

Carrington, R. 1958. *Elephants. A short account of their natural history, evolution and influence on mankind.* Basic Books, New York.

Case, J. 1966. *Sensory Mechanisms.* Macmillan, New York.

Chapin, J.P. 1932. The birds of the Belgian Congo. Part I. *Bulletin of the American Museum of Natural History,* 75.

Chauvin, Remy. 1963. Translation 1968. *Animal societies: from the bee to the gorilla.* Hill and Wang. New York.

Chitty, D. 1952. Mortality among voles (*Microtus agrestis*) at Lake Vyrnwy, Montgomeryshire in 1936–1939. *Philosophical Transaction of the Royal Society of London,* B, 236:505–552.

_____ . 1957. Self-regulation in numbers through changes in viability. *Symposia of Quantitative Biology,* 22:277–280.

_____ . 1967. What regulates bird populations? *Ecology,* 48:698–701.

Christian, J.J. 1961. *Proceedings of the National Academy of Science,* 47:428–449.

_____ . 1963. Endocrine adaptive mechanisms and the physiologic regulation of population growth. In *Physiological mammalogy,* ed. by W.V. Mayer and R.G. van Gelder. Academic Press, New York, pp. 189–353.

————— . 1968. The potential role of the adrenal cortex as affected by social rank and population density on experimental epidemics. *American Journal of Epidemiology*, 87:255–66.

Clulow, F.V. and J.R. Clarke, Jr. 1968. Pregnancy block in *Microtus agrestis* and induced ovulation. *Nature*, 219:511.

Cody, M.L. 1969. Convergent characteristics in sympatric species: A possible relation to interspecific competition and aggression. *Condor*, 71:222–239.

————— and J.H. Brown. 1970. Character convergence in Mexican finches. *Evolution*, 24: 304–310.

Collias, N.E. 1944a. Aggressive behavior among vertebrate animals. *Physiological Zoology*, 17: 83–123.

————— . 1944b. Aggressive behavior and evolution. Excerpted in *Animal Aggression*, ed. by C.H. Southwick (1970). Van Nostrand Reinhold Co., New York.

————— . 1960. An ecological and functional classification of animal sounds. In *Animal sounds and communication*, ed. by W.E. Lanyon and W.N. Tavolga. American Institute of Biological Sciences Publication No. 7. Washington, D.C. pp. 368–391.

————— . 1963. A spectrographic analysis of the vocal repertoire of the African village weaverbird. *Condor*, 65:517–527.

————— , M. Brandman, K. Victoria, L.F. Kiff and C.E. Rischer. 1971. Social facilitation of nest-building in experimental colonies of a weaverbird: Effects of varying the sex ratio. *Ecology*, 52:829–836.

————— and L.R. Jahn. 1959. Social behavior and breeding success in Canada geese (*Branta canadensis*) confined under semi-natural conditions. *Auk*, 76:478–509.

————— , J. K. Victoria and R.J. Shallenberger. 1971. Social facilitation in weaverbirds: importance of colony size. *Ecology*, 52:823–828.

Collins, C.W. and S.F. Potts. 1932. Attractants for the flying gypsy moth as an aid in locating new infestations. *U.S. Department of Agricultural Technology Bulletin*, 336:1–43.

Connell, J.H. 1961. The influence of interspecific competition and other factors on the distribution of the barnacle *Chthamalus stellatus*. *Ecology*, 42:710–723.

Corning, W.C. and E.R. John. 1961. Effect of ribonuclease on retention of conditioned response in regenerating planaria. *Science*, 134: 1363–1365.

Corso, J.F. 1967. *The experimental psychology of sensory behavior*. Holt, Rinehart and Winston, Inc., New York.

Cott, H.B. 1957. *Adaptive coloration in animals*. Methuen and Co., London.

Coulson, J.C. 1968. Differences in the quality of birds nesting in the centre and on the edges of a colony. *Nature*, 217:478–479.

————— and E. White. 1960. The effect of age and density of breeding birds on the timing of breeding of the kittiwake *Rissa tridactyla*. *Ibis*, 102:71–86.

Cowley, J.J. 1970. Food intake and the modification of behaviour. In *Animal populations in relation to their food resources*, ed. by A. Watson, Blackwell, Oxford.

Cragg, J.F. 1955. The natural history of sheep blowflies in Britain. *Annals of Applied Biology*, 42:197–207.

Craig, W. 1918. Appetites and aversions as constituents of instincts. *Biological Bulletin*, 34: 91–107.

————— . 1928. Why do animals fight? *International Ethics*, 31:264–278.

Crane, J. 1952. A comparative study of innate defensive behavior in Trinidad mantids (Orthoptera, Mantoidea). *Zoologica*, 37:259–293.

————— . 1955. Imaginal behavior of a Trinidad butterfly, *Heliconius erato hydara* Heivitson, with special reference to the social use of color. *Zoologica*, 40:167–196.

————— . 1957. Basic patterns of display in fiddler crabs (Ocypodidae, genus *Uca*). *Zoologica*, 42:69–82.

————— . 1966. Combat, display and ritualization in fiddler crabs. *Philosophical Transactions of the Royal Society of London B*, 251: 459–472.

Crook, J.H. 1961. The basis of flock organization in birds. In *Current problems in animal behaviour*, ed. by W.H. Thorpe and O.L. Zangwill.

Cambridge University Press, New York, pp. 125–149.

_____ . 1963. Comparative studies on the reproductive behaviour of two closely related weaver bird species (*Ploceus cucullatus* and *Ploceus nigerrimus*) and their races. *Behaviour*, 21:177–232.

_____ . 1964. The evolution of social organization and visual communication in the weaver birds (Ploceinae). *Behaviour* supplement no. 10.

_____ . 1965. The adaptive significance of avian social organizations. Social organizations of animal communities. *Symposia of the Zoological Society of London*. 14. pp. 181–218.

_____ . 1966. Gelada baboon herd structure and movement: a comparative report. *Symposia of the Zoological Society of London*, 18:237–258.

_____ . 1969. Functional and ecological aspects of vocalization in weaver birds. In *Bird vocalizations*. ed. by R.A. Hinde. Cambridge. pp. 265–290.

_____ . 1970a. The socio-ecology of primates. In *Social behaviour in birds and mammals*, ed. by J.H. Crook. Academic Press, New York, pp. 103–159.

_____ . 1970b. Social organization and the environment: Aspects of contemporary social ethology. *Animal Behavior*, 18:197–209.

_____ . 1970c. Sources of cooperation in animals and man. Smithsonian Society for Scientific Information, 9:27–48.

_____ and J.S. Gartlan. 1966. Evolution of primate societies. *Nature*. 210:1200–1203.

Crowell, K. 1962. Reduced interspecific competition among the birds of Bermuda. *Ecology*, 43:75–88.

Cullen, E. 1957a. Adaptations in the kittiwake in the British Isles. *Bird Study*, 10:147–179.

_____ . 1957b. Adaptations in the kittiwake to cliff nesting. *Ibis*, 99:275–302.

_____ . 1960. Experiments on the effects of social isolation on reproductive behaviour in the three-spined stickleback. *Animal Behavior*, 8:235.

Cullen, J.M. 1959. Behaviour as a help in taxonomy. *Pub. Syst. Assoc.* 3:131–140.

_____ and N.P. Ashmole. 1963. The black noddy *Anous tenuirostris* on Ascension Island. Part 2, Behaviour. *Ibis*, 103b:423–446.

Daanje, A. 1950. On locomotory movements in birds and the intention movements derived from them. *Behaviour* 3:48–99.

Darling, F.F. 1938. Bird flocks and the breeding cycle: A contribution to the study of avian sociality. Cambridge University Press, Cambridge.

Davidson, J. and H.G. Andrewartha. 1948a. Annual trends in a natural population of *Thrips imaginis* (Thysanoptera). *Journal of Animal Ecology*, 17:193–199.

_____ . 1948b. The influence of rainfall, evaporation and atmospheric temperature on fluctuations in size of a natural population of *Thrips imaginis* (Thysanoptera). *Journal of Animal Ecology*, 17:200–202.

Darwin, C.R. 1859. *The origin of species*. John Murray, London.

_____ . 1871. *The descent of man and selection in relation to sex*. John Murray, London.

_____ . 1890. *The Descent of Man*. 2nd ed. Murray, London.

Davis, D.E. 1942. The phylogeny of social nesting habits in the Crotophaginae. *Quarterly Review of Biology*, 17:115–134.

_____ . 1946. A seasonal analysis of mixed flocks of birds in Brazil. *Ecology*, 27:168–181.

Delius, J.D. 1965. A population study of skylarks, *Alauda arvensis*. *Ibis*, 107:465–492.

Dethier, V.G. and E. Stellar. 1961. *Animal behavior*. Prentice-Hall, Inc., Englewood Cliffs.

De Vore, I. (ed.). 1965. *Primate behavior: field studies of monkeys and apes*. Holt, Rinehart and winston, New York.
behavior. In *Primate Behavior*, ed. by I. DeVore. Holt, Rinehart and Winston, New York. pp. 53–110.

Diamond, J.M. and J. Terborgh. 1967. Observations on bird distribution and feeding assemblages along the Rio Callaria, Department of Loreto, Peru. *Wilson Bulletin*, 79:273–282.

DiCara, L.V. 1970. Learning in the autonomic nervous system. *Scientific American*, 222:30–39.

Dilger, W.C. 1956. Hostile behavior and reproductive isolating mechanisms in the genera *Catharus* and *Hylocichla*. *Auk*, 73:313-353.

Dilger, P.C. 1960. The comparative ethology of the African parrot genus *Agapornis*. *Zeitschrift für Tierpsychologie*, 17:649–685.

———— . 1962. The behavior of love birds. *Scientific American*, 206:88–98.

Dimond, S.J. 1970. The social behaviour of animals. B.T. Batsford, Ltd., London.

Dixon, K. 1961. Habit distribution and niche relationships in North American species of *Parus*. In *Vertebrate Speciation*, ed. by W.F. Blair. Texas University Press, Austin. pp. 179–216.

Dobzhansky, Th. 1937, 3d edition, 1951. *Genetics and the origin of the species*. Columbia University Press, New York.

———— . 1950. Evolution in the tropics. *American Scientist*, 38:209–221.

Dollard, J.; L. Doob; N. Miller; O. Mowrer; R. Sears. 1939. *Frustration and aggression*. Yale University Press. New Haven.

Dorst, J. 1962. *The migration of birds*. Houghton Mifflin Co., Boston.

Doty, R.W. and J.F. Bosma. 1956. An electromyographic analysis of reflex deglutination. *Journal of Neurophysiology*, 19:44–60.

Dufay, C. 1957. Sur l'attraction sexuelle chez *Lasiocampa quercus* L. (Sep., Sasio-campidae). *Bulletin de la Société d'Entomologië*, France, 62:61–64.

Earhart, C.M. and N.K. Johnson. 1970. Size dimorphism and food habits of North American owls. *Condor*, 72:251–264.

Eccles, J.C. 1953. *The neurophysiological basis of mind: The principles of neurophysiology*. Oxford University Press, London.

Edney, E.B. 1954. Woodlice and the land habitat. *Biological Review*, 29:185–219.

Ehrlich, P.R. and L.C. Birch. 1967. The "balance of nature" and "population control." *American Naturalist*, 101:97.

———— and A.H. Ehrlich. 1970. *Population, resources, environment*. W.H. Freeman, San Francisco.

———— . 1953. *The dancing bees*. Methuen and Co., London.

Eibl-Eibesfeldt, I. 1950. Über die Jungendentwicklung des Verhaltens eines männlichen Dachses (*Meles meles* L.) unter besonderer Berücksichtigung des spieles. *Zeitschrift für Tierpsychologie*, 7:327–355.

———— . 1959. Der Fisch *Aspidontus taeniatus* als Nachahmer des Putzers *Labroides dimidiatus*. *Zeitschrift für Tierpsychologie*, 16:19–25.

———— . 1961a. The fighting behavior of animals. *Scientific American*, 205:122–121.

———— . 1961b. The interactions of unlearned behaviour patterns and learning in mammals. In *Brain mechanisms and learning*, ed. by J.F. Delafresnage. Blackwell, pp. 53–73.

———— . 1963. Angeborenes und Erworbenes im Verhalten einiger Säuger. Zeitschrift für *Tierpsychologie*, 20:705–754.

———— . 1967. Concepts of ethology and their significance for the study of human behavior. In *Early behavior: comparative and developmental approaches*, ed. by H.W. Stevenson. Wiley, New York, pp. 127–146.

———— . 1970. *Ethology, the biology of behavior*. Holt, Rinehart and Winston, New York.

Eisner, T. 1970. Chemical defense against predation in arthropods. In *Chemical ecology*, ed. by E. Sondheimer and J.B. Simeone. Academic Press, New York, pp. 157–217.

Elkan, E. 1960. The common toad (*Bufo bufo* L.) in the laboratory. *British Journal of Herpetology*, 2:177–182.

Emlen, J.T. and R.L. Penney. 1964. Distance navigation in the Adélie penguin. *Ibis*, 106:417–431.

———— and F.W. Lorenz. 1942. Pairing responses of free-living valley quail to sex hormone pellet implants. *Auk*, 59:369–378.

Emlen, S.T. 1967. Migratory orientation in the indigo bunting, *Passerina cyanea*. Part I. Evidence for use of celestial cues; Part II. Mechanism of celestial orientation. *Auk*, 84:309–342, 463–389.

———— . 1971. Adaptive aspects of coloniality in the bank swallow. *American Zoologist*, 11.

Errington, P.L. 1943. An analysis of mink predation upon muskrats in northcentral United States. *Research Bulletin of the Iowa Agri-*

cultural Experiment Station, 320:797–924.

——— . 1945. Some contributions of a fifteen year local study of the northern bobwhite to a knowledge of population phenomena. *Ecological Monographs*, 15:1–34.

——— . 1946. Predation and vertebrate populations. *Quarterly Review of Biology* 21: 145–177, 221–245.

Estes, W.K.; S. Koch; K. McCorquodale; P.E. Meehl; C.G. Mueller; W.N. Schoenfeld; and W.S. Verplanck. 1954. *Modern learning theory*. Appleton-Century-Crofts, New York.

Etkin, W. 1964. Cooperation and competition in social behavior. In *Social behavior and organization among vertebrates*, ed. by W. Etkin. University of Chicago Press, Chicago, pp. 1–34.

——— . 1967. *Social behavior from fish to man*. University of Chicago Press, Chicago.

Evans, H.E. 1953. Comparative ethology and the systematics of spider wasps. *Systematic Zoology*, 2:155–172.

Evans, S.M. and G.R. Patterson. 1971. The synchronization of behavior in flocks and estrildine finches. *Animal Behavior*, 19:429–438.

Ewer, R.F. 1968. *Ethology of mammals*. Plenum Press, New York.

Festetics, A. 1959. Okologische Untersuchungen an Brutvögeln des Saser. *Vogelwelt*, 80:1–21.

Fischer, J. 1954. Evolution and bird sociality. In *Evolution as a process*, ed. by J. Huxley, A.C. Hardy, and E.B. Ford. Allen and Unwin, London, pp. 71–83.

——— and R.T. Peterson. 1964. *The world of birds*. Doubleday and Co., Inc., Garden City, N.Y.

Fisher, R.A. 1930. *The genetical theory of natural selection*. Dover, New York.

Fitch, H.S. 1948. Ecology of the California ground squirrel on grazing lands. *American Midland Naturalist*, 39:513–596.

Flickinger, G.L. 1966. Responses of the testes to social interaction among grouped chickens. *General Comparative Endocrinology*, 6:89–98.

Fraenkel, G.S. and D.L. Gunn. 1940. *The orientation of animals*. Oxford University Press, London.

Free, J.B. 1965. The allocation of duties among worker honeybees. Social organization of animal communities. *Symposia of the Zoological Society of London*, 14. pp. 173–178.

Fretwell, S.D. 1969. The adjustment of birth rate to mortality in birds. *Ibis*, 111:624–627.

Friedmann, H. 1929. *The cowbirds*. Thomas, Baltimore.

Frings, H.; M. Frings; J. Jumber; R. Busnel; J. Giban; P. Gramet. 1958. Reactions of American and French species of *Corvus* and *Larus* to recorded communication signals tested reciprocally. *Zoology*, 39:126–131.

Frisch, K. von. 1950. Bees: their chemical senses, vision, and language. Cornell University Press, Ithaca.

——— . 1964. *Biology*. Harper and Row, New York.

Fromme, H.G. 1961. Untersuchungen über das Orientierungsvermögen nächtlich ziehender Kleinvögel (*Erithacus rubecula, Sylvia communis*). *Zeitschrift für Tierpsychologie*, 18: 205–220.

Fuller, J.L. and W.R. Thompson. 1960. *Behavior genetics*. John Wiley and Sons, New York.

Gartlan, J.S. 1968. Structure and function in primate society. *Folia Primat.*, 8:89–120.

Gause, G.F. 1934. *The struggle for existence*. Williams and Wilkins, Baltimore.

Geist, V. 1966a. The evolutionary significance of mountain sheep horns. *Evolution*, 20:558–66.

——— . 1966b. Evolution of horn-like organs. *Behavior*, 27:175–214.

Gerard, R.W. 1961. The fixation of experience. In *Brain mechanisms and learning*, ed. by J.F. Delafresnaye. Blackwell, Oxford, pp. 21–35.

Gerdes, K. 1962. Richtungstendenzen vom Brutplatz verfrachteter Lachmöven (*Larus ridibundus* L.) unter Ausschluss visueller Gelände und Himmelsmarken. *Zeitschrift für Wissenschaftliche Zoologie*, 166:352–410.

Gershenson, S. 1945. Evolutionary studies on the distribution and dynamics of melanism in the hamster (*Cricetus cricetus* L.). *Genetics*, 30: 207–251.

Gilliard, E.T. 1963. The evolution of bowerbirds. *Scientific America*, 209:38–46.

Goethe, F. 1954. Vergleichende Beobachtungen zum Verhalten der Silbermowe (*Larus argentatus*) und der Heringsmowe (*Larus fuscus*). Proc. XI *International Ornithological Congress*, pp. 577–582.

Gompertz, T. 1961. The vocabulary of the great tit. *British Birds*, 54:369–394, 404–418.

Goodwin, B. 1963. *Temporal organization in cells.* Academic Press, New York.

Goss-Custard, J.D. 1970. Feeding dispersion in some overwintering wading birds. In *Social behavior in birds and mammals,* ed. by J.H. Crook. Academic Press, New York, pp. 3–34.

Grant, P.R. 1965. The adaptive significance of some size trends in island birds. *Evolution,* 19:355–367.

_____. 1966a. Ecological compatability of bird species on islands. *American Naturalist,* 100:451-462.

_____. 1966b. The density of land birds on the Tres Marias Islands in Mexico. I. Numbers and biomass. *Canadian Journal of Zoology.,* 44:391–400.

_____. 1968. Bill size, body size, and the ecological adaptations of bird species to competitive situations on islands. *Systematic Zoology,* 17:319–333.

_____. 1969. Community diversity and the coexistence of congeners. *American Naturalist,* 103:552–556.

_____. 1971. Comment on Simberloff's letter. *American Naturalist,* 105:194–197.

Grant, V. 1963. *The origin of adaptations.* Columbia University Press, N.Y.

Griffin, D.R. 1955. Bird navigation. In *Recent studies in avian biology,* ed. by A. Wolfson. University of Illinois Press, Urbana, pp. 154–1972

_____. 1958. *Listening in the dark.* Yale University Press, New Haven.

_____. 1964. *Bird migration.* Doubleday & Company, Inc., Garden City, New York.

Guhl, A.M. and L.L. Ortman. 1953. Visual patterns of recognition of individuals among chickens. *Condor,* 55:287–298.

Guthrie, R.D. and R.G. Petocz. 1970. Weapon automimicry among mammals. *American Naturalist,* 104:585–588.

Hailman, J.P. 1964. Breeding synchrony in the equatorial swallow-tailed gull. *American Naturalist,* 98:79–83.

_____. 1965. Cliff-nesting adaptations of the Galápagos swallow-tailed gull. *Wilson Bulletin,* 77:346–362.

_____. 1969. How an instinct is learned. *Scientific America,* 221:98–106. June.

Hairston, N.G., F.E. Smith and L.B. Slobodkin. 1960. Community structure, population control, and competition. *American Naturalist,* 94:421–425.

Halberg, F. 1960. Temporal coordination of physiologic function. *Cold Spring Harbor Symposia on Quantative Biology,* 25:289–308.

Haldane, J.B.S. 1932. *The causes of evolution.* Longmans, Green, London.

Hall, J.R. 1970. Synchrony and social stimulation in colonies of the Blackheaded Weaver *Ploceus cucullatus* and Vieillot's black weaver *Melanopteryx nigerrimus. Ibis,* 112:93–103.

Hall, K.R.L. 1964. Aggression in monkey and ape societies. In *The Natural History of Aggression,* ed. by J.D. Carthy and F.J. Ebling. Academic Press, New York, pp. 51–64.

_____. 1965a. Ecology and behavior of baboons, patas and vervet monkeys. *Proceedings of the 1st International Conference on the baboon as an experimental animal,* San Antonio, Texas.

Hall, K.R.L. 1965b. Social organization of the old-world monkeys and apes. Social organization of animal communities. *Symposia of the Royal Society of London,* 14, pp. 265–289.

_____ and I. DeVore. 1965. Baboon social behavior. In *Primate behavior,* ed. by I. DeVore. Holt, Rinehart and Winston, New York, pp. 53–110.

Hall, M.F. 1962. Evolutionary aspects of estrildial song. *Symposia of the Zoological Society of London,* 8:3.

Hamilton, W.D. 1963. The evolution of altruistic behavior. *American Naturalist,* 97:354–356.

_____. 1964a. The genetic evolution of social behaviour. I. *Journal of Theoretical Biology,* 7:1–16.

_____. 1964b. The genetic evolution of social behaviour. II. *Journal of Theoretical Biology,* 7:17–52.

Hamilton, T.H. 1962. Species relationships and adaptations for sympatry in the avian genus *Vireo*. *Condor*, 64:40–68.

———— and R.H. Barth, Jr. 1962. The biological significance of season change in male plumage appearance in some new world migratory bird species. *American Naturalist*, 96: 123–144.

Hansen, E.W. 1966. The development of maternal and infant behavior in the rhesus monkey. *Behavior*, 27:107–149.

Hardin, G. 1960. The competitive exclusion principle. *Science*, 131:1291–1297.

Harker, J.E. 1958. Diurnal rhythms in the animal kingdom. *Biological Review*, 33:1–52.

Harlow, H.F. 1932. Social facilitation of feeding in the albino rat. *Journal of General Psychology*, 41:211–221.

———— . 1949. The formation of learning sets. *Psychology Review*, 56:51–65.

———— . 1958. The nature of love. *American Psychologist*, 13:673–685.

Harper, J.L. et al. 1961. The evolution and ecology of closely related species living in the same area. *Evolution*, 15:209–227.

Hartley, P.H.T. 1949. The biology of the mourning chat in winter quarters. *Ibis*, 91:393–413.

———— . 1953. An ecological study of the feeding habits of the English titmice. *Animal Ecology*, 22:261–288.

Hartry, A.L. P. Keith-Lee and W.D. Morton. 1964. Planaria, memory transfer through cannibalism reexamined. *Science*, 146:274–275.

Hartshorne, C. 1958. The relation of bird song to music. *Ibis*, 100:421–445.

Hasler, A.D. 1960. Guideposts of migrating fishes. *Science*, 132:785–792.

Hastings, J.W. 1970. In *The Biological Clock: two views*, by F.A. Brown, J.W. Hastings, J.D. Palmer. Academic Press, New York, pp. 63–94.

Hatch, J. 1966. Collective territories in Galápagos mockingbirds, with notes on other behavior. *Wilson Bulletin*, 78:198–207.

Hebb, D.O. 1953. Heredity and environment in animal behavior. *British Journal of Animal Behavior*, 1:43–47.

Hediger, H. 1948. Die Zucht des Feldhasen (*Lepus europaeus* Pallus) in Gefangenschaft. *Physiologia Comparata et Oecologia*, 1:46–62.

———— . 1955. *Studies of the psychology and behavior of captive animals in zoos and circuses*. Butterworth & Co., London.

Heinroth, O. 1910. Beiträge zur Biologie, nämentlich Ethologie and Physiologie der Anatiden. *Verhandlungen der Internazionalen Ornotologischen Kongres*, pp. 589–702.

———— . 1930. Über bestimmte Bewegungsweisen bei Wirbeltieren. *S.B. Ges. naturf. Fr. Berl. Feb.*

Hensley, M.M. and J.B. Cope. 1951. Further data on removal and repopulation of the breeding birds in a spruce-fir forest community. *Auk*, 68:483–493.

Hess, W.R. 1943. Das Zwischenhirn als Koordinationsorgan. *Helvetica Physiologica Acta*, 1:549–565.

———— . 1956. Space perception in the chick. *Scientific America*, 195:71–80.

———— . 1962. Ethology: an approach toward the complete analysis of behavior. In *New directions in Psychology*. Holt, Rinehart and Winston, New York, pp. 159–266.

Hilgard, E.R. 1956. *Theories of learning*. Appleton-Century-Croft, New York.

———— and D.G. Marquis. 1961. *Conditioning and learning*. Revised G.A. Kimble. Methuen, London.

Hinde, R.A. and J. Fisher. 1951. Further observations on the opening of milk bottles by birds. *British Brids*, 44:393–396.

Hinde, R.A. 1952. The behavior of the great tit (*Parus major*) and some other related species. *Behavior*, Suppl. 2, pp. 1–201.

———— . 1956a. Ethological models and the concept of drive. *British Journal of Philosophical Science*, 6:321–331.

———— . 1956b. Territories of birds. *Ibis*, 98: 340–369.

———— . 1959. Unitary drives. *Animal Behavior*, 7:130–141.

Hinde, R.A. 1960a. Energy models of motivation. *Symposia of the Society for Experimental Biology*, 14:199–213.

_____ . 1960b. Factors governing the changes in strength of a partially inborn response, as shown by the mobbing behaviour of the chaffinch (*Fringilla coelebs*): III. The interaction of short-term and long-term incremental and decremental effects. *Proceedings of the Royal Society of Social Service* B, 153:398–420.

_____ . 1970 (2nd ed.) *Animal behaviour: A synthesis of ethology and comparative psychology*. McGraw-Hill, New York.

_____ and J. Fisher. 1952. Further observations on the opening of milk bottles by birds. *British Birds*, 44:393–396.

_____ and N. Tinbergen. 1958. The comparative study of species-specific behavior. In *Behavior and evolution*, ed. by A. Roe and G.G. Simpson. Yale University Press, New Haven, pp. 251–268.

Hirsch, J. (ed.) 1967. *Behavior-genetic analysis*. McGraw-Hill, New York.

Hoffman, K. 1954. Versuche zu der im Richtungsfinden der Vögel enthaltenen Zeitschätzung. *Zeitschrift für Tierpsychologie*, 11:453–475.

Hokanson, J.E. and S. Shetler. 1961. The effect of overt aggression on Physiological Tension Level. *Journal of Abnormal Social Psychology*, 63:446–448.

Holling, C.S. 1959. The components of predation as revealed by a study of small-mammal predation on the European sawfly. *Canadian Entomology*, 5:293–320.

_____ . 1968. Tactics of a predator. *Insect Abundance Symposium of the Royal Entomological Society of London*, 4, pp. 47–58.

Holmes, R.T. 1970. Differences in population density, territoriality and food supply of dunlin on arctic and subarctic tundra. In *Animal populations in relation to their food resources*, ed. by A. Watson. Blackwell, Oxford, pp. 303–322.

Holst, E. von. 1935. Über den Lichtrückenreflex bei Fischen. *Publicazioni della Stazione Zoologica di Napoli*, 15:143–158.

Hoogland, R., D. Morris; and N. Tinbergen. 1957. The spines of sticklebacks (*Gasterosteus* and *Pygosteus*) as means of defense against predators (*Perca* and *Esox*). *Behavior*, 10:205–236.

Horn, H.S. 1968. The adaptive significance of colonial nesting in the Brewer's blackbird (*Euphagus cyanocephalus*). *Ecology*, 49:682–694.

Howard, H.E. 1920. *Territory in bird life*. Antheneum, New York.

_____ . 1929. An introduction to the study of bird behavior. Cambridge University Press, Cambridge.

Hüchtker, R. and J. Schwartzkopff. 1958. Soziale Verhaltensveisen bei hörenden and gehörlosen Compfaffen (*Pyrrhula pyrrhula* L.). *Experientia*, 14:106–107.

Hunsaker, D. 1962. Ethological isolating mechanisms in the *Sceloporus torquatus* group of lizards. *Evolution*, 16:62–74.

Hunter, J.L. 1965. *Acoustics*. Prentice-Hall, Inc. Englewood Cliffs, N.J.

Hutchinson, G.E. 1959. Homage to Santa Rosalia or why are there so many different kinds of animals? *American Naturalist*, 93:145–159.

_____ and E.S. Deevey, Jr. 1949. Ecological studies on populations. *Survey of Biological Progress*, 1:325–359.

Huxley, J.S. 1942. *Evolution: the modern synthesis*. George Allen and Unwin, London.

_____ . 1934. A natural experiment on the territorial instinct. *British Birds*, 27:270–277.

_____ . 1938. Threat and warning coloration in birds, with a general discussion of the biological functions of color. *Proceedings of the 8th International Ornithological Congress*, Oxford: 430–455.

_____ . 1959. *Clades and grades*. Systematics Association Publication No. 3, 21–22.

Iersel, J.J.A. van. 1953. An analysis of the parental behavior of the male three-spined stickleback. *Behavior Supplement*, 3:1–159.

Immelmann, K. 1962. Biologische Bedeutung optischer und akustischer Merkmale bei Prachtfinken (Aves: Spermestidae). *Verhandlungen der Deutschen Zoologischen Gesellschaft*, Zoologischer Anzeiger Supplement, 25:369–374.

Itani, J. 1958. On the acquisition and propagation of a new food habit in the troop of Japanese monkeys at Takasakiyama. *Primates*, 1: 84–98.

_____ . 1959. Paternal care in the wild Japanese monkey, *Macaca fuscata. Primates,* Japan, 2:61–93.

Jacobs, W. 1953. Verhaltensbiologische Studien an Feldheuschrecken. Beiheft 1: *Zeitschrift für Tierpsychologie.*

Janzen, D.H. 1971. Escape of juvenile *Dioclea megacarpa* (leguminosae) vines from predators in a deciduous tropical forest. *American Naturalist,* 105:97–112.

Jarman, P. 1968. The effect of the creation of Lake Kariba upon the terrestrial ecology of the Middle Zambezi valley, with particular reference to the large mammals. Ph.D. thesis. Manchester University.

Jenkins, D. 1961. Population control in protected partridges (*perdix perdix*). *Journal of Animal Ecology,* 30:235–258.

———— . 1963. Population control in red grouse (*Lagopus lagopus scoticus*). *Proceedings of the XIII International Ornithological Congress,* pp. 690–700.

Jenkins, D.; A. Watson; and G.R. Miller. 1963. Population studies on red grouse, *Lagopus l. scoticus. Journal of Animal Ecology,* 36:97–122.

———— . 1964. Predation and red grouse populations. *Journal of Applied Ecology,* I: 183–195.

Jespersen, P. 1929. On the frequency of birds over the high Atlantic Ocean. *Verhandlung der Internationalen Ornithologischen Kongres,* 6:163–172.

Johnsgard, P.A. 1965. *Handbook of waterfowl behaviour.* Constable, London.

———— . 1967. *Animal behavior.* Wm. C. Brown, Dubuque, Iowa.

Kaada, B. 1967. Brain mechanisms related to aggressive behaviour. UCLA Forum in Medical Science. In *Aggression and defense. Neural mechanisms and social pattern.* ed. by C.D. Clemente and D.B. Lindsley. University of California Press, Berkeley.

Kagan, J. and H.A. Moss. 1962. *Birth to maturity.* John Wiley, New York.

Kahn, M.W. 1951. The effect of severe defeat at various age levels on the aggressive behavior of mice. *Journal of Genetic Psychology,* 79: 117–130.

Kalleberg, H. 1958. Observations in a stream tank of territoriality and competition in juvenile salmon and trout (*Salmo salar* L. and *S. trutta* L.). *Report of the Institute of Freshwater Research.* Drottningholm, 39:55–98.

Kalmus, H. 1955. The discrimination by the nose of the dog of individual human odours and in particular the odours of twins. *British Journal of Animal Behavior,* 3:25–31.

Kawai, M. 1965. Newly acquired pre-cultural behavior of the natural troop of Japanese monkeys on Koshima Islands. *Primates,* 6:1–30.

Kear, J. 1961. Food selection in finches with special reference to interspecific differences. *Proceedings of the Zoological Society of London,* 138:163–204.

Keenleyside, M.H.A. 1955. Some aspects of the schooling behaviour of fish. *Behaviour,* 8: 183–249.

———— and F.T. Yamamoto. 1962. Territorial behaviour of juvenile Atlantic salmon (*Salmo salar* L.). *Behaviour,* 19:139–69.

Keeton, W.T. 1969. Orientation by pigeons: Is the sun necessary? *Science,* 1965:922–928.

Kemp, G.A. and L.B. Keith. 1970. Dynamics and regulation of red squirrel (*Tamiasciurus hudsonicus*) populations. *Ecology,* 51:763–779.

Kendeigh, S.C. 1941. Territorial and mating behavior of the house wren. *Illinois Biological Monographs,* 10–1–120.

Kenney, N.T. 1968. Sharks: wolves of the sea. *National Geographic,* 133(2):222–257.

Kettlewell, H.B.D. 1956. Further selection experiments on industrial melanism in the Lepidoptera. *Heredity,* 10:287–301.

Kiester, A.R. 1971. Species density of North American amphibians and reptiles. *Systematic Zoology,* 20:127–137.

Kilham, L. 1958. Territorial behavior of wintering red-headed woodpeckers. *Wilson Bulletin,* 70: 347–348.

———— . 1958. Sealed-in winter stores of red-headed woodpeckers. *Wilson Bulletin,* 70: 107–113.

———— . 1965. Differences in feeding behavior of male and female hairy woodpeckers. *Wilson Bulletin,* 77:134–145.

———— . 1970. Feeding behavior of downy woodpeckers. I. Preference for paper birches and sexual differences. *Auk*, 87:544–556.

King, J. 1955. Social behavior, social organization and population dynamics in a black-tailed prairie dog town in the Black Hills of South Dakota. *Contributions Laboratory Vertebrate Biology*. University of Michigan, No. 67. Ann Arbor.

Klomp, H. 1954. De terreinkeus van de Kievit, *Vanellus vanellus* (L). *Ardea*, 42:1–140.

Klopfer, P.H. 1961. Observational learning in birds: the establishment of behavioral modes. *Behaviour*, 17:1–80.

——— . 1962. *Behavioral aspects of ecology.* Prentice Hall, Englewood Cliffs, N.J.

——— . 1969. *Habitats and territories.* Basic Books, New York.

——— and J.P. Hailman. 1965. Habitat selection in birds. In *Advances in the study of behavior,* ed. by D.S. Lehrman, R.A. Hinde, E. Shaw. Academic Press, New York, pp. 279–304.

——— and ——— . 1967. *Ethology's first century—An introduction to animal behavior.* Prentice-Hall. Englewood Cliffs, N.J.

——— and R.H. MacArthur. 1961. On the causes of tropical species diversity: niche overlap. *American Naturalist*, 95:223–226.

Kluijver, H.N. 1951. The population ecology of the great tit *Parus m. major* L. *Ardea*, 39:1–135.

——— and N. Tinbergen. 1953. Regulation of density in titmice. *Archives Neerlandaises de Zoologie*, 10:265–289.

——— . 1963. The determination of reproductive rates in Paridae. *Proceedings of the International Ornithological Congress*, 13:706–716.

Koch, S. 1959. *Psychology, a study of science. Study I, conceptual and systematic.* Vols. 1 and 2, McGraw-Hill, New York.

Koivisto, I. 1965. Behaviour of the black grouse *Lyrurus tetrix* (L.) during the spring display. *Finnish Game Reserve*, 26:60.

Konishi, M. 1970. Evolution of design features in the coding of species specificity. *American Zoologist*, 10:67–72.

Kormondy, E.J. 1969. *Concepts of Ecology.* Prentice-Hall, Englewood Cliffs, N.J.

Kortlandt, A. 1938. De uitdrukkingsbeweginben en -geluiden van *Phalacrocorax carbo sinensis* (Shaw and Nodder). *Ardea*, 27:1–40.

——— . 1940. Wechselwirkung zwischen Instinkten. *Archives Neerlandaises de Zoologie*, 4:442–520.

——— . 1940. Eine übersicht der angeborenen Verhaltungsweisen des Mittel-Europäischen Kormorans (*Phalacrocorax carbo sinensis* Shaw and Nodd), ihre Funktion, ontogenetische Entwicklung und phylogenetische Herkunft. *Archives Neerlandaises de Zoologie*, 4:401–442.

Kramer, G. 1949. Über Richtungstendenzen bei dernächtlichen Zugunruhe gekäfigter Vögel. In *Ornithologie als biologische Wissenschaft*. Heidelberg.

——— . 1957. Experiments in bird orientation and their interpretation. *Ibis*, 99:196–227.

——— . 1961. Long-distance orientation. In *Biology and comparative physiology of birds*, ed. by A.J. Marshall. London, pp. 341–371.

Kress, S.W. 1967. *A robin nests in winter. Wilson Bulletin*, 79:245–246.

Kruuk, H. 1964. Predators and anti-predator behavior of the black-headed gull (*Larus ridibundus* L.) *Behavior Supplement*, 11:1–129.

Kuhme, W. 1965. Freilandstudien zur Sociologie des Hyanenhundes. *Zeitschrift für Tierpsychologie*, 22:495–541.

Kullenberg, B. 1961. Studies in *Ophrys* pollination. *Zool. Bridrag*, Uppsala, 34:1–340.

Kuo, Z.Y. 1960. Studies on the basic factors in animal fighting. *Journal of Genetic Psychology*, 96:201–239.

——— . 1961. Studies on the basic factors in animal fighting. *Journal of Genetic Psychology*, 97:181–209.

Laarman, J.J. 1960. The plasticity of response patterns in host-seeking mosquitoes. *Proceedings of the XI International Congress on Entomology,* Vol. 3. Symp. 5:60–61.

Lack, D. 1933. Habitat selection in birds. *Journal of Animal Ecology*, 2:239–262.

——— . 1939. The display of the blackcock. *British Birds*, 32:290–303.

——— . 1944. Ecological aspects of species-formation in passerine birds. *Ibis*, 86:260–286.

———— . 1954. *The natural regulation of animal numbers.* Clarendon Press, Oxford.

———— . 1968. *Ecological adaptations for breeding in birds.* Methuen & Co., Ltd., London.

———— . 1969. Subspecies and sympatry in Darwin's finches. *Evolution*, 23:252–263.

———— . 1970. Introduction. In *Animal populations in relation to their food resources,* ed. by A. Watson. Blackwell, Oxford.

———— and E. Lack. 1958. The nesting of the long-tailed tit. *Bird Study*, 5:1–19.

Lanyon, W.E. 1960a. The middle American populations of the crested flycatcher *Myiarchus tyrannulus. Condor*, 62:341–350.

———— . 1960b. The ontogeny of vocalization in birds. In *Animal sounds and communication,* ed. by W.E. Lanyon and W.W. Tavolga. American Institute of Biological Sciences. Publication no. 7. Washington, D.C.

———— . 1963. Experiments on species discrimination in *Myiarchus* fly catchers. *American Museum Novitates*, No. 2126:1–16.

———— and W.N. Tavolga (eds.). 1960. *Animal sounds and communication.* American Institute of Biological Sciences, Washington, D.C.

Van Lawick-Goodall, J. 1971. *In the shadow of man.* Houghton Mifflin Co., Boston.

Leck, C.F. 1971a. Cooperative feeding in *Leucophoyx thula* and *Podilymbus podiceps* (Aves). *American Midland Naturalist*, 86:241–242.

———— . 1971b. Measurement of social attractions between tropical passerine birds. *Wilson Bulletin*, 83:278–283.

Lehrman, D.S. 1953. A critique of Konrad Lorenz's theory of instinctive behavior. *Quarterly Review of Biology*, 28:337–363.

———— . 1955. The physiological basis of parental feeding behaviour in the ringdove (*Streptopelia risoria*). *Behaviour*, 7:241–286.

———— . 1970. Semantic and conceptual issues in the nature-nurture problem. In *Development and evolution of behavior,* ed. by L.R. Aronson, E. Tobach, D.S. Lehrman, J.S. Rosenblatt. W.H. Freeman, San Francisco, pp. 17–52.

Leopold, A. 1933. *Game management.* Charles Scribner's Sons, New York.

Levene, H. 1953. Genetic equilibrium when more than one ecological niche is available. *American Naturalist*, 87:331–333.

Lewontin, R.C. 1965. Selection for colonizing ability. In *The genetics of colonizing species,* ed. by H.G. Baker and G.L. Stebbins. Academic Press, New York, pp. 77–91.

Leyhausen, P. 1956. Verhaltensstudien an Katzen. Beiheft 2 zur *Zeitschrift für Tierpsychologie.*

———— . 1965. The communal organization of solitary mammals. *Symposium of the Zoological Society of London*, 14:279–263.

Lindauer, M. 1964. Allgemeine Sinnesphysiologie: Orientierung im Raum. *Fortschritte der Zoologie*, 16:58–140.

———— . 1965. Social behavior and mutual communication. In *The physiology of insecta,* ed. by M. Rockstein. Vol. 2. Academic Press, New York, pp. 124–187.

Linicone, D.R. 1971. The goodness of parasitism: a new hypothesis. In *Aspects of the biology of symbiosis,* ed. by T.C. Cheng. University Park Press, Baltimore, pp. 139–227.

Lissmann, H.W. 1951. Continuous electrical signals from the tail of a fish *Gymnarchus niloticus. Nature* (London), 167:201–202.

Loeb, J. 1901. *Comparative physiology of the brain and comparative psychology.* London.

Lockie, J.D. 1966. Territory in small carnivores. *Symposia of the Zoological Society of London*, 18:143–65.

Lockley, R.M. 1967. *Animal navigation.* Hart Publishing Co. Inc., New York.

Lorenz, K.Z. 1931. Beiträge zur Ethologie sozialer corviden. *Journal für Ornithologie*, 79:67–127.

———— . 1935. Der Kumpan in der Umwelt des Vogels. *Journal für Ornithologie*, 83:37–213, 289–413.

———— . 1937a. Über den Begriff der Instinkthandlung. *Folia Biotheoretica*, 2:17–50.

———— . 1937b. Über die Bildung des Instinktbegriffes. *Naturwissenschaften* 25:289–300, 307–318, 324–331. (English translation in C.H. Schiller, 1957).

———— and N. Tinbergen. 1938. 1957. Taxis and Instinct. In C.H. Schiller (ed.), *Instinctive behavior*. (1957) International Universities Press, New York, pp. 176–208.

————. 1939. *Vergleichende Verhaltensforschung. Zoologishes Anzug Supplement (Verhandlung der deutschen zoologischen Gesellschaft* 41), 12:69–102.

———— and N. Tinbergen, 1939. Taxis und Instinkthandlung in der Eirollbewegung der Graugans I. *Zeitschrift für Tierpsychology.* 2:1–29.

————. 1941. Vergleichende Bewegungstudien an Anatinen. *Journal für Ornithologie,* Leipzig, 89:94–293.

————. 1950. The comparative method in studying innate behaviour patterns. *Symposium of the Society of Experimental Biology,* 4:221–268.

————. 1952. *King Solomon's ring,* trans. by M.K. Wilson. Thomas Y. Crowell, New York.

————. 1957. Companionship in bird life and other essays. In *Instinctive behavior,* ed. by C.H. Schiller. International Universities Press, New York.

————. 1958. The evolution of behavior. *Scientific American,* 199:67–78.

————. 1961. Phylogenetische Anpassung und adaptive Modifikation des Verhaltens. *Zeitschrift für Tierpsychologie,* 18:139–187.

————. 1963. *On Aggression.* (transl. 1966) *Zeitschrift für Tierpsychologie,* Harcourt, Brace and World, New York.

————. 1965. *Evolution and modification of behavior.* University of Chicago Press, Chicago.

————. 1969. Innate bases of learning. In *On the biology of learning,* ed. by K.H. Pribram. Harcourt, Brace and World. New York, pp. 13–93.

Lotka, A.J. 1925. *Elements of physical biology.* Baltimore.

MacArthur, R.H. 1959. On the breeding distribution pattern of North American migrant birds. *Auk,* 76:318–325.

———— and R. Levins. 1964. Competition, habitat selection and character displacement in a patchy environment. *Proceedings of the National Academy of Science, U.S.A.,* 51:1207–1210.

———— and E.O. Wilson. 1963. An equilibrium theory of insular zoogeography. *Evolution,* 17:373–387.

————. 1967. *The theory of island biogeography.* Princeton University Press. New Jersey.

McConnell, J.V. 1962. Memory transfer through cannibalism. *Journal of Neuropsychiatry,* 3:542–548.

————; A.L. Jacobson; and D.P. Kimble. 1959. The effects of regeneration upon retention of a conditioned response in the planarian. *Journal of Comparative Physiological Psychology,* 52:1–5.

McDougall, W. 1905. *Physiological psychology.* London.

Magnus, D. 1958. Experimentalle Untersuchungen zur Bionomie und Ethologie des Kaisermantels *Argynnis paphia* L. (Lep. Nymph). I. Uber optische Auslöser von Angliegeralktionen und ihre Bedeutung für das Sichfinden der Geschechter. *Zeitschrift für Tierpsychologie,* 15:397–426.

Maier, R.A. and B.M. Maier. 1970. *Comparative animal behavior.* Brooks/Cole. Belmont, Calif.

Makkink, G.F. 1942. Contribution to the knowledge of the behaviour of the oyster catcher (*Haematopus ostralegus* L.) *Ardea,* 31:23–74.

Manning, A. 1959. The sexual behaviour of two sibling *Drosophila* species. *Behaviour,* 15:123–145.

————. 1961. The effects of artificial selection for mating speed in *Drosophila melanogaster. Animal Behavior,* 9:82–92.

————. 1965. *Drosophila* and the evolution of behaviour. *Viewpoints in Biology,* 4:125–169.

————. 1967. *An introduction to animal behavior.* Addison-Wesley. Reading, Mass.

————. 1971. Evolution of behavior. In *Psychobiology,* ed. by J.L. McGaugh. Academic Press, New York, pp. 1–52.

Marler, P. 1956. The voice of the chaffinch and its function as a language. *Ibis,* 98:231–261.

————. 1957a. Specific distinctiveness in the communication signals of birds. *Behaviour,* 11:13–39.

————. 1957b. Studies of fighting in chaffinches (4.). *Appetitive and consummatory behavior*, 5:29–37.

_____ . 1959. Developments in the study of animal communication. In *Darwin's Biological work*, ed. by P.R. Bell. Cambridge University Press, Cambridge, pp. 150–206.

_____ . 1961a. The evolution of visual communication. In *Vertebrate speciation*, ed. by W.F. Blair. University of Texas Press, Austin, pp. 96–121.

_____ . 1961b. The filtering of external stimuli during instinctive behavior. In *Current problems in animal behavior*, Cambridge University Press, New York, pp. 150–166.

_____ and W.J. Hamilton, III. 1966. *Mechanisms of animal behavior*. John Wiley and Sons, Inc., New York.

_____ and M. Tamura. 1962. Song "dialects" in three populations of white crowned sparrows. *Condor*, 64:368–377.

Martin, M.M. 1970. The biochemical basis of the fungus-attine ant symbiosis. *Science*, 169: 16–20.

Mason, W.A. 1965. The social development of monkeys and apes. In *Primate behavior*, ed. by I. De Vore. Holt, Rinehart and Winston, New York.

Matthews, G.V.T. 1955. *Bird navigation*. Cambridge University Press, Cambridge.

_____ . 1963. The orientation of pigeons as affected by the learning of landmarks and by the distance of displacement. *Animal Behavior*, 11:310–317.

_____ . 1968. *Bird navigation* (2nd ed.). Cambridge University Press, Cambridge.

Mayersbach, H. von. 1967. *The cellular aspects of biorhythms*. Springer, New York.

Mayr, E. 1942. *Systematics and the origin of the species*. Columbia University Press, New York.

_____ . 1948. The bearing of the new systematics on genetical problems. The nature of species. *Advances in genetics*, 2:205–237.

_____ . 1958. Behavior and systematics. In *Evolution and behavior*, ed. by A. Roe and G.G. Simpson. Yale University Press, New Haven, pp. 341–362.

_____ . 1963. *Animal species and evolution*. Harvard University Press, Cambridge.

_____ . 1965. The nature of colonization in birds. In *Genetics of colonizing species*, ed. by H.G. Baker and G.L. Stebbins. Academic Press, New York.

Meisenheimer, J. 1921. *Geschlecht und Geschlechter im Tierreich*. Jena.

Menaker, M. 1969. Biological clocks. *Bioscience*, 19:681–689.

Meyer, M.E. 1964. Discriminative basis for astronavigation in birds. *Journal of Comparative Physiology and Psychology*, 58:403–406.

Meyer-Holzapfel, M. 1958. Soziale Beziehungen bei Saugetieren. In *Gestaltungen sozialen Lebens bei Tier und Mensch*, ed. F.E. Lehmann. Franke, Bern. pp. 86–109.

Miller, N.E. 1961. Integration of neurophysiological and behavioral research. *Annals of the New York Academy of Science*, 92:830–839.

_____ . 1969. Learning of visceral and glandular responses. *Science*, 163:434–445.

_____ and A. Carmona. 1967. Modification of a visceral response, salivation in thirsty dogs, by instrumental training with water reward. *Journal of Comparative Physiology and Psychology*, 63:1–6.

_____ and L.V. DiCara. 1967. Instrumental learning of heart rate changes in curarized rats: shaping, and specificity to discriminative stimulus. *Journal of Comparative Physiology and Psychology*, 63:12–19.

Moment, G. 1962. Variation in brittle stars. *Science*, 136:262–263.

Montagu, M.F. 1962. *Culture and the evolution of man*. Oxford University Press. New York.

Monteith, L.G. 1958. Influence of food plant of host on attractiveness of the host to tachinid parasites with notes on preimaginal conditioning. *Canadian Entomology*, 90:478–482.

Moreau, R.E. 1966. *The bird faunas of Africa and its islands*. Academic Press, New York.

Morgan, L.C. 1894. *Introduction to comparative psychology*. Arnold. London.

Morris, D. 1957. "Typical intensity" and its relation to the problem of ritualisation. *Behaviour*, 11:1–12.

_____ . 1962. The behavior of an experimental colony of wild rabbits, *Oryctalagus cuniculus* (L), III Second breeding season. *Wildlife research*. 5:120.

Morse, D.H. 1969. Ecological aspects of some mixed-species foraging flocks of birds. *Ecological Monographs,* 40:119–168.

———— . 1971. The foraging of warblers isolated on small islands. *Ecology,* 52:216–228.

Moynihan, M. 1960. Some adaptations which help to promote gregariousness. *Proceedings of the 12th International Ornithological Congress,* 523–541.

———— . 1962a. Hostile and sexual behavior patterns of South American and Pacific Laridae. *Behaviour Supplement,* 8, pp. 1–365.

———— . 1962b. The organization and probable evolution of some mixed species flocks of neotropical birds. *Smithsonian Miscellaneous Collection,* 143:1–140, No. 7.

———— . 1963. Inter-specific relations between some Andean birds. *Ibis,* 105:327–339.

———— . 1968. Social mimicry: character convergence versus character displacement. *Evolution,* 22:315–331.

———— . 1971. Successes and failures of tropical mammals and birds. *American Naturalist,* 105:371–383.

———— and F. Hall. 1953. Hostile sexual and other social behaviour patterns of the spice finch (*Lonchura punctulata*) in captivity. *Behaviour,* 7:33–77.

Mueller, H.C. and D.D. Berger. 1970. Prey preferences in the sharp-shinned hawk: the roles of sex, experience and motivation. *Auk,* 87:452–457.

Muir, R.C. 1954. Calling and feeding rates of fledged tawny owls. *Bird Study,* 1:111–117.

Murdoch, W.W. 1966. Community Structure, Population Control, and Competition: A Critique. *American Naturalist,* 100:219–226.

Murie, A. 1944. The wolves of Mount McKinley. *Fauna of the national parks of the U.S.A.* Fauna Series, 5.

Murphy, R.C. 1936. *Oceanic birds of South America.* Macmillan Co., New York.

Murray, B.G. 1971. The ecological consequences of interspecific territorial behavior in birds. *Ecology,* 52:414–423.

Murton, R.K.; A.T. Isaacson; and K.T. Westwood. 1964. The relationships between woodpigeons and their clover food supply and the mechanism of population control. *Journal of Applied Ecology,* 3:55–96.

Myers, K. 1966. The effects of density on sociality and health in mammals. *Proceedings of the Ecological Society of Australia,* 1:40–64.

Nelson, J.B. 1967. Etho-ecological adaptations in the Great Frigate-bird. *Nature,* 214:318.

Nice, M.M. 1937. Studies in the life history of the song sparrow. I. *Transactions of the Linnaean Society,* New York, 4.

———— . 1943. Studies in the life history of the song sparrow, I, II. *Transactions of the Linnaean Society,* N.Y., 4:1–247, 6:1–328.

Nicholson, A.J. 1933. The balance of animal populations. *Journal of Animal Ecology,* 2: 132–178.

———— and V.A Bailey. 1935. The balance of animal populations. *Proceedings of the Zoological Society of London,* 1935:551–598.

———— . 1954. An outline of the dynamics of animal populations. *Australian Journal of Zoology,* 2:9–65.

———— . 1957. Comments on paper of T.B. Reynoldson. Cold Spring Harbor Symposia on Quantitative Biology, 22:326.

———— . 1958. The self-adjustment of populations to change. In *Population studies: Animal ecology and demography.* Cold Spring Harbor Symposia on Quantitative Biology, Vol. XXII. Cold Spring Harbor, L.I. pp. 153–172.

Noble, G.K. 1936. Courtship and sexual selection of the flicker (*Colaptes auratus lutus*). *Auk,* 53:269–282.

Odum, E.P. 1942. Annual cycle of the black-capped chickadee. *Auk,* 59:499–535.

———— . 1971. *Fundamentals of ecology.* 3rd ed., W.B. Saunders. Philadelphia.

Orians, G.H. 1961. Social stimulation within blackbird colonies. *Condor,* 63:330–337.

———— and G. Collier. 1963. Competition and blackbird social systems. *Evolution,* 17:449–459.

———— and M.F. Willson. 1964. Interspecific territories of birds. *Ecology,* 45:736–745.

Osche, G. 1962. Okologie des Parasitismus und der Symbiose. *Fortschrift der Zoologie,* 15: 125–164.

_____ . 1966. Amniotic contractions and embryonic motility in the chick embryo. *Science*, 152:528–529.

Palmer, J.D. 1970. In *The biological clock: two views*. By F.A. Brown, J.W. Hastings, J.D. Palmer. Academic Press, New York, pp. 3–12.

Patterson, I.J. 1965. Timing and spacing of broods in the blackheaded gull (*Larus ridibundus*). *Ibis*, 107:433–459.

Paulson, D.R. 1969. Commensal feeding in grebes. *Auk*, 86:759.

Pavlov, I.P. 1927. Conditioned reflexes: an investigation of the activity of the cerebral cortex. *Transaction of G.V. Anrep*. London.

Pearson, O.P. 1947. The rate of metabolism of some small mammals. *Ecology*, 28:127–145.

Peckham, G.W. and E.G. Peckham. 1898. On the instincts and habits of the solitary wasps. *Wisconsin Geology and Natural History Survey Bulletin*, No. 2.

Pelkwijk, J.J. Ter and N. Tinbergen. 1937. Eine reizbiologische Analyse einiger Verhaltensweisen von *Gasterosteus aculeatus* L. *Zeitschrift für Tierpsychologie*, 1:193–204.

Penney, R.L. and J.T. Emlen. 1967. Further experiments on distance navigation in the Adélie penguin. *Ibis*, 109:99–109.

Phillips, R.E. 1964. "Wildness" in the mallard duck: effects of brain lesions and stimulation on "escape behavior" and reproduction. *Journal of Comparative Neurology*, 122:139–155.

Pianka, E. 1970. On r- and K- selection. *American Naturalist*, 104:592–597.

Pielowski, Z. 1961. Über die Vertikalverteilung der Vögel in einem Pineto-Quercetum Biotop. *Ekologia Polska Seria* A, 9:1–23.

Pitelka, F.A. 1942. Territoriality and related problems in North American hummingbirds. *Condor*, 44:189–204.

Pittendrigh, C.S. and D.H. Minis. 1964. The entrainment of circadian oscillations by light and their role as photoperiodic clocks. *American Naturalist* 98:261–294.

Pribram, K.H. (ed.). 1969. *On the biology of learning*. Harcourt, Brace and World, New York.

Pritchatt, D. 1968. Avoidance of electric shock by the cockroach *Periplaneta americana*. *Animal Behavior*, 16:178–185.

Rand, A.L. 1954. Social feeding behavior of birds. *Fieldiana: Zoologica*, 36:1–71.

Rasa, O.A.E. 1969. The effect of pair isolation on reproductive success in *Etroplus maculatus* (Cichlidae). *Zeitschrift für Tierpsychologie*, 19:645–651.

Rheingold, H.L. 1963. Maternal behavior in mammals. John Wiley & Sons. New York.

Ripley, S.D. 1961. Aggressive neglect as a factor in interspecific competition in birds. *Auk*, 78:366–371.

Ritter, W.E. 1938. *The California woodpecker and I*. University of California Press, Berkeley.

Roberts, B.B. 1934. Notes on the birds of central and south-east Iceland. *Ibis*, 4:239–264.

Romane, A. 1961. Gedanken zum Problem: Homologie und Analogie, Praeadaptation und Parallelitat. *Zoologischer Anzeiger*, 166:447–470.

Romer, A.S. 1941. *Man and the vertebrates*. 3rd. ed. University of Chicago Press, Chicago.

_____ . 1958. Phylogeny and behavior with special reference to vertebrate evolution. In *Behavior and evolution*, ed. by A. Roe and G.G. Simpson. Yale University Press, New Haven, pp. 48–75.

_____ . 1970. *The vertebrate body*. W.B. Saunders, Philadelphia.

Rooke, K.B. 1947. Notes on robins wintering in North Algeria. *Ibis*, 89:204–210.

Rosen, D.E. and M. Gordon. 1953. Functional anatomy and evolution of male genitalia in poecilid fishes. *Zoologica* (N.Y.), 38:1–47.

Rosenbaum, L.A. and R.W. Cooper. 1968. *The squirrel monkey*. Academic Press, New York.

Roth, L.M. and E.R. Willis. 1952. A study of cockroach behaviour. *American Midland Naturalist*, 47:66–129.

Rothenbuhler, W.C. 1964a. Behaviour genetics of nest cleaning in honeybees. I. Responses of four inbred lines to disease-killed brood. *Animal Behaviour*, 12:578–583.

_____ . 1966b. Behavior genetics of nest cleaning in honeybees. IV. Responses of F_1 and backcross generations to disease-killed brood. *American Zoologist*, 4:111–123.

Rothstein, S.I. 1970. An investigation of the defenses of the hosts of the parasitic brown-headed cowbird (*Molothrus ater*). Ph.D. Dissertation. Yale University, New Haven.

Rowell, T.E. 1966. Hierarchy in the organization of a captive baboon group. *Animal Behavior*, 14:420–443.

Rowley, I. 1965. The life history of the superb blue wren, *Malarus cyancus*. *Emu*, 64:251–297.

Ruiter, L. de 1955. Countershading in caterpillars. *Archives Neerlandaises de Zoologie*, 11:1–57.

Sackett, G.P. 1966. Monkeys reared in visual isolation with pictures as visual input. Evidence for an innate releasing mechanism. *Science*, 154:1468–1472.

Sauer, F. 1955. Uber Varcatonen der Artgesange bie Grasmücken. *Journal für Ornithologie*, 96:129–146.

————. 1957. Die Sternenorientierung nachtlich ziehender Grasmücken (*Sylvia atricapilla, borin* und curruca). *Zeitschrift für Tierpsychologie*, 14:29–70.

———— and E.M. Sauer. 1955. Zur Frage der nächtlichen Zugorientierung von Grasmücken. *Revue Suisse de Zoologie*, 62:250–259.

Saunders, J.W. and M.W. Smith. 1962. Physical alteration of stream habitat to improve trout production. *Transactions of the American Fisheries Society*, 91:185–8.

Schaller, G.B. 1963. *The mountain gorilla*. University of Chicago Press, Chicago.

———— and G.R. Lowther. 1969. The relevance of carnivore behavior to the study of early hominids. *Southwestern Journal of Anthropology*, 24:307–341.

Schenkel, R. 1966. Zum Problem der Territorialität und des Markierens bei Säugern—am Beispiel des Schwarzen Nashorns und des Löwen. *Zeitschrift für Tierpsychologie*, 23:593–626.

Schiller, C.H. 1957. *Instinctive behavior: the development of a modern concept*. International Universities Press, New York.

Schmidt-Koenig, K. 1965. Current problems in bird orientation. In *Advances in the study of behavior*, ed. by E. Hinde, K. Lehrman, and E. Shaw. New York, pp. 217–278.

Schneider, D. 1962. Electrophysiological investigation on the olfactory specificity of sexual attracting substances in different species of moths. *Journal of Insect Physiology*, 8:15–30.

Schneirla, T.C. 1956. The interrelationships of the "innate" and the "acquired" in instinctive behavior. In *L'instinct dans le comportement des animaux et de l'homme*. Masson, Paris. pp. 387–452.

————. 1959. An evolutionary and developmental theory of biphasic processes underlying approach and withdrawal. *Nebraska Symposium on Motivation*, 1–42.

————. 1966. Behavioural development and comparative psychology. *Quarterly Review of Biology*, 41:283–302.

Schoener, T.W. 1965. The evolution of bill size differences among sympatric congeneric species of birds. *Evolution*, 19:189–213.

————. 1968. Sizes of feeding territories among birds. *Ecology*, 49:123–141.

————. 1970. Size patterns in West Indian Anolis lizards. II. Correlations with the sizes of particular sympatric species-displacement and convergence. *American Naturalist*, 104:155–174.

Schüz, E. 1949. Die Spät-Auflassung ostpreussischer Jungstörche in West-Deutschland durch die Vogelwaste Rossitten 1933. *Vogelwarte*, 15:63–78.

Schwink, I. 1958. A study of olfactory stimuli in the orientation of moths. *Proceedings of the Xth International Congress on Entomology*, (1956), 2:577–582.

Scott, J.P. 1945. Social behavior, organization and leadership in a small flock of domestic sheep. *Comparative Psychology Monograph* No. 96, 18:1–29.

————. 1960. *Aggression*. University of Chicago Press, Chicago.

————. 1966. Agonistic behavior of mice and rats: a review. In *Animal Aggression; selected readings*, ed. by C.H. Southwick. Van Nostrand Reinhold, New York, pp. 103–128.

Seilacher, A. 1967. Fossil Behavior. *Scientific American*, 217(2):72–80.

Seitz, A. 1940. Die Paarbildung bei einigen Chichliden. I. Die Paarbildung bei *Astatotilapia strigigena* (Pfeffer). *Zeitschrift zür Tierpsychologie*, 4:40–84.

———— . 1942. Die Paarbildung bei einigen Cichliden. II. Die Paarbildung bei *Hemichromis bimaculatus*. *Zeitschrift zür Tierpsychologie*, 5:74–101.

Selander, R.K. 1965. On mating systems and natural selection. *American Naturalist*, 99:129–141.

———— . 1966. Sexual dimorphism and differential niche utilization in birds. *Condor*, 68:113–151.

Shaw, C.E. 1948. The male combat "dance" of some crotalid snakes. *Herpetologica*, 4:137–145.

Sherrington, C.S. 1906. *The integrative action of the nervous system*. New York.

Short, L.L. Jr. 1961. Interspecies flocking of birds of montane forest in Oaxaca, Mexico. *Wilson Bulletin*, 73:341–347.

———— . 1970. The habits and relationships of the Magellanic woodpecker. *Wilson Bulletin*, 82:115–129.

Sibley, C.G. 1957. The evolutionary and taxonomic significance of sexual dimorphism and hybridization in birds. *Condor*, 59:166–191.

———— . 1961. Hybridization and isolating mechanisms. In *Vertebrate speciation*, ed. by W.F. Blair:69–88. University of Texas Press, Austin.

Siebenaler, J.B. and D.K. Caldwell. 1956. Cooperation among adult dolphins. *Journal of Mammology*, 37:126–128.

Simberloff, D. 1970. Taxonomic diversity of island biotas. *Evolution*, 24:22–47.

———— . 1971. Population sizes of congeneric bird species on islands. *American Naturalist*, 105:190–193.

Simmons, R.E.L. 1951. Interspecific territorialism. *Ibis*, 93:407–418.

Simmons, K.E.L. 1970. Ecological determinants of breeding adaptations and social behaviour in two fish-eating birds. In *Social behaviour in birds and mammals*, ed. by J.H. Crook. Methuen, London, pp. 37–77.

Simpson, G.G. 1958. Behavior and evolution. In *Behavior and evolution*, ed. by A. Roe and G.G. Simpson. Yale University Press, New Haven, pp. 7–26, 507–535.

———— . 1961. *Principles of animal taxonomy*. Columbia University Press, New York.

Skinner, B.F. 1938. *The behavior of organisms*. Appleton-Century-Croft, New York.

Skutch, A.F. 1961. Helpers among birds. *Condor*, 63:198–226.

Slobodkin, L.B. 1968. How to be a predator. *American Zoologist*, 8:43–51.

Smith, F.E. 1961. Density dependence in the Australian thrips. *Ecology*, 42:403–407.

Smith, J.M. 1964. Group selection and kin selection. *Nature*, 201:1145-1147.

———— and M.G. Ridpath. 1972. Wife sharing in the Tasmanian native hen, *Tribonex mortierii*: A Case of Kin Selection? *American Naturalist*, 106:447–452.

Smythe, N. 1970. On the existence of "pursuit invitation" signals in mammals. *American Naturalist*, 104:491–494.

Solomon, M.E. 1957. Dynamics of insect populations. *Annual Review of Entomology*, 2:121–142.

Soulé, M. 1970. A comment on the letter by Van Valen and Grant. *American Naturalist*, 104:590–591.

———— and B.R. Stewart. 1970. The "niche-variation" hypothesis: a test and alternatives. *American Naturalist*, 104:85–97.

Southwick, C.H. 1955. The population dynamics of confined house mice supplied with unlimited food. *Ecology*, 36:212–25.

———— . 1970. *Animal aggression: selected readings*. Van Nostrand Reinhold Co., New York.

———— , M.A. Beg and M.R. Siddigi. 1965. Rhesus monkeys in North India. In *Primate behavior*, ed. by I. DeVore. Holt, Rinehart and Winston, New York.

Sperry, R.W. 1958. Developmental basis of behavior. In *Behavior and evolution*, ed. by A. Roe and G.G. Simpson. Harvard University Press, New Haven, pp. 128–139.

Spieth, H.T. 1952. Mating behavior within the genus *Drosophila* (Diptera). *Bulletin of the American Museum of Natural History*, 99:401–474.

Stenger, J. 1958. Food habits and available food of ovenbirds in relation to territory size. *Auk*, 75:335–346.

Stewart, R.E. and J.W. Aldrich. 1951. Removal and repopulation of breeding birds in a spruce-fir forest community. *Auk*, 68:471–482.

Stoddard, H.L. 1931. *The bobwhite quail: its habits, preservation and increase.* Scribner's. New York.

Stokes, A.W. 1962a. Agonistic behaviour among blue tits at a winter feeding station. *Behaviour*, 19:118–138.

————. 1962b. Comparative ethology of great, blue, marsh and coal tits at a winter feeding station. *Behaviour*, 19:208–218.

————. 1969. Aggressive man and aggressive beast. 39th Honor Faculty Lecture. Utah State University.

Stonehouse, B. 1960. The King Penguin *Aptenodytes pategonica* of South Georgia. I. Breeding behaviour and development. *Scientific Reports on the Falkland Islands Dependencies Survey*, 23:1–181.

Stoner, E.A. 1947. Anna hummingbirds at play. *Condor*, 49:36.

Storer, R.W. 1952. Variation in the resident sharp-shinned hawks of Mexico. *Condor*, 54:283–289.

Stout, J.F. 1963. The significance of sound production during the reproductive behaviour of *Notropis analostanus* (Family Cyprinidae). *Animal Behavior*, 11:83–92.

Stride, G.O. 1958. On the courtship behavior of a tropical mimetic butterfly, *Hypolimnas misipus* L. (Nymphalidae). *Proceedings of the Xth International Congress of Entomology* (1956), 2:419–424.

Sweeney, B.M. 1969. *Rhythmic phenomena in plants.* Academic Press. New York.

Svärdson, G. 1949. Competition and habitat selection in birds. *Oikos*, 1:157–174.

Tavolga, W.M. 1956. Visual, chemical and sound stimuli as cues in sex discriminatory behavior of the Gobiid fish, *Bathygobius sporator*. *Zoologica*, 41:49–64.

————. 1960. Sound production and underwater communication in fishes. In *Animal sounds and communication*, ed. by W.E. Lanyon and W.N. Tavolga. AIBS. Washington, D.C., pp. 93–136.

————. (ed.). 1964. Sonic characteristics and mechanisms in marine fishes. In *Marine bioacoustics*. Macmillan, New York.

Taylor, D.H. and D.E. Ferguson. 1970. Extraoptic celestial orientation in the southern cricket frog *Acris gryllus*. *Science*, 168:390–392.

Telle, H.J. 1966. Beitrag zur Kenntnis der Verhaltensweise bei Ratten, vergleichend dargestellt bei *Rattus norvegicus* und *Rattus rattus*. *Angewandte Zoologie*, 9:129–196.

ter Pelkwijk, J.N., and N. Tinbergen. Eine reizbiologische analyse einiger Verhaltensweisen von Gasterosteus aculeatus L., *Zeitschrift für Tierpsychologie*, 1, 1937, 193–200.

Thayer, G.H. 1909. *Concealing-coloration in the animal kingdom.* Macmillan, New York.

Thielcke, G. 1961. Stammesgeschichte und geographische Variation des Gesanges unserer Baumlaufer (*Certhis familiaris* L. und *Certhis brachydactyla* Brehm). *Zeitschrift für Tierpsychologie*, 18:188–204.

Thompson, W.R. 1939. Biological control and the theories of the interactions of populations. *Parasitology*, 31:299–388.

Thorndike, E.L. 1911. *Animal intelligence.* New York.

Thorpe, W.H. 1961. *Bird Song: The biology of vocal communication and expression in birds.* Cambridge University Press, Cambridge.

————. 1963. (first edition 1956). *Learning and instinct in animals.* Harvard Press, Cambridge.

———— and O.L. Zangwill. 1961. *Current problems in animal behavior.* Cambridge University Press, Cambridge.

Tiger, L. 1969. *Men in groups.* Random House, New York.

Tinbergen, N. 1940. Die Ubersprungbewegung. *Zeitschrift für Tierpsychologie*, 4:1–40.

————. 1942. An objectivistic study of the innate behaviour of animals. *Bibliotheca Biotheoretica*, Leiden, 1:37–98.

————. 1948a. Social releasers and the experimental method required for their study. *Wilson Bulletin*, 60:6–52.

————. 1948b. Dierkundeles in het meeuwendiun. *De Levende Natuur*, 51:49–56.

————. 1951. *The study of instinct.* Oxford University Press, London.

_____ . 1952a. Derived activities: their causation, function and origin. *Quarterly Review of Biology*, 27:1–32.

_____ . 1952b. On the significance of territory in the herring gull. *Ibis*, 94:158–159.

_____ . 1952c. The curious behavior of the stickleback. In *Psychobiology. Readings from Scientific American* (1966). W.H. Freeman, San Francisco. pp. 5–9.

_____ . 1953a. *Social behaviour in animals, with special reference to vertebrates.* Methuen, London.

_____ . 1953b. Specialists in nest building. *Country Life*, Jan. 30, 270–271.

_____ . 1953c. The herring gull's world. Collins. London.

_____ . 1958. *Curious naturalists.* Basic Books. New York.

_____ and D.V. Kuenen, Uber die auslösenden und die richtunggebenden Reizsituationen der Sperrbewegung von jungen Drosseln (Turdus m. merula und T. e. erictorum Turton), *Zeitschrift für Tierpsychologie*, 15 1958, 340–380.

_____ . 1959. Comparative studies of the behaviour of gulls (Laridae): a progress report. *Behaviour*, 15:1–70.

_____ . 1962. The evolution of animal communication—a critical examination of methods. *Symposia of the Zoological Society of London*, no. 8, pp. 1–6.

_____ . 1963. On aims and methods of ethology. *Zeitschrift für Tierpsychologie*, 20:410–433.

_____ . 1964. *Social behaviour in animals.* Barnes & Noble, New York.

_____ . 1965a. *Animal behavior.* Time, Incorporated, New York.

_____ . 1965b. Behavior and natural selection. In *Ideas in evolution and behavior*, ed. by J.A. Moore. Vol. 6. *Proceedings of the XVIth International Congress of Zoology.* Natural History Press. New York.

_____ . 1967. Adaptive features of the Black-Headed Gull (*Larus ridibundus* L.). *Proceedings of the XIVth International Ornithological Congress*, Oxford, 1966. Blackwell. Oxford, pp. 43–59.

_____ . 1968. On war and peace in animals and men. *Science*, 160:1411–1418.

Tinbergen, N., G.J. Brockhuysen, F. Feekes, J.C.W. Houghton, H. Kruuk and E. Szulc. 1962. Eggshell removal by the black-headed gull, *Larus ridibundus* L.: a behavior component of camouflage. *Behaviour*, 19:74–118.

_____; M. Impekoven; and D. Franck. 1967. An experiment in spacing-out as a defense against predation. *Behaviour*, 28:307–321.

_____ and D.J. Kuenen. 1939. Uber die auslosenden und die richtunggebenden Reizsituationen der Sperrbewegung von jungen Drosseln (*Turdus m. merula* L. und *T. e. ericetorum* Turton). *Zeitschrift für Tierpsychologie*, 3:37–60.

_____ and A.C. Perdeck. 1950. On the stimulus situation releasing the begging response in the newly hatched herring gull chick (*Larus argentatus argentatus* Pont). *Behaviour*, 3:1–39.

Todd, J.H. 1971. The chemical language of fishes. *Scientific American*, 224:98–108.

Tolman, E.C. 1937. The acquisition of string-pulling by rats—conditioned response or sign gestalt? *Psychology Review*, 44:195–211.

Tompa, F.S. 1962. Territorial behavior: the main controlling factor of a local song sparrow population. *Auk*, 79:687–697.

_____ . 1964. Factors determining the numbers of song sparrows *Melospiza melodia* (Wilson) on Mandarte Island, B.C. Canada. *Arcta Zool. fenn.*, 109, 1–68.

Trager, W. 1970. *Symbiosis.* Van Nostrand Reinhold Co., New York.

Trowill, J.A. 1967. Instrumental conditioning of the heart rate in the curarized rat. *Journal of Comparative Psychology*, 63:7–11.

Ulrich, J. 1938. The social hierarchy in albino mice. *Journal of Comparative Physiology and Psychology*, 25:373–413.

Van den Assem, J. 1967. Territory in the three-spined stickleback *Gasterosteus aculeatus*. L. *Behaviour supplement*, 16.

Van Valen, L. 1965. Morphological variation and width of ecological niche. *American Naturalist*, 99:377–390.

———— and P.R. Grant. 1970. Variation and niche width reexamined. *American Naturalist*, 104:589–590.

Varley, G.C. 1941. On the search for hosts and the egg distribution of some chalcid parasites of the Knapweed Gall-fly. *Parasitology*, 33: 47–66.

———— . 1953. Ecological aspects of population regulation. *Transactions of the IXth International Congress of Entomology*, 2:210–214.

Vernberg, J.F. and W.B. Vernberg. *The animal and the environment*. Holt, Rinehart and Winston, New York.

Volterra, V. 1926. Variazioni e fluttuzaioni del numero d'individui in specie animale conviventi. *Atti dell' Accademia Nazionale dei Lincei Memorie* (6), 2:31–113.

Voute, A.D. 1946. Regulation of the density of the insect populations in virgin forests and cultivated woods. *Archives Neerlandaises de Biologie*, 7:435–470.

Vowles, D.M. 1954. The orientation of ants. I. The substitution of stimuli. *Journal of Experimental Biology*, 31:341–355.

Vuilleumier, F. 1967. Mixed species flocks in Patagonian forest, with remarks on interspecies flock formation. *Condor*, 69:400–404.

Wahlert, Gerd von. 1965. The role of ecological factors in the origin of higher levels of organization. *Systematic Zoology*, 14:288–300.

Walcott, C. and M. Michener. 1967. Analysis of single tracks of homing pigeons. *Proceedings of the XIVth Ornithological Congress*, 311–329.

Wall, W. van de. 1963. Bewegungsstudien an anatinen. *Journal für Ornithologie*, Leipzig, 104:1–15.

Wallace, B. and A.M. Srb. 1964. *Adaptation*. Prentice-Hall, Englewood Cliffs, New Jersey.

Wallace, R.A. 1969. Sexual dimorphism, niche utilization, and social behavior in insular species of woodpeckers. Ph.D. Dissertation. University of Texas at Austin. Austin, Texas.

Walther, F.R. 1958. Zum Kampf-und Paarungsverhalten einiger Antilopen. *Zeitschrift für Tierpsychologie*, 15:340–380.

———— . 1961. Enlwickungszüge im Kampf und Paarungsverhalten der Horntiere. *Jahrbuch der Gesellschaft von Opel-Freigehege Tierforschung*, 3:90–115.

Ward, P. 1965. Feeding ecology of the black-faced dioch *Quelea quelea* in Nigeria. *Ibis*, 107:173–214.

Washburn, S.L. and V. Avis. 1958. Evolution of human behavior. In *Evolution and behavior*, ed. by A. Roe and G.G. Simpson. Yale University Press, New Haven, pp. 421–436.

———— and D.A. Hamburg. 1965. The study of primate behavior. In *Primate behavior*, ed. by I. DeVore. Holt, Rinehart and Winston, New York, pp. 1–13.

Watson, A. 1964. Aggression and population regulation in red grouse. *Nature*, London, 202: 506–7.

———— . 1967. Population control by territorial behavior in the red grouse. *Nature*, 215:1274–1275.

———— and R. Moss. 1970. Dominance, spacing behaviour and aggression in relation to population limitation in vertebrates. In *Animal populations in relation to their food resources*, ed. by A. Watson. Blackwell, Oxford, pp. 167–220.

Watson, G.E. 1962. Three sibling species of *Alectoris* partridge. *Ibis*, 104:353–367.

Watson, J.B. 1913. Psychology as the behaviorist views it. *Psychology Review*, 20:158–177.

Watts, C.R. and A.W. Stokes. 1971. The social order of turkeys. *Scientific American*, 224: 112–118 (June).

Weeden, J.S. and J.B. Falls. 1959. Differential responses of male ovenbrids to recorded songs of neighboring and more distant individuals. *Auk*, 76:343–351.

Weichert, C.K. 1965. *Anatomy of the chordates*. McGraw-Hill, New York.

Weiss, P.A. 1941. Self-differentiation of the basic patterns of coordination. *Comparative Psychology Monographs*, 17:1–96.

Wells, M.J. 1959. Functional evidence for neurone fields representing the individual arms within the central nervous system of *Octopus*. *Journal of Experimental Biology*, 36:501–511.

Wenner, A. 1971. *The bee language controversy*. Educ. Programs Improvement Corp., Boulder Colo.

Wertheimer, M. 1912. Experimentelle Studien über das Sehen von Bewegung. *Z. Psychol.*, 61:161–265.

Whitman, C.O. 1899. Animal behavior. Biological Lectures, Summer Session, 1897–1898, Wood's Hole. pp. 285–338.

———— . 1919. The behavior of pigeons. Posthumous works of C.O. Whitman, 3:1–161. Ed by H.A. Parr. Publ. Carneg. Instn., 257.

Whittaker, R.H. 1970. Communities and ecosystems. Macmillan. New York.

———— and P.P. Feeny. 1971. Allelochemics: Chemical interactions between species. *Science*, 171:757–770.

Wickler, W. 1961. Okologie und Stammesgeschichte von Verhaltensweisen. Fortschrift für Zoologie, 13:303–365.

———— . 1968. *Mimicry in plants and animals.* McGraw-Hill, New York.

Wigglesworth, V.B. 1953. *The principles of insect physiology* (5th Edition). Methuen and Co., London.

Wiley, R.H. 1971. Cooperative roles in mixed flocks of antwrens (Formicariidae). *Auk,* 88:881–892.

Wilkinson, D.H. 1952. The random element in bird "navigation." *Journal of Experimental Biology*, 29:532–560.

Williams, L. 1942. Display and sexual behavior of the Brandt cormorant. *Condor*, 43:85–104.

Willis, E.O. 1966a. Interspecific competition and the foraging behavior of plain-brown woodcreepers. *Ecology*, 47:667–672.

———— . 1966b. The role of migrant birds at swarms of army ants. *Living Bird*, 5:187–236.

———— . 1967. The behavior of bicolored antbirds. University of California Publications on Zoology, 79:1–132.

Willson, M.F. 1971. Ecological overlap and bill size differences: A comment. *American Midland Naturalist*, 86:215–217.

Wilson, E.O. 1965. The challenge from related species. In *The genetics of colonizing species*, ed. by H.G. Baker and G.L. Stebbins. Academic Press, New York, pp. 7–24.

———— . 1971. The prospects for a unified sociobiology. *American Scientist*, 59:400–407.

Wilson and Bossert. 1963. Chemical communication among animals. *Recent Progress in Hormone Research*, 19:673–716.

Wiltschko, W. 1968. Uber den Einfluss statischer Magnetfelder auf die Zugorientiesung der Rotkehlchen (*Erithacus rubecula*). *Zeitschrift für Tierpsychologie*, 25:537–558.

Wing, L. 1946. Species association in winter flocks. *Auk,* 63:507–510.

Wynne-Edwards, V.C. 1962. *Animal dispersion in relation to social behaviour.* Oliver and Boyd, London.

———— . 1965. Self-regulating systems in populations of animals. *Science,* 147:1543–1548.

Yarrow, L.J. 1964. Separation from parents during early childhood. In *Review of child development research.* Vol. I, ed. by M.L. Hoffman and L.W. Hoffman. Russell Sage Foundation, New York, pp. 89–136.

INDEX